Seen

To Tristan,

From

Pete.

Capitalism and Freedom

Anthem Studies in Development and Globalization

Fullbrook, Edward (ed.) *Real World Economics* (2007)
Ellman, Michael (ed.) *Russia's Oil and Natural Gas* (2007)
Rangaswamy, Vedavalli *Energy for Development* (2007)
Ringmar, Erik *Why Europe was First* (2006)
Buira, Ariel (ed.) *Reforming the Governance of the IMF and the World Bank* (2006)
Ringmar, Erik *Surviving Capitalism* (2006)
Saquet, Anne-Marie *World Atlas of Sustainable Development* (2005)
Ritzen, Jozef *A Chance for the World Bank* (2005)
Buira, Ariel (ed.) *The IMF and the World Bank at Sixty* (2005)
Assayag, Jackie & Fuller, Chris (eds) *Globalizing India* (2005)
Nolan, Peter *Transforming China* (2004)
Standing, Guy *Promoting Income Security as a Right* (2004)
Chang, Ha-Joon (ed.) *Rethinking Development Economics* (2003)
Chang, Ha-Joon *Kicking Away the Ladder* (2003)

Capitalism and Freedom

The Contradictory Character of Globalisation

PETER NOLAN

ANTHEM PRESS
LONDON · NEW YORK · DELHI

Anthem Press
An imprint of Wimbledon Publishing Company
www.anthempress.com

This edition first published in UK and USA 2007
by ANTHEM PRESS
75-76 Blackfriars Road, London SE1 8HA, UK
or PO Box 9779, London SW19 7ZG, UK
and
244 Madison Ave. #116, New York, NY 10016, USA

Copyright © Peter Nolan 2007

The moral right of the author has been asserted.
All rights reserved. Without limiting the rights under copyright reserved above,
no part of this publication may be reproduced, stored or introduced
into a retrieval system, or transmitted, in any form or by any means
(electronic, mechanical, photocopying, recording or otherwise),
without the prior written permission of both the copyright
owner and the above publisher of this book.

British Library Cataloguing in Publication Data
A catalogue record for this book is available from the British Library.

Library of Congress Cataloging in Publication Data
Nolan, Peter, 1949-
Capitalism and freedom : the contradictory character of globalisation / Peter Nolan.
    p. cm. — (Anthem development studies and globalization)
Includes bibliographical references.
ISBN-13: 978-1-84331-280-2
ISBN-10: 1-84331-280-8
1. Capitalism—Social aspects. 2. Globalization—Social aspects. 3. Liberty. I. Title.

HB501.N653 2007
306.3'42—dc22
2007026381

1 3 5 7 9 10 8 6 4 2

ISBN-13: 978 1 84331 280 2 (Hbk)
ISBN-10: 1 84331 280 8 (Hbk)

Printed in India

For Siobain and our children,
Dermot and Maeve

Also by Peter Nolan

Growth Processes and Distributional Change in a South Chinese Province: The Case of Guangdong
(1983, London: School of Oriental and African Studies, University of London)

with T. J. Byres, *Inequality: India and China Compared, 1950 – 1970*
(1976, Milton Keynes: Open University Press)

*The Political Economy of Collective Farms: An Analysis of
China's post-Mao Rural Economic Reforms*
(1988, Cambridge: Polity Press)

State and Market in the Chinese Economy: Essays on Controversial Issues
(1993, Basingstoke: Macmillan)

China's Rise, Russia's Fall: Politics, Economics and Planning in the Transition from Stalinism
(1995, Basingstoke: Macmillan)

*Indigenous Large Firms in China's Economic Reform: The Case of
Shougang Iron and Steel Corporation*
(1998, London: School of Oriental and African Studies, University of London)

Coca-Cola and the Global Business Revolution: A Study with Special Reference to the EU
(1999, Cambridge: Judge Institute of Management)

China and the Global Business Revolution
(2001, Basingstoke: Palgrave)

China and the Global Economy
(2001, Basingstoke: Palgrave)

China at the Crossroads
(2003, Cambridge: Polity Press)

Transforming China: Globalization, Transition and Development
(2004, London: Anthem Press)

with J. Zhang and C. Liu, *The Global Business Revolution and the Cascade Effect:
Systems Integration in the Global Aerospace, Beverage and Retail Industries*
(2007, Basingstoke: Palgrave)

CONTENTS

Acknowledgements ix

Prologue: Conflict or Cooperation? 1

    Humanity at the Crossroads 2
    Negative Freedom: Aggression, Competition,
    Selfishness and Masculinity 3
    Positive Freedom: Cooperation, Love, Benevolence
    and Femininity 18
    Search for the 'Mean' 38

Part 1. Capitalism's Contradictory Character 43

  1.1 What is 'Globalisation'? 44
        Pre-Modern Capitalism 44
        Capitalism 1750–1914 45
        Capitalism 1914–1970s 46
        Capitalism Since the Mid-1970s 47

  1.2 Capitalist Rationality in the Epoch of the Global
       Business Revolution 48
       1.2.1 Capitalism and Coordination 49
       1.2.2 Finance and Development 59
       1.2.3 Competition, Industrial Concentration
             and Technical Progress 65
       1.2.4 Expanding Human Freedom 76

  1.3 Capitalist Irrationality in the Epoch of the Global
       Business Revolution 92
       1.3.1 Capitalism's Two-Edged Sword 92
       1.3.2 The Natural Environment 92
       1.3.3 The Challenge of the Global Business
             Revolution 104

	1.3.4	Class Structure in the Epoch of Globalisation	120
	1.3.5	Finance	131
	1.3.6	Conclusion	143

Part 2. Groping for a Way Forward: Conflict or Cooperation?   **145**

	Introduction		146
2.1	The United States and China		146
	2.1.1	China	147
	2.1.2	The United States	171
	2.1.3	Resolving the Contradictions: Conflict or Cooperation?	179
	2.1.4	Conflict?	179
	2.1.5	Cooperation?	194
	2.1.6	Conclusion	205
2.2	The United States and Islam		207
	2.2.1	Islam and the West	208
	2.2.2	Capitalism, Development and Islam	242
	2.2.3	Conclusion	271
		Edward Said on Conflict	279

Conclusion: Searching for the Middle Way   **281**

Introduction	282
The Contradictions of Capitalist Globlisation	283
Globalisation and the Clash of Civilisations	286
Possibilities for Cooperation and Mutual Understanding	288
Nationalism and Globalisation	290
Capitalist Contradictions and Revolution	292
Conclusion	293
Tables	297
Notes	307
Bibliography	331
Index	341

ACKNOWLEDGEMENTS

I am grateful to Dr Jin Zhang and Dr Chunhang Liu for innumerable discussions surrounding the issues raised in this book; to Dr Charles Curwen for his careful reading of the whole manuscript and for many valuable observations; and to Elizabeth Briggs for her expert editing. Responsibility for the opinions expressed in the book rests entirely with me.

It was the best of times, it was the worst of times, it was the age of wisdom, it was the age of foolishness, it was the epoch of belief, it was the epoch of incredulity, it was the season of Light, it was the season of Darkness, it was the spring of hope, it was the winter of despair, we had everything before us, we had nothing before us,...

(Charles Dickens, *A Tale of Two Cities*)

PROLOGUE: CONFLICT OR COOPERATION?

After making a final check of his instrumentation, Tibbets pushed forward the throttles at 2.45 and Enola Gay began to roll down the runway ... At exactly 8.15:17 a.m., the 'Little Boy' was released from the bomb bay of the Enola Gay ... [A]s the 'Little Boy' reached 1900 feet, the proximity fuse fired, sending the U235 bullet down the short barrel of the gun assembly into its U235 target. The super-critical mass was formed, drenched in neutrons by the polonium/beryllium initiator, and an uncontrolled chain reaction went through eighty generations before the expanding uranium core was too large to sustain it ... As Tibbets strained to get the Enola Gay away to the south, 'A bright light filled the plane' ...

President Truman was travelling back from the Potsdam conference aboard the USS Augusta when he was told the news; he told sailors in the mess deck where he was dining, that 'This was the greatest thing that has ever happened' ...

Otto Frisch was working at the Los Alamos laboratory when somebody opened the door and shouted 'Hiroshima has been destroyed!'. About a hundred thousand people were thought to have been killed. 'I still remember the feeling of unease, indeed nausea, when I saw how many of my friends were rushing to the telephone to book tables at the La Fonda hotel in Santa Fe, in order to celebrate' ... That same evening at Los Alamos, [Robert] Oppenheimer made a speech in the auditorium, after walking through a cheering crowd of scientists pumping his fists in the air.

(Weale, 1995: 134–8, and 171–4)

Humanity at the Crossroads

Since ancient times the exercise of individual freedom has been inseparable from the expansion of the market, driven by the search for profit. This force, namely capitalism, has stimulated human creativity and aggression in ways that have produced immense benefits. As capitalism has broadened its scope in the epoch of globalisation, so these benefits have become even greater. Human beings have been liberated to an even greater degree than hitherto from the tyranny of nature, from control by others over their lives, from poverty, and from war. The advances achieved by the globalisation of capitalism have appeared all the more striking, when set against the failure of non-capitalist systems of economic organisation.

However, capitalist freedom is a two-edged sword. In the epoch of capitalist globalisation, its contradictions have intensified. They comprehensively threaten the natural environment. A ferocious international struggle is under way to secure access to scarce resources. It has contributed to intensified global inequality within both rich and poor countries, and between the internationalised global power elite and the mass of citizens rooted within their respective nations. It has produced a world of potentially extreme financial instability. The world's dominant economic, political and cultural power, the United States, refuses to dismantle its vast stock of nuclear arms, sufficient to obliterate the entire global civilisation. That country benefits in numerous ways from global capitalism. It also feels under intense threat, both internally and externally from those same forces.

The present stage of development of global capitalism has produced in even more intense form the contradictions latent within the nature of the capitalist system. As human beings have taken to new heights their ability to free themselves from fundamental constraints through the market mechanism, so they also have reached new depths in terms of the uncontrollability of the structures they have created. Global capitalism has created uniquely intense threats to the very existence of the human species at the same time that it has liberated humanity more than ever before from fundamental constraints.

If humanity cannot find a 'mean', its prospects for survival are bleak. The destruction of human civilisation may arise either from the internal self-destructiveness of extreme free market individualism, or from the nihilistic response of those excluded and angered by the globalisation of the free market.

Since ancient times, philosophers have debated about the essential features of human nature, and the relationship of these features to the market economy. It has long been recognised that human beings are inherently contradictory. Within themselves they have the capacity for selfish, aggressive and warlike behaviour (the 'death instinct'), alongside a capacity for cooperative, benevolent and loving behaviour (the 'love instinct'). Can human beings find a path between these warring tendencies within their personality?

Negative Freedom: Aggression, Competition, Selfishness and Masculinity

Odysseus hurled his boast at Socus: 'Poor man, headlong death is about to overtake you! A dark bloody doom will take you down today – gouged by my spear you'll give me glory now, you'll give your life to the famous horseman Death!' Odysseus plunged a spear in his back between the shoulders – straight through his chest the shaft came jutting out and down Socus crashed, Odysseus vaunting over him: 'Socus, son of Hippasus, skilled breaker of horses, so Death in its rampage outraced you – no escape. No, poor soldier. Now your father and noble mother will never close your eyes in death – screaming vultures will claw them out of you, wings beating your corpse'. He dragged the heavy spear of hardened Socus squelching out of his own wound and bulging shield. As the fighter tore it out the blood came gushing forth and his heart sank.

(Homer, *The Iliad*, Book 11, 'Agamemnon's Day of Glory')

Competitive markets are the essence of capitalism. Competition by its very nature involves aggression. Capitalist dynamism stems from the energy arising from aggression. Among small firms there is a remorseless battle for survival. Often, the competitor is another small firm fighting within the local market. If the product is sold in distant markets, the competitors consist of anonymous small firms in far off places. For large firms, the competitors are other large firms, with identities that are well-known to each other. Large firms fight with each other for a share of the market. They market their products aggressively to persuade customers to buy them. In raw capitalism, unconstrained by guilds, custom or government regulation, the competitive battle is a ferocious life-and-death struggle. Successful firms defeat other firms. The defeated firm either dies or is taken prisoner by the successful firm, living on inside the victorious firm.

The key incentive for firms in the competitive struggle is the pursuit of profits. Profits are pursued because they provide wealth, power and status, either directly to owner-managers or indirectly to shareholders. Firms compete by investing in new technologies and by reducing costs of production. Firms battle with their suppliers to lower the costs of purchased inputs. Owners battle with workers to keep wage costs low, pushing them to increase the intensity of labour by working longer and harder, and organising the work process in ways that raise productivity. Workers fight managers and owners to increase their earnings and achieve a larger share of value-added. Employees compete with each other to move up the hierarchy within the firm. Top-level managers fight with each other to win the leading positions in the firm. Successful firms, like successful armies, have tight internal discipline to ensure success in the competitive battle.

There is a long tradition that views human beings as essentially aggressive and competitive, and regards this competition as beneficial for human progress, subject to a minimum of intervention and rule-setting by the government. Capitalist aggression, the foundation of capitalist dynamism is inseparable from human beings' aggressive instincts. Many social thinkers who deplore the social and psychological consequences of capitalist aggression acknowledge the dynamism that stems from that aggression.

Aristotle

Even in ancient Greece the market economy was already well-developed. Aristotle was deeply interested in markets, money and acquisitiveness. He considered that exchange of goods in the market originally was simply for the two parties to mutually benefit from the division of labour, and that this was 'in accordance with nature'. However, he considered that the pursuit of wealth for its own sake was 'contrary to nature':

> One form of property-getting is, in accordance with nature, a part of household management ... And it looks as if wealth in its true sense consists of property such as this. For the amount of property of this kind which would give self-sufficiency for a good life is not limitless ... But there is another kind of property-getting to which the term 'acquisition of goods' is generally and justly applied; and it is due to this that there is thought to be no limit to wealth or property... [O]ne is natural, the other is not (Politics, 79–80).

> Some people ... never cease to believe that their store of coined money ought to be either hoarded or increased without limit ... The reason why some people get this notion into their heads may be that they are eager for life but not for the good life; so the desire for life being unlimited, they desire also an unlimited amount of what enables it to go on. Others again, while aiming at the good life, seek what is conducive to the pleasure of the body. So, as this too appears to depend on the possession of property, their whole activity centres on business, and the second mode of acquiring goods owes its existence to this. For where enjoyment consists in excess, men look for that skill which produces the excess that is enjoyed. And if they cannot procure it through money-making, they try to get it by some

other means, using all their faculties for this purpose, which is contrary to nature ... [T]hese people turn all skills into skills for acquiring goods, as though that were the end and everything had to serve that end (Politics, 85).

Aristotle believed that a new motive quickly comes to dominate commercial transactions, namely the pursuit of profit as an end in itself:

Once a currency was provided, development was rapid and what started as a necessary exchange became trade, the other mode of acquiring goods. At first it was probably quite a simple affair, but then it became more systematic as men became more experienced at discovering where and how the greatest profits might be made out of exchanges ... [T]here is indeed no limit to the amount of riches to be got from this mode of acquiring goods. [T]here is no limit to the end which this kind of acquisition has in view, because the end is wealth in that form, i.e. the possession of goods (Politics, 83–4).

He deeply disapproved of charging people interest for the loan of money, which consisted in 'making money from money':

The acquisition of goods is then, ... of two kinds; one, which is necessary and approved of, is to do with household management; the other, which is to do with trade and depends on exchange, is justly regarded with disapproval, since it arises not from nature but from men's gaining from each other. Very much disliked also is the practice of charging interest; and the dislike is fully justified, for the gain arises out of currency itself, not as a product of that for which the currency was provided. Currency was intended as a means of exchange, whereas interest represents an increase in the currency itself. Hence its name,[1] for each animal produces its like, and interest is currency born of currency. And so of all types of business this is the most contrary to nature (Politics, 87).

Smith

Smith considered that the individual's freedom to dispose of his labour and property within the market economy was the foundation upon which could take place the liberation of human energies:

The property which every man has in his own labour, as it is the original foundation of all other property, so it is the most sacred and inviolable ...

to hinder him from employing this strength and dexterity in what manner he thinks proper without injury to his neighbour, is a plain violation of this most sacred property. It is a manifest encroachment upon the just liberty both of the workman, and of those who might be disposed to employ him (Smith, 1976, Vol. 1: 136).

Few propositions in economics have been as much quoted as Adam Smith's about the pursuit of individual self-interest serving the collective good:

The natural effort of every individual to better his own condition, when suffered to exert itself with freedom and security, is so powerful a principle that it is alone, and without any assistance, not only capable of carrying on the society to wealth and prosperity, but of surmounting a hundred impertinent obstructions with which the folly of human laws encumbers its operation ... (Smith, 1976, Vol. 2: 49–50).

For Smith the peculiar wonder of the autonomous-functioning market mechanism was that it produced deep cooperation without any sense of benevolence for people's fellow human beings, but takes place instead through the pursuit of self-interest:

In civilised society [man] stands at all times in need of the cooperation and assistance of great multitudes, while his whole life is scarce sufficient to gain the friendship of a few other persons. In almost every other race of animals each individual, when it is grown up to maturity, is entirely independent, and in its natural state has occasion for the assistance of no other living creature. But man has almost constant occasion for the help of his brethren, and it is in vain for him to expect it from their benevolence only. He will be more likely to prevail if he can interest their self-love in his favour, and show them that is for their own advantage to do for him what he requires of them. Whoever offers another a bargain proposes to do this. Give me that which I want, and you shall have this which you want, is the meaning of every such offer; and it is in this manner that we obtain from one another the far greater part of those good offices which we stand in need of. It is not from the benevolence of the butcher, the brewer, or the baker, that we expect our dinner, but from their regard for their own interest. We address ourselves not to their humanity but to their self-love, and never talk to them of our own necessities but of their advantages (Smith, 1976, Vol. 1: 18).

Smith believed that a central explanation for eighteenth century Britain's relative prosperity was due to the removal of state intervention, which allowed capital accumulation to thrive:

> In the midst of all the exactions of government, this capital has been silently, gradually, accumulated by the private frugality and good conduct of individuals, by their universal, continual, and uninterrupted effort to better their condition. It is this effort, protected by law, and allowed by liberty to exert itself, in the manner that is most advantageous, which has maintained the progress of England towards opulence and improvement (Smith, 1976, Vol. 1: 367).

He considered that individual businessmen are far more competent than politicians to judge resource allocation, since their own interests are directly at stake:

> [B]y directing his industry in such a manner as its produce may be of the greatest value, he intends only his own gain, and he is in this, as in many other cases, led by an invisible hand to promote an end which was not part of his intention ... What is the species of domestic industry which his capital can employ, and of which the produce is likely to be of the greatest value, every individual it is evident can, in his local situation, judge much better than any statesman or lawgiver can do (Smith, 1976, Vol. 1: 478).

Mill

Mill has inspired liberal social thinkers since the mid-nineteenth century.[2] The cornerstone of his view of the world was the political rights of the individual: '[T]he only purpose for which power can rightfully be exercised over any member of a civilised community, against his will, is to prevent harm to others' (Mill, 1988: 78).[3]

Alongside these political rights, Mill also considered that competition was central to economic progress (Mill, 1998). Pursuit of profit was central to his analysis of the economic system. He criticised contemporary socialists who failed to understand the central role played by competition in stimulating human energies and achieving economic progress:

> One of [the Socialists] greatest errors ... is to charge upon competition all the economical evils which at present exist. They forget that wherever competition is not, monopoly is; and that monopoly, in all its forms, is the taxation of the industrious for the support of indolence, if not

plunder. They forget, too, that with the exception of competition among labourers, all other competition is for the benefit of labourers, by cheapening the articles they consume ... Competition may not be the best conceivable stimulus, but it is at present a necessary one, and no one can foresee the time when it will not be indispensable to progress. Instead of looking upon competition as the baneful, and anti-social principle which it is held to be by the generality of Socialists, I conceive that, even in the present state of society and industry, every restriction of it is an evil, and every extension of it ... is always an ultimate good. To be protected against competition is to be protected in idleness, in mental dullness; to be saved the necessity of being as active and as intelligent as other people ... [T]he time has come when the interest of universal improvement is no longer promoted by prolonging the privileges of the few (Mill, 1998: 156–8).

Mill was fully aware of the brutal nature of competition in Victorian England:

I am not charmed with the ideal of life held out by those who think that the normal state of human beings is that of struggling to get on: that the trampling, crushing, elbowing, and treading on each other's heels, which form the existing type of social life, are the most desirable lot of human kind, or anything but the disagreeable symptoms of one of the phases of human progress (Mill, 1998: 126).

Mill said that the driving force of the capitalist progress in nineteenth century England, was 'energies of mankind, [which are] harnessed by the struggle for riches, as they were formerly by the struggle of war' (Mill, 1998: 127). He contrasts the 'progress' in terms of human ingenuity and productivity with the conditions of work for most people:

Hitherto it is questionable if all the mechanical inventions yet made have lightened the day's toil of any human being. They have enabled a greater population to live the same life of drudgery and imprisonment, and an increased number of manufacturers and others to make fortunes. They have increased the comforts of the middle class. But they have not yet begun to effect those great changes in human destiny, which it is their nature and in their futurity to accomplish (Mill, 1998: 129).

Freud

The publication of Sigmund Freud's study 'Civilisation and its Discontents' in 1930 was a milestone in the history of psychoanalysis. The First World War had a profound impact upon Freud's understanding of human instincts. He concluded that human beings are 'creatures among whose instinctual endowments is to be reckoned a powerful share of aggressiveness' (Freud, 2001b: 110). When the mental counter-forces which ordinarily inhibit it are out of action, man is revealed as 'a savage beast to whom consideration towards his own kind is something alien … In consequence of this primary mutual hostility of human beings, civilised society is perpetually threatened with disintegration' (Freud, 2001b: 112).

Freud considered that the instinct of aggressiveness and destruction, when successfully 'moderated and tamed', provides the ego with 'the satisfaction of its vital needs and with the control over nature' (Freud, 2001b: 121). Freud thought that ethics were critical to the survival of the human species: 'Civilisation has to use its utmost efforts in order to set limits to man's aggressive instincts and to hold the manifestations of them in check by psychical reaction-formations' (Freud, 2001b: 112). He attached particular importance to 'what is probably the most recent of the cultural commands of the super-ego, the commandment to love one's neighbour as oneself' (Freud, 2001b: 142). However, he was uncertain if human beings' mental constitution was able to bear the weight of this severe instruction: 'The cultural super-ego issues a command and does not ask whether it is possible for people to obey it' (Freud, 2001b: 143).

Lorenz

Konrad Lorenz's book *On Aggression*, had a tremendous impact on its publication in 1966. He believes that human beings' essential characteristic is aggression, which he argues is the basis of life throughout the animal kingdom. Lorenz considered that the animal kingdom is characterised by widespread aggression, which is used as a means to preserve the species rather than to destroy it. In other words, aggression has a positive role to play in Darwinian evolution in large parts of the natural world. Lorenz focused on the role intra-species aggression can play in determining access to food supply and to females: 'It is always favourable to the future of the species if the stronger of two rivals takes possession of the territory or of the desired female' (Lorenz, 1966: 23).

He believes that in the long millennia of human evolution towards settled civilisations, human beings developed powerful instinctive drives towards aggression. Lorenz argues that in prehistoric times, as populations of hunters and gatherers expanded and pressure on resources grew, 'intra-specific selection bred into man a measure of aggression drive for which in the social order today he finds no adequate outlet' (Lorenz, 1966: 209). In the prehistoric context aggression served a Darwinian function in helping to ensure the survival of the human species: '[I]t is more than probable that the destructive intensity of the aggression drive, still a hereditary evil of mankind, is the consequence of a process of intra-specific selection which worked on our forefathers for roughly forty thousand years, that is throughout the early Stone Age' (Lorenz, 1966: 34). Due to their superior strength, males bear the brunt of being warriors, and consequently, are the main repositories of the instincts of aggression and destructiveness.

Patterns of violence and destructiveness that served a positive Darwinian function in the long early millennia of their evolution threaten the human species in the modern world, in which human beings have developed extraordinarily destructive weaponry:

> An unprejudiced observer from another planet, looking upon man as he is today, in his hand the atom bomb, the product of his intelligence, in his heart the aggression drive inherited from his anthropoid ancestors, which his nature cannot control, would not prophesy a long life for the species ... Knowledge of the fact that the aggression drive is a true, primarily species-preserving instinct enables us to recognise its full danger: it is the spontaneity that makes it so dangerous (Lorenz, 1966: 40).

These instincts are dangerously inappropriate to an age with the instruments of modern warfare. Other species evolved much more slowly and lacked human beings' capability of developing tools and weapons. Those species which had evolved the ability to kill others easily through powerful claws, beaks, teeth and wings, developed patterns of behaviour that enabled them to resolve disputes in ways that did not lead to violent intra-species conflict: 'These inhibitions are most important and consequently most highly differentiated in those animals which are capable of killing living creatures of about their own size' (Lorenz, 1966: 206). All heavily-armed carnivores 'possess sufficiently reliable inhibitions which prevent the self-destruction of the species' (Lorenz, 1966: 207). In human evolution, 'no inhibitory mechanisms preventing sudden manslaughter were necessary, because quick killing was impossible', until 'all of a sudden, the invention of artificial weapons upset the equilibrium of killing potential and social inhibitions' (Lorenz, 1966: 207).

According to Lorenz, human aggressive energy has been channelled into creative activities, especially science, among which is the application of science to weaponry:

> It is a curious paradox that the greatest gifts of man, the unique faculties of conceptual thought and verbal speech which have raised him to a high level above all other creatures and given him mastery over the globe, are not altogether blessings, or at least are blessings that have to be paid for very dearly indeed. All the great dangers threatening humanity with destruction are direct consequences of conceptual thought and verbal speech... Man is... by nature a jeopardised creature (Lorenz, 1966: 204).

Lorenz was mesmerised by the thought that human beings' instinctive aggression inherited from the far distant past was now allied with the technical capability of destroying the human species. The sophistication of human beings' weapons also allows them to kill at a distance from the fellow members of their species being killed, especially with modern weapons: 'The man who presses the releasing button is so completely screened against seeing, hearing or otherwise emotionally realising the consequences of his action, that he can commit it with impunity' (Lorenz, 1966: 208).

Like Freud, Lorenz places a critical weight on ethics to resolve the tension between the instinctive, inherited aggression drive and the weaponry at human beings' disposal through their own creation. He is uncertain if the weight of human beings' ethical advance can resolve the contradiction:

> [T]he task of compensation devolving on responsible morality increases at the same rate at which the ecological and sociological conditions created by culture deviate from those to which human instinctive behaviour is phylogenetically adapted. Not only does this deviation continue to increase, but it does so with an acceleration that is truly frightening. The fate of humanity hangs on the question of whether or not responsible morality will be able to cope with its rapidly growing burden (Lorenz, 1966: 218).

Social Darwinism

In modern times, the idea of individual self-interest serving the interests of the whole of human society received apparently strong support from Darwin's theory of human evolution, as expressed in his *Descent of Man* (2004). The powerful idea of the 'survival of the fittest' provided the intellectual foundation for 'Social Darwinism', which reached an apogee of influence in the United States in the late nineteenth century. Social Darwinists argue that aggression is the key instinct of all animals, including human beings. They argue that cooperation based on benevolent feelings will fail because of the innate selfishness exhibited by individuals throughout the animal kingdom. They view competition between members of the same species as a fundamental driver of evolution.

Darwin's *Descent of Man* was immensely popular with the Victorian middle class in both Britain and America (Moore and Desmond, 2004). It appeared to provide them with an intellectual justification for their 'progressive' role in human evolution. In England, the *Descent of Man* sold for 24 shillings, more than a week's wages for an average worker. It was seized upon as a 'piece of self-congratulatory science for the Liberal nouveau riche and emerging agnostic liberals of middle England: the rising businessmen, industrialists and professionals' (Moore and Desmond, 2004: liv). Darwin himself was emphatically a part of the wealthy middle class: 'cocooned with his inherited fortune, [he] never had to compete himself' (Moore and Desmond, 2004: liii). Darwin was opposed to Unions and Cooperatives, which he said 'opposed ... competition', and were 'a great evil for the future progress of mankind' (Darwin in 1872, quoted in Moore and Desmond, 2004: liv).

At the heart of the rise of Social Darwinism in America was the struggle over the meaning of the word 'freedom': 'Freedom has always been a terrain of conflict, subject to multiple and competing interpretations, its meaning constantly created and re-created' (Foner, 1998: xv). At the heart of the struggle for the meaning of 'freedom' in the United States was the battle over the role of the state, and its function in the achievement of 'negative' and 'positive' freedoms. Was the US state to serve purely as the guardian of individual liberties or 'negative freedoms', or was the state to serve as the instrument for the achievement of the positive freedoms of all citizens to enable them to be fulfilled human beings? These struggles over the interpretation of 'freedom' have existed in America since the eighteenth century.

Darwin's ideas were seized upon by sociologists, notably Herbert Spencer, who advocated deregulation and unhampered individual competition. Social Darwinism provided capitalism with a sociology that could 'help to contain the demands of labour as economies restructured': 'Unfettered rivalry in the market place, among men, races and nations, the belief that the mighty inherit the earth and progress depends on reformers and their governments letting them get on with it' (Moore and Desmond, 2004: lv). The leading exponent of Social Darwinism in the United States was Yale professor William Graham Sumner. For Sumner, freedom properly understood meant the 'abnegation of state power and a frank acceptance of inequality'. In his view society faced only two possible alternatives: 'liberty, inequality and the survival of the fittest; not-liberty, equality, survival of the unfittest' (quoted in Foner, 1998: 122). The task of social sciences, wrote iron manufacturer, Abram Hewitt, was to devise ways of making 'men who are equal in liberty' content with the 'inequality in distribution' inevitable in modern society (Foner, 1998: 119).

Social Darwinism was a political philosophy that was strongly opposed to any form of state interference with the 'natural' workings of society. Laws regulating labour conditions were seen as a form of slavery, since they interfered in the rights of free agents to dispose of their property as they saw fit. The idea that 'freedom' essentially meant freedom of contract became the bedrock of 'liberal' thinking at the end of the nineteenth century: 'As long as economic processes and labour relations were governed by contracts freely arrived at by autonomous individuals, Americans had no grounds to complain about loss of freedom' (Foner, 1998: 120). In this view, the true realm of freedom, was 'the liberty to buy and sell, and mend and make, where and how we please, without interference from the state' (Foner, 1998: 120).

Under the impact of the Great Depression and post-war construction in the 1940s and 1950s, Social Darwinism faded from view as a mainstream political philosophy in the United States. After the 1960s, the growing influence of social thinkers such as Friedrich von Hayek and Milton Friedman helped to propel the philosophy into the mainstream once again. The dominant view of 'freedom' in the United States once again equated 'freedom' with individual choice in the market place with minimal interference from the state. As the US business system became increasingly powerful globally, the idea gained force that the United States should lead the world towards a single universal free market. One of the earliest expressions of this vision of a 'New World Order' led by the United States was provided by Barry Goldwater, during the 1964 election campaign. In his acceptance speech for the Republican Party's nomination for presidential candidate, he said that God had intended 'this mighty republic to be ... the land of the free, and invoked a vision of a world united, under American leadership, in "a mighty system" of freedom, prosperity and interdependence' (quoted in Foner, 1998: 313). The collapse of the USSR reinforced Americans' confidence in the free market, and in the country's duty to lead the world towards this as a universal form of socio-economic organisation. By the 1990s, in the United States there was no serious intellectual challenge to the economic philosophy of the free market.

Hayek

Hayek's ideas, especially those contained in his book *The Road to Serfdom* (1944), were a 'clarion call for conservatives to reclaim the word "freedom", which, he charged, had been usurped and distorted by socialists' (Foner, 1998: 236).[4] For Hayek, the foundation of a good society was individual economic freedom. He believed that this was a unique product of Western civilisation and the growth of the market economy in this part of the world over hundreds of years. It is this individualism which 'from elements provided by Christianity and the philosophy of classical antiquity, was first fully developed during the Renaissance and has since grown and spread into what we know as Western European civilisation – the respect for the individual man *qua* man, that is the recognition of his own views and tastes as supreme in his own sphere' (Hayek, 1944: 14). For Hayek, competition is the key driver of economic progress: 'Perhaps the greatest result of the unchaining of individual energies was the marvellous growth of science which followed the march of individual liberty from Italy to England and beyond' (Hayek, 1944: 15–16). Where the barriers to the 'free exercise of human ingenuity were removed', man became 'rapidly able to satisfy ever-widening ranges of desire' (Hayek, 1944: 16). Competition is favoured because it is the 'only method by which our activities can be adjusted to each other without coercive or arbitrary intervention of authority' (Hayek, 1944: 38).

Hayek believed that the market is the most effective mechanism for coordinating the efforts of the myriad of individuals in the economic system. At its heart is the price mechanism: 'Any attempt to control prices or quantities of particular commodities deprives competition of its power of bringing about an effective coordination of individual efforts, because price changes then cease to register all the relevant changes in circumstances and no longer provide a reliable guide for the individual's actions' (Hayek, 1944: 38).

The theme of the *Road to Serfdom* was simple: 'planning for freedom' was an oxymoron, since 'planning leads to dictatorship' (Foner, 1998: 235). Hayek argued that all planning restricted individual liberty, and without 'freedom in economic affairs', political and personal freedom were impossible. He argued strongly against a 'Middle Way':

> [M]ost people still believe that it must be possible to find some Middle Way between 'atomistic' competition and central direction. Yet mere common sense proves a treacherous guide in this field ... Both competition and central direction become poor and inefficient tools if they are incomplete; they are alternative principles used to solve the same problem, and a mixture of the two means that neither will really work and that the result will be worse than if either system had been consistently relied upon (Hayek, 1944: 43).

Hayek's ideas had a massive influence:

> In effectively equating fascism, and the New Deal, and identifying economic planning with a loss of freedom, he helped lay the foundation for the rise of modern conservatism, offering a powerful weapon with which to attack liberalism and the left and inspiring a revival of classic economic thought (Foner, 1998: 236).

Friedman

For classical liberal political economists and philosophers, individual economic freedom is the foundation of political freedom. The two are seen to be inextricably intertwined. Classical liberalism emphasises the individual as the 'ultimate entity in the society' (Friedman, 1962: 5). Liberals believe that the foundation of a good society is private property. The scope of government should be limited, confined to preserving law and order, enforcing private contracts, and fostering competitive markets (Friedman, 1962: 2). They see the central feature of the market system of economic activity as the fact that it 'prevents one person from interfering with another in respect of most of his activities' (Friedman, 1962: 14).

Political freedom is interpreted as meaning the 'absence of coercion of a man by his fellow men' (Friedman, 1962: 15). In other words, the essential freedom is viewed as being 'negative freedom': 'The notion of "negative" freedom: I am normally said to be free to the degree to which no man or body of men interferes with my activity. Political liberty in this sense is simply the area within which a man can act unobstructed by others' (Berlin, 1969: 122). Liberals view the freedom of the individual as the 'ultimate goal in judging social arrangements' (Friedman, 1962: 12).

Classical liberals accept that the market will produce unequal outcomes. The liberal 'distinguishes sharply between equality of rights and equality of opportunity on the one hand, and material inequality or equality of outcomes on the other' (Friedman, 1962: 195). Liberals contrast their view of the inequality of outcomes with the view of 'egalitarians': 'The egalitarian ... will defend taking from some to give to others ... on the grounds of "justice". At this point, equality comes sharply into conflict with freedom: one must choose. One cannot be both an egalitarian, in this sense, and a liberal' (Friedman, 1962: 195).

The ethical principle that they use to justify the distribution of income in a free market society is: 'To each according to what he and the instruments he owns produces' (Friedman, 1962: 161–2). A large part of the inequality that results 'reflects differences in endowments, both of human capacities and property' (Friedman, 1962: 164). A fundamental tenet of classical liberals is the right of inheritance of property: 'Is there any greater ethical justification for the high returns to the individual who inherits from his parents a peculiar voice for which there is a great demand than for the high returns to the individual who inherits property?' (Friedman, 1962: 164). Such a society is acknowledged to be 'in practice characterised by considerable inequality of income and wealth' (Friedman, 1962: 168). Classical liberals believe that 'narrowly materialistic interests dominate the bulk of mankind' (Friedman, 1962: 201). They consider that 'one of the strongest and most creative instincts known to man' is the 'attempt by millions of individuals to promote their own interests' (Friedman, 1962: 200). They consider that the exercise of these instincts through the market has been the central force in human progress.

Classical liberals acknowledge that some people are fortunate to be born into better circumstances than others, whether richer families or richer countries, or by extension, families with greater human capital.[5] Milton Friedman raises the imaginary case of four Robinson Crusoes marooned on desert islands. Three of them are on 'small and barren' islands and one of them is on a 'large and fruitful' island. He asks: 'Of course, it would be generous of the Crusoe on the large island if he invited the others to join him and share its wealth. But suppose he does not. Would the other three be justified in joining forces and compelling him to share his wealth with them?' (Friedman, 1962: 165). Friedman answers emphatically that this would be an infringement of the freedom of the Crusoe on the large island: 'The unwillingness of the rich Crusoe to share his wealth does not justify the use of coercion by the others' (Friedman, 1962: 165). Friedman broadens the argument to a global scale: 'Are we prepared to urge on ourselves or our fellows that any person whose wealth exceeds the average of all persons in the world should immediately dispose of the excess by distributing it equally to all the rest of the world's inhabitants? We may admire and praise such action when undertaken by a few. But a universal "potlatch" would make a civilised world impossible' (Friedman, 1962: 165).

Bush

Social Darwinist ideas reached a new apogee under President George W. Bush. His National Security Strategy document of September 2002 (Bush, 2002) was entitled 'How the US will lead "freedom's triumph"'. The Report states: 'Freedom is the non-negotiable demand of human dignity; the birthright of every person – in every civilisation ... Today, humanity holds in its hands the opportunity to further freedom's triumph over all [its] foes. The US welcomes our responsibility to lead in this great mission'. It commits the United States to 'defend liberty and justice because these principles are right and true for all people everywhere'. It commits the United States to 'stand firmly for the non-negotiable demands of human dignity: the rule of law; limits on the absolute power of the state; free speech; freedom of worship; equal justice; respect for women; religious and ethnic tolerance; and respect for private property'. The 'equation of [America's] national interests with the liberation of mankind and of its antagonists with hostility to freedom' is not something new. From the earliest days of American territorial expansion, it has 'infused the rhetoric of American statecraft to the present day, often to the bemusement and annoyance of other nations' (Foner, 1998: 78).

In the wake of September 11, the US Government is even more firmly convinced of its historic function to spread the moral principle of the free market across the whole world:

> The great struggles of the twentieth century between liberty and totalitarianism ended with a decisive victory for the forces of freedom – and a single sustainable model for national success: freedom, democracy and free enterprise. Today, the US enjoys a position of unparalleled military strength, and great economic and political influence ... We seek to create a balance of power that favours human freedom ... The US will use this moment of opportunity to spread the benefits of freedom across the globe ... We will make freedom and the development of democratic institutions key themes in our bilateral relations (Bush, 21 September 2002).

It says that the United States will 'use this moment of opportunity to extend the benefits of freedom across the globe'. In other words, September 11 is viewed as an 'opportunity' to push forward, under the guise of a 'War on Terrorism', US conceptions of a new world order based on the US model.

The idea that the free market is a moral concept stands at the centre of political discourse in the United States at the start of the twenty-first century. President Bush's Security Strategy declaration of September 2002 states: 'The concept of "free trade" arose as a moral principle even before it became a pillar of economics. If you can make something that others value, you should be able to sell it to them. If others make something that you value you should be able to buy it. This is real freedom, the freedom for a person – or nation – to make a living' (Bush, 21 September 2002). In his speech to the West Point Military Academy in 2002, President Bush said: 'Moral truth is the same in every culture, in every time, in every place' (quoted in *Financial Times*, 7 February 2003). In his State of the Union Address to Congress in 2003, he said: 'The liberty we prize is not America's gift to the world, it is God's gift to humanity' (quoted in *Financial Times*, 7 February 2003). The *Financial Times* commented: 'Put another way, America's unparalleled might is to be deployed on the side of indisputable right. You have to go back a while to find such a stark assertion of moral certitude and strategic power' (*FT*, 7 February 2003).

Positive Freedom: Cooperation, Love, Benevolence and Femininity

Once they'd bathed and smoothed their skin with oil, they took their picnic, sitting along the river's banks and waiting for all the clothes to dry in the hot noon sun. Now fed to their heart's content, the princess and her retinue threw their veils to the wind, struck up a game of ball. White-armed Nausicaa led their singing, dancing beat ... The ball – the princess suddenly tossed it to a maid but it missed the girl, it splashed in a deep swirling pool and they all shouted out – and that woke Odysseus ... Nausicaa called out ... 'Here's an unlucky wanderer strayed our way and we must tend him well ... So quick, my girls, give our newfound friend some food and drink and bathe the man in the river wherever you find some shelter from the wind'.

(From Homer, *The Odyssey*, Book 6: 'The Princess and the Stranger')

Today, the world is looking into the abyss. This is most obvious in relation to ecology, not least global warming. It is true also in relation to a potential global financial crisis. These issues are set against a background of large changes in the distribution of income and wealth within both rich and poor countries, closely linked to capitalist globalisation. They are also set against the background of the divergence between nationally rooted populations and the global capitalist business elite. Behind these issues is the potential conflict between countries with different national interests and worldviews. Behind this in turn is the reality of massive stocks of nuclear weapons, which can destroy human civilisation in the twinkling of an eye. Only internationally cooperative solutions can resolve these sharp and potentially disastrous inter-related contradictions. Is there any possibility of a cooperative outcome?

There is a long tradition of social movements inspired by the idea of building a society based around selfless behaviour and benevolence, in which the selfish, competitive behaviour of the market economy would be eliminated. The essence of such movements has been the notion that people are basically cooperative, not competitive in nature. In this view, the animal world is driven as much by cooperation, by mutual affection and love, as by competition and violence.

Many influential social thinkers have argued that for its long-term survival, the human species needs cooperation, not competition.

Plato

Plato believed that avarice was the path to unhappiness and an imperfect society. Such a society 'elevates the element of desire and profit-seeking to the throne, and lets it govern like an oriental despot with tiara, chain and sword ... While reason and ambition squat in servitude at its feet, reason forbidden to admire or value anything but wealth and the wealthy, or to compete for anything but the acquisition of wealth and whatever leads to it' (Plato, 1987: 370–1). Such a society 'inevitably splits into two factions, the rich and the poor, who live in the same place and are always plotting against each other': 'The more [the ruling class] go in the process of accumulating wealth, the more they value it and the less they value goodness. For aren't wealth and goodness related like two objects in a balance, so that when one rises, the other must fall?' (Plato, 1987: 368). In such a society, 'honour and admiration are preserved for the rich, and the poor are despised' (Plato, 1987: 367).

For Plato, in a good society, 'the beast in us' is subject to 'our human, or perhaps I should say, our divine element', while in the imperfect, avaricious society, 'our humaner nature [sic]' is 'subject to the beast' (Plato, 1987: 417). For Plato, the good society was one in which 'as many people as possible use the words "mine" and "thine" in the same sense of the same things':

> And is not cohesion the result of the common feelings of pleasure and pain which you get when all members of a society are glad or sorry at the same successes and failures? ... Such a community will regard the individual who experiences pain or loss as part of itself, and be glad or sorry accordingly ... Our citizens, then, are devoted to a common interest, which they call *my own; and in consequence entirely share each other's feelings of joy and sorrow* (Plato, 1987: 247 and 249) (My emphasis: PN).

The rulers of such a society should be people who are 'truly rich', 'that is those whose riches consist not of gold, but of the true happiness of a good and rational life': 'if you get men in public affairs whose life is impoverished and destitute of personal satisfactions, but who hope to snatch some compensation for their own inadequacy from a political career, there can never be good government' (Plato, 1987: 235).

Plato envisaged a society in which the rulers themselves are assured of internal harmony and social cohesion by means of the principle of 'all things in common between friends'. The rulers should have 'no private property beyond the barest essentials' (Plato, 1987: 184). They should 'eat together in messes like soldiers in camp', with 'food provided by other citizens as an agreed wage for the duties they perform as Guardians' (Plato, 1987: 184). They 'must be told that they have no need of mortal and material gold and silver, because in their hearts they have heavenly gold and silver given them by the gods as a permanent possession, and it would be wicked to pollute the heavenly gold in their possession by mixing it with earthly, for theirs is without impurity, while that in currency among men is a common source of wickedness' (Plato, 1987: 184). Rulers of this type would be 'very happy indeed' (Plato, 1987: 185), and in the best position to 'promote not the particular happiness of a single class, but, as far as possible, of the whole community' (Plato, 1987: 186–7).

From the ancient Greeks onwards, utopian ideas such as those of Plato have had a consistent appeal. These have typically been based on common property, which eliminates the profit motive and selfish behaviour, and restricts social inequality. Such societies have attempted to establish social cohesion derived from the benevolent concern of all citizens for other members of the society. Education in the elements of the 'good society' has been central to such ideas. Happiness is sought through non-material paths of self-fulfilment for all members of the society, including science, the arts, and harmony with nature.

Aristotle

Aristotle considered that the essence of morally 'right' and 'fine' behaviour was benevolence towards one's fellow human beings, considering their interests out of an appreciation of their feelings and an understanding of their situation:

> [T]he man of good character ... performs many actions for the sake of his friends and his country, and if necessary even dies for them. For he will sacrifice both money and honours and in general the goods that people struggle to obtain, in the pursuit of what is [morally] fine (Ethics, 302).

> It is those who desire the good of their friends for their friends' sake that are the most truly friends, because each loves the other for what he is, and not for any incidental quality (Ethics, 263).

He acknowledged that some people might behave considerately towards others for motives of utility, involving benefit for themselves or those close to them. While not as morally desirable as pure benevolence, it was preferable to selfishness:

> [T]hose who love each other on the ground of utility do not love each other for their personal qualities, but only insofar as they derive some benefit from each other (Ethics, 261).

> ... [T]hose whose friendship is based on goodness are eager to benefit each other ... and where there is this sort of rivalry there is no occasion for complaints or quarrels ... But utilitarian friendship does give rise to complaints, because since each associates with the other for his own benefit, they are always wanting the better of the bargain, and thinking that they have much less than they should, and grumbling because they do not get as much as they want (Ethics, 282).

Aristotle considered that benevolent behaviour is the essential bond that holds a community together:

> ... [T]he affection of parent for child and of child for parent seems to be a natural instinct not only in man but in birds and most animals; and similarly the mutual friendliness between members of the same species, especially of the human species; that is why we commend those who love their fellow men ... Friendship also seems to be the bond that holds communities together (Ethics, 258).

He considered that 'right' behaviour would be 'selfish', since it was in accordance with people's essential nature, and would, therefore, lead to their happiness:

> [I]f everyone were striving for what is fine, and trying his hardest to do the finest deeds, then both the public welfare would be truly served, and each individual would enjoy the greatest of goods, since virtue is of this kind ... so it is right for the good man to be self-loving, because he will be both benefited himself by performing fine actions and also help others (Ethics, 302).

Smith

Smith unquestionably believed that the self-interested, competitive market economy was the most powerful force for stimulating economic progress. However, he was deeply conscious of the damaging effects of the competitive market economy. He considered that the fundamental impulse for business activity was the pursuit of profits and wealth. This powerful impulse paradoxically stimulated business people to achieve immense progress, but it was also a 'deception':

> The pleasures of wealth and greatness, ... strike the imagination as something grand and beautiful and noble, of which the attainment is well worth all the toil and anxiety which we are apt to bestow upon it. And it is well that nature imposes upon us in this manner. It is this deception which rouses and keeps in continual motion the industry of mankind. It is this which first prompted them to cultivate the ground, to build houses, to found cities and commonwealths, and to invent and improve all the sciences and arts, which ennoble human life; which have entirely changed the whole face of the globe, have turned the rude forests of nature into agreeable and fertile plains, and made the trackless and barren ocean a new fund of subsistence, and the great high road of communication to the different nations of the earth. The earth by these labours of mankind has been obliged to redouble her natural fertility, and to maintain a greater number of inhabitants (Smith, 1982: 183–4).

Smith considered that this path was a 'deception' because of the negative consequences for human beings in relation to their own psychology and happiness:

> Power and riches then appear to be, what they are, enormous and operose [sic] machines contrived to produce a few trifling conveniences to the body, consisting of springs the most nice and delicate, which must be kept in order with the most anxious attention, and which, in spite of all our care are ready every moment to burst into pieces, and to crush in their ruins their unfortunate possessor ... How many people ruin themselves by laying out money on trinkets of frivolous utility ... All their pockets are stuffed with little conveniences ... They walk about loaded with a multitude of baubles ... If we consider the real satisfaction which all these things are capable of affording, by itself and separated from the beauty of the arrangement which is fitted to promote it, it will appear in the highest degree contemptible and trifling ... [W]ealth and greatness are mere trinkets of frivolous utility, no more adapted for procuring ease of body or tranquillity of mind than the tweezer-cases of the lovers of toys (Smith, 1982: 180–1, 183–4).

For Smith, the key to human happiness is found in tranquillity, not wealth and greatness:

> Happiness is tranquillity and enjoyment. Without tranquillity there can be no enjoyment; and where there is perfect tranquillity there is scarce anything which is not capable of amusing ... [T]he pleasures of vanity and superiority are seldom consistent with perfect tranquillity, the principle and foundation of all real and satisfactory enjoyment (Smith, 1982: 149–50).

Smith considered that human psychology required social cohesion as the foundation of a good society in which all citizens could achieve happiness:

> All the members of human society stand in need of each others assistance ... . Where the necessary assistance is reciprocally afforded from love, from gratitude, from friendship, and esteem, the society flourishes and is happy. All the different members of it are bound together by the agreeable bonds of love and affection, and are, as it were, drawn to one common centre of mutual good offices (Smith, 1982: 85).

The foundation of such cohesion is 'benevolence':

> [T]o feel much for others and little for ourselves, to restrain our selfish, and to indulge our benevolent affections, constitutes the perfection of human nature; and can alone among mankind produce that harmony of sentiments and passions in which consists their whole grace and propriety (Smith, 1982: 25).

In Smith's view, the division of labour is a two-edged sword, which powerfully stimulates productivity growth, but at the same time has deeply damaging effects on workers' lives:

> In the progress of the division of labour, the employment of the far greater part of those who live by labour, that is the great body of the people, comes to be confined to a few very simple operations, frequently to one or two. But the understanding of the greater part of men are necessarily formed by their ordinary employments. The man whose life is spent in performing a few simple operations, of which the effects too are, perhaps, always the same, or very nearly the same, has no occasion to exert his understanding, or to exercise his invention in finding out expedients for removing difficulties which never occur. He naturally loses, therefore, the

habit of such exertion, and generally becomes as stupid and ignorant as it is possible for a human creature to become ... But in every improved and civilised society, this is the state into which the labouring poor, that is, the great body of the people, must necessarily fall, unless government takes some pains to prevent it (Smith, 1976, Vol. 2: 302–3).

The division of labour stimulates growth of average real incomes, but at the same time the natural tendency of the workings of the market economy is towards socio-economic inequality:

It is in the most thriving [countries], or those which are growing the fastest, that the wages of labour are the highest ... Wherever there is great property, there is great inequality. For every rich man, there must be at least five hundred poor, and the affluence of the few supposes the indigence of the many (Smith, 1976, Vol. 2: 232).

Smith considered that in a market economy, there was a strong propensity for society to be pervaded by admiration for success in the pursuit of wealth and position, and, correspondingly to look down upon poor people. For Smith, this constituted a deep corruption of a society's ethical foundation:

[T]he disposition to admire, and almost to worship, the rich and powerful, and to despise, or at least, to neglect persons of poor and mean condition, though necessary to maintain the distinction of ranks and the order of society, is at the same time, the great and most universal cause of the corruption of our moral sentiments (Smith, 1982: 61).

Despite Smith's hostility to state intervention, he recognised that there were critically important functions for the state to undertake. In Smith's view, the potential scope for such action was extremely wide, and was likely to vary depending on the time and place:

[The third duty of government] is erecting and maintaining those public institutions and those public works which, though they may be in the highest degree advantageous to a great society are, however, of such a nature that the profit could never repay the expence to any individual or small number of individuals, and which it therefore cannot be expected that any individual or small number of individuals should erect or maintain. The performance of this duty requires, too, very different degrees of expence in the different periods of society[6] (Smith, 1976, Vol. 2: 244).

Mill

John Stuart Mill considered that the key social problem of the future would be 'how to unite the greatest individual liberty of action with a common ownership in the raw materials of the globe, and an equal participation of all in the benefits of combined labour' (Mill, 1998: xvii). He believed that the requisite social transformation would involve 'an equivalent change of character ... both in the uncultivated herd who now compose the labouring masses, and in the immense majority of their employers' (Mill, 1998: xvii). Both these classes needed to learn to 'combine for generous, or at all events for public and social purposes, and not, as hitherto, solely for narrowly interested ones': 'But the capacity to do this has always existed in mankind, and is not, nor is ever likely to be, extinct ... The deep-rooted selfishness which forms the general character of the existing state of society, is *so* deeply rooted only because the whole course of existing institutions tends to foster it' (Mill, 1998: xvii). Mill considered that 'the idea is essentially repulsive of a society only held together by the relations and feelings arising out of pecuniary interests', and that 'there is something naturally attractive in a form of society abounding in strong personal attachments and disinterested self-devotion' (Mill, 1998: 133).

Mill believed that the cooperative movement was the main path through which society could gradually establish new forms of social consciousness. J. S. Mill believed that such a form of socialism contained far fewer dangers than the proposals of the radical socialists who proposed 'the management of the whole productive resources of the country by one central authority, the general government' (Mill, 1998: 414).[7] He took the idea of establishing a communist idea very seriously indeed. However, he thought that the psychology of the mass of the population was not yet ready to make a communist system work effectively:

> The one certainty, is that communism, to be successful requires a high standard of both moral and intellectual education in all members of the community – moral, to qualify them for doing their part honestly and energetically in the labour of life under no inducement but their share in the general interest of the association, and their feeling of duty and sympathy towards it; intellectual, to make them capable of estimating distant interests and entering into complex considerations, sufficiently at least to be able to discriminate, in these matters, good counsel from bad (Mill, 1998: 426).

Mill was emphatic in his insistence on the eventual possibility of establishing a communist morality, but believed that it would take a long time to achieve the moral and intellectual pre-requisites for such a society. Like the classical

Greeks, Plato and Aristotle, in which Mill was deeply versed, he believed that education was critical to establishing the sort of benevolent morality that is the basis for a good society, in which all citizens can fulfil their human potential:

> Now I reject altogether the notion that it is impossible for education and cultivation such as is implied in these things to be made the inheritance of every person in the nation; but I am convinced that it is very difficult, and that the passage to it from our present condition can only be slow. I admit that in the points of moral education on which the success of communism depends, the present state of society is demoralising, and that only a communist association can effectually train mankind for communism. It is for communism, then, to prove by practical experiment, its power of giving this training (Mill, 1998: 426–7).

Mill regarded the proper role of the government as one of the great issues of political economy. However, he acknowledged that it was an immensely complex subject, which 'does not admit of any universal solution' (Mill, 1998: 325).[8] He was in favour of 'restricting to the narrowest compass the intervention of a public authority in the business of the community' but acknowledged that government interference was warranted wherever it was 'required by some great good' (Mill, 1998: 334–5). The possible array of such circumstances could be very wide indeed. Mill rejected the dogmatic arguments of the extreme 'laissez-faire' school, which 'have a disposition to restrict the interference of government within the narrowest bounds', confining it 'to the protection of person and property against fraud' (Mill, 1998: 159 and 324). He believed that the government should undertake 'anything which it is desirable should be done for the general interests of mankind or of future generations, or for the present interests of those members of the community who require external aid, but which is not of a nature to remunerate individuals or associations for undertaking it' (Mill, 1998: 366).[9] He recognised that the sphere of necessary government activity would be different in different circumstances:

> In the particular circumstances of a given age or nation, there is scarcely anything really important to the general interest, which may not be desirable, or even necessary, that the government should take upon itself, not because private individuals cannot effectually perform it, but because they will not. At some times and places, there will be no roads, docks, harbours, canals, works of irrigation, hospitals, schools, colleges, printing-presses, unless the government establishes them; the public being too little advanced in intelligence to appreciate the ends, or not sufficiently practised in joint action to be capable of the means[10] (Mill, 1998: 366).

Darwin

At the core of Darwin's theory of natural selection was the principle of Natural Selection: 'Owing to this struggle for life, any variation, however slight and from whatever cause proceeding, if it be profitable to an individual of any species, in its infinitely complex relations to other organic beings and to external nature, will tend to the preservation of that individual, and will generally be inherited by its offspring' (Darwin, 1985: 115). Darwin insisted upon the term being taken in its 'large and metaphorical sense, including dependence of one being on another, and including (which is more important) not only the life of the individual, but success of the progeny' (Darwin, 1985: 116). Darwin's ideas were far removed from those of the Social Darwinists.

In *The Descent of Man* Darwin pays the closest attention to the evolution of moral qualities in human beings. He ascribes a central role in human evolution to the development of 'social instincts'. While these have evolved from similar instincts in the rest of the animal kingdom, Darwin believes that these are far more developed in human beings: '[O]f all the differences between man and lower animals, the moral sense is by far the most important' (Darwin, 2004: 120). He ranges widely in exploring the origins of these instincts among human beings. The instincts include 'love', 'mutual love', 'sympathy', 'sympathetic feelings', 'instinctive sympathy', 'the all-important emotion of sympathy', 'sympathetic kindness to others', 'mutual aid', 'fidelity', and 'benevolent actions' (Darwin, 2004: chapters 4–5). He uses the word 'love' more than ninety times in the *Descent of Man* (Darwin, 2004: lxiii).

Darwin argues that primeval men, the ape-like progenitors of man, became social beings through the acquisition of 'the same instinctive feelings, which impel other animals to live in a body': 'They would have felt uneasy when separated from their comrades, from whom they would have felt some degree of love; they would have warned each other of danger, and have given mutual aid in attack or defence. All this implies some degree of sympathy, fidelity, and courage' (Darwin, 2004: 154–5). Darwin emphasised that these qualities were of 'paramount importance to the lower animals', and believed that they were probably acquired in a similar manner by humans, namely by natural selection, aided by inherited habit. Darwin linked the development of these qualities closely to competition between tribes of human beings who vie with each other for access to limited resources. The successful tribe would be that which includes the greater number of 'courageous, sympathetic and faithful members, who were always ready to warn each other of danger, to aid each and defend each other' (Darwin, 2004: 155).

Darwin believed that 'primitive men' at a 'very remote period' were influenced by the praise and blame of their fellows, and through this acquired social instincts that helped them to succeed in competition with other groups of their own species. He believed that the foundation-stone of morality became 'do unto others as ye would they should do unto you'. As human society evolved, people's moral sense or conscience also became more complex, 'originating in the social instincts, largely guided by the approbation of [their] fellow-men, ruled by reason, self-interest, and in later times, by deep religious feelings, and confirmed by instruction and habit' (Darwin, 2004: 157).

There is no doubt that Darwin considered benevolence and sympathy as central factors in human evolution. However, there is equally no doubt that he considered that this instinct originated in inter-tribe aggression in the early phase of human evolution. He visualised intense sociability within the given society of human beings as perfectly compatible with violent conflict with other social groups: 'It is no argument against savage man being a social animal, that the tribes inhabiting adjacent districts are almost always at war with each other; for the social instincts never extend to all the individuals of the same species' (Darwin, 2004: 132). He emphasises that in tribal societies the social virtues are 'practised almost exclusively in relation to the men of the same tribe', whereas, 'their opposites are not regarded as crimes in relation to the men of other tribes' (Darwin, 2004: 141).

However, Darwin clearly visualised that the 'social instincts', which initially were confined to individual tribes among 'savages' and 'primeval man', would extend across much wider spans of humanity among 'civilised' people: '[T]he so-called moral sense is aboriginally derived from the social instincts, *for both relate at first exclusively to the community*' (Darwin, 2004: 143) (My emphasis: PN). Darwin thought that a chief cause of the 'low morality of savages, as judged by our standards', was the '*confinement of sympathy to the same tribe*' (Darwin, 2004: 143) (My emphasis: PN). In other words, Darwin believed that a critical part of the evolution of human beings' morality was the generalisation of the social instincts of love, sympathy, and benevolence, to an ever-wider circle of human beings: 'At all times throughout the world tribes have supplanted other tribes; and as morality is one important element in their success, the standard of morality and the number of well-endowed men will thus everywhere tend to rise and increase' (Darwin, 2004: 158). Darwin considered that the principal mechanisms through which superior moral standards would spread more widely were firstly, through the extension of the powers of the 'civilised races' so as to 'take the place of the lower races', and secondly, through an increase in the 'number of men endowed with high intellectual and moral faculties' (Darwin, 2004: 160 and 166).[11]

Kropotkin

Kropotkin was born in 1842. During his youth he made long journeys in vast expanses of Eastern Siberia and Northern Manchuria: 'Even in those few spots where animal life teemed in abundance I failed to find – although I was eagerly looking for it – that bitter struggle for the means of existence, which was considered by most Darwinists (though not always by Darwin himself) as the dominant characteristic of struggle for life, and the main factor of evolution' (Kropotkin, 1939: 12). Kropotkin came to the conclusion that in the animal kingdom 'sociable habits' are of 'overwhelming importance'. They secure for animals 'a better protection from their enemies, facilities for getting food (winter provisions, migrations, etc.), longevity, and, therefore, a greater development of intellectual faculties' (Kroptokin, 1939: 18). Kropotkin was fully aware of the 'immense amount of warfare and extermination going on amidst various species, especially amidst various classes of animals'. However, he believed that there is 'as much, or perhaps even more, of mutual support, mutual aid and mutual defence amidst animals belonging to the same species, or at least, to the same society: Sociability is as much a law of nature as mutual struggle' (Kropotkin, 1939: 24).

Darwin argued that the 'struggle for existence' is 'almost invariably most severe between the individuals of the same species, for they frequent the same districts, require the same food, and are exposed to the same dangers' (Darwin, 1985: 126). He also argued that 'the struggle will generally be almost equally severe ... between varieties of the same species' (Darwin, 1985: 126). Kropotkin observes that Darwin's statement, which has been widely generalised in different ways in other fields, is based on the flimsiest of evidence, which is uncharacteristic of Darwin: 'The struggle between individuals of the same species is not illustrated by even one single instance: it is taken as granted; and the competition between closely-allied animal species is illustrated by but five examples, out of which one at least, is now proved to be doubtful' (Kropotkin, 1939: 63). Kropotkin was greatly influenced by the Russian zoologist, Kessler, who said: 'Zoology and those sciences which deal with man, continually insist upon what they call the pitiless law of struggle for existence. But they forget the existence of another law which may be described as the law of mutual aid, which law, at least for the animals, is far more essential than the former' (quoted in Kropotkin, 1939: 25).[12]

Kropotkin chronicles in great detail the ways in which animals, from the smallest to the largest, cooperate. His account begins with the ants:

> The ants and the termites have renounced their 'Hobbesian war', and they are the better for it. Their wonderful nests, their buildings, superior in

relative size to those of man; their paved roads and overground vaulted galleries; their spacious halls and granaries; their corn-fields, harvesting and 'malting' of grain; their rational methods of nursing their eggs and larvae, and of building special nests for rearing the aphides ... ; and finally, their courage, pluck, and superior intelligence – all these are the natural outcome of the mutual aid which they practise at every stage of their lives (Kropotkin, 1939: 30).

On birds, Kropotkin writes:

[A]t nesting time ... our trees are crowned with groups of crows' nests; our hedges are full of nests of smaller birds; our farmhouses give shelter to colonies of swallows; our old towers are the refuge of hundreds of nocturnal birds; and pages might be filled with the most charming descriptions of the peace and harmony which prevail in almost all nesting associations ... Life in societies does not cease when the nesting period is over ... Social life is practised at that time chiefly for its own sake – partly for security, but chiefly for the pleasures derived from it. ... And, finally, we have that immense display of mutual aid among birds – their migrations ... So far from migrating isolately, in order to secure for each separate individual the advantages of better food or shelter which are to be found in another district – they always wait for each other, and gather in flocks, before they move north or south, in accordance with the season (Kropotkin, 1939: 47).

Turning to consideration of larger animals Kropotkin writes:

Not long ago the small streams of Northern America and Northern Siberia were peopled with colonies of beavers, and up to the seventeenth century like colonies swarmed in Northern Russia. The flat lands of the four great continents are still covered with countless colonies of mice, ground-squirrels, marmots, and other rodents. In the lower latitudes of Asia and Africa the forests are still the abode of numerous families of elephants, rhinoceroses, and numberless societies of monkeys. In the far north, the reindeer aggregate in numberless herds; while still farther north we find herds of the musk-oxen and numberless bands of polar foxes. The coasts of the ocean are enlivened by flocks of seals and morses; its waters by shoals of sociable cetaceans; and even in the depths of the wild plateau of Central Asia we find herds of wild horses, wild donkeys, wild camels and wild sheep. All these mammals live in societies and nations sometimes numbering hundreds of thousands of individuals, although now, after three centuries of gunpowder civilisation, we find but the debris of the immense aggregations of old (Kropotkin, 1939: 48).

Kropotkin believed that the same forces of mutual aid have played a central role in human evolution, and that they have given to human beings, 'in addition to the same advantages, the possibility of working out those institutions which have enabled mankind to survive in its hard struggle against Nature, and to progress, not withstanding all the vicissitudes of its history' (Kropotkin, 1939: 18).

Freud

In the last years of his life, Freud came to the conclusion that human behaviour was the result of the interaction of two different kinds of instinct: 'those which seek to lead what is living to death, and others, the sexual instincts, which are perpetually attempting and achieving a renewal of life' (Freud, 2001a: 46). He believed that in this respect, the human instincts mimicked those of the wider world of living things, with the objective of 'bringing people together into large unities' (Freud, 2001b: 103):

> [T]he union of a number of cells into a vital association – the multicellular character of organisms – has become a means of prolonging their life. One cell helps to preserve the life of anoher, and the community of cells can survive even if individual cells have to die ... [W]e might attempt to apply the libido theory which has been arrived at in psychoanalysis to the mutual relationship of cells ... The germ cells require their libido, the activity of their life instincts, for themselves, as a reserve against their later momentous constructive activity ... In this way the libido of our sexual instincts would coincide with the Eros of the poets and philosophers which holds all living things together (Freud, 2001a: 50).

Freud suggests that 'living substance at the time of its coming into life was torn apart into small particles, which ever since endeavoured to reunite through the sexual instinct' (Freud, 2001a: 58). He considered that love is one of the 'foundations of civilisation': 'The love which founded the family ... carries on its function of binding together considerable numbers of people, and it does so in a more intensive fashion than can be effected through the interest of work in common' (Freud, 2001b: 101–2). Freud viewed civilisation as 'a process in the service of Eros', whose purpose is to 'combine single individuals and after that families, then races, peoples and nations into one great unity, the unity of mankind' (Freud, 2001b: 122). In recent times, the neurologist, Oliver Sacks has echoed Freud's sentiments of the function of Eros: 'One sees that beautiful and ultimate metaphysical truth, which has been stated by poets and physicians and metaphysicians in all ages – by Leibniz and Donne and Dante and Freud: that Eros is the oldest and strongest of the gods; that love is the alpha and omega of being; and that the work of healing, of rendering whole is first and last, the business of love' (Sacks, 1982: 239–40).

Fromm

The view is widely held that 'the more primitive the man, the more aggressive he is' (Fromm, 1997: 180). Fromm presents a wide range of anthropological evidence to suggest a different view of human aggression. The vast bulk of man's history has been lived as a hunter: '[W]e owe our biology, psychology, and customs to the hunters of the time past' (Fromm, 1997: 180). Fromm assembles evidence from a range of archaeologists and anthropologists about 'primitive' hunters and gatherers during the Stone Age to conclude that the qualities often attributed to human nature of destructiveness, cruelty and associability ' ... are remarkably missing in the least civilised men' (Fromm, 1997: 190). E. S. Service's study of ancient hunters and gatherers observes that 'primitive peoples ... "give things away", they admire generosity, they expect hospitality, they punish thrift and selfishness' (quoted in Fromm, 1997: 193). Service argues that 'in no primitive band is anyone denied access to the resources of nature ... The natural resources on which the bands depend are collective, or communal, property ... [T]he most primitive societies are at the same time the most egalitarian ... [which] must be related to the fact that because of rudimentary technology this kind of society depends more fully more of the time than any other' (quoted in Fromm, 1997: 196).

At the heart of these attitudes was the fact that due to low population pressure over hundreds of thousands of years in the early evolution of mankind, there was an abundance of resources and little need for conflict (Fromm, 1997: 200–01). It is only as resources begin to become scarce that war becomes more common. Fromm argues that 'warlikeness is not a function of man's natural drives that manifest themselves in the most primitive form of society, but of his development in civilisation' (Fromm, 1997: 205). Glover and Ginsberg conclude: [I]f the facts do not support the view of a primitive idyllic peace, they are perhaps compatible with those who think that primary or unprovoked aggressiveness is not an inherent element of human nature' (quoted in Fromm, 1997: 207).

Once mankind reached the Neolithic period, from around 9000-7000 BC onwards, the situation changes. Until this point human beings were completely dependent on nature. As population densities grew, so too did pressure on natural resources, and human beings needed to develop their skills and inventiveness to transform nature in order to support themselves.[13] Human beings needed to 'plant more seed, to till more land, and to breed more animals' in order to meet growing population densities. Human beings needed to 'use their will and intention to make things happen ... [T]he discovery of agriculture was the foundation of all scientific thinking and later technical development' (Fromm, 1997: 210). There is much evidence from this period to show the central role of women in society: 'Following the older division of labour, where men hunted and women gathered roots and fruits, agriculture was most likely the discovery of women, while animal husbandry was that of men' (Fromm, 1997: 213). Fromm hypothesises that 'the earth and women's capacity to give birth ... quite naturally gave the mother a supreme place in the world of early agriculturalists' (Fromm, 1997: 213–4). Women are likely to have had a central role in developing storage vessels for food. This period saw the invention of the art of pottery: '[The potter] can form her lump [of clay] as she wishes; she can go on adding to it without any doubts as to the solidity of the joints. In thinking of "creating", the free activity of the potter in "making form where there was no form" constantly recurs to man's [sic] mind' (V. G. Childe, quoted in Fromm, 1997: 211). Religion often centred around the figure of the mother-goddess: 'The mother-goddess of the Neolithic religion is not only the mistress of wild animals. She is also the patroness of the hunt, the patroness of agriculture, and mistress of plant life' (Fromm, 1997: 215).[14]

In Fromm's view, Neolithic society was typically 'unaggressive and peaceful': 'The reason for this lies in the spirit of affirmation of life, [the] lack of destructiveness was an essential trait of all matriarchal societies' (Fromm, 1997: 217). The way of life of Neolithic people was 'conducive to the development of cooperation and peaceful living ... Prehistoric hunters and agriculturalists had no opportunity to develop a passionate striving for property or envy of the "haves", because there was no private property to hold on to and no important economic differences to cause envy' (Fromm, 1997: 219).

However, in around the fourth and third millennium BC a new kind of society developed under the pressure of increased population densities. Within a relatively short period of time, historically speaking, human beings learned to harness the physical energy of oxen and the energy of the winds. Mankind invented the plough, the wheeled cart, and the sailing boat, discovered the chemical processes involved in smelting copper ores and the physical properties of metals, and began to work out a solar calendar. The way was prepared for the art of writing and standards and measures: 'In no period of history until the days of Galileo was progress in knowledge so rapid and far-reaching discoveries so frequent' (V. G. Childe, quoted in Fromm, 1997: 221). These changes were accompanied by a profound social transformation. States based on bureaucratic elites emerged. Urban centres, specialisation and trade began to assume centre stage. The production of an economic surplus for exchange became a central goal of economic life. Human beings began to be widely used as an economic instrument for the production of marketed goods. Class differentiation developed. War in the pursuit of economic resources assumed centre stage.

The role of women in society and religion changed dramatically: 'No longer was the fertility of the soil the source of life and creativity, but the intellect which produced new inventions, techniques, abstract thinking, and the state with its laws ... [T]he mind became the creative power, and simultaneously, not women, but men, dominated society' (Fromm, 1997: 224–5). In this patriarchal society, control was of central importance, including 'control of slaves, women and children: 'The new patriarchal man literally "makes" the earth. His technique is not simply modification of the natural processes, but their domination and control by man, resulting in new products which are not found in nature' (Fromm, 1997: 225).

Fromm's concludes that human beings are not innately aggressive. They have become so only in the relatively short period of time during which the competitive market economy has come to dominate human beings' lives. The productivity and creativity of the market economy has allowed the vast expansion of human population and the immense increase in productivity. However, the price has been domination by aggression, masculinity and warfare: 'The history of civilisation, from the destruction of Carthage and Jerusalem to the destruction of Dresden, Hiroshima, and the people, soil, and trees of Vietnam, is a tragic record of sadism and destructiveness' (Fromm, 1997: 227). Fromm believes that it is possible to 'complete the full circle and construct a society in which no one is threatened: not the child by the parent; not the parent by the superior; no social class by another; no nation by a super-power ... [T]he empirical data shows that a real possibility exists to build such a world in a foreseeable future if the political and psychological road-blocks are removed' (Fromm, 1997: 575).

United States

Within the United States there has been intense debate over the role of competition and aggression in economic life. The American Economics Association was founded in 1885, at the high-point of the 'Gilded Age', with the express purpose of combating both Social Darwinism and 'laissez-faire orthodoxy'. The founder of the AEA, Richard T. Ely, wrote: 'We regard the state as an educational and ethical agency whose positive assistance is one of the indispensable conditions of human progress (quoted in Foner, 1998: 130).[15] Many younger economists believed that private property had become a 'means of depriving others of their freedom', and that 'poverty posed a far graver danger to the republic than an activist state' (Foner, 1998: 130).

During the Progressive Era leading up to the First World War, a broad coalition of forces emerged in America to nourish the idea of an activist national state to enable the realisation of 'freedom' for the mass of people. Laissez-faire became 'anathema among the lovers of liberty'. It was thought that only 'energetic government' was able to 'create the social conditions for freedom'. The Progressives were wedded to the idea that freedom required conscious creation of the social conditions for full human development.

T. H. Green, the British philosopher, made a profound impact with his lectures in the United States in which he argued that freedom was a 'positive concept'. Green's ideas on 'positive freedom' far precede similar notions propounded by such late twentieth century philosophers as Isaiah Berlin (Berlin, 1969) or A. K. Sen (e.g., Dreze and Sen, 1989). Berlin's treatment of the notion of 'positive freedom' remains abstract and philosophical: 'The "positive" sense of the word "liberty" derives from the wish on the part of the individual to be his own master. I wish my life and decisions to depend on myself, not on external forces of whatever kind. I wish to be the instrument of my own, not of other men's, acts of will. I wish to be a subject, not an object; to be moved by reasons, by conscious purposes, which are my own, not by causes which affect me, as it were, from outside. I wish to be somebody, not nobody' (Berlin, 1969: 131). Unlike T. H. Green, Berlin does not link the concept of positive freedom with the conditions necessary for people to realise their positive freedoms, namely education, health, housing, and other cultural and material prerequisites for a 'fulfilled life'. If one does so, then the notion of positive freedom immediately raises the question of the degree to which different segments of society have the wherewithal to be positively free, to be fulfilled and whether the possession of those capabilities by some people is at the expense of others.

Leading Progressive thinker John Dewey argued: 'Effective freedom [is] far different from the highly formal and limited concept of autonomous individuals that need to be protected from outside restraint' (quoted in Foner, 1998: 153). For Dewey, freedom meant 'effective power to do specific things', and it was therefore, 'a function of the distribution of powers that exists at a given time'. William F. Willoughby argued that Progressivism 'looks to state action as the only practicable means now in sight, of giving to the individual, all individuals, not merely a small economically strong class, real freedom' (quoted in Foner, 1998: 153).

The influence of the Progressive movement reached its highpoint in the 1912 election, a four way contest between incumbent Republican president William Howard Taft, former president Theodore Roosevelt, now running as a candidate for the Progressive Party, Democrat Woodrow Wilson, and Eugene V. Debs, representing the Socialist Party, now at the height of its influence. The central theme of the campaign was the relationship between political and economic freedom in the age of the large corporation. Debs' Socialist Party campaigned with the ultimate goal of abolishing the capitalist system altogether, propelling the country 'from wage slavery to free cooperation, from capitalist oligarchy to industrial democracy'. Although his party was thoroughly permeated with laissez-faire ideology, under the influence of the widespread Progressive thinking, Woodrow Wilson maintained: 'freedom today is something more than being left alone. The program of a government of freedom must in these days be positive, not negative merely' (quoted in Foner, 1998: 159).[16]

The Great Depression had a major impact on the struggle over the interpretation of 'freedom' in the United States. By 1932, the United States' GNP had fallen by one-third, prices by nearly one-half, and over 15 million Americans were out of work. For those able to find jobs, real wages fell precipitously: 'Hungry men and women lined the streets of major cities; thousands more inhabited the ramshackle shanty towns called Hoovervilles that sprang up in parks and on abandoned land ... No part of America was untouched by the crisis. When he assumed the Presidency in 1933, Franklin D. Roosevelt proclaimed: 'For too many Americans, life is no longer free; liberty no longer real; men can no longer follow the pursuit of happiness' (quoted in Foner, 1998: 196). Under Roosevelt's guidance, the Democratic Party led the country towards large-scale state intervention to reconstruct the economy and provide citizens with social security. The Depression discredited the idea that social progress rested on the unrestrained pursuit of wealth and transformed expectations of government. It reinvigorated the Progressive conviction that the national state must protect Americans from the vicissitudes of the marketplace. It placed 'social citizenship', with a broad public guarantee of economic security, at the forefront of American discussions of freedom.

These ideas remained as the mainstream of US political thought for long into the post-war world, reinforced by the massive task of economic and social reconstruction in war-ravaged Europe. For example, in 1975, Arthur Okun, chairman of the President's Council for Economic Advisors, and of course, a 'child of the Depression', said: 'The market needs a place and the market should be kept in its place ... Given the chance, it would sweep away all other values and establish a vending-machine society. I would not give it more than two cheers' (quoted in Yergin and Stanislav, 1998: 375).

Mao Zedong

China under Chairman Mao attempted to build a communist society based on principles of selfless benevolence and maximum opportunities for the whole society to achieve positive freedoms. This amounted to nothing less than an attempt to transform people's work motivation, to overcome the classic 'principal-agent' problem, by liberating human productive energies from the link with material reward. 'Serve the people' (*wei renmin fuwu*) was the foundation of Maoist ideology. The phrase was first enunciated by Chairman Mao in 1944, in a speech at the memorial meeting in honour of Zhang Side.

Chairman Mao believed that under the leadership of the communist party it would be possible to build a non-capitalist, humane society which provided the opportunity for the whole population to fulfil its human potential. It was a philosophy that was powerfully driven by the intention to restrict drastically the population's 'negative' freedoms to act in accordance with its individual wishes free of external restriction, while providing the maximum equality of opportunity for citizens to achieve their 'positive freedoms'.

During the Great Leap Forward and again in the Cultural Revolution, the Party leadership led the drive to drastically reduce inequalities in the workplace. It was accepted that, as in the USSR, it was necessary in the 'socialist' phase to stimulate workers' enthusiasm through the principle of 'from each according to their labour', which Marx termed 'bourgeois right':

> Under this mode of distribution, each and every person's labour is rewarded on the basis of an equal standard – labour is the measure and from that perspective [the reward] appears equal. But great differences exist in the conditions of individual labourers: some are stronger, some weaker; some have a higher cultural level, some a lower one; some have more mouths to feed, some fewer and so forth. Therefore, to use a unified measure of labour as the measure of distribution and to apply this to very unequal individuals must result in real inequality and differences of living standards. The peculiarities of bourgeois right manifest themselves; equal right will in fact be the premise of inequality (Comrades, 1974: 596–7).

The explicit goal of the Party, under Chairman Mao's leadership was to lead society towards the goal of 'communism', beyond even the 'socialist' stage. Especially during the Great Leap Forward (1958–59) and the Cultural Revolution (1966–76), under Chairman Mao's leadership, the attempt was made to push forward towards a communist society: 'In a socialist society, it is necessary to acknowledge the differences in the rewards for labour, but the differences ought not to be too great. We must actively create the conditions for communist society's stage, "from each according to their abilities, to each according to their needs", and should constantly strive to lessen the three great differences and increasingly extirpate the influence of the bourgeois right' (Comrades, 1974: 597). Under Chairman Mao's leadership, the Party attempted 'gradually lessening differences' and 'gradually increasing the element of "distribution according to need"' (Comrades, 1974: 597). It was argued that various types of welfare measures and so forth were in reality the 'sprouts of communist distribution according to need': 'We ought to rationally and gradually shrink, not expand, the distance between the individual incomes of the masses of the people and those of the functionaries in the party, the national government, in industry, and in the people's communes' (Comrades, 1974: 598). The Party leadership advocated 'resolutely upholding the principle of the Paris Commune and opposing the system of high salaries (for the few)': '[This] has the advantage of promoting intimate relations between the party and the masses, provides a style of plain living and hard struggle, and contributes the revolutionisation of the thinking of many cadres' (Comrades, 1974: 597–8).

Search for the 'Mean'

> *We were inclined to think of the psychological crisis of the waking worlds as being the difficult passage from adolescence to maturity; for in essence it was an outgrowing of juvenile interests, a discarding of toys and childish games, and a discovery of the interests of adult life. Tribal prestige, individual dominance, military glory, industrial triumphs lost their obsessive glamour, and instead the happy creatures delighted in civilised social intercourse, in cultural activities, and in the common enterprise of world-building.*

> *On my native planet ... I had taken comfort in the thought that at least the massed effect of all our blind striving must be the slow but glorious awakening of the human spirit ... But now I saw that there was no guarantee of any such triumph. It seemed that the universe, or the maker of the universe, must be indifferent to the fate of worlds ... [T]hat all struggle should be finally absolutely in vain, must be sheer evil. In my horror it seemed to me that Hate must be the Star Maker.*

(Olaf Stapledon, *Star Maker*, 1937: 51 and 130)

The force of individual self-interest exercised through the market mechanism and the pursuit of profit has been a hugely progressive force historically. The stimulus this has provided to savings, investment, and technical progress has served to promote economic development and the achievement of national wealth. It has widened the scope for individual freedom from control by others over people's lives, and provided the foundation of democratic institutions. It has stimulated the reduction in poverty through the impact on economic growth and the advance of the productive forces. It has contributed to peace among nations thanks to the market's function of nurturing contacts and trust across national boundaries.

However, the market mechanism is a two-edged sword. The pursuit of individual freedom through the market mechanism and the profit motive is a force that human beings create, but which contains its own deep contradictions. These contradictions have reached new heights in the epoch of modern globalisation at the same time that the achievements of free market capitalism have also reached a new apogee. Social thinkers as different as Karl Marx, Adam Smith and John Stuart Mill have recognised the inherent contradictions within capitalism. They each greatly admired its dynamic force, but deeply feared its uncontrolled character and the fact that it unleashed and nourished the selfish, materialistic, non-benevolent aspect of human nature.

In the epoch of the Global Business Revolution, the stimulation of individualism, selfishness and greed has reached a new intensity. This has powerfully affected people's lives as both producers and consumers. From the perspective of people as producers, business leaders' daily lives are built around a remorseless global struggle for competitive success in the pursuit of profit. The battlefield struggle governs their lives. New information technology has allowed this abstract force to dominate their existence at every hour of the day. Pressures from globally integrated markets feed through into the lives of the workforce in companies at every level in the global value chain. From the perspective of human beings as consumers, new information technologies, new marketing techniques and increasingly powerful global mass media companies ever more effectively stimulate increased individual consumption of goods and services as the path through which people are promised individual satisfaction.

In the epoch of capitalist globalisation, the force of self-interest, the market mechanism and the profit motive has produced unique threats to sustainability of the human species. These include the unprecedented threat to the global environment, with the possibility that many deep ecological problems already are irreversible. They include the disorganised international financial system. It is now more deeply interconnected than ever before across countries and regions, and faces the possibility of a global financial crisis that involves the whole world. The threats include the fact that globalisation has intensified class inequalities within both rich and poor countries. A truly global class has emerged that lacks any particular national allegiance, while the mass of citizens in both rich and poor countries are tied to their national place of residence and identity. They include the threat to global political stability posed by the challenge of the emerging capitalist countries in the face of inevitable decline in the relative position of the United States. The potential sources of conflict arising from capitalist globalisation include the struggle over scarce resources, especially energy, conflict over the deterioration of the global ecology, and the fact that the world's dominant power is still wedded to its defence through nuclear weapons. A financial crisis in the United States would powerfully and rapidly affect the American economy. This would in turn be likely to lead to a social and political crisis. It is possible to imagine a variety of scenarios in which this would lead ultimately to military conflict between the United States and China. It would be hard to prevent this developing into a global disaster.

Capitalist globalisation is witnessing ever wider penetration of the operations of large firms and their supply chains. The tensions of globalisation are created by the giant firms pursuing profits in the interests of satisfying their customers' wants. However, the main location of political life and regulation remains the nation state, to which most people are bound by virtue of the accident of their birth. The central actors on the global stage, who will determine whether this critical phase of capitalist globalisation is sustainable, are the United States, on the one hand, the world's most hegemonic power, and, on the other hand, the rising force of China, with a population of 1.3 billion people, and the transnational force of the Islamic world, also with the a population of 1.3 billion people. Between them these two sets of people comprise two-fifths of the world's population, contained within relatively unified cultural environments. The future of the world hangs in the balance: is the United States, with the dominance of its individualistic, materialistic, Social Darwinist philosophy capable of interacting with the ancient Islamic and Chinese civilisations to produce a peaceful cooperative solution to the common problems that confront humanity at this critical stage in human beings' evolution? Is it conceivable that under its leadership the United States will be able to cooperate with these two giant groups of people to construct global institutions that can control, regulate and direct capitalist globalisation in ways that ensure a sustainable future for human beings?

From ancient times to the present day, philosophers and political thinkers have sought to find a 'middle way' between competing extremes as the ethical foundation for the good society. Humanity faces a choice of no choice. The human species cannot survive without a sustainable ethic. Neither extreme negative nor extreme positive freedom offers the solution. Human beings must find a common ethical ground from across the different world civilisations, 'using the past to serve the present' to form a common ethic for global survival, which answers people's deep spiritual needs to form the basis of a simple rational philosophy that all people can understand. Human beings have no choice, but to accept their essential duality. They will forever be tortured by the very nature of their existence, by their incomprehension of their purpose and the torture of the prospect of death, and face the certainty that at the end of their life they will not be a single scintilla further advanced towards understanding who they are and why they exist. Human beings socially must do what they have to do individually, namely, to live with their duality, and find ways to balance their destructive, death instincts with their constructive cooperative instincts. They must learn to tame and civilise the market economy in a new way in the context of global capitalism, to serve the collective social purpose on a global scale. The solution to sustainable development lies neither in the utopia of a purely benevolent, selfless, non-competitive world, nor in the anarchy of an unconstrained, individualistic, competitive global capitalism.

Human beings cannot avoid the duality that is at the centre of their being, the struggle between cooperative, loving instincts, and destructive, death instincts. They have no choice but to live with this duality. They must cooperate and love, while living with their fears and instincts to behave aggressively. Freud poses the choice facing mankind with characteristic clarity: '[T]he meaning of the evolution of civilisation is no longer obscure to us. It must present the struggle between Eros and Death, between the instinct of life and the instinct of destruction, as it works itself out in the human species. This struggle is what all life essentially consists of, and the evolution of civilisation may therefore be simply described as the struggle for life of the human species' (Freud, 2001b: 122).

If humanity cannot find a 'mean' that meets deep human needs, its prospects for survival are bleak. The destruction of human civilisation may arise either from the internal self-destructiveness of extreme free market individualism, from the nihilistic response of those excluded and angered by the globalisation of the free market, or, most importantly, from the destructive behaviour of nations fighting each other.

The challenges that are faced by human beings are the product of people's own purposive activities, expressed mainly through the economic system. It is within their collective power to resolve these contradictions. The very depth of the challenges they now face may shock them into the action necessary to ensure the survival of the species. Alongside human beings competitive and destructive instincts are their instincts for species survival through cooperation. However great the challenge may be, human beings have the capability to solve the contradictions that are of their own making. It may only be the approaching 'final hour' which finally forces human beings to grope their way towards globally cooperative solutions.

PART 1.
CAPITALISM'S CONTRADICTORY CHARACTER

Most disputes are due to the fact that there are many scholars, and many ignorant men, so constituted that they can never see more than one side of a fact or idea; and each man claims that the aspect he has seen is the only true and valid aspect.

(Honoré de Balzac,
letter to Don Michele Angelo Cajetani, Prince of Teano,
dedication in *Cousine Bette*)[1]

1.1 What is 'Globalisation'?

The recent explosive changes in the world business system constitute a surge forward of capitalism to a global scale.[2] However, despite the dramatic advance of capitalism, it constitutes only the most recent stage in an evolving process that has been under way since human beings' early history. For several thousand years, human history has been organised to an ever-increasing extent around the division of labour, the extension of the scope of the market, and the pursuit of profit. This force has been the central factor in technical progress. Until the early modern period, the main consequence of technical progress was to enable population growth and output more or less to keep pace with each other, advancing together in a complex symbiotic relationship.[3] However, around 200 years ago, a new relationship between population and per capita output emerged. Population growth and per capita output and income began an unprecedented, simultaneous acceleration.

Pre-Modern Capitalism

Capitalism, in the sense of production for profit for the market, is an ancient phenomenon. The incentive to 'truck and barter' has been a central part of the history of the world since ancient times. The evolution of capitalism in early modern Western Europe, within the overall feudal socio-economic structure, has been deeply studied.[4] However, large parts of the world outside Europe contained significant pockets of capitalism within overall non-capitalist socio-economic structures. These involved urban trading centres and specialist production for both local and distant markets.[5] For millennia in many parts of the world there has been extensive local trade in goods such as grain, vegetables, herbs, furniture, metallurgical products, building materials, and low value textiles and pottery, and long-distance trade in products such as precious metals, minerals, spices, salt, sugar, tea, coffee, and high value textiles and pottery. There is now a rich historical literature on the extensive pockets of capitalism in East[6] and South Asia,[7] as well as on the Middle East.[8] Large parts of the pre-modern world were linked by long-distance international trade in products with high value to weight ratios, from China through South and Southeast Asia, the Middle East, coastal Africa, and Europe.

Industrial production in the pre-modern world was widely dispersed, including specialised industries such as food processing, metallurgy, mining, textiles, carpets, pottery, shipbuilding, salt, sugar, and tea, as well as the construction of canals, ports, roads, bridges and buildings. These often involved relatively large-scale enterprises, amidst a myriad small-scale 'proto-industrial' production. It is estimated that in 1750, China accounted for around one-third of total world manufacturing output, and South Asia for around one-quarter, while 'the West' still accounted for only around 18 per cent (Bairoch, 1982). Commercial growth interacted with institutional change, stimulating the evolution of urban-based legal and financial mechanisms to facilitate commerce.

Research in recent decades has shown that technical changes in the non-Western world played a far more important role in global pre-modern technical progress than was once thought to be the case.[9] Many of the key technical innovations of the late Middle Ages in Europe either originated in Asia, or were independently invented there.[10] Typically, technical progress occurred through innovations by profit-seeking entrepreneurs who responded to commercial opportunities.

The development of capitalism in early modern Europe has been deeply studied by generations of scholars. However, it is becoming increasingly clear that there was powerful embryonic capitalism in other regions of the world prior to that in Europe. Two of the most important examples of this occurred in the Islamic world and in China, which will be examined in more detail in Part 2.

Capitalism 1750–1914

The technical advances that had slowly evolved within the capitalist segments of the non-European world made their way to Europe in the Middle Ages. These interacted with indigenously evolving technical progress and with the fast-evolving capitalist institutions to produce the European Industrial Revolution. Technical progress accelerated far beyond the rates that had previously been achieved. In the eighteenth century, global markets for British-made goods expanded at a fierce rate, with great fluctuations from one period to another. The search for profits to enable British manufacturers to benefit from this process greatly stimulated the search for innovations in manufacturing technologies.

By the middle of the nineteenth century, industrial capitalism had spread across Europe. It was taking firm root in North America behind high protectionist barriers, with unified national capitalist markets ensured by violent civil war. By 1900, the share of 'The West' in global manufacturing output had risen to over three-quarters, from less than one-fifth a mere 150 year previously. The share of China and South Asia together had shrunk to less than one-tenth of the world total, from nearly three-fifths in the mid-eighteenth century (Bairoch, 1982). From the perspective of Europe and North America in the nineteenth century, the non-Western world increasingly assumed the character of a homogenously 'stagnant' economy and society, 'vegetating in the teeth of time'.

Large parts of the 'non-Western' world were integrated through military conquest into global industrial capitalism, including China, South and

Southeast Asia, Australia, South America, the North American 'West', and Africa. The period witnessed explosive growth of international trade, facilitated by technical progress in transport, including the railway, the steamship, and refrigeration. Merchandise exports as a share of GDP for the whole world rose from 1.0 per cent in 1820 to 7.9 per cent in 1914 (Wolf, 2004: 110). International movements of capital accelerated, especially in the latter part of the period. Foreign assets as a share of world GDP rose from 6.9 per cent in 1870 to 17.5 per cent in 1914 (Wolf, 2004: 113). By the end of the nineteenth century, industrial capitalism had enjoyed over a century of high-speed growth, with large parts of the world integrated by relatively open trade systems and free movement of capital. The integration of global markets reached levels far beyond those of the pre-modern epoch. The world appeared to be on the threshold of limitless expansion of global capitalism.

Capitalism 1914–1970s

The remorseless advance of global capitalism was interrupted rudely in 1914. A succession of phenomena stifled its growth for much of the twentieth century. These included the impact of the Civil War and anti-Japanese Wars in China, the war in the Pacific, and the First and Second World Wars.

In the high-income countries, the searing impact of the Great Depression led to the introduction of 'beggar-my-neighbour' policies of high tariff protection in the inter-war years, and a sharp decline in the growth of world trade.[11] Exchange controls were applied widely. In the post-war period, trade protection in the manufacturing sector[12] of the high-income countries was gradually reduced.[13] In the inter-war years, capital flows out of the high-income countries slumped, and in the post-war period, high-income countries maintained severe restrictions on international capital flows.[14] In addition, in the post-war period, most of the Western European countries nationalised large swathes of the economy, including a large part of the steel, oil and chemical, coal, automobile, aerospace, post and telecommunications, rail, port, airport, gas and electricity networks.

The Russian Revolution ushered in a series of communist revolutions, including those in Eastern Europe, in China and in Southeast Asia. By 1950, a 'sea of communism' extended from the Elbe in the West to China and Vietnam, committed to establishing a 'non-capitalist economy', from which the anarchy of the market was eliminated.[15] The communist economies drastically limited their interaction with global capitalism, cutting off vast swathes of the world, containing around two-fifths of the world's population from the reach of industrial capitalism.

Developing countries, which were heavily dependent on primary product exports, were devastated by the impact of the Great Depression and the associated collapse of primary product prices. Post-war economic policies in developing countries were influenced deeply by this experience. In addition, the Soviet Union appeared to offer an alternative route towards self-reliant development, freed from the disruptive effects of the 'anarchic' international economic system. In the post-war period, throughout the non-communist developing world, economic policies focused on import substituting industrialisation. Most countries heavily protected indigenous manufacturing and established large state-owned enterprises as the core of the manufacturing sector. The philosophy of the 'Big Push', led by the state, dominated development philosophy. It was hoped that the resulting structural transformation would free developing countries from reliance on primary products with their associated price instability and perceived 'unequal exchange' with manufactured goods imports,[16] and permit accelerated growth through more extensive indigenous manufactured goods production, which was thought to be characterised by greater opportunities to benefit from economies of scale and technical progress.

Capitalism Since the Mid-1970s

The net effect of the phenomena outlined in the previous section was to stifle the expansion of global capitalism that had been unfolding in the nineteenth century and up to the First World War. From the mid-1970s onwards a series of far-reaching changes set the scene for the renewal of the spread of global capitalism. Like a spring that has been held under pressure, the release of pressure was followed by an explosive expansion.

In the high-income countries, the mid-1970s saw the start of far-reaching institutional and policy changes. In 1974, following the first oil crisis, after decades of restrictions on international capital flows, the high-income countries moved decisively towards floating exchange rates and freedom of international capital movements. The massive increase in international capital flows meant that foreign assets as a share of world GDP increased from 17.7 per cent in 1980 to 56.8 per cent in 1995 (Wolf, 2004: 113). In the 1980s and 1990s, Europe's vast structure of state-owned enterprises was almost completely privatised. Numerous of these large and technically powerful but poorly-run firms were transformed into global business giants by the turn of the twenty-first century.[17]

In the communist world, the death of Chairman Mao in 1976 began a period of comprehensive system reform. In China, reform was gradual, 'touching stones to cross the river', with steadily deepening penetration of market forces under the leadership of the Chinese Communist Party (CCP).

The 'Chinese wall' between the domestic and global economy was dismantled brick by brick. By 2004, China had risen to be the world's third largest exporter[18] and the largest recipient of annual flows of FDI, with an accumulated stock of almost US$ 500 billion. In the former USSR and Eastern Europe, after a period of experimentation with gradual economic reform, Communist Party rule collapsed. In the 1990s the whole region opened up to international investment and trade.[19]

In the non-communist developing world, there was wide dissatisfaction with the pace of growth of output and living standards. Across most of the developing world, average annual growth rates of output per head were around 2–3 per cent per annum (Wolf, 2004: 107). It was felt widely that in many areas 'import substituting growth' had run its course,[20] and that only more comprehensive integration with the international economy would enable output and income growth to accelerate.[21] The 'conventional wisdom' in development thinking shifted profoundly, and turned full circle compared with that of the 1950s and 1960s. In the 1980s and 1990s, non-communist developing countries carried out comprehensive privatisation of state assets, dismantled protectionist barriers and opened their economies to international investment. Between 1990 and 2002, foreign trade as a share of the GDP of low and middle-income countries rose from 33 per cent to 52 per cent; the annual flow of FDI to low and middle-income countries rose from US$ 24 billion to US$ 147 billion; and stock market capitalisation as a share of the GDP of low and middle-income countries rose from 19 per cent to 33 per cent (World Bank, 2004).

From the 1970s onwards, the global economy took up where it had left off before the First World War. Once again, private enterprise dominated, international trade was relatively unregulated and capital could flow freely across national borders.[22] Leading global firms increasingly were international in terms of their markets, employees and the composition of ownership. The principal difference with the period before 1914 was the migration of people. In the former period there were massive international migrations to the 'lands of recent settlement', but in the present period, international migration, especially of poor people, is severely restricted. However, in most respects the world economy has again entered a period of free markets and a 'global level playing field' comparable to the late nineteenth century, the previous highpoint of the liberal economy.

1.2 Capitalist Rationality in the Epoch of the Global Business Revolution

The battle of competition is fought by cheapening commodities. The cheapness of commodities depends, ceteris paribus, *on the productiveness of labour, and this again on the scale of production. Therefore the larger capital beats the smaller ... Everywhere the increased scale of industrial establishments is the starting-point for a more comprehensive organization of the collective work of many, for a wider development of their material motive force - in other words, for the progressive transformation of isolated processes of production, carried on by customary methods, into processes of production socially combined and scientifically arranged.*

(Marx, 1967: 626–7)

Big industry universalized competition ... established means of communication and the modern world market ... By universal competition it forced individuals to strain their energy to the utmost ... It produced world history for the first time, insofar as it made all civilized nations and every individual member of them dependent for the satisfaction of his wants on the whole world, thus destroying the formal natural exclusiveness of separate nations.

(Marx, 1960: 56)

Free Trade dissolves the hitherto existing nationalities and pushes to its climax the tension between proletariat and bourgeoisie. In one word, the system of free trade precipitates the social revolution.

(Marx, *Selected Works*, Vol. 1: 64–5, quoted in Avineri, 1968: 252)

The bourgeoisie, by the rapid development of all instruments of production, by the immensely facilitated means of communication, draws all, even the most barbarian, nations into civilization. The cheap prices of its commodities are the heavy artillery with which it batters down all Chinese walls, with which it forces the barbarians' intensely obstinate hatred of foreigners to capitulate. It compels all nations, on pain of extinction, to adopt the bourgeois mode of production; it compels them to introduce what it calls civilization into their midst, that is, to become bourgeois themselves. In one word it creates a world after its own image.

(Marx and Engels, 1968: 38–9)

1.2.1 Capitalism and Coordination

Since the earliest days of the emergence of capitalist markets, the market mechanism has acted as an instrument for coordinating the activities of individual economic agents each engaged in their own special function within the overall division of labour. However, the nature of that coordinating mechanism has shifted greatly over time, not least in the epoch of the Global Business Revolution.

The Invisible Hand

Through the process of the division of labour and exchange, human beings establish complex forms of inter-dependence and cooperation, even though they may not intend that this is so and may be only dimly aware of it. Economists have long marvelled at the independently functioning market, which allows the actions of market participants to be 'magically' coordinated without any apparent guiding hand. Markets were coordinated in this fashion throughout the trading centres of the Islamic world, in South Asia and in China, long before the European countries entered their period of early modern market expansion.

Smith, capitalism and the scientific revolution. Writing on the eve of the Industrial Revolution, Adam Smith produced the most famous of all analyses of the division of labour and the impact upon cooperation among people. Smith places the central role of the division of labour at the heart of his analysis of economic development, making it the first sentence of the first chapter of the *Wealth of Nations*: 'The greatest improvement in the productive powers of labour, and the greater part of the skill, dexterity, and judgement with which it is any where directed, or applied, seem to have been the effects of the division of labour' (Smith, 1976, Vol. 1: 7). Smith examines closely the variety of objects in the accommodation of 'the most common artificer or day-labourer in a civilized and thriving country', and concludes that 'the number of people of whose industry a part, though but a small part, has been employed in procuring him this accommodation, exceeds all computation' (Smith, 1976, Vol. 1: 15): 'If we examine, I say, all these things, and consider what a variety of labour is employed about each of them, we shall be sensible that without the assistance and cooperation of many thousands, the very meanest person in a civilized country could not be provided, even according to what we very falsely imagine, the easy and simple manner in which he is commonly accommodated' (Smith, 1976, Vol. 1: 16). The division of labour does not evolve through conscious human agency: 'The division of labour, from which so many advantages are derived, is not originally the effect of any human wisdom, which foresees and intends that general opulence to which it gives occasion. It is the necessary, though very slow and gradual, consequence of a certain propensity in human nature which has in view no such extensive utility; the propensity to truck, barter, and exchange one thing for another' (Smith, 1976, Vol. 1: 17).

For Smith, the market was not simply a mechanism for achieving greater output from given resources, it was the essential mechanism for raising the productivity of resources through technical progress. Capital accumulation and the ways in which capital could become more productive through technical progress were central to Smith's analysis of the economy. He devoted great care to analysing the process of technical progress. He distinguished between three different sources of technical progress. First, there are technologies that are developed by specialist 'philosophers and men of speculation, whose trade it is to observe everything; and who, on that account are often capable of combining together the powers of the most distant and dissimilar objects'. These are in their turn, 'subdivided into a great number of different branches'. As a result, each individual becomes 'more expert in his own peculiar branch, more work is done on the whole, and the quantity of science is considerably increased by it'. Secondly, many improvements in machines are made by 'the ingenuity of the makers of the machines, when to make them became the business of a particular trade'. Thirdly, technical progress is also achieved by 'the inventions of common workmen, who, being each of them employed in some very simple operation, naturally turned their thoughts towards finding out easier and readier methods of performing it' (Smith, 1976, Vol. 1: 13–4).

For Smith, market exchange was a mechanism through which participants could mutually benefit due to the division of labour. In other words, the market could be viewed as a giant mechanism for the achievement of 'non-zero-sum' outcomes of mutual benefit (see below). This aspect of the division of labour and capitalist markets has become an important part of modern micro-economics. The more extensive is the market, and the lower are the transaction costs, which are reduced through advances in transport and communication technologies, the greater are the gains from non-zero-sum interactions between the market participants. Dense populations tend to reduce transaction costs and the non-zero-sum benefits from exchange.[23]

The impact of the 'invisible hand' of capitalism upon technical progress can be seen operating powerfully in the critically important period of European and, indeed, of world history, namely the period of the Scientific Revolution from the fourteenth to the seventeenth centuries (Bernal, 1965, White, 1972). This period saw the emergence of an increasingly powerful capitalist class in Western Europe (Hilton, 1976, Dobb, 1963). Europe's population more or less doubled from the fourteenth century to the middle of the eighteenth century.[24] During this long persistent increase in Europe's population, revolutionary technological advances took place. These incorporated a great deal of technical progress from the Islamic world and from China (see Part 2 below). The revolutionary advances in Europe laid the foundations for the Industrial Revolution, which is best seen as part of a process that began at the start of the European Middle Ages (Lilley, 1973: 187–191).[25]

Technological changes interacted in symbiotic fashion with the extension of the market. The core of technical changes has always been in the transformation of capital goods. During this extraordinary period, the widening market provided a steadily expanding source of profit to reward innovation in capital goods. These were increasingly produced by specialist industrial enterprises.

In agriculture, the spread of the heavy plough, the efficient harnessing of horses and the horseshoe, contributed to greatly increased land productivity. The expansion of international trade led to the introduction of a wide variety of new crops from the Middle and Far East, including mulberries and silkworms, durum wheat and rice, as well as new fruits and vegetables, such as asparagus, artichokes and apricots. These improved people's diet.

Water-mills had first appeared in Europe in the first century BC, but the windmill did not appear in Europe until the twelfth century. During the Middle Ages, the use of both water- and wind-mills spread rapidly across Europe: 'During the later Middle Ages there was a passion for the mechanisation of industry such as no other culture had known' (White, 1972: 156). Initially, their main purpose was to grind grain, but eventually they were used to mechanise almost all major industrial processes, manufacturing beer, processing hemp, fulling cloth, stamping ore, grinding knives, powering forges, cutting and drawing metal, sawing planks, polishing armaments, and pounding herbs (White, 1972: 156–7). Wind- and water-mills needed to be made and serviced, a task which was beyond the skill of most village smiths, so 'there grew up a trade of millwrights who went about the country making and mending mills ... These men were the first mechanics in the modern sense of the word. They understood how gears could be made and how they worked as well as the management of dams and sluices which made them hydraulic as well as mechanical engineers' (Bernal, 1965, Vol. 1: 315).

The advances in gearing, metallurgy, cranks, and rotary motion, coalesced in the efforts to produce clocks and, eventually, watches. By the 1330s, the main technical problems had been overcome, with the development of the verge and the wheel escapements. There followed an explosive expansion of the use of clocks. The clock was an extraordinarily sophisticated machine, with complex gearing and hundreds of moving parts. The rapidly expanding use of clocks created an increasing corps of craftsmen to make and mend them.

The European Middle Ages witnessed tremendous advances in navigation techniques. The arrival of the compass in Europe from China stimulated an industry of map-making. This allowed safer and more direct voyages between ports. Shipbuilding techniques altered greatly. During the fourteenth century the sternpost rudder replaced the lateral oar and allowed voyages across open seas to be undertaken more safely, since the new rudder was less liable to break (White, 1972: 167). Also, the new rudder allowed ships to sail closer to the wind, which in turn led to the development of the for-and-aft sail to replace the older lateen sail (Bernal, 1965, Vol. 1: 319). These developments 'threw the oceans, for the first time, open to exploration, war and trade' (Bernal, 1965, Vol. 1: 319). The rapid growth of open-sea voyages stimulated the development of a 'new quantitative geography, and of instruments for use on shipboard: The need for compasses and other navigating instruments brought into being a new skilled industry, that of the card and dial makers, whose subsequent influence on science, particularly in setting higher and higher standards for accurate measurement, was enormous' (Bernal, 1965, Vol. 1: 320).

A series of technical innovations took place, which greatly helped the spread of knowledge. Paper made its way to Europe via the Islamic world in the eighth century. However, it was not until new techniques of paper manufacture were developed in the thirteenth century, using water-powered mills to prepare pulp, that relatively cheap paper became available. In the 1440s, Gutenberg developed cast movable type printing. The combination of printing and cheap paper ushered in an era of relatively cheap books, and brought about a revolution in book manufacture.[26] By the second half of the fifteenth century, printing had become a major industry. Advances in optics in Medieval Europe owed a great deal to the absorption of knowledge from the Islamic world (Bernal, 1965, Vol. 1: 278). The discovery of lenses led to the invention of spectacles in 1350 (Bernal, 1965, Vol. 1: 320). Around the same time Europeans developed the technique of making clear glass, which allowed the manufacture of spectacles to grow rapidly. The demand for spectacles gave rise to the trades of the lens grinders and spectacle makers (Bernal, 1965, Vol. 1: 320).

The driver of all these, and many other, technical changes during the technological revolution in the European Middle Ages,[27] was the pursuit of profit through sales in the market. The contribution of a specialist body of scientific knowledge was quite limited. Rather, the main channel of technical progress was through the body of craftsmen, especially the engineers, who produced the capital goods. They benefited from the codification of knowledge in books, which were increasingly available, but the relationship of specialist scientific speculation to the day-to-day process of product innovation was typically remote. Bernal concludes that up until the end of the eighteenth century, 'science drew far more from industry than it could yet give back' (Bernal, 1965, Vol. 2: 491). Even during the phase of explosive technical change in the last quarter of the eighteenth century, despite the contribution of the steam engine, 'it cannot be claimed that science was a major factor in effecting the decisive change from hand to machine production' (Bernal, 1965, Vol. 2: 505). It was only at the end of the nineteenth century that 'industries that started and remained scientific, such as the chemical and electrical industries, began to take form, and their full development was not seen until the twentieth century' (Bernal, 1965, Vol. 2: 505).

In the European Middle Ages, technical progress by the makers of capital goods revolutionised production processes across almost every sector of the economy. Technical progress in agriculture enabled a larger population to be supported, which permitted greater densities of population, thereby reducing transport costs and allowing more rapid spread of knowledge. Technical progress in paper-making and printing enabled new ideas to spread more rapidly. It enabled knowledge to diffuse more deeply into the social structure, and allowed the craftsmen to acquire new technical knowledge more easily. Advances in lens-making and spectacles enabled people to spend more of their life reading. Advances in transport, especially in shipbuilding and navigation, reduced transport costs and allowed the distance over which it was profitable to transport goods to increase. The technological revolution was not driven mainly by the state or by scientific research in universities. The state's direct involvement in production was mainly evident in the manufacture of warships and weapons, though much military equipment was purchased from the private sector. The main generators of technical progress were the makers of diverse types of capital goods. Their principal incentive was to make money by meeting the needs of their customers through the provision of better and cheaper products. Through this mechanism capitalism in the Middle Ages achieved immense progress. The capitalist market economy was like a giant reciprocating engine in which the parts constantly interacted to mutual benefit.

The modern economy is vastly more complicated than that which surrounded Adam Smith. Its ability to coordinate economic activity is even more an object of wonder today than it was in the eighteenth century. Eric Beinhocker has suggested that in New York alone, the number of distinct products or 'stock-keeping units' may be around 10 billion, compared with a 'few hundred' in the Stone Age: 'The economy is a marvel of complexity, yet no one designed it and no one runs it' (quoted in *Financial Times*, 17 January 2007). Markets do not simply coordinate information in a static fashion. They also provide dynamic feedback effects from customers to producers, which is at the heart of technical progress. According to Beinhocker, 'markets win over command and control, not because of their efficiency at resource allocation in equilibrium, but because of their effectiveness in disequilibrium'. Markets can be viewed as 'hugely powerful evolutionary mechanisms because they are innovation machines' (Martin Wolf, *FT*, 17 January 2007).

Non-zero-sum. Robert Wright's writings on this topic have been extremely influential.[28] In his view, human beings are, indeed, characterised by 'firm self-interest', rather than by 'true, pure altruism, indifferent to ultimate payoff' (Wright, 2000: 25). He believes that human beings have an 'innate tendency to monitor the contributions of others' (Wright, 2000: 25). However, he believes that through the market mechanism human beings have over millennia been able to achieve non-zero-sum outcomes from their interactions and this has been the fundamental instrument allowing human progress:

> The successful playing of a non-zero-sum game amounts to a growth of social complexity. The players must coordinate their behaviour, so people who might otherwise be off on their own orbits come together to form a single solar system, a larger synchronised whole. And typically there is division of labour within the whole ... Complex coherence has materialised ... New technologies create new chances for positive sum games and people manoeuvre to seize those sums, and social structure changes as a result (Wright, 2000: 21).

Wright argues that people are often unaware that they are interacting with each other in a mutually profitable fashion, but 'reciprocal altruism' to achieve 'beneficial exchange' is deeply built into human nature, and 'rooted ultimately in the genes' (Wright, 2000: 22). The only difference between the modern economy and that of our distant ancestors is the degree of complexity: 'At the heart of every modern capitalist economy – as at the heart of the hunter-gatherer economies from which they evolved – is the principle of exchange. One hand washes the other, and both are better off than they would be if they played alone – the very definition of a well-played non-zero-sum game' (Wright, 2000: 26).

Wright believes that 'non-zero-sumness' is the fundamental characteristic of evolution. Both organic and human history involve the playing of 'ever more complex games, ever larger, and ever more complex non-zero-sum games': 'It is the accumulation of these games – game upon game – that constitutes the growth of biological and social complexity that people like Bergson and Teilhard de Chardin have talked about' (Wright, 2000: 7). Wright views globalisation as simply the culmination of a process that began before human beings evolved: 'Globalisation has been on the cards ... since the invention of life. The current age, in which relations among nations grew more non-zero-sum year by year, is the natural outgrowth of several billion years of unfolding non-zero-sum logic' (Wright, 2000: 7). He believes that today ' a magnificent new social structure – our future home – is being built before our very eyes' (Wright, 2000: 16). Wright considers that humanity is 'approaching a culmination of sorts', in which the human species faces 'a kind of test toward which basic forces of history have been moving us for millennia' (Wright, 2000: 9). Wright feels that the current era has the 'aura of a threshold': '[I]t has that unsettling, out-of-control feeling that can portend a major shift' (Wright, 2000: 9). He is optimistic that the 'current turbulence' will give way to 'an era when global political, economic and social structures have largely tamed the new forms of chaos', and the period we are now entering will 'in retrospect look like the storm before the calm' (Wright, 2000: 9).[29]

The Visible Hand

The traditional American and European business firm of the early Industrial Revolution was a single-unit business enterprise. The activities of these small, personally owned and managed enterprises were coordinated and monitored by the 'anonymous' market and price mechanisms. In the late nineteenth century in the United States and Europe, the 'modern firm' emerged. These firms brought many different units under their control, operating in different locations, and entering different lines of business through vertical and horizontal integration. These complex internal business relationships became monitored and coordinated by salaried employees rather than by the market mechanism. By the middle of the twentieth century this type of firm had become dominant in all the high-income countries. They employed large numbers of middle and top managers who supervised the work of tens of hundreds of thousands of employees working in hundreds of operating units (Chandler, 1977). Within such firms, the boundaries of the firm had shifted decisively compared with the enterprise of the early Industrial Revolution (Coase, 1988), and goods and services that had formerly been purchased through the 'anonymous' market were instead produced within the firm.

Instead of an arms-length relationship mediated through price, large areas of business transaction were internalised within the firm, and became subject to the 'visible hand' of planned resource allocation within the vertically and horizontally integrated firm (Chandler, 1977). Prior to the 1930s, economists were reluctant even to acknowledge the existence of such firms, and 'since then they have looked on large-scale business enterprise with deep suspicion' (Chandler, 1977: 4). Even today much economic theory is grounded on the assumption that most production and distribution is managed by the invisible hand of the market. The small and medium-sized anonymous firm is taken as the foundation of economic analysis. It is believed that this form of business organisation is preferable to the large-scale modern enterprise, which is regarded as 'an aberration and an evil one at that' (Chandler, 1977: 4). Its existence is explained mainly by the desire to establish monopoly power rather than by the benefits from economies of scale and scope.

While the internal mechanism of the large corporation became a form of planned economy governed by a 'visible hand', large firms persistently struggled against each other to achieve dominance in their respective markets. They battled to achieve technical progress and lower the costs of production. While the 'visible hand' of planning came to dominate their internal structure, the 'invisible hand' of ferocious oligopolistic competition persisted in the conduct of their relationships with each other. Chandler has demonstrated the central role of the large, oligopolistic firm in technical progress. This was, in its turn, central to the whole growth dynamic of modern capitalism. In the late nineteenth century, especially in the United States, the first-mover large firms 'established themselves as dominant oligopolistic players' and became 'the fertile learning ground for technological, managerial, and organizational knowledge for an entire economy' (Chandler, *et al.*, 1997: 25). These were primarily in the manufacturing sector that constituted the Second Industrial Revolution, including especially such capital-intensive activities as primary metals, petroleum refining, chemicals, electrical products and transport equipment. In these oligopolistic industries, there took place a switch from price to non-price competition:

> [O]ligopolistic firms competed even more effectively through functional and particularly strategic effectiveness: that is, by carrying out processes of production and distribution more capably; by improving both product and process through systematic research and development; by identifying more suitable sources of supply; by providing more effective marketing services; by product differentiation (in branded packaged products primarily through the advertising); and by moving more quickly into expanding markets and out of declining ones (Chandler *et al.*, 1997: 31).

In this climate of oligopolistic competition, 'market share and profits changed constantly, which kept oligopolies from becoming stagnant and monopolistic' (Chandler *et al.*, 1997: 31).

Technological advances achieved by large firms in these industries had powerful beneficial effects on the rest of the economy. They contributed to improved productivity in a wide range of other industries, including transport, communication and financial services (Chandler *et al.*, 1997: 25): 'These enterprises became a rich spring of managerial and organizational information as well as technological knowledge, all of which spilled over into the wider spheres of domestic and international economies by means of networks, spin-offs and even ordinary market transactions' (Chandler *et al.*, 1997: 25). The Third Industrial Revolution during and after the Second World War was also 'dominated by large enterprises'. This revolution involved new technologies in chemicals, pharmaceuticals, aerospace, and electronics. Indeed, with the exception of electronic data-processing technologies, 'the new technologies were commercialized by large, well-established enterprises rather than start-ups' (Chandler *et al.*, 1997: 33). The modern industrial enterprise 'played a central role in creating the most technologically advanced, fastest growing industries of their day'. These industries, in turn, were 'the pace-setters of the industrial sector of their economies'. They provided an underlying dynamic in the development of modern industrial capitalism (Chandler, 1990: 593).

The External Firm

In the current capitalist epoch, the boundaries of the firm have not only shifted in the 'Coasian' sense (Coase, 1988), but the very boundaries have become 'blurred', with functions of control and coordination extending across the boundaries of the legally defined firm. Through the hugely increased planning function undertaken by systems integrators, facilitated by recent developments in information technology, the boundaries of the large corporation have not only 'shifted', so that a wider range of goods and services is procured from outside the firm, but the very boundaries of the firms have become blurred. The core systems integrators across a wide range of sectors have become the coordinators of a vast array of business activity outside the boundaries of the legal entity in terms of ownership. The relationship extends far beyond the purchase price. In order to develop and maintain their competitive advantage, the systems integrators deeply penetrate the value chain both upstream and downstream, becoming closely involved in business activities that range from long-term planning to meticulous control of day-to-day production and delivery schedules. Competitive advantage for the systems integrator requires that it must consider the interests of the whole value chain in order to minimise costs across the whole system. As we will see in more detail later, the core systems integrator interacts in the deepest, most intimate fashion with the major segments of the value chain, both upstream and downstream, across a wide range of business types, from fast-moving consumer goods to aircraft manufacture. One of the most remarkable features of the Global Business Revolution is the persistence of intense oligopolistic competition between giant global firms, which have sophisticated internal planning systems (the 'visible hand') and a vast 'external firm' coordinated by them.

1.2.2 Finance and Development

Finance has always stood at the centre of economic advance. Availability of credit has been central to the smooth conduct of trade. Availability of sophisticated payments systems through banking systems that allow safe carriage of goods over long distances without the need to carry money has been critical to the development of long-distance trade wherever capitalism has matured beyond a certain point. This was true for the world of medieval Islam, South Asia and China, as it was for Europe in the late Middle Ages in early modern period. During and after the Industrial Revolution, financial institutions reached new heights of sophistication, facilitating further development of capitalism. In the epoch of the Global Business Revolution, financial institutions and financial flows have taken another leap forward in size and sophistication, standing at the heart of the new phase of global capitalist development.

Private Capital Flows

Policy shift. In the epoch of the Global Business Revolution a consensus grew up among the 'Bretton Woods' institutions (the World Bank and the IMF), which argued that there are large benefits for both rich and poor countries alike to be gained by liberalisation of international capital flows, including freedom of movement on the capital account. The so-called 'Washington Consensus' argued that 'the size of the financial sector alone, regardless of its sophistication, has a strong causal effect on economic performance' (Wolf, 2004: 285). Measures which stimulate the development of national financial systems will enhance productivity by facilitating transactions and leading to improved resource allocation (Singh, 2002). In terms of its impact on growth, the most important effect seems to be on productivity, through improved resource allocation, rather than through the impact on the accumulation of capital (Wolf, 2004: 285). Allowing free access to international finance and international financial institutions is the most immediate and powerful way to stimulate 'financial deepening' in developing countries, whose financial systems not only were 'repressed' by government intervention, but also very small compared to those of the high-income countries.[30]

Underlying the Washington Consensus' approach is an ethical argument, namely that one of people's fundamental 'human rights' is that of exercising their free choice about where to lodge their capital: 'It is not difficult to see why full convertibility of the currency might be desirable ... One good reason is given by Hayek. If we regard choices as valuable in their own right, then there are few choices more important than those to travel and, if necessary, to escape oppressive, exploitative or predatory regimes' (Wolf, 2004: 284).

The economic argument rests on a simple proposition: 'Free markets are more efficient, [and] greater efficiency allowed for faster growth' (Stiglitz, 2002: 66). Stanley Fischer, the former Deputy Managing Director of the IMF argued that capital account liberalisation leads to global economic efficiency, by allocating savings to those who can use them most productively. Citizens of countries with free capital movements can benefit from diversifying their portfolios, and thereby increase their risk-adjusted rate of return. It enables firms to raise capital at lower cost in international markets (Singh, 2002).

Pressure from global capital markets serves as an important discipline on government macro-economic and other policies 'which improves overall economic performance by rewarding good policies and penalising bad' (quoted in Singh, 2002). Removal of restrictions on the international movement of capital acts as a pressure on the state in developing countries to 'force review and reform of the financial sector', including breaking 'the connections between financial institutions and borrowers', and 'establishing an effective bankruptcy regime', which might thereby help to provide foreign capital with 'protection of its property rights' (Wolf, 2004: 287–8). In addition, capital controls are costly to enforce and are a source of corruption (Wolf, 2004: 287).

The Washington Consensus argued that it is beneficial for developing countries to allow free access to international financial firms, in order to benefit from their size and associated economies of scale and skill. However, it is agued that the only way to attract them and to benefit from their size and skills was to allow them 'to repatriate their capital and remit earnings ... [and have] access to global financial markets' (Wolf, 2004: 284–6).

The IMF's Interim Committee meeting held in Hong Kong in April 1997, proposed that the IMF's Articles of Agreement should be amended to extend the Fund's jurisdiction to capital movements: 'This agreement would make liberalisation of capital movements a central purpose of the Fund' (Singh, 2002). In September 1997, the world's financial leaders again met in Hong Kong for the annual meeting of the World Bank and the IMF. Even as the Asian Financial Crisis began to unfold, at this meeting IMF officials were 'so sure of their advice that they even asked for a change in its charter to allow it to put *more* pressure on developing countries to liberalise their capital markets' (Stiglitz, 2002: 93). As Stanley Fischer put it: 'In a nutshell, the prime goal of the amendments would be to enable the Fund to promote the orderly liberalisation of capital movements' (quoted in Singh, 2002).

The outcome. Private capital flows include both debt and non-debt instruments. Private debt flows include commercial bank lending, bonds, and other private credits. Non-debt flows include foreign direct investment and portfolio equity investment. During the epoch of the Global Business Revolution, overall private capital flows have increased enormously, albeit with large fluctuations. Gross private capital flows to low and middle-income countries doubled their share of GDP from 5.9 per cent in 1990 to 11.9 per cent in 2004 (World Bank, WDI, 2006: 318). Foreign direct investment has been the largest and most stable element in such flows. Private debt flows and portfolio equity investment have been more volatile. A major source of international capital flows involved participation in the widespread privatisation of infrastructure. This process took off in the 1990s: 'developing countries have been at the head of this wave, pioneering better approaches to providing infrastructure services and reaping the benefits of greater competition and customer focus' (World Bank, WDI, 2004: 257). In the period 1990–2002, a total of 2500 infrastructure projects attracted investment commitments of US$ 750 billion, of which around 46 per cent went into telecommunications and 33 per cent into energy (World Bank, WDI, 2004: 256).

Global economic integration has greatly increased opportunities for migrants from poor countries to earn income abroad. The total level of officially recorded remittances received by low and middle-income countries from workers abroad rose from US$ 31 billion in 1990 to US$ 161 billion in 2004 (World Bank, WDI, 2006: 362).

Foreign direct investment.[31] Liberalisation of international capital flows since the 1970s has facilitated a large rise in foreign direct investment. Global stocks of FDI rose from US$ 699 in 1980 to US$ 7.123 in 2002 (UNCTAD, 2003: 257–9). Over two-thirds of this increase involved flows between developed countries, a large part of which involved mergers and acquisitions across national boundaries, and reflected the growth of international production systems in the epoch of the Global Business Revolution.

Liberalisation of rules on foreign investment allowed the annual flow of FDI into low and middle-income countries to rise from US$ 23 billion in 1990 to US$ 211 billion in 2004 (World Bank, WDI, 2006: 342). The inward stock of FDI in developing countries rose from US$ 307 billion in 1980 to US$ 2340 billion in 2002, an average annual growth rate of almost 10 per cent (UNCTAD, 2003: 257). The stock was heavily concentrated regionally. A group of just ten developing countries, with around 36 per cent of the population of low and middle-income countries accounts for around 69 per cent of total FDI stocks in developing countries (UNCTAD, 2003).[32] In these countries, local production systems built by multinational firms have grown into critically important parts of the local economy. For example, in Brazil, which has US$ 175 billion of FDI, in 2001, multinational firms accounted for 14 of the top 25 'Brazilian' firms.[33] In China, which had US$ 448 billion of FDI by 2002, the local production systems of multinational firms accounted for a large share of domestic markets in many sectors producing final products for middle class consumers or capital goods for the modern sector.[34] Large parts of the developing world and 'transition' economies received only negligible amounts of FDI.

Although FDI is still a relatively small part of total investment in developing countries,[35] the subsidiaries established by multinational firms in developing countries have a powerful influence on the modern sector of the local economy. Large manufacturing assembly facilities owned by multinational firms tend to stimulate the development of clusters of supplier companies, often encouraging other multinationals to invest to meets the needs of their global customers, contributing to the technical upgrading of the whole supply chain. Multinational firms tend to produce globally standardised products, whether they are final consumer goods for the global middle class or capital goods for other companies, making use of standard global machine tools, components and capital-labour ratios. Consequently, FDI in developing countries contributes to the spread of global production technologies, management systems and employee skills. Multinationals in developing countries also can take advantage of global procurement to lower unit costs of inputs of goods and services. Global oligopolistic firms also tend to carry their intense competition into developing countries, whether in the production of final consumer goods or capital goods for intermediate customers.

Stock markets. Stock markets have played a central role in capitalist development in most of today's high-income countries. Stock markets can have several positive functions in stimulating capitalist development in developing countries. In the view of the World Bank, both banks and stock markets are central to economic development: 'Well functioning financial systems provide good and easily accessible information. That lowers transaction costs, which, in turn, improves resource allocation and boosts economic growth. Both banking systems and stock markets enhance growth, the main factor in poverty reduction' (World Bank, WDI, 2004: 269). Stock markets can provide a mechanism for shareholders to monitor standards of corporate governance. They can constitute a vehicle for stimulating savings and channelling them into investment. They can provide a mechanism for facilitating mergers and acquisitions, and allowing benefits from economies of scale. They can contribute to social stability by providing pension funds with a channel through which to diversify their investments.

The epoch of the Global Business Revolution has seen a significant expansion of the role of stock markets in developing countries' economies. The number of firms floated on stock markets in low and middle-income countries rose from less than 8000 in 1990 to 21 000 in 2003 (World Bank, WDI, 2004: 268). Total stock market capitalisation in low and middle-income countries increased from US$ 375 billion in 1990 to US$ 3433 billion in 2005, and stock market capitalisation as a share of GDP rose from 18.8 per cent in 1990 to 43.8 per cent in 2005 (World Bank, WDI, 2004: 268 and WDI, 2006: 280). Although the total stock market capitalisation of low and middle-income countries is still only a small fraction of that of the high-income countries (less than 10 per cent in 2005), flows of funds from high-income to low and middle-income countries have played an important role in stock market development in the latter group of countries. The total net portfolio investment flow (bonds plus equities) to low and middle-income countries rose from US$ 4.5 billion in 1990 to US$ 80.6 billion in 2004 (World Bank, WDI, 2006: 342). In order to attract international capital, standards of corporate governance of firms in developing countries have needed to rise. International equity holders now constitute an important fraction of share ownership in many developing countries that were formerly substantially closed to multinational equity investors, and these have had a substantial influence on the nature of corporate governance.[36]

Financial Institutions

Since the 1970s, large-scale changes have taken place in the conditions affecting financial services institutions, including the reduction of obstacles to mergers and acquisitions across the boundaries of different segments of the industry, across regions within large countries (especially in the United States), and across national boundaries.[37] International mergers and acquisitions by large financial firms form an important part of the international merger and acquisition explosion since the 1970s. The institutional structure of financial firms has been strongly affected by the transformation of their customers, both business and private, who increasingly seek global services from financial institutions. The large economies of scale and scope derived from procurement of IT hardware and software acts as a powerful driver of institutional change in financial services, as it does in the manufacturing sector. Financial firms benefit also from economies of scale in branding and marketing, and in human resource acquisition.

The period of the Global Business Revolution has seen a powerful process of merger and acquisition in this sector. A group of super-large financial firms has emerged. In the banking sector these include Citigroup,[38] Deutsche Bank,[39] HSBC,[40] JPMorgan Chase,[41] and Bank of America.[42] The industry has become increasingly bifurcated into a small group of immensely powerful firms and a large number of small firms serving local markets and global niche markets. The world's leading financial institutions are rapidly penetrating the financial services industry of developing countries.

Following financial liberalisation in most developing countries, global giant financial firms rapidly increased their acquisition activity. By 2001, within Latin America, the share of foreign banks in total bank assets had risen to 90 per cent in Mexico, 62 per cent in Peru, 61 per cent in Argentina and Chile, 59 per cent in Venezuela, and 49 percent in Brazil (Chang Song, 2005). In Mexico, the four leading banks that had been acquired by international banks alone accounted for around nine-tenths of the entire country's banking assets (*FT*, 18 September 2002).[43] Following the acquisition of Mexico's Banamex by Citigroup, the *Financial Times* commented: 'The acquisition [of Banamex] underscored the rapacious appetite of Citigroup ... for assets in the developing world, and Citigroup executives made it clear that they will pursue similar deals in other emerging markets' (*FT*, 18 May 2001).[44] By 2001, in Eastern Europe the share of foreign banks in total bank assets stood at 99 per cent in Estonia, 90 per cent in the Czech Republic and Poland, 89 per cent in Hungary, 86 per cent in Slovakia, 78 per cent in Lithuania, and 75 per cent in Bulgaria (Chang Song, 2005). By 2005 China had begun to implement the WTO Agreement under which global financial institutions would be allowed to increase their ownership share in local financial firms.

The penetration of developing countries' financial markets by global financial firms has brought powerful benefits for both individuals and businesses. The threat of competition from global banks can force local banks to improve their operating mechanisms. Global giant banks can spread risk across numerous markets. They have access to vast global assets and possess sophisticated IT systems with which to evaluate risk. They have also established a culture built around strict internal control systems, and have long experience of operating under the sophisticated financial regulations within the high-income countries. Global giant banks operate according to rigorous and systematic procedures, so that lending tends to be based on strict commercial criteria to a much greater extent than in many developing countries' banking systems. This increases the possibility that loans will be made to firms that are able to employ them effectively. This may tend to help more effective use of savings and thereby stimulate growth, as well as tending to reduce the risk of bad loans and of a financial crisis. Financial reforms in developing countries have often found it difficult to break the link between bankers and local political power holders. The entry of global banks can help to break the link more effectively. Multinational firms tend to find that working with global banks can stimulate their growth in developing countries, by enabling them to benefit from lower-priced and higher quality services supplied to them on a global basis. Local depositors may also benefit from the presence of global banks, by having greater security for their deposits and more opportunity to benefit from global wealth management. Local pension funds may benefit by having access to the global asset management services of global banks.

The World Bank believes that those 'transition economies' that have been more willing to 'cede majority control of their banks to foreign interests' have enjoyed higher growth rates than their neighbours (World Bank, 2002). It is widely argued that 'countries with a higher proportion of foreign-owned banks are ... less prone to financial crises, perhaps because foreign banks are better regulated, better managed or merely more immune to pressure for imprudent lending' (Wolf, 2004: 285).

Global Financial Risk

The global financial system has undergone tremendous change in the past two decades. The financial system has 'deepened' across much of the developing world, gradually supplanting the former 'repressed' financial structures. Advances in information technology and in financial instruments have greatly improved risk control in commercial banks. New financial instruments have distributed risk widely throughout the economic system.[45] Alan Greenspan believes that there is a 'new paradigm' of 'active credit management which makes the global financial system far more robust. Credit derivatives permit risks to be unbundled and transferred to those players who are best able to absorb them. Hedge funds' arbitrage activity makes markets more efficient and 'keeps the financial system fluid and flexible' (*FT*, 16 February 2005). The global financial system demonstrated its newly-found robustness by surviving intact a series of severe bouts of turbulence since the 1980s, including the Mexican 'Tequila' crisis, the Asian Financial Crisis, the Russian and Argentinian financial crises, and 9/11. In the view of many financial experts, the global financial system is now so 'thick' as to be nearly indestructible. The IMF believes: 'Short of a major and devastating geopolitical incident undermining, in a significant way, consumer confidence, and hence financial asset valuation, it is hard to see where systemic threats could come from in the short-term' (quoted in *Financial Times*, 16 February 2005).

1.2.3 Competition, Industrial Concentration and Technical Progress

Contrasting Views

The nature and determinants of industrial structure is one of the most important issues in economics. In the history of economics, there have been radically contrasting views on the basic determinants of industrial structure. For most of the twentieth century, industrial structure was heavily influenced by state industrial policy. Since the 1980s, the end of communist central planning and of inward-looking development strategies in poor countries, together with widespread privatisation and liberalisation, ushered in the epoch of 'globalisation'.[46] This provides an opportunity to test the validity of the competing views of the determinants of industrial structure under free market conditions.

There is a substantial empirical literature analysing the nature and determinants of industrial structure prior to the epoch of modern 'globalisation'.[47] However, there is still a dearth of empirical analysis of the nature and causes of the trends in industrial structure in the epoch of globalisation, and of the implications of these trends for both theory and policy. The assembly and interpretation of evidence on this issue is critical for understanding the current epoch.

The issue of industrial structure is closely related to that of the determinants of technical progress, which is the central issue of economic progress: 'If there had been no technical progress, the whole process of accumulation would have been much more modest' (Maddison, 1994: 53).

Mainstream view. The 'mainstream', 'neo-classical' view of the competitive process believes that the perfectly competitive model best describes the essence of capitalist competition. Departures from it are viewed as exceptional and typically arising from government intervention, including protection and nationalisation. At the heart of the mainstream view is the self-equilibrating mechanism of market competition. It is believed that the basic driver of the capitalist process, competition, ensures that if any firm enjoys super-normal profits rivals will soon enter to bid away those profits and undermine any temporary market dominance that the incumbent enjoys. The neo-classical approach emphasises the importance of competition among small firms as the explanation for the prosperity of the advanced economies. Milton Friedman, for example, believed that there is 'a general bias and tendency to overemphasize the importance of the big versus the small': 'As I have studied economic activities in the United States, I have become increasingly impressed with how wide is the range of problems and industries that can be treated as if they were competitive' (Friedman, 1962: 120–3).

Mainstream economists tend to believe that managerial diseconomies of scale set in after firms reach a certain size. The classic expression of this view was contained in Marshall's *Principles of Economics*:

> [H]ere we may read a lesson from the young trees of the forest as they struggle upwards through the benumbing shade of their older rivals.

Many succumb on the way, and a few only survive: those few become stronger with every year, they get a larger share of light and air with every increase of their height, and at last in their turn they tower above their neighbors, and seem as though they would grow on for ever and for ever becoming stronger as they grow. But they do not. One tree will last longer in full vigour and attain a greater size than another; but sooner or later age tells on them all. Though the taller ones have a better access to light and air than their rivals, they gradually lose vitality; and one after another they give place to others, which though of less material strength, have on their side the vigour of youth ... [I]n almost every trade there is a constant rise and fall of large businesses, at any one moment some firm being in the ascending phase and others in the descending (Marshall, 1920: 315–6).

Despite the fact that during the epoch of globalisation, mergers and acquisitions have reached new heights,[48] it is widely argued that global concentration levels have not increased.[49] It is observed that there is a high rate of disappearance of companies from the *Fortune 500* (Wolf, 2004: 226). Based mainly on the analysis of shareholder returns, mainstream economists believe that mergers and acquisitions mostly fail.[50] The explanation that is usually advanced for mergers and acquisitions is the pursuit of power and wealth by CEOs, who are alleged to pursue their own interests at the expense of shareholders, rather than industrial logic. It is argued also that in the epoch of globalisation markets have become so large that it is hard for any firm or small group of firms to dominate a given sector.

Insofar as there was evidence of increased industrial concentration over the course of the twentieth century, the argument was made by mainstream economists that this was due to government policies rather than to the advantages of large-scale production. Hayek argued that it was 'largely due to the influence of German socialist theoreticians, particularly Sombart, generalising from the experience of their country, that the inevitable development of the competitive system into "monopoly capitalism" became widely accepted' (Hayek, 1944: 49). He asks the question: Is it true that 'large firms are everywhere underbidding and driving out the small ones', and that 'this process must go on till in each industry only one or at most a few giant firms are left' (Hayek, 1944: 47). He answers emphatically that there is 'little support from serious evidence' (Hayek, 1944: 47). He quotes from the US Congress' Report on the Concentration of Economic Power (1941): 'The superior efficiency of large establishments has not been demonstrated: the advantages that are supposed to destroy competition have failed to manifest themselves in many fields ... The conclusions that the advantages of large-scale production must lead inevitably to the abolition of competition cannot be accepted' (quoted in Hayek, 1944).

In recent years, the argument has gained ground that advances in information technology have created the possibility of a radical change in the nature of the firm. Activities that it was formerly rational to carry out within the firm can now be performed by networks of small firms connected by the internet (Castells, 2000). In his widely-read book, *The Company of Strangers* (2005), Seabright argues that in the last 25 years, technological changes have transformed the business to the disadvantage of large firms: 'In the two and a half decades since [Alfred Chandler published *The Visible Hand*], more and more large firms, particularly in the traditional production industries, have found themselves outperformed by smaller, nimbler competitors' (Seabright, 2005: 166).[51]

This is widely thought to herald the rise of a new form of 'Post-Fordist' economic system based around 'clusters' of small businesses that can both compete and cooperate at different times (Piore and Sabel, 1984; Porter, 1990). This view appears to be strongly reinforced by the rapid rise in the extent of outsourcing activities that were formerly carried on within the firm. In Coasian terms (see above) the boundaries of the firm have shifted. Many researchers argue that the large corporation is being 'hollowed out', and rapidly becoming an 'endangered species': 'While big companies control ever larger flows of cash, they are exerting less and less direct control over business activity. They are, you might say, growing hollow' (Malone and Laubacher, 1998: 147).

The spread of global markets has greatly reinforced the belief that 'catch-up' at the level of the firm is the normal path of capitalist development. In this view, there are limitless opportunities for firms from developing countries to 'catch-up' if they compete on the free market of the 'global level playing field'. This view is expressed powerfully in Thomas Friedman's book *The World is Flat* (Friedman, 2005) 'The explosion of advanced technologies now means that suddenly, knowledge pools and resources have connected all over the planet, leveling the playing field as never before, so that each of us is potentially an equal – and competitor – of each other' (Friedman, 2005).[52] The view that the 'World is Flat' is strongly reinforced by the explosive growth of China during the epoch of globalisation. The world is widely thought to have become 'flat' for individuals, countries and firms from developing countries, due to liberalisation, privatisation and the IT revolution.

Non-mainstream view. From the earliest stages in the development of modern capitalism, there were economists who believed that capitalism contained an inherent tendency towards industrial concentration. Marx, in *Capital* Vol. 1 argued that there was a 'law of centralization of capital' or the 'attraction of capital by capital'. The driving force of concentration was competition itself, which pressured firms to cheapen the cost of production by investing ever larger amounts of capital in new means of production and in 'the technological application of science', which in turn creates barriers to entry. In the early 1970s, on the eve of the modern epoch of globalisation Hymer visualised the possible outcome of the capitalist process if existing restrictions on merger and acquisition were lifted:

> Suppose giant multinational corporations (say 300 from the US and 200 from Europe and Japan) succeed in establishing themselves as the dominant form of international enterprise and come to control a significant share of industry (especially modern industry) in each country. The world economy will resemble more and more the US economy, where each of the large corporations tends to spread over the entire continent, and to penetrate almost every nook and cranny (Hymer, 1972).

In fact, Marshall's *Principles of Economics* provides numerous reasons to explain 'the advantages that a large business of almost any kind, nearly always has over a small one' (Marshall, 1920: 282). These include economies in procurement, transport costs, marketing, branding, distribution, knowledge, human resources, and management (Marshall, 1920: 282–4). By contrast, his explanation of 'managerial diseconomies of scale' resorts to an analogy ('the trees in the forest') without logic or evidence.

Penrose's path-breaking book *The theory of the growth of the firm* addresses directly the issue of possible limits to the growth of the firm. Like Marshall, she identifies a number of potential advantages that can be enjoyed by the large firm (Penrose, 1995: 89–92). She considers that the most significant advantages for the large firm are those that she terms 'managerial economies'. Penrose concludes that there are no theoretical limits to the size of the firm: 'We have found nothing to prevent the indefinite expansion of firms as time passes, and clearly if some of the economies of size are economies of expansion, there is no reason to assume that a firm would ever reach a size in which it has taken full advantage of all these economies' (Penrose, 1995: 99).

Chandler has demonstrated the central role of the large, oligopolistic firm in technical progress in the business history of today's high-income countries. This was, in its turn, central to the whole growth dynamic of modern capitalism. He has shown that the modern industrial enterprise 'played a central role in creating the most technologically advanced, fastest growing industries of their day'. These industries, in turn, were 'the pace-setters of the industrial sector of their economies'. They provided an underlying dynamic in the development of modern industrial capitalism (Chandler, 1990: 593). Chandler emphasises the paradox that even as the number of firms in a given sector shrinks, competition between increasingly powerful firms can intensify: 'market share and profits changed constantly, which kept oligopolies from becoming stagnant and monopolistic' (Chandler *et al.*, 1997: 31).

The succession of studies which purport to show the irrationality of mergers and acquisitions are almost entirely based on the analysis of the consequences for shareholder value in the short-term. The much smaller number of studies which analyse the long-term impact of mergers and acquisitions on business survival and growth show a different story (Chandler, 1990; Nolan, 2001a and 2001b; and Boston Consulting Group, 2004). They suggest, rather, that well-selected and well-executed mergers and acquisitions that have a clear strategic purpose can increase the business capability of the firm concerned. They can strengthen the firm's presence in given geographical markets, increase their access to technologies they formerly did not posses, acquire scarce human resources, add valuable brands to their portfolio, and enable long-term savings through economies of scale and scope in procurement, research and development, and marketing.

The Evidence on Industrial Concentration

The period since the 1970s has provided an ideal opportunity to test competing theories of the basic tendencies of capitalism once the constraints are removed. The period has seen a drastic reduction of state intervention, with comprehensive privatisation, drastic reduction of state support for national industries, removal of protectionist barriers on cross-border mergers and acquisitions, and extension across the entire globe of markets for most goods and services.[53]

The period has seen a large change in the nature of business organisation, amounting to nothing less than a 'business revolution'. As global markets have opened up, multinational companies typically have responded by divesting their 'non-core' businesses to focus on a small array of closely related products in which they have global leadership, achieved through the possession of a combination of superior brand and technology, and through economies of scale and scope in both areas. The large size and business focus of leading firms has enabled them to benefit greatly from economies of scale in procurement. Leading global firms have increasingly outsourced manufacturing and 'non-core' service functions, to focus on the 'brain' functions of design, product development, final assembly, marketing and financing. Alongside the growth of outsourcing, they have also developed skills in systems integration and coordination of their supply chain. Leading global firms have also been able to attract the best employees in the international 'battle for talent'.

In almost every sector, the period since the 1970s has seen an unprecedented amount of merger, acquisition and divestment, with leading firms using this to consolidate their position at the centre of global markets by achieving focus and scale. In addition to highly publicised large-scale mergers there has been a continuous process of smaller-scale acquisitions, with leading companies each acquiring numerous small and medium-sized firms annually in order to enhance their leading positions in their respective markets.

Levels of global industrial consolidation within each sector have advanced remorselessly. The process has affected almost every sector, from the world's most sophisticated, high technology capital goods, to the simplest consumer goods. It is as though a law has come into play, under which in every sector, the top half dozen systems integrator firms, with superior brands and/or technologies account for over one half of the entire global market in the particular product. This is the case in industries as diverse as large commercial airliners, automobiles, gas turbines, farm equipment, lifts, construction equipment, chemicals, pharmaceuticals, consumer electronics, telecommunications equipment, servers, semiconductors, digital cameras, personal computers, IT software, carbonated soft drinks, salty snacks, beer, confectionary, ice cream, hair colourants, camera film, cigarettes, recorded music, media and marketing, investment banking, accountancy, foreign exchange trading, and water management, Moreover, in different sub-categories within each broad product category, levels of industrial concentration are typically even higher.[54] These dramatic developments are consistent with the persistence in most sectors of a large number of small and medium-sized firms, which produce mainly non-branded, low technology products, supplying local markets, and which collectively occupy a small share of total global markets. These parts of the segmented industrial structure typically supply the lower groups within each country's income distribution.

The explosive advance in industrial consolidation among systems integrator firms has produced a powerful consequential impact on industrial structure, which has been termed the 'cascade effect' (Nolan, 2001a). The global industry leaders in each sector have used their procurement power to exert intense pressure on their supply chains, typically requiring leading firms in the upper tiers of the supply chain to supply inputs on a 'just-in-time' basis to production sites around the world. This has intensified the pressure upon supplier firms to build global networks to feed the needs of global customers. The leading systems integrators place intense pressure on their suppliers to achieve technical progress in order to supply inputs of improving technical quality so that they can meet the demands of final customers. Moreover, they exert remorseless pressure on their suppliers to lower prices for a given product quality. This has, in turn, resulted in intense pressure upon supplier firms themselves to merge and acquire, and to divest non-core business, in order to gain scale and focus, enabling them to achieve economies of scale in research and development, procurement, human resources, and subsystems integration.

Technical Progress

The impact of this process upon technical progress has been striking. The world's research and development expenditure is highly concentrated. The United Kingdom's Department of Trade and Industry compiles an annual survey of the R&D spending of the top 1250 companies globally, the '*Global 1250*' (DTI, 2006). These companies are at the heart of the global economic system. In 2005–06, the firms in the Global 1250 list invested around US$ 430 billion in R&D. They employed around 32 million people, generated sales revenues of around US$ 11 800 billion, earned operating profits of around US$ 1300 billion (11 per cent of sales revenue), and had a market capitalisation of around US$ 14 600 billion (DTI, 2006). Expenditure on R&D is growing fast.

The Global 1250 constitutes the core of global technical progress. The list is 'strongly concentrated by company, sector and country' (DTI, 2006, Vol. 1: 43). The United States accounts for 41.3 per cent of the total number of companies in the Global 1250, and Japan accounts for 19.5 per cent (DTI, 2006, Vol. 1: 45). The top ten countries (all high-income),[55] account for 94 per cent of the total (DTI, 2006, Vol. 1: 45). The top 100 companies account for 61.4 per cent of the total expenditure of the Global 1250 while the bottom 150 companies account for just 1.3 per cent of the total (DTI, 2006, Vol. 1: 45). The top 20 companies alone spend a total of US$ 112 billion (US$ 5.6 billion per company), and account for 26.2 per cent of the total (DTI, 2006, Vol. 1: 39).

The Global 1250 reveals a picture in which global technical progress in each sector is dominated by a small number of powerful firms:

- The Information Technology Hardware sector has a total of 225 companies in the Global 1250. The top five companies account for 25 per cent of total R&D expenditure, 28 per cent of total revenues, and 33 per cent of profits, while the top ten account for 42 per cent of R&D expenditure, 43 per cent of revenues and 51 per cent of profits (DTI, 2006, Vol. 2: 118–9). In the more broadly-defined 'technology hardware' sector, the top company, Hitachi, was granted 1968 US patents in 2005, compared with 410 for Ericsson, the twentieth-ranked company, 200 for Qualcomm, the thirtieth-ranked, and 87 for Mitsubishi Electric, the fortieth-ranked (DTI, 2006, Vol. 2: 225–6).
- The Pharmaceutical and Biotechnology sector has a total of 152 firms in the Global 1250. Of these, the top five account for 57 per cent of R&D

expenditure, 58 per cent of revenue, and 69 per cent of profits (DTI, 2006, Vol. 2: 108–9). The top company in the sector, Pfizer, was granted 349 US patents in 2005, compared with just 12 for the thirtieth-ranked company in the sector (DTI, 2006, Vol. 2: 224).
- The Software and Computer Services sector has a total of 111 companies in the Global 1250. The top five account for 57 per cent of R&D expenditure, 61 per cent of revenues and 70 per cent of profits (DTI, 2006, Vol. 2: 114). The top company in the sector, IBM, was granted 2962 US patents in 2005, compared with just 20 for the tenth-ranked company in the sector (DTI, 2006, Vol. 2: 225).
- The Electronics and Electrical Equipment sector has a total of 102 firms in the Global 1250. Of these, the top five account for 53 per cent of R&D expenditure, 41 per cent of revenues, and 41 per cent of profits (DTI, 2006, Vol. 2: 92). The top company in the sector, Matsushita Electric, was granted 1904 US patents in 2005, compared with 156 for the twentieth-ranked company in the sector (DTI, 2006, Vol. 2: 223).
- The Automobile and Parts sector has a total of 78 firms in the Global 1250. Of these, the top five firms account for 43 of the total R&D expenditure, 46 per cent of the revenue and 36 per cent of profits (DTI, 2006, Vol. 2: 84). The top company among the auto assemblers, the Honda Motor Co., was granted 822 US patents in 2005, compared with 55 for the tenth-ranked company. Among the auto component makers, the top-ranked company, Bosch, was granted 794 US patents in 2005, compared with 77 for the tenth-ranked company (DTI, 2006, Vol. 2: 222).
- The Aerospace industry has a total of 34 firms in the Global 1250. Of these the top five firms account for 63 per cent of the total R&D expenditure, and 45 per cent of both the revenues and profits (DTI, 2006, Vol. 2: 84). The top-ranked company, Boeing, was granted 413 US patents in 2005, compared with 62 for the tenth-ranked company in the sector (DTI, 2006, Vol. 2: 222).

Far from witnessing a 'reduction in the level of competition', the recent period has seen a drastic increase in the intensity of competition, and investment in technical progress is a key source of competitive advantage: 'Large companies are pouring money into research and development at an unprecedented rate, in response to growing competition ... In many sectors profits are growing strongly and companies can afford to spend more on R&D ... Where profits are weak, such as in the automobile industry, the competition is so fierce that companies dare not cut their investment' (DTI economist, quoted in *Financial Times*, 30 October 2006). Between 2001–02 and 2005–06 total R&D expenditure by the Global 1250 rose by 23 per cent (DTI, 2006, Vol. 2: 170).

The increased focus on core business among the world's leading systems integrators and subsystems integrators has enhanced the effectiveness of R&D expenditure, allowing benefits from economies of scale and scope. Technical progress in the instruments of R&D, especially IT hardware and software, has further enhanced the effectiveness of R&D spending. In addition, the world's leading firms are rapidly increasing their R&D bases in low and middle-income countries, which enables them to obtain greater amounts of knowledge per dollar spent on R&D. The share of developing countries' R&D undertaken by multinational firms in many developing countries is now very high. In 2003, the share of foreign affiliates in total R&D is estimated to be 48 per cent in Brazil, 24 per cent in China, 47 per cent in the Czech Republic, and 63 per cent in Hungary, while it stood at 46 per cent in Mexico in 2000 (UNCTAD, 2005: 292–3).

Meaningful measurement of technical progress has eluded economists.[56] The pace of technical progress during the epoch of the Global Business Revolution cannot be unambiguously compared with previous periods of rapid technical progress. However, it is self-evident that the period has seen one of the fastest periods of technical progress in human history, led by the oligopolistic firms that dominate the apex of global supply chains, which have in turn powerfully stimulated technical progress at lower levels in the supply chain. I shall examine briefly technical progress in four sectors in the past two decades.

Information technology. The IT revolution has been at the heart of technical progress in all sectors. The IT hardware and software sector is by far the most important in terms of global technical progress. In 2005–06, the total R&D expenditure of the companies in this sector within the Global 1250, amounted to US$ 111 billion (DTI, 2006, Vol. 1: 49). Within the Global 1250 companies, the IT Hardware, Software, and Computer Services sectors contain a total of 326 companies accounting for 25.8 per cent of the total R&D spending (DTI, 2006, Vol. 1: 50). The massive spending of the world's leading IT companies over the past two decades has stimulated a revolution in information generation and transmission. The revolution in IT has transformed both the nature of capital goods and the nature of a large fraction of final consumption. Goods and services in almost every sector have been comprehensively changed by this technical revolution, from complex engineering products, including aeroplanes, automobiles, farm equipment, and all types of manufacturing machinery, to almost every imaginable service, including mass media, retail, banking, insurance, tourism, transport, and marketing. The IT revolution has universally lowered costs and prices of IT goods and services. It has allowed a dramatic fall in the cost of global communications, transformed the cost and nature of R&D, and facilitated a profound change in the nature of the global firm and its relationship to the surrounding value chain.

Automobiles. In the epoch of the Global Business Revolution, both passenger and commercial vehicles have altered radically, with huge reductions in weight, due mainly to advances in technologies embodied in steel, aluminium and plastics; large increases in fuel economy, due both to weight reduction and advances in engine technologies; large increases in vehicle safety, comfort, ease of use, reliability and longevity; and large reductions in polluting emissions. The application of advances in information technology has penetrated every aspect of vehicle operation.

Aerospace. In the aerospace industry, enormous changes have taken place in the nature of passenger aircraft. Large weight reductions per passenger carried have taken place due to advances in aircraft design, through improvements in each type of construction material, and through increased use of composite materials; large advances have taken place due to continuous progress in engine technologies, including weight reduction, increased fuel efficiency, reduced engine noise, increased engine reliability, and advances in ease of engine maintenance; and large advances have taken place in aircraft safety, due to advances in avionics and flight control systems, and advances in the design and reliability of aircraft components, including seats, engines, landing gear, avionics, and tyres.

Beverages. In the beverage industry, including both soft drinks and beer, quite limited changes have taken place in the nature of the product, but enormous technical progress has taken place in the nature of the processes involved in producing and distributing beverages. Filling machinery has greatly increased in speed, reliability, and fuel efficiency, alongside reductions in variability of filling height and bottle damage. Packaging technologies have altered radically. Metal cans and PET bottles have joined glass bottles to constitute the three main forms of primary packaging. The introduction of metal cans and PET allowed enormous changes in the appearance of primary packaging, increasing customer satisfaction through increased ease of use and attractiveness of designs. Improved packaging technologies have increased longevity of beverages at peak condition. All three types of primary packaging have achieved large reductions in package weight, which economises on use of raw materials, reduces weight in transport and improves ease of use by the final customer. These advances have occurred through intense interaction between leading beverage companies and the suppliers of packaging materials (including steel, aluminium, PET and glass), as well as with the firms that make machinery to produce primary packaging. Large advances have taken place in the machine building industry to produce 'PET pre-forms', PET blowing equipment, can-making machinery and glass bottle machinery. They have increased speed and reliability, reduced raw material and fuel consumption per unit, and improved packaging design capabilities. Distribution of beverages is enormously intensive in the use of road transport. Improvements in commercial vehicle technologies have greatly increased fuel efficiency in the distribution of beverages.

As these four examples indicate, increased focus on core business and increased firm size among both systems integrators and suppliers has increased economies of scale and scope at every level in the value chain. This applies to almost every sector. Alongside dramatic advances in product and process technologies, there has taken place a near universal decline in unit costs and advance in product quality. The epoch of the Global Business Revolution has seen a dramatic rise in levels of industrial concentration. Ferocious oligopolistic competition has penetrated almost every level of the supply chain, from the systems integrators downwards. Oligopolistic competition at lower levels in the supply chain has been stimulated by intense pressure from above, which 'cascades' down through the whole system. Instead of the technical stagnation and real price increase that were predicted by most economists, both 'radical' and mainstream, the epoch has witnessed intense oligopolistic competition, which has been responsible for this epoch's extraordinary technological dynamism. This reality has hardly begun to be absorbed and analysed by economists.[57] For Marx or Schumpeter, the nature and consequences of the Global Business Revolution would be unsurprising.

1.2.4 Expanding Human Freedom

Through the ages, the pursuit of profit by business people has stimulated them to respond to the expansion of markets by saving and investing, and achieving technical progress. This has led the way to a progressive expansion of the realm of individual freedom from the numerous forces that constrain the lives of ordinary people. In the epoch of the Global Business Revolution, these forces have intensified, producing powerful stimuli for the advance of human freedoms from numerous constraints on their lives.

Freedom from the Tyranny of Nature

Technical progress and nature. One of the central forces in Adam Smith's growth model was the accumulation of capital, and the central motive for the application of capital was to obtain profit derived from the use of capital. Smith believed that behind this lay an even deeper psychological drive, namely the desire to acquire 'wealth and greatness'. Smith enumerates the dramatic effects of the application of this 'industry', impelled by the pursuit of 'wealth and greatness':

> It is this which first prompted them to cultivate the ground, to build houses, to found cities and commonwealths, and to invent and improve all the sciences and arts, which ennoble human life; which have entirely changed the whole face of the globe, have turned the rude forests of nature into agreeable and fertile plains, and made the trackless and barren ocean a new fund of subsistence, and the great high road of communication to the different nations of the earth. The earth by these labours of mankind has been obliged to redouble her natural fertility, and to maintain a greater number of inhabitants (Smith, 1982: 183–4).

The pace of expansion accelerated after the Industrial Revolution. Economists as different as Marx and J. S. Mill, writing in the midst of this revolutionary process, regarded the profit motive and the extension of markets as fundamental to the liberation of human creative capabilities, which underpinned the technical progress that in turn transformed people's dependence on nature. Writing in 1848 Marx and Engels wrote:

> The bourgeoisie, during its rule of scarce one hundred years, has created more massive and more colossal productive forces than have all the preceding generations together. Subjection of Nature's forces to man, machinery, application to industry and agriculture, steam-navigation, railways, electric telegraphs, clearing whole continents for cultivation, canalisation of rivers, whole populations conjured out of the ground – what earlier century had even a presentiment that such productive forces slumbered in the lap of social labour (Marx and Engels, 1968)?

In the same year, J. S. Mill wrote:

> Of the features which characterise this progressive economical movement of civilised nations, that which first excites attention, through its intimate connection with the phenomena of Production, is the perpetual, and so far as human foresight can extend, the unlimited, growth of man's power over nature. Our knowledge of the properties and laws of physical objects shows no sign of approaching its ultimate boundaries: it is advancing more rapidly, and in a greater number of directions at once than in any previous age or generation, and affording such frequent glimpses of unexplored fields beyond, as to justify the belief that our acquaintance with nature is still almost in its infancy. This increasing physical knowledge is

now, too, more rapidly than at any former period, converted, by practical ingenuity, into physical power (Mill, 1998: 66).

These forces, which appeared 'magical' in the nineteenth century, have accelerated in the epoch of the Global Business Revolution, driven by the same forces of capitalist competition, but reaching new heights of human inventiveness. The array of choices facing people has expanded at a dizzying pace. Technical progress has combined with intense competitive pressure among large capitalist firms and their supply chains, to lower real prices, increase consumer choice and advance human welfare. So great has been the pace and ubiquity of technical progress during the epoch of the Global Business Revolution that it has become impossible to measure the real pace of advance in real incomes.

Energy availability. Energy supply is central to the world economy. Human ingenuity has hugely increased the availability of primary energy, continually disappointing fears that the global economy would 'run out of primary energy'. In 1865, Stanley Jevons, the distinguished British economist, believed that the progressive exhaustion of Britain's coal reserves would spell disaster for the British economy: 'It will appear that there is no reasonable prospect of any release from future want of the main agent of industry' (quoted in Lomborg, 2001: 124). Jevons hugely underestimated the capacity of human ingenuity to find new sources of energy and to use old ones in more inventive ways.

As well as liberating people from the tyrannies of nature, technology has also produced difficulties. In the view of Lord Broers, technology produces many problems, but it also contains the capability of solving the same problems: 'technology is our friend' (Broers, 2005). In the view of Lord Browne, Chief Executive of BP, fears that the world will run out of energy are based on 'linear thinking'. He believes that this view hugely underestimates human beings' capability to 'innovate in the face of adversity', and considers that the stimulus of demand and price will ensure that 'innovation occurs at the right time in order to avoid catastrophe' (Browne, 2005).

(a) Fossil fuels. Around four-fifths of global primary energy supply today comes from fossil fuels. Most transport, building, heating and electricity generation technologies are built around the use of fossil fuels.

It is widely thought that the prospects for fossil fuel supply are strictly limited. At today's level of consumption, it is predicted that there are only 40 more years of oil reserves, and 70 years of gas reserves, while coal reserves may last for 200 years. In addition, the rate of increase of demand for primary energy in the low and middle-income countries is accelerating, so that the prospects for global energy supply and demand look even bleaker.

However, the reserves of fossil fuel are not absolutely fixed. The data available for 'reserves' are those recoverable at given prices. However, the size of recoverable reserves alters greatly as the price of fossil fuels changes: 'At US$ 70 per barrel, oil reserves are to all intents and purposes infinite' (Chris Mottershead, BP, 2005). At higher prices, recovery becomes worthwhile using technologies that enable the extraction of a higher proportion of oil, gas and coal from existing fields. Some estimates of the world's coal reserves consider that there is more than 1500 years'-worth of supply at present levels of consumption (Lomborg, 2001: 127).

Higher prices also mean that sources of fossil fuels that were uneconomic become economically viable. For example, oil can be recovered from tar sands and shale oil. Techniques are now available to produce oil from these sources at around US$ 11 per barrel. At a price of around US$ 70 per barrel, there are 'at least 200 years of oil reserves contained in tar sands' (Mottershead, 2005). Shale oil contains an estimated eight times more energy than in all other forms of fossil fuel combined (including oil, gas, coal, peat, and tar sands): 'This stunning amount of energy is the equivalent of our present *total* energy consumption for more than 5000 years' (Lomborg, 2001: 128). The coastlines of most countries have huge amounts of gas contained within crystals. The total reserves of 'gas in crystals' are 'larger than all known reserves of fossil fuels added together', and the techniques for gaining access to these gases could be commercially viable within fifteen years (Mottershead, 2005).

(b) Nuclear power. After years of stagnation, the increased price of oil, fears of national energy security and concerns over global warming have led to a widespread reconsideration of the place of nuclear energy within the energy portfolio in all countries: 'Nuclear power generation has made great strides. After a period when it was believed to be hopelessly uneconomic, it is now close to competing in real economic terms with gas-powered generation. And even after making allowance for decommissioning costs, nuclear power is significantly cheaper than wind or wave power' (Lord Broers, president of the United Kingdom's Royal Academy of Engineering and former Vice-Chancellor of the University of Cambridge, quoted in *Financial Times*, 18 May 2005).

Technical progress has greatly reduced the construction and operational costs of nuclear power stations, and increased their safety. Modern nuclear fission reactors are 'designed to shut down in the absence of constant intervention'. Fast breeder reactors will greatly reduce the demand for uranium, so that there will be almost unlimited availability of the basic raw material for energy generation. In addition, nuclear fusion, which uses ordinary sea water as its fuel, and hence has virtually limitless fuel availability, may become commercially viable within a few decades. Such notable figures in the Green Movement as James Lovelock, the originator of the 'Gaia' theory, which sees the earth as a self-regulating mechanism, has shifted to support for nuclear energy.

Key developing countries, such as China and India, have committed themselves to large increases in the numbers of nuclear power stations. China plans to build up to forty nuclear power reactors by 2020: 'International companies with nuclear expertise, such as the United States' Westinghouse [acquired by Toshiba in early 2006] and France's Framatome ANP, are salivating at the prospect' (*FT*, 28 October 2005).

(c) Renewable energy. Hydro power has already made large strides using well-established technologies. In countries that are well-endowed with water resources, such as Brazil, hydro power accounts for nine-tenths of total electricity generation. However, globally, its share is only around 6.6 per cent of total primary energy supply (Lomborg, 2001: 130), and it is not thought likely that it can significantly increase its share of the global total (Mottershead, 2005).

Wind power was for a long time regarded as an eccentric technology that would never contribute substantially to global primary energy supply. However, in recent years there has been a large increase in investment in wind turbines, with consequential declines in the costs of production, installation and operation. GE demonstrated its commitment to wind power through the acquisition of the wind generation assets of Enron, and its wind division had a turnover of US$ 2 billion in 2005 (*FT,* 1 July 2005).

By far the most abundant source of primary energy is that which comes from the sun. Science fiction writers such as Olaf Stapledon (1930 and 1937), looking far into the future, have long thought that human beings' technical ingenuity would eventually enable them to harness solar energy as their main source of primary energy. They viewed reliance on fossil fuels as a short-term phenomenon associated with an early, primitive phase in human development. It is estimated that the influx of solar energy is equivalent to about 7000 times today's global energy consumption.

Solar energy can be exploited both directly and indirectly. The indirect route is via plant life, which in the very long term provides the basis of fossil fuels. However, in the short term, solar energy can be harnessed through growing plants. A large advantage of 'biomass' as a source of energy is that they are 'carbon neutral', since the emission of carbon dioxide when they are burned, either as primary fuels or as secondary fuels (such as ethanol) is counterbalanced by their absorption of carbon dioxide during their growth. There has been a great deal of recent technical progress that enables more intensive use of the energy stored within plants, such as that in new types of power stations and domestic heating equipment.

Much the most effective way to make use of solar energy is through the generation of electricity through the use of solar cells or photovoltaic cells. Even with today's technologies, it is estimated that an area of around 250 000 square kilometres (0.15 per cent of the earth's land mass) in the tropics could provide all current global energy requirements. Also, solar cells and photovoltaic cell technologies have been advancing rapidly, allowing rapid advances in the effectiveness of capture of solar energy and declines in the price of harnessing solar energy. Leading international energy companies such as BP are now at the forefront of solar energy technologies.

Energy efficiency. Technical progress in automobile engines, power generation equipment, building design and packaging, have contributed to large advances in energy efficiency. GDP per unit of energy use has risen globally from US$ 3.5 (at constant PPP prices) per kilogram of oil equivalent in 1990 to 4.2 kilograms in 2001 (World Bank, WDI, 2004: 146). Progress has been especially striking in low and middle-income countries, where the impact of global production technologies in energy generation, transport and packaging have helped to raise GDP per unit of energy use from US$ 2.8 in 1990 to US$ 3.7 in 2001 (World Bank, WDI, 2004: 146).

Pollution

(a) Carbon dioxide. It can be seen that there is an almost limitless availability of fossil fuel. The world is now going through a second 'energy shock', linked to the rise of China and India, with huge and fast-growing energy needs, political instability in the Middle East, and fears over global warming. These factors have affected both government regulation of the energy sector, notably through the Kyoto Agreement, and energy prices, though the long-term prospect for the likely course of energy prices is still highly uncertain. The main factor in global warming is production of carbon dioxide by fossil fuels, which produces the 'greenhouse effect', which traps reflected radiation from the sun in the earth's atmosphere. The level of carbon dioxide production has risen from under 2 billion tons per year in 1950 to around 7 billion tons in 2000 (Mottershead, 2005). In the absence of government regulation or technical progress, and using current projections of global output growth, it is predicted that the level of carbon dioxide production would rise to around 14 billion tons by 2050. However, using technical knowledge that either already exists, or which could soon be brought into existence based on current knowledge, there are numerous ways in which the projected rise in global output could be achieved without any increase in global carbon dioxide output.

BP has identified seven 'one billion ton wedges' that could form part of the 'stabilisation triangle' of carbon dioxide output without any major technological breakthrough. Each one gigawatt 'wedge' is the equivalent to 'taking 250 000 vehicles off the road'. The 'wedges' could include 700 1GW nuclear power stations; improving building techniques so that the amount of energy used to heat buildings remains constant (40 per cent of primary energy is used to heat buildings); a fifty-fold increase in global wind turbine capacity; doubling the rate of re-forestation; 2500 fossil-fuelled hydrogen power stations, which sequester carbon dioxide in oil fields; a 700-fold increase in photovoltaic cells; and re-powering 1400 GW of coal-fired power stations with gas.

There are large opportunities for the more general use of carbon sequestration technologies so that extensive use can continue to be made of the world's massive coal reserves without contributing to global warming. This is especially important for the world's two largest coal users, China and the United States, which generate 70 per cent and 50 per cent of their electricity respectively from coal.

A variety of possibilities exist through which technical progress might allow large increases in vehicle use to take place without substantial growth of carbon dioxide emissions (Oliva, 2005). These include improvements in internal combustion engine technologies; the use of hybrid vehicles which combine the internal combustion engine with the addition of an electric motor; pure electric vehicles which may ultimately be powered with electricity generated from renewable sources, eventually from solar power, or from fossil fuels accompanied by carbon dioxide sequestration; and expanded use of biofuels, which are carbon dioxide neutral.

(b) Airborne particulates. For a prolonged period, as average incomes increased, today's developed countries saw large increases in levels of air pollution. As late as the early 1950s, airborne particulates in cities such as London caused severe smogs that caused large-scale loss of life. Government regulation such as Britain's Clean Air Act (1955) and later regulation to restrict the sale of leaded petrol, stimulated technical progress through such measures as the introduction of smoke scrubbing equipment at power stations, increased use of low-sulphur coal, and improved fuels for vehicles. Particulates in the atmosphere fell dramatically thereafter reaching levels that today are only a tiny fraction of those in the early 1950s (Lomborg, 2001: 168). Many of the technical advances that helped reduce airborne particulates in high-income countries were embodied in global products that were later sold in developing countries, including power stations, automobile and aircraft engines, and fuels for transport equipment. This might tend to reduce the level of particulate emissions in developing countries compared with those experienced in high-income countries at similar levels of real output per person (Lomborg, 2001: 176–7).

Transport. Technical progress in transport has comprehensively transformed the choices facing people in terms of personal movement. Since the 1970s the real prices of automobiles and air travel have fallen tremendously, which has allowed people with ever lower income levels to acquire cars and travel long journeys on aeroplanes. In low and middle-income countries, the number of passenger cars per 1000 people rose from 16 in 1990 to 28 in 1999–2001 (World Bank, WDI, 2004: 162).

Health. Technical advances in medicines and medical equipment, increasing real consumption levels, improvement in national and international government agencies' delivery systems, improved food security, as well as advances in infrastructure provision and better access to reliable drinking water,[58] and improved sanitation,[59] have contributed to improvements in health, helping to free people from the threat of illness, pain and premature death. This has been crucially important for the standard of living in developing countries. In these countries, between 1970 and 2002, infant mortality rates fell from 108 per thousand live births to 61 per thousand in 2002, and under-five mortality rates fell from 166 per thousand to 89, while fertility rates fell from 5.4 births per woman in 1970–75 to 2.9 per woman in 2002–05 (UNDP, 2004: 155 and 171). Life expectancy at birth in developing countries rose from 56 years in 1970–75 to 65 years in 2000–05 (UNDP, 2004: 171).[60] Even in the least-developed group of countries, life expectancy rose from 44 in 1970–75 to 51 in 2000–05.

Telecommunications. Revolutionary technical advances, especially in semiconductors, have contributed to enormous progress in the nature and price of electronic consumer durables. The transformation of the telecommunications industry has been especially significant for advances in the standard of living of people in developing countries. Increases in average incomes in developing countries have helped to stimulate growth of expenditure on telecommunications goods and services. In developing countries between 1990 and 2002, the number of telephone mainlines per 1000 people rose from 29 to 96 and the number of cellular phone subscribers rose from zero per 1000 people to 101 (UNDP, 2004: 183). By 2002, for every 1000 people in developing countries, there were 257 radios, 190 TV sets and 28 personal computers (World Bank, WDI, 2004: 296). The technical and business transformation of the global media industry, as well as liberalisation of national controls, has hugely widened the range of broadcast information to which people of almost all segments of the income distribution can have access.[61] These developments have helped to provide people with enormously enhanced freedom of choice both for entertainment and knowledge acquisition.

Agriculture. In low-income countries, population grew by 2.2 per cent per annum between 1980 and 2002 (from 1.6 billion to 2.5 billion), while the amount of arable land per person shrank from 0.23 hectares to just 0.17 hectares in the same period. (World Bank, WDI, 2004: 40). Without large improvements in agricultural productivity in this period, food output per person would have declined and developing countries' susceptibility to famine would have greatly increased. In fact, this period saw unprecedented advances in agricultural technology and rapid farm modernisation in developing countries, including seeds, farm equipment, transport infrastructure and information technology. In low-income countries, between 1979–81 and 2000–02 the amount of fertiliser applied per hectare of arable land rose from 289 grams to 717 grams, the number of tractors per square kilometre of arable land rose from 20 to 66 and irrigated land increased its share of total cropland from 19.8 per cent to 26.4 per cent (World Bank, WDI, 2004: 122–3). As a consequence of this immense technical progress, per capita food output in low-income countries grew by 0.8 per cent per annum (World Bank, WDI, 2004: 40 and 126). The improvement in agricultural performance in developing countries has played a central role in confining famines to Sub-Saharan Africa, whereas formerly they affected large parts of the developing world.

Freedom from Control by Others

Urbanisation. The advance of market forces in pursuit of profit has been associated with rapid urbanisation and decline in rural living during the epoch of the Global Business Revolution. Where data are available they show large declines in the proportion of the population in developing countries that is dependent on agriculture.[62] In low and middle-income countries, the share of agriculture in GDP fell from 31 per cent in 1965 (World Bank, 1990: 183) to 11 per cent in 2002 (World Bank, WDI, 2004: 188). Living patterns altered drastically as people moved away from primary reliance on agriculture into urban environments and closer contact with the market economy and complex division of labour. The share of the urban population in low and middle-income countries rose from 24 per cent in 1965 (World Bank, 1990: 39) to 42 per cent in 2002 (World Bank, WDI, 2004: 154). The total urban population in developing countries rose from 782 million in 1975 to 2.04 billion in 2002 (UNDP, 2004: 155).[63] The fact that nearly one half the population of developing countries now lives and works in an urban capitalist environment has radically changed the consciousness of the populations of developing countries. The pace of change has been accelerated by the transformations in the mass media facilitated by institutional change and technical progress in telecommunications and electronic consumer goods.

The transformation in the living and working environment from a rural, isolated setting, with limited connection to markets, negligible opportunities for occupational and residential change, and a restricted, unchanging set of interpersonal relationships, to an urban capitalist environment, intimate engagement with the market for one's labour power, wide opportunities for occupational and residential change, and access to a wide and changing set of inter-personal relationships, has comprehensively changed the outlook of the new generation of urban dwellers. The outlook of their children contrasts even more with that of their parents and grandparents. The new generation of urban dwellers operating in a capitalist environment is vastly more independent than their forbears, with far greater opportunities to resist pressures from parents and kin groups, and (in the case of wives and female children) from husbands, fathers and brothers.

Democratisation. In the political realm, the Global Business Revolution, the accompanying process of capitalist urbanisation and the transformation of consciousness of the urban population has seen a powerful growth of demands for political liberties, paralleling the movements that emerged in Europe in the nineteenth century as capitalist urbanisation advanced. Across the developing world, the epoch saw large advances in political liberties. Whereas in 1985 38 per cent of the world's population lived in the world's 'most democratic countries', by 2000, the share had risen to 57 per cent (UNDP, 2002: 15). The share living in 'authoritarian regimes' had fallen from 45 per cent to 30 per cent (UNDP, 2002: 15).

Inequality. Growth rates of national output per person have been somewhat faster in developing countries than in high-income countries. Between 1975 and 2002, the growth of per capita GDP in the OECD countries was 2.0 per cent per annum, compared with 2.3 per cent per annum in developing countries as a whole (UNDP, 2004: 184–7). Moreover, the growth of GDP per capita in the most populous developing countries, namely India and China, has been even higher, at 3.3 per cent and 8.2 per cent respectively between 1975 and 2002. Studies which measure global inequality using country averages weighted by population totals, have found there has been a small decline in the global Gini coefficient during the last quarter of a century (Sutcliffe, 2002: 14).[64] Using the data from these different international studies, Sutcliffe has calculated that the global Gini coefficient of the distribution of world income fell from around 0.58–0.62 in 1980 to around 0.52–0.56 in 1998 (Sutcliffe, 2002: 14).

Freedom from Poverty

During the period 1975–2002, output per person in developing countries rose by around 2.3 per cent per annum, and in the years 1990–2002, the period in which globalisation intensified, the growth rate accelerated to 2.8 per cent per annum (UNDP, 2004: 187). The rapid increase in output per person during the period of the Global Business Revolution has contributed to a massive reduction in global poverty. Between 1981 and 2002, the share of people living on less than US$ 1 per day in developing countries is estimated to have fallen from 40 per cent to 19 per cent (World Bank, WDI, 2006: 73). In the same period, the share of those living on less than US$ 2 per day in developing countries is estimated to have fallen from 67 per cent to 50 per cent.

Freedom from War

It is widely assumed that national identification is 'so natural, primary and permanent as to precede history'. In fact 'in its modern and basically political sense the concept *nation* is historically very young' (Hobsbawm, 1990: 14–8). It is closely associated with industrialisation and the growth of the state, emerging in Europe with the mercantilist epoch in the sixteenth to eighteenth centuries, and reaching its full development with state-led industrialisation in the nineteenth century.

During the early phase of capitalist industrialisation from the late eighteenth to the mid-nineteenth century, most economists considered that the emerging market economy was essentially international, not national. It was thought that the global market economy would erode national cultural differences, including language. Much of the economics of the period was focused on individual units, whether people or firms, 'rationally maximising their gains and minimising their losses in a market which had no specific spatial dimension' (Hobsbawm, 1990: 26). Adam Smith's *Wealth of Nations* is directed against the concept of a protected national economy based on mercantilist principles. It argued for a cosmopolitan, international economy in which the extent of the market and the division of labour would become ever wider, not halting at national boundaries.

It was widely held that the trend of world history was towards unification of small states into larger ones and, eventually, into a world state alongside a global market. The process of nation building was viewed as but a step on that path, with the combination of formerly separate nationalities into a single larger national entity:

> Experience proves that it is possible for one nationality to merge and be absorbed into another ... Nobody can suppose that it is not more

beneficial for a Breton or a Basque of French Navarre to be … a member of the French nationality, admitted on equal terms to all the privileges of French citizenship … than to sulk on his own rocks, the half-savage relic of past times, revolving in his own little mental orbit, without participation in the general movement of the world (J. S. Mill, quoted in Hobsbawm, 1990: 34).

In 1784, Emmanuel Kant wrote his essay called 'Idea for a Universal History with a Cosmopolitan Purpose', in which he suggested that history embodied a 'hidden plan of nature': [S]uch a plan opens up the comforting prospect of a future in which all the germs implanted by nature can be developed fully, and in which man's destiny can be fulfilled here on earth' (Kant, 1991: 52–3). He considered that the 'highest purpose of nature' was a 'universal cosmopolitan existence', and that this would eventually be realised as the 'matrix within which all the original capacities of the human race may develop' (Kant, 1991: 51).[65]

Marx and Engels were merely giving voice to this widely held view about the internationalist character of the trend of history, with the market economy at its core, when they wrote in the *Communist Manifesto*:

The bourgeoisie has through its exploitation of the world market given a cosmopolitan character to production and consumption in every country … In place of their old local and national seclusion and self-sufficiency, we have intercourse in every direction, universal inter-dependence of nations. As in material so also in intellectual production. The intellectual creations of individual nations become common property. National one-sidedness and narrow-mindedness become more and more impossible … National differences and antagonisms between peoples, are daily more and more vanishing, owing to the development of the bourgeoisie, to freedom of commerce, to the world market, to uniformity in the mode of production and in the conditions of life corresponding thereto (Marx and Engels, 1968: 55).

In fact, the widely anticipated move towards a peaceful global capitalism did not take place. The 'late industrialising countries' caught up with the First Industrial Nation, England, through powerful state action, especially protection, to support the growth of the national bourgeoisie and to construct strongly-felt national identities. The emergence of distinct national identities was stimulated by the spread of universal education, necessary to produce capable workers for a modern economy, and the closely associated construction of a unified national language.[66] Markets cannot function without trust and commonly accepted rules of operation. Despite intense national economic rivalry, rules were established that provided a mutually agreed structure for the peaceful conduct of international trade, investment flows and migration. During the whole of the first century of modern industrial capitalism, from 1815 to 1914 there was no major international conflict among the world's leading economic powers. However, the strains stimulated by intensifying nationalistic rivalries between leading capitalist countries finally erupted in the World Wars of 1914–18 and 1939–45.

The establishment after 1945 of a set of international institutions, although not directly aimed at preventing conflict, helped to do so by greatly increasing the sense of shared global responsibility felt by the separate countries. The most important of these institutions were established under the auspices of the United Nations. They provided mechanisms for the mutually accepted conduct of international relations, principally, but not exclusively, in the economic sphere. These included the World Bank, the International Monetary Fund (IMF), the General Agreement on Tariffs and Trade (GATT),[67] the UN Conference on Trade and Development (UNCTAD), the Food and Agriculture Organisation (FAO), the International Telecommunications Union (ITU), the International Labour Organisation (ILO) and the World Health Organisation (WHO). Regional political and economic entities such as the EU, NAFTA, ASEAN and 'APEC' also may be viewed as part of the march towards global political unity.

Membership of each of these organisations involved the sacrifice of a degree of autonomy by participating states. Under the GATT, successive rounds of reform resulted in large reductions in trade restrictions. At least as significant was the decision taken in 1994 to establish the World Trade Organisation (WTO) as a successor to the GATT. The GATT had confined itself essentially to cross-border transactions. The WTO was not only concerned with trade in the strict sense, but also with the rights of international firms to establish service activities within other countries, to invest in other countries without the requirements to transfer technology or join partnerships with local firms, with their right to have equal access with indigenous firms to local markets, and to protect the use of their intellectual property in other countries. The World Bank and the IMF originally had relatively limited objectives, essentially to support long-term investments and relieve short-term balance of payments difficulties respectively. Over time their original, limited objectives were extended deeper and deeper into conditionality requirements for loan recipients to undertake comprehensive system reform, including privatisation, price de-regulation, public sector reform, improvements in corporate governance, labour standards and environmental regulation. The trend in all these cases has been towards international harmonisation and 'deep integration' with conditions in other countries. Through these steadily advancing arrangements, individual countries sacrifice their autonomy in the interests of establishing their own markets as part of a unified global capitalist market.[68]

Up until the 1970s, most countries still implemented interventionist policies in important aspects of international economic relations. Most governments supported the national bourgeoisie in various ways, including protection (albeit declining), state ownership of key industries supporting the indigenous private sector, support from the local banking industry and resistance to foreign acquisition of local firms. However, the web of mutually agreed international economic and political arrangements deepened, reducing the possibility of conflict. In the last resort, this growing network of global regulations helped to prevent military conflict among capitalist countries by building a common interest in international arrangements that were mutually beneficial economically.[69]

The role of international trade has sharply increased during the period of capitalist globalisation. Global prosperity is more reliant than ever before on the maintenance of friendly relations between trading partners. Exports of goods and services rose from just 11 per cent of world GDP in 1965 to 24 per cent in 2004 (World Bank, WDR, 1992: 235; and World Bank, WDI, 2006: 224). Total trade in goods and services rose from 40 per cent of GDP in 1990 to 55 per cent in 2004 (World Bank, WDI, 2006: 318). The standard of living of consumers in high-income countries has become intimately linked to international trade. Imports of manufactured goods by high-income countries from low and middle-income countries rose from US$ 414 billion in 1994 to US$ 1382 billion in 2004 (World Bank, WDI, 2006: 327–8). A large fraction of these imports are consumer goods, the real price of which has fallen heavily during this period, contributing significantly to advances in living standards in the high-income countries.

Since the 1970s, massive changes have taken place in the way in which national and international economic policies are conducted. National governments across the world have abandoned protectionist, state-led strategies. Support for a 'national bourgeoisie' has almost disappeared as barriers to international capital flows have been universally dismantled.[70] For the first time, production systems are being established by firms across national boundaries on a global basis, with closely integrated international division of labour within the supply chain of large firms.

Liberalisation of international capital flows means that a large shift has taken place in ownership structures. It is increasingly likely that foreigners will own a substantial share of the equity of a firm headquartered in a given country. These developments mean that firms from capitalist countries are more deeply embedded than ever before in each other's business systems. Leading international firms typically have more than half their assets, employment and sales in countries other than those in which they have their headquarters.

The degree of internationalisation of the world's leading firms has risen steadily in the epoch of globalisation, as capitalist firms have, in the words of

Marx and Engels, 'nestled everywhere, settled everywhere, and established connections everywhere'. By 2003, the 100 largest transnational corporations had an average of 50 per cent of their assets and employment, and 54 per cent of their sales, in foreign countries (UNCTAD, 2005: 17).

The nature of ownership has altered greatly in the period of capitalist globalisation. The structure of equity ownership has altered sharply. Institutional owners now constitute the bulk of owners of large modern firms. Owners are less and less 'national'. For example, BP, formerly 'British Petroleum', is now a truly global company. Only 44 per cent of its shares are owned by British entities, and these are mainly institutions. Thirty-nine per cent of BP's shares are owned by Americans (mainly institutions), and the rest by other nationalities. Other leading UK-based companies, such as WPP and Vodafone, have a large fraction of their shares (54 per cent and 49 per cent respectively) held by foreign individuals and institutions. The former French state-owned 'national champion', Saint-Gobain, has 47 per cent of its shares owned by foreign institutions. Only 48 per cent of the German carmaker DaimlerChrysler is owned by Germans.[71]

The fact that mergers and acquisitions have advanced at high speed, reaching an historic peak in 2006, has resulted in an increasing number of 'national' firms being absorbed by firms which have their headquarters in other countries. Between 1995 and 2004 there were more than 800 'large' cross-border mergers and acquisitions valued at over US$ 1 billion each (UNCTAD, 2005: 9). In other words, over 800 large 'national firms' lost their national identity, and became 'foreign firms'. As a result a large swathe of firms were absorbed into a new corporate entity, with their headquarters in another country. Famous symbols of national economic success, such as Volvo, Saab, Mannesman, Usinor, BOC, Marconi, Pilkington Glass, Chrysler, Amoco, Arco, Castrol Burmah, Jaguar, Morgan Grenfell, Warburgs, Smiths, and BAA, all were absorbed into international firms with their headquarters 'abroad'.

The corporate culture of successful global firms is increasingly similar Most leading global firms conduct their internal communications in English. Intense mergers and acquisitions in the firms that provide services to other international firms has helped to produce an increasing homogeneity of corporate culture. Most international firms are advised by the same narrow group of international investment banks, accountants and consultants, and human resource advisors, and have their brands shaped by the same narrow group of leading international marketing firms. Corporate identity is less and less associated with a particular nation. This is reflected in the proliferation of corporate names that are simply initials, such as BP, AXA, ENI, UBS, RWE, E.ON, HSBC, BAE, NEC, BASF, SBC, BT, AIG and ING. Business leaders are increasingly recruited from a common pool of educational institutions. A large fraction of the world's top business leaders have, at some point in their career, participated in courses at the world's leading business schools, which teach courses that are almost indistinguishable from each other.

Ordinary citizens also have been pulled together by the forces of capitalist globalisation. English has increasingly become the common global language. Citizens across the world share a common culture on global mass media. Together, they watch the Olympic Games, the World Cup, English football, or 'Friends' or 'Big Brother'. They participate in programmes with a common international format, like 'Who wants to be a millionaire'.

Knowledge about other countries and cultures has accelerated. The period of capitalist globalisation has seen a large increase in mass literacy and educational levels (see below). The instruments of mass communication have become ubiquitously available. By 2004, 54 per cent of households in low and middle-income countries had a television set (World Bank, WDI, 2006: 304). International tourism has grown into a mass phenomenon, facilitated by increases in per capita income, by economies of scale in tourism and hotel companies, which has lowered the real price of tourist lodgings, and by technical progress in airplanes, which has allowed a drastic decline in the real price of air travel, and stimulated by the global mass media. In 2004, there were 259 million outbound tourists from low and middle-income countries, and 470 million from high-income countries. The number of inbound tourists going to low and middle-income countries was 350 million compared with 429 million to high-income countries (World Bank, WDI, 2006: 366). Total tourist arrivals increased from 450 million in 1990 to over 700 million in 2004 (World Bank, WDI, 2006: 367).

Few people now believe that there is any possibility of a global military conflict. For almost everyone, it is unimaginable that a global economy, with deeply intertwined economic relations and a global culture could have a global military conflict. The world can now look back upon more than half a century of peaceful relations among the leading capitalist countries. Increasingly, the period from 1914–45 appears as an aberration in the long march towards global unification achieved by the modern capitalist market economy. The stresses in the international political system that existed in this period can be viewed as the outcome of strains arising from the nation-based pattern of industrialisation that was specific to a particular epoch in capitalist development: '[L]ooking back over the development of the modern world economy we are inclined to see the phase during which economic development was integrally linked to the "national economies" of a number of developed territorial states as situated between two essentially transnational eras' (Hobsbawm, 1990: 25). As the capitalist world economy begins finally to take shape after a delay of one hundred years, we may be witnessing today the beginnings of the global government structure that was envisioned by nineteenth century liberal economists as the natural consequence of the global economy.[72] In such an environment, the possibility of major international military conflict would cease to exist, thanks ultimately to the 'cement' produced by the international capitalist economy.

1.3 Capitalist Irrationality in the Epoch of the Global Business Revolution

The mirage of the nineteen twenties was, as we now know, the belated reflexion of a century beyond recall - the golden age of continuously expanding territories and markets, of a world policed by the self-assured and not too onerous British hegemony, of a coherent 'Western civilization' whose conflicts could be harmonised by a progressive extension of the area of common development and exploitation, of the easy assumptions that what was good for one was good for all and that what was economically right could not be morally wrong. The reality which had once given content to this utopia was already in decay before the nineteenth century had reached its end. The utopia of 1919 was hollow and without substance. It was without influence on the future because it no longer had any roots in the present.

(Carr, 2001: 207)

1.3.1 Capitalism's Two-Edged Sword

Mankind's embracing of the forces of capitalist competition can be compared with the pact between Faust and Mephistopheles. The drive to make profits has stimulated human ingenuity over millennia. As we have seen this intense force operates even more powerfully in the epoch of the 'Global Business Revolution' than in previous epochs. It is a force that they themselves have created. However, this force also enslaves them. Through the force of the pursuit of profit, mankind is allowed to win ever-greater mastery over nature, and achieve ever-greater levels of consumption, but at a huge price. As with Faust, the pact may be of fixed duration. Eventually, in return for the transitory pleasures that he has been granted, Faust must give up his life. Mankind may stand at a crossroads in which the very existence of the human species is threatened through the 'magical' forces that it has conjured up itself.

1.3.2 The Natural Environment

Deforestation

Between 1950 and 1994, the FAO estimates that the global total of forest cover rose marginally, from 30.0 per cent to 31.0 per cent (Lomborg, 2001: 111).

However, important changes have taken place in the distribution and composition of the forested area.

In the high-income countries, a number of factors contributed to a sustained growth in the forested area, all of which reflected the high standard of living achieved in these countries. These included population stability, de-industrialisation, government regulation, secure property rights over forests, and the establishment of large areas as nationally protected wilderness areas.[73] Between 1990 and 2000, the forested area in high-income countries grew by 0.1 per cent per annum (World Bank, WDI, 2004: 130). However, the high-income countries account for only around one-fifth of the world's total forested area.

In low and middle-income countries between 1990 and 2000, the forested area fell by around 0.3 per cent per annum, a much faster rate than that at which it is expanding in the high-income countries, so that overall, the world's forested area contracted by around 0.2 per cent per annum in the 1990s (World Bank, WDI, 2004: 130). This meant that over the course of the decade, the world's total forested area had contracted by 2.4 per cent. The pressures that led to this decline are rooted in underdevelopment. At best, it will be many decades before the population of low and middle-income countries achieve the income levels of today's high-income countries. Therefore, it is likely that the current trends of severe contraction of the forested area in developing countries will continue for several decades hence. The global consequences of this are especially significant due to the fact that the largest declines in forested area took place in tropical or sub-tropical regions. Within the overall decline in forested area in developing countries between 1990 and 2000, Brazil alone accounted for over one-fifth and ten developing countries (including Brazil) accounted for almost four-fifths of the total.

Species Loss

A large fraction of the forest loss took place in tropical or sub-tropical areas. This has had serious consequences for biodiversity, due to the far greater density of species diversity in such forests compared with temperate forests. Numerous species of mammals, birds and plants in fast-growing developing countries are threatened with extinction. The proportion of mammal species threatened with extinction in China is estimated to be 16 per cent, compared with 20 per cent in India and 22 per cent in Indonesia (World Bank, WDI, 2006, Table 3.4). Nearly 34 000 plant species, or 12.5 per cent of the total number recorded, are threatened with extinction (World Bank, WDI, 2004: 131).[74]

The consequence of uncontrolled pursuit of profit by global capitalism is vividly seen in the case of the fishing industry. This sector has witnessed high-speed advances in technology in recent years, including the use of information technology to identify the location of large concentrations of fish. Demand for fish is rising fast as incomes increase in developing countries. The incomes elasticity of demand for fish at low levels of income is high. A report in *Science* in November 2006 presented a dire warning of the consequences of uncontrolled fishing in the 'global commons' of the high seas. It estimated that the proportion of fish species that have collapsed rose from zero in 1950 to around 40 per cent in 2003. It concluded that, if commercial fishing continues at present levels, there would be a complete collapse of fish species by around 2050, which means that there would be no commercial fishing at all within forty years (*FT*, 3 November 2006). It predicts that by 2048 stocks of all the species currently fished for food will collapse to less than ten per cent of the maximum recorded catches. This would make fishing impossible and render the recovery of stocks unlikely. The report noted that the over-fishing of one species of fish has a knock-on effect on others, and reduces the resilience of the ocean eco-system and its ability to recover stocks. It found that in areas where over-fishing had continued beyond a certain point, it was impossible for fish stocks to recover. The effects of over-fishing have been compounded by pollution and global warming, which have both tended to reduce fish stocks.

Just as with climate change, the solution is international agreement to control levels of fishing and ensure replenishment of stocks. However, it has proved impossible to achieve, despite the self-evident nature of the problem and its solution. Less than one per cent of the world's ocean surface is protected from over-fishing. There is no global agreement to prevent over-fishing, except for a moratorium on commercial whaling. Even in the EU, which is a relatively small 'club' of high-income countries, it has proved impossible to devise an effective policy that all members will agree to implement, since each country pursues its own selfish national interest, and the voice of the fishing lobby is powerful. The *Financial Times* notes: 'Without proper regulation, the raw pursuit of private interest in exploiting common goods such as the atmosphere and the oceans, results in despoiling them for all mankind' (*FT*, 4 November 2006).

Ecological Transition

Developing countries: general. The ability to provide a clean environment is closely related to levels of per capita income. In the high-income countries most measures of environmental standards have steadily improved since the 1970s. However, in fast-growing developing countries, ecological conditions have deteriorated seriously, and it will be a huge challenge for policy-makers to prevent further environmental degradation. The most likely prospect is that the low and middle-income countries will endure a long period of output growth in which they continue to be heavily polluted before they can become rich and clean.[75]

Urban air quality in fast-growing developing countries has deteriorated seriously since the 1970s. Levels of particulates, sulphur dioxide, and nitrogen dioxide, in the major cities in China and India are now far above those in the industrialised world, posing enormous challenges to the health of their citizens. For example, the level of particulates in Paris is 15 micrograms per cubic metre and 22–23 micrograms in London and New York, compared with 99 in Beijing, 115 in Jakarta, 137 in Chongqing, 145 in Calcutta, 159 in Cairo, and 177 in New Delhi (World Bank, WDI, 2006, Table 3.13). Environmental degradation in developing countries is not confined to the cities. Across the low and middle-income countries, between 1990 and 2005 the forested area declined by an annual average of 91 million sq. km., compared with an annual increase of seven million sq. km. in the high-income countries (World Bank, WDI, 2006, Table 3.4).

The governments of developing countries face a massive environmental challenge. Not only are they struggling to devise policies that protect their own people from the awful environmental consequences of early stage industrialisation, but, as we shall see, the high-income countries increasingly expect them to grow in a fashion that does not damage the rest of the world through global warming.

Developing countries: China. In terms of conventional measures of growth of output and income, China is the most remarkable success story of the past two decades. However, its environment has been deeply damaged by the rampant growth of the market economy. The UNDP's Report on the Chinese environment described China's environmental situation as 'perilous' (UNDP, 2002b: 39). It concludes that China faces the world's 'most daunting environmental problems', with 'persistent environmental degradation' and 'ever-worsening industrial pollution' (UNDP, 2002b: 1).

(a) Land. China's grassland area has been receding by around 1 million hectares per annum in recent years, and around nine-tenths of the country's grasslands are 'degraded to varying degrees' (UNDP, 2002b: 17). China's 'large and ambitious reforestation programmes' have produced poor results. China's reserves of high quality mature trees in the northeast and southwest have fallen steadily alongside extensive plantings, often of single species, in other parts of the country. The percentage of mature trees has fallen to only around 28 per cent of the total (UNDP, 2002b: 19). China's intense and growing population pressure means that the amount of arable land per person is among the lowest in the world, standing at only around 0.10 hectares, compared with a world average of 0.24 hectares (UNDP, 2002b: 20). The average quality of farmland is falling due to the conversion of high quality land, especially in Eastern China, to industrial and residential use. By the 1980s, China was already one of the world's most seriously eroded countries. Since then the amount of land that suffers from erosion has increased by 20–30 per cent (UNDP, 2002b: 21). From the 1950s to the 1970s around 1500 sq. kms of land annually became desertified. By the 1990s it had reached 2500 sq kms per year. Nearly a quarter of China's rivers fail to meet irrigation standards. Pesticide residues are found in more than half of the foods grown in the suburbs of major cities (UNDP, 2002b: 22).

(b) Biodiversity. Official Chinese data estimate that more than one-tenth of the country's vertebrate species and about 15–20 per cent of its higher plants are endangered species. The main causes of the decline in biodiversity include the sharp reduction in the amount of natural forest, reclamation of forests and wetlands for agriculture and construction, and industrial and human pollution.

(c) Water. Overall, China is not short of water. However, distribution is highly uneven, and nearly half of the population lives in critically water short areas in northern China. Groundwater levels over large parts of the North China Plain have fallen due to over-extraction for irrigation and urban water supply. Out of a total of 600 major cities, 300 face severe water shortages and in 100 cities the situation is severe (UNDP, 2002b: 24). In 2000, only 19 per cent of the Chinese population, mainly those in cities, had access to tap water. However, in only six of China's 27 largest cities does drinking water quality meet state standards. Groundwater does not meet state standards in 23 of these cities (UNDP, 2002b: 33). An absolute majority of industrial wastewater is untreated or has passed only rudimentary pre-treatment processes. Wastewater and hazardous waste discharge at most 'township and village enterprises' is unmonitored. Since their activities are widely scattered across the country, 'their wastes endanger the health of many people' (UNDP, 2002b: 33). Less than one-tenth of municipal wastewater receives any form of treatment (UNDP, 2002b: 25). Roughly 200 million people live in 20 000 small towns without any sanitation 'other than maybe pipes that might lead wastewater to the nearest ditch' (UNDP, 2002b: 25). China's 20 000-kilometre long coastline has suffered 'severe damage and degradation' over the past two decades. Estuaries and coastal areas are threatened by 'increasingly intensive occurrences of red tides, oil spills and pollution from inland sources' (UNDP, 2002b: 26). A combination of pollution and over-fishing has led to a sharp drop in fish catches from coastal waters in recent years (UNDP, 2002b: 26).

(d) Solid waste. Generation of waste in large Chinese cities is growing by around 10 per cent annually. Although waste treatment has made progress, official data estimate that less than one-half of municipal waste is treated. Chinese industry generates five times as much solid waste as the municipalities. Of this, less than 10 per cent is reported to be 'discharged'. Of the remaining 90 per cent, a considerable amount is dumped in an uncontrolled manner, 'leading to pollution of land as well as adjacent surface and groundwater sources and air' (UNDP, 2002b: 31). Official data on hazardous waste estimate that les than one half is treated to a reasonable degree or re-used, while 'the rest joins the uncertain fate of other industrial solid waste streams' (UNDP, 2002b: 31).

(e) Air. Air quality in many Chinese cities falls well below international standards. Sixteen of the world's twenty most polluted cities are in China (UNDP, 2002b: 26). Air pollution in Chinese cities associated with direct burning of coal and lead from car exhausts has declined due to strict government regulation. However, the volume of motor traffic is rising at high speed (see below). By 2010 it is predicted that vehicles will account for over three-quarters of Shanghai's emissions of nitrogen oxide, carbon monoxide and hydrocarbons (UNDP, 2002b: 28). The area affected by acid rain has grown steadily, and now affects around one-third of the whole country (UNDP, 2002b: 28). The steady march of desertification has led to increasingly frequent sandstorms in northern cities, including Beijing. The vast number of rural 'township and village enterprises' are frequently in heavy industries such as cement, chemicals and metallurgy. They account for a growing fraction of China's carbon dioxide and sulphur dioxide emissions.

Global Warming

Lock-in. Technical progress has greatly reduced the consumption of energy and other inputs per unit of final product. However, in the epoch of the Global Business Revolution, the pace of growth of final output has been so great that the total amount of environmental damage has greatly advanced. Human ingenuity has been outpaced by total consumption growth. At the centre of the intensification of environmentally damaging processes is a 'locked-in' pattern of economic development. A huge inter-related structure of personal consumption and road transport is at the heart of the capitalist free market system. Within this system, individual consumer freedom and rights dominate. Consumers' freedom and right to consume is nurtured intensely by giant capitalist firms whose interests are served by increased personal consumption. The day has yet to appear in which the marketing by global firms in financial services, retailing, automobiles, airlines, holidays, food and drink, electronic goods, and IT equipment and services, encourages people to borrow less, spend less, and pursue greater happiness rather than increased consumption.

Under capitalist globalisation consumers are locked in to a pattern of final consumption organised around packaged and processed goods, which in their turn support a global packaging industry that uses plastics, steel and aluminium. The intermediate and final products are distributed mainly by road-based commercial transport systems. Roads require a network of supplier industries, including cement and steel. The production of commercial vehicles requires a global network of supplier industries, including steel, aluminium, plastics, and glass. Individuals have exercised their freedom of choice by demanding individualised transport systems in the shape of the automobile. Low and middle-income countries have, without exception, allowed the same pattern of development in their transport systems and the same freedom of individual consumer choice as exists in the high-income countries. Technical progress has reduced the consumption of energy and other inputs per unit of final product. However, the pace of growth of final consumption, based around the locked-in pattern of production and distribution, is producing large rates of increase in the consumption of primary energy, including oil.

Energy consumption. Global energy use is rising rapidly. Between 1990 and 2003, the world as a whole increased its consumption of primary energy by 22 per cent (World Bank, WDI, 2006, Table 3.7). The prospects are for continued rapid growth of global primary energy consumption. In 2003, levels of per capita energy use in low-income countries still stood at only 501 kg. per capita, compared with 1373 kg. in middle-income countries and 5410 kg. in the high-income countries. In 2003, the number of motor vehicles per 1000 people still stood at just 47 in the low and middle-income countries, compared with 623 in the high-income countries and 808 in the United States (World Bank, WDI, 2006, Table 3.12). As developing countries achieve increases in per capita incomes, they will move steadily towards the levels of primary energy use of today's high-income countries. Moreover, even the high-income countries are still expanding their consumption of primary energy. Between 1990 and 2003, their total primary energy consumption rose by 23 per cent, and accounted for over one half of the total global increase (World Bank, WDI, 2006, Table 3.7).

Greenhouse gases. It is now accepted by almost everyone that the production of carbon dioxide has caused an increase in the earth's temperature through the impact of the 'greenhouse effect'. The most authoritative report to date on global warming is that of the UN's Intergovernmental Panel on Climate Change (IPCC), published in February 2007. The IPCC comprises 2500 climate experts, and was the fruit of six years of research, and forms the basis for a possible successor to the Kyoto Protocol after it expires in 2012. It concluded that there is 'unequivocal' evidence that climate change is caused by fossil fuel combustion (*FT*, 3 February 2007). A decade ago, the IPCC was only able to say that 'on balance' human actions were the likely cause (*FT*, 2 February 2007).

The vast bulk of primary energy worldwide is from fossil fuels. Automobiles almost entirely use fossil fuels. In 2003, nuclear power and hydropower each accounted for only around 16 per cent of global primary energy for electricity generation, or less than one-third of the total (World Bank, WDI, 2006, Table 3.9). Coal accounted for 40 per cent, gas for 19 per cent and oil for just 7 per cent.

The level of carbon dioxide in the earth's atmosphere is estimated to have risen from around 260 parts per million (ppm) before the Industrial Revolution[76] to 315 ppm in 1958, increasing still further to 397 ppm in 2005. If current trends in the use of fossil fuels were to continue then it is predicted that levels would rise to 400 ppm by 2015 and 800 ppm in 2100 (King, 2005). The increased production of carbon dioxide is attributed primarily to increased burning of fossil fuels, and secondarily to cement production.[77] The IPCC's report in 2007 predicts that global temperatures will rise by around 3 degrees centigrade by 2100, with the range of predictions, varying between 2–4.5 degrees centigrade (*FT*, 2 February 2007).

If this continues it will pose 'a real threat to our global civilisation' (King, 2005). The threat will take the form of a rise in the global sea level, increased extreme weather events, and damage to agriculture.[78] It is thought likely that the Arctic Ice Cap will 'disappear completely by 2060' whatever action is taken in the next few years, since it takes many years for carbon dioxide to disperse from the atmosphere. Managing the consequences of global warming will pose a large challenge even for high-income countries, but for poor countries, especially those in Asia, the challenge will be even more serious. In the view of the United Kingdom's Chief Scientific Officer, Sir David King, a 'global turning point has been reached' and 'a choice must be made within this decade' if a 'disaster for the earth' is to be avoided.[79]

Under the Kyoto Protocol, the main body of high-income countries, apart from the United States and Australia, will attempt to restrict their carbon dioxide emissions by the year 2012 to roughly the level of 1990.[80] The principal mechanism through which they hope to achieve this is by trading carbon permits. These are allocated to production establishments in the main polluting industries, which can trade the resulting right to pollute, selling them if they produce less than the fixed target, and buying them if they over-pollute relative to the target for the particular establishment. It is by no means certain that the signatories will achieve their intended goal. The carbon trading system only went into force in 2005, which is just five years before the expiry of the Kyoto Agreement. It is uncertain what form of agreement, if any, will operate after 2012.

The developing countries were not required to implement the conditions of the Kyoto Protocol. By the year 2000, their emissions of carbon dioxide had almost caught up with those from the high-income countries, standing at 49 per cent of the world's total emissions. However, carbon emissions per capita in developing countries were less than one-fifth of those of the high-income countries. In the absence of technical progress, the process of catch-up in developing economies would lead to globally unsustainable increases in carbon dioxide emissions. If the development of solar energy technology is successful, then this may eventually lead to a widespread substitution of fossil fuels by solar energy, including in developing countries. However, even the most optimistic predictions do not consider that this is likely to begin to take place before 2030–40, 'ending in the 2060s' (Lomborg, 2001: 286). Despite increases in the use of nuclear power stations, wind power and hydro power, it is likely that fossil fuels will remain the main source of primary energy for the next several decades. Indeed, in many developing countries, coal will continue to be used as the main source of primary energy due to its low price and widespread availability. Moreover, there is every prospect that automobile use for passengers and freight will hugely expand in developing countries in the next several decades.

The period between today and the possible widespread use of solar energy will be extremely challenging for global policy makers. During this phase it will be necessary that technical progress and its application in developing countries (and in the United States) occurs at such a pace as to ensure that increases in carbon dioxide emissions from fossil fuels are kept within sustainable levels for the planet. The interests of developing countries are primarily those of increasing national income. The negative consequences stemming from continued use of polluting fuels and technologies will take place at a global level. Action by any individual developing country to limit carbon dioxide emissions has little benefit for the country concerned, but may involve large sacrifices in terms of extra costs required to provide energy for economic growth. Managing these conflicts between national and global interests will be a major challenge for the capacity of human beings to work harmoniously and achieve outcomes that are in their collective interest.

Energy and International Relations

The competition for exhaustible resources. There is little prospect for renewable energy to replace fossil fuels in the coming decades. Coal is likely to remain the most important source of primary energy for electricity generation for the foreseeable future. However, oil is critically important for transport, which is growing at a high rate, especially in developing countries.

Global consumption of oil is increasing rapidly. Total oil consumption increased by 19 per cent from 1995–2005, with increases of 17 per cent in the United States and 33 per cent in the Asia-Pacific Region (BP, 2006: 11). The United States consumes 17 per cent of the world total, compared with 33 per cent in the Asia-Pacific Region (BP, 2006: 11).[81]

Oil production in the United States is falling and oil production in the Asia-Pacific is stagnant. Consequently, oil imports in both regions are rising rapidly. Global oil imports rose by 24 per cent from 1998–2005 (BP, 1999: 19, and BP, 2006: 20–1). The United States accounted for 33 per cent of the increase and the Asia-Pacific Region for 49 per cent (China accounted for 25 per cent of the total world increase and the rest of the Asia-Pacific Region, excluding Japan, for 24 per cent).[82]

As developing countries raise their level of per capita income, and expand their transport systems, their demand for oil will expand greatly. For most of the Asia-Pacific Region, increased oil consumption will need to be satisfied mainly through increased imports.[83] However, the United States is likely to remain the most important importer of oil for a long period ahead. By 2004, US net oil imports amounted to 58 per cent of its total oil consumption (BP, 2005), and it is predicted that by 2025 oil imports will account for as much as 68 per cent of US consumption (Klare, 2004: 76).

As we will see later, the possibility of conflict over access to finite oil supplies has become an increasingly important issue in international relations, not least in respect to the US and China.

Global warming. Oil has been a key part of past international relations conflicts. Many commentators have voiced concern at the prospect of conflict between the United States and the large oil-importing regions of the world as demands accelerate in the period ahead. With only 16 per cent of the world's population, the high-income countries account for 52 per cent of the world's carbon dioxide production.[84] Despite technical progress to increase the amount of GDP generated per unit of energy use,[85] low and middle-income countries are fast increasing their production of carbon dioxide as their per capita income advances.[86] India and China together increased their production of carbon dioxide by 54 per cent from 1990–2002, and their share of global carbon dioxide production rose from 14.5 per cent in 1990 to 19.4 per cent in 2002 (World Bank, WDI, 2006: Table 3.8). However, their levels of carbon dioxide production per person are still far below those of the high-income countries.

The United States refused to participate in the Kyoto Protocol. Under President Clinton, the United States Senate refused, by a majority of 95–0 to ratify the Treaty. The United States produces 24 per cent of global carbon dioxide emissions (World Bank, WDI, 2006, Table 3.8). Its level of emissions rose by 21 per cent between 1990 and 2002, accounting for 21 per cent of the total global increase. The rise was largely due to the increase in the number of motor vehicles and the distance travelled per person.[87] The United States consumes annually over 1600 litres of petrol per capita compared with 250 litres in Europe (*FT*, 25 January 2007). Faced with the growing evidence of global warming and its relationship to fossil fuel burning, the United States still refuses to introduce measures that would interfere with 'Americans' long love-affair with the automobile', including congestion charges, incentives to car-pool, increased public transport, or an increase in excise taxes on gasoline: 'It is hard to find a Republican or a Democrat who will admit to supporting higher taxes' (*FT*, 25 January 2007). Americans think they live in one of the most heavily taxed countries in the world, but in fact it is one of the lightest: 'Taxes are a no-go area' (Dan Becker, Head of the Sierra Club's Global Warming unit, quoted in *Financial Times*, 25 January 2007). The United States refuses to raise the fuel economy standard. The current standard of 27.5 miles per gallon was fixed in the mid-1970s and has been unchanged ever since then (*FT*, 25 January 2007).

Even though the countries of the EU are signatories of the Kyoto Agreement, there is intense pressure from consumers and, especially, from industry lobbies to resist sharp reductions in carbon dioxide emissions. In early 2007, in the face of 'fierce lobbying from Ms Merkel [Germany's Chancellor] and the car sector' the EU scaled back its plans to reduce car emissions (*FT*, 31 January 2007). The European car-makers lobbied successfully to prevent the implementation of a target of carbon dioxide emissions of 120 kgs per km by 2012, fixing the target instead at 130 kgs per km. The EU car companies warned that the lower target would make large parts of the European industry unprofitable. VW, DaimlerChrysler, BMW, Opel and Ford all warned that the stricter target was 'unrealistic' and 'technically unfeasible'. For their part, European consumers are 'reluctant to pay extra for clean cars'.

The developing countries were not signatories to the Kyoto Agreement. Fast-growing developing countries are strongly committed to using motor vehicles as the core of their transport systems both for people and goods. Governments and consumers in these countries feel that they have the right to replicate the pattern of development of today's high-income countries. Already in the year 2002, the emissions of carbon dioxide from the low and middle-income countries stood at 48 per cent of the world's total emissions (World Bank, WDI, 2006, Table 3.8). However, in 2002 per capita carbon emissions in low and middle-income countries amounted to just 2.2 metric tons, compared with 12.8 metric tons in the high-income countries, and 20.2 in the United States. In the absence of extremely rapid technical progress and/or fundamental changes in the nature of economic development, the process of catch-up in developing economies will lead to globally unsustainable increases in carbon dioxide emissions.

It would require an immense effort of creativity by the governments of developing countries to develop a new approach to transport and consumption that was built around a different pattern of development, avoiding the 'lock-in' that characterises today's high income countries. This would mean far-thinking efforts to control the market and to resist the push upon government policy that arises from the free market. With the rapidly increased presence in developing countries of global firms in both the automobile and closely-related sectors, the possibility of such a creative policy response is fast receding.

There are possibilities for deep conflicts of interest between different segments of the world population over an issue of fundamental importance to the sustainability of human life on the planet.

Conclusion

The driving force of capitalist globalisation is the freedom of capitalist businesses to nurture individual wants through the mass media and global marketing machines.[88] The exercise of individual freedom of choice in consumption has allowed patterns of consumption, production and distribution that are deeply damaging to the natural environment of the whole world. These not only damage the global environment for today's inhabitants. They threaten the future for the generations yet to come. Within the existing 'locked in' structure there is a huge and growing gap between private short-run costs and benefits, and long-run costs and benefits for the world, including its future inhabitants. Human beings' growing mastery over nature has taken place alongside a disintegrating control over the direction in which the whole structure is moving in respect to the natural environment. Many of these processes already are irreversible. The effects of some of them may only become apparent in terms of their full impact at some point in the future. Freedom for the individual has been achieved at the expense of anarchy for the whole system in terms of the impact on the natural environment.

1.3.3 The Challenge of the Global Business Revolution

In the 1990s, many of the constraints on firm growth were removed. Vast regions of the world were opened for competition. Privatisation was enacted across almost all countries. Cross-border restrictions on mergers and acquisitions were removed from all but a few sectors. China joined the WTO at a time of unprecedented concentration among the world's leading 'systems integrators'. However, the depth of this challenge is even greater than it appears at first sight due to the profound changes taking place through the 'cascade' effect. In addition to intense concentration among 'systems integrators', an explosive process of industrial concentration has taken place at the level of the upper reaches of the global value chain. The invisible changes which have taken place 'below the water level' of the 'iceberg' of industrial concentration are at least as powerful as those that are more easily visible 'above the water level'.

Systems Integrators

The Global Business Revolution witnessed massive asset restructuring, with firms extensively selling off 'non-core businesses' in order to develop their 'core businesses' and upgrade their asset portfolios. The goal for most large firms became the maintenance or establishment of their position as one of the handful of top companies in the global market-place. Although the intensity abated in the wake of the collapse of the late 1990s stock market bubble, the merger and acquisition process has continued at a high level in recent years. An unprecedented degree of industrial concentration has been established among leading firms in sector after sector. By the 1980s, there was already a high degree of industrial concentration within many sectors of the individual high-income countries (Pratten, 1971, Prais, 1981). However, the Global Business Revolution saw for the first time the emergence of widespread industrial concentration across all high-income countries, as well as extending deeply into large parts of the developing world.

By the early 2000s, within the high value-added, high technology, and/or strongly branded segments of global markets, which serve mainly the middle and upper income earners who control the bulk of the world's purchasing power, a veritable 'law' had come into play: a handful of giant firms, the 'systems integrators', occupied upwards of 50 per cent of the whole global market.[89] The top two firms accounted for 100 per cent of the entire global market for large commercial aircraft and 70 per cent of the carbonated soft drinks market; the top three firms accounted for over 80 per cent of the gas turbine market and for 70 per cent of the farm equipment market, for over 60 per cent of the mobile phone market, and over 50 per cent of the market for LCD TVs; the top four firms accounted for over 60 per cent of the elevator market; the top five firms accounted for over 80 per cent of the digital camera market; the top six firms accounted for over 70 per cent of the auto industry market and the top ten firms accounted for over 50 per cent of the pharmaceutical market.[90]

Cascade Effect

The process of concentration through simultaneous de-merger of non-core businesses and merger of core businesses is cascading across the value chain at high speed. In sector after sector, leading firms, with powerful technologies and marketing capabilities, actively select the most capable among their numerous suppliers, in a form of 'industrial planning', adopting 'aligned suppliers' who can work with them across the world. Thus, across a wide range of activities a 'cascade effect' is at work in which intense pressures develop for first tier suppliers of goods and services to the global giants to themselves merge and acquire, and develop leading global positions. These, in their turn, pass on intense pressure upon their own supplier networks. The result is a fast-developing process of concentration at a global level in numerous industries supplying goods and services to the systems integrators.

Planning and Coordination: The External Firm

Through the hugely increased planning function undertaken by systems integrators, facilitated by recent developments in information technology, the boundaries of the large corporation have not only 'shifted', so that a wider range of goods and services is procured from outside the firm, but the very boundaries of the firms have become blurred. The core systems integrators across a wide range of sectors have become the coordinators of a vast array of business activity outside the boundaries of the legal entity in terms of ownership. The relationship extends far beyond the purchase price. In order to develop and maintain their competitive advantage, the systems integrators deeply penetrate the value chain both upstream and downstream, becoming closely involved in business activities that range from long-term planning to meticulous control of day-to-day production and delivery schedules. Competitive advantage for the systems integrator requires that it must consider the interests of the whole value chain in order to minimise costs across the whole system.

If we define the firm not by the entity which is the legal owner, but, rather, by the sphere over which conscious coordination of resource allocation takes place, then, far from becoming 'hollowed out' and much smaller in scope, the large firm can be seen to have enormously increased in size during the Global

Business Revolution. As the large firm has 'disintegrated', so has the extent of conscious coordination over the surrounding value chain increased. In a wide range of business activities, the organisation of the value chain has developed into a comprehensively planned and coordinated activity. At its centre is the core systems integrator. This firm typically possesses some combination of a number of key attributes. These include the capability to raise finance for large new projects, and the resources necessary to fund a high level of R&D spending to sustain technological leadership, to develop a global brand, to invest in state-of-the-art information technology and to attract the best human resources. Across a wide range of business types, from fast-moving consumer goods to aircraft manufacture, the core systems integrator interacts in the deepest, most intimate fashion with the major segments of the value chain, both upstream and downstream.

Upstream. The relationship of the core systems integrator with the upstream first tier suppliers extends far beyond the price relationship. Increasingly, leading first tier suppliers across a wide range of industries have established long-term 'partner' or 'aligned supplier' relationships with the core systems integrators. There are some key aspects of the intimate relationship between systems integrators and upstream firms. First, leading first tier suppliers plan the location of their plants in relation to the location of the core systems integrator. Secondly, it is increasingly the case that the aligned supplier produces goods within the systems integrator itself. It is common for leading suppliers of specialist services, such as data systems, to physically work within the premises of the systems integrator. Thirdly, leading first tier suppliers plan their R&D in close consultation with the projected needs of the core systems integrator. An increasing part of R&D is contracted out to small and medium-sized firms. This is typically under the close control of the systems integrator. Fourthly, product development is intimately coordinated with the systems integrator. Finally, precise product specifications are instantaneously communicated to the leading suppliers through newly developed information technology. The production and supply schedules of leading first tier suppliers are comprehensively coordinated with the systems integrator to ensure that the required inputs arrive exactly when they are needed and the inventory of the systems integrator is kept to a minimum.

Downstream. Planning by systems integrators extends downstream also. Manufacturers of complex capital goods, increasingly are interested in the revenue stream to be derived from maintaining their products over the course of their lifetime. New information technology is increasingly being used to monitor the performance of complex products in use, with continuous feedback to the systems integrator in order to construct optimum servicing schedules. Through this pervasive process, systems integrators deeply penetrate a wide range of firms that use their products. However, penetration of the downstream network of firms is not confined to complex capital goods. Systems integrators in the fast-moving consumer goods (FMCG) sector increasingly coordinate the distribution process with specialist logistics firms in order to minimise distribution costs. They work closely with grocery chains and other selling outlets, such as theme parks, movie theatres, oil companies (petrol stations have become major locations for retailing non-petrol products), and quick-service restaurants, to raise the technical efficiency in the organisation of the selling process. The FMCG systems integrators often have their own experts working within the retail chain.

Employment. A large corporation may have a total procurement bill of several billions of dollars. The procurement could involve purchases from numerous firms that employ a much larger number of full-time equivalent employees 'working for' the systems integrator than are employed within the core firm itself. A leading systems integrator with 100–200 000 employees could easily have the full-time equivalent of a further 400–500 000 employees 'working for' the systems integrator, in the sense that their work is coordinated in important ways by the core firm. In this sense, we may speak of an 'external firm' of coordinated business activity that surrounds the modern global corporation and is coordinated by it.

Competition

From a mainstream perspective, 'greater competition' is equated with a larger number of firms in a given sector. In the non-mainstream, view, 'greater competition' is equated with increased intensity of competition between powerful oligopolistic firms. Far from stifling 'competition', powerful oligopolies can produce increasingly intense competition as giant global firms struggle with other such firms, applying greater resources in R&D and marketing, and leveraging greater procurement budgets to lower costs and stimulate technical progress across the supply chain.

We have seen that the period since the 1980s has seen a remorseless process of industrial consolidation across almost every industrial sector, from aerospace to financial services. The firms that have their headquarters in the high-income countries stand at the centre of the global business system. In the epoch of the 'global level playing field', the landscape of industrial competition is extraordinarily uneven. The high-income economies contain just 15 per cent of the world's total population. Firms headquartered in these countries account for 94 per cent of the companies listed in the '*Fortune 500*', which ranks firms by sales revenue (Table 1). They account for 96 per cent of the firms in the '*FT 500*' list of the world's leading firms, ranked by market capitalisation. They account for almost 100 per cent of the firms included in the list of the world's top 700 firms ranked by expenditure on research and development, which is a critical indicator of the distribution of global business power (Table 1). There is not a single firm from the low and middle-income countries in the list of the world's 'top 100 brands' (Sorrell, 2004).

The Cascade Effect: Aerospace, Automobiles, Telecommunications and Beverages

A single large commercial aircraft costs over US$ 200 million. A single serving of a soft drink or a beer costs only around one dollar. However, as we will see in this section, common processes are at work in both industries through the impact of the 'cascade effect', as well as in industries as diverse as telecommunications and automobiles.

Aerospace. Large commercial aircraft and advanced military aerospace equipment contain bundles of the world's most advanced technologies. The design, assembly, marketing and upgrading of this equipment embodies powerful economies of scale and scope. The design of a new aircraft requires enormous investments with significant up-front costs during the launch stage. While the cost of failure is high, so is the reward for success. A successful new plane can lock up its chosen market segment for over 20 years, producing sales of US$ 25–40 billion and huge profits. Due to the 'bet-the-firm' nature of new aircraft launches, every new aircraft design therefore requires rigorous market analysis based upon the company's deep knowledge of its customers. The industry has large economies of scale in assembly, which come from spreading planning efforts and high tooling costs over large outputs of one type of aircraft. There are economies achieved through learning effects, obtained in the course of producing more units of a given aircraft model. Having a family of aircraft with common platforms enables the manufacturer to spread given R&D outlays over a larger number of aircraft, and to obtain economies of scale in procurement of components, and to achieve large operating benefits for customers. Branding is critical in the aerospace industry. A large installed base itself is the best demonstration of product reliability, operating efficiency and technology leadership.

By the late 1960s, the US commercial airplane industry had reduced to just three main producers: Boeing, McDonnell Douglas, and Lockheed. The competitive pressure from Boeing on its rivals was intense. By the mid-1990s, Lockheed had ceased production of the Tristar and McDonnell Douglas was in deep financial difficulties in its commercial aeroplane division. In 1997 came the path-breaking merger of Boeing and McDonnell Douglas. Following the merger Boeing accounted for over four-fifths of the world's total commercial aircraft in service. From the 1950s to the 1970s, there were several European companies each manufacturing large jet airliners (by the standards of the time).[91] By the late 1960s it was apparent that none of them was able to compete with Boeing. In 1970, France and Germany decided to join forces to build a family of large commercial aeroplanes that could challenge Boeing's dominance, and preserve a wide array of high technology supplier industries within Europe. They were later joined by Britain and Spain. Without massive support from the respective governments, Airbus could never have become established. By the early 2000s, Airbus had overtaken Boeing in the market for large commercial aircraft. The two companies are now locked in head-to-head duopolistic rivalry. Boeing has staked much of its future on the medium-sized 787 ('Dreamliner'), while Airbus has done the same with the super-large A380. The USSR possessed a highly sophisticated aerospace industry that produced thousands of large jet passenger planes.[92] If the USSR had followed a suitable path of system reform, the Soviet aircraft industry could have become a formidable challenger to the West's leading companies in both civilian and military sectors (Nolan, 1995). Today, the industry is in ruins.[93]

The systems integrators, Airbus and Boeing, have huge procurement budgets, totaling more than US$ 29 billion annually in Boeing's case. They focus increasingly on coordinating and planning the supply chain, rather than direct manufacture. As much as 60–80 percent of the end-product value of aerospace products is now derived from the external supply network (Murman *et al.*, 2002: 18). Airbus pioneered the concept of final assembly of large subsystems. However, Boeing has taken the lead over Airbus in reorganising its supply chain. In each aircraft programme, Boeing selects risk-sharing partners that develop and design important subsystems of the aircraft. These require massive R&D investments. Boeing's top suppliers invest hundreds of millions of dollars in R&D annually and they own increasing amounts of the intellectual property embedded in the aircraft. As aircraft technology becomes more complex and the cost pressure increases, the systems integrators have pushed more development and design activities down the supply chain to its subsystems integrators.

In 2000, Boeing started to implement the Toyota Production System (TPS), converting its production system from batch processes to assembly line processes. TPS requires just-in-time delivery of parts, which in turn calls for changes in suppliers' operations. In 1999, Boeing centralised the procurement function and radically pruned the number of suppliers. Between 2000 and 2005, it reduced direct suppliers from 3600 to 1200. In the supplier structure for the new B787, Boeing deals directly with just seven or eight first tier suppliers. The reduction in the number of direct suppliers allows Boeing to form closer collaboration with its direct suppliers and maintain tight control over the aircraft design and assembly as technology and cost requirements continue to increase.

The way in which Airbus and Boeing reorganised the institutional structure of the supply chain in order to reduce the number of suppliers and nurture large-scale subsystems integrators constitutes a form of industrial policy, with the systems integrators picking and nurturing 'winners'. They each penetrate deeply into their respective supply chain. Surrounding each of them is an 'external firm' in which control by the core systems integrator extends across the boundary of the legally-owned entity: 'If we are to succeed in the face of increasing global competition and greater demands for cost improvements from our customers, then *our entire extended enterprise* must operate under Lean principles and a Lean philosophy.' (Mike Sears, former Boeing CFO) (Sears, 2001).

In order to meet the demands of the systems integrators, the major subsystem and key component suppliers themselves need to invest heavily in research and development, and to expand in order to benefit from cost reduction through economies of scale and scope. A powerful merger movement has taken place at all levels of the supply chain and the level of concentration in the upper reaches of the aircraft industry supply chain has increased rapidly. Through continuous merging and acquiring 'core businesses' that meet their strategic goals, and through divesting 'non-core businesses' in order to 'upgrade' their asset portfolio, a group of giant subsystems integrators have established or strengthened their competitive position in businesses covering one or more aircraft subsystems. All of these suppliers are headquartered in, and have their main production facilities in developed countries, especially the United States. Leaders in their respective industries, all of them are global giants themselves with billions of dollars in revenues and large R&D outlays (Table 2). They dominate every major subsystem of the aircraft.

Engines are by far the most expensive aircraft subsystem, requiring enormous development costs and R&D outlays. There are now only three engine makers that are able to produce large modern jet aircraft engines that meet the continuously advancing demands of Boeing and Airbus. These are GE, Rolls-Royce, and United Technology (Pratt & Whitney). Aircraft structures are dominated by a handful of companies, including Vought Aircraft (which is the sole supplier of major structures for the B747), BAE Systems (which is the sole supplier of wings for Airbus), Finnemeccanica (Alenia), Mitsubishi Heavy Industries, Fuji Heavy Industries and Kawasaki Heavy Industries. Honeywell is by far the most powerful firm in the supply of avionics systems, including communication and navigation systems, flight instrument systems, flight management systems, as well as traffic alert and collision avoidance technologies. It is also at the forefront of power distribution, pneumatic and landing systems. Honeywell was selected to supply the core avionics systems for both the A380 and the B787. Smiths Industries, Goodrich, and Rockwell Collins are major competitors in the supply of avionics and other control systems. Each of them supplies subsystems to both Boeing and Airbus, and each has positions on both the A380 and B787. The supply of landing gear, wheel and braking systems is dominated by Snecma's Messier-Bugati and Messier Dowty subsidiaries, and by Goodrich. Each of these supplies complete landing subsystems to both Boeing and Airbus. Between them they have close to 80 per cent of the global market for brakes on commercial aircraft (company websites).

Even the smaller subsystems on the large airplane are dominated by a small number of powerful subsystems integrators. The wiring systems on large commercial aircraft are immensely complex. Snecma (through its subsidiary Labinal) is the world leader in the supply of wiring systems. It supplies the main part of the wiring systems for both the A380 and the B787. Jamco is sole supplier to Boeing for aircraft lavatories. Meggitt supplies the fire and smoke detectors for almost all large commercial aircraft. Recaro and B/E Aerospace account for most of the market for seats on large commercial aircraft. Many critically important components and materials are supplied by specialist aerospace divisions of giant global firms. Michelin, Goodyear and Bridgestone are the only firms capable of supplying tyres for large commercial aircraft. Saint-Gobain is the sole supplier of aircraft glass to Airbus. Alcoa and Alcan account for most of the world's supply of aluminium for aircraft assembly. Each A380 will use around one million Alcoa 'lockbolts'.

Automobiles. The global stock of automobiles has grown from around 150 million in 1950 to around 800 million in 2000, and is predicted to rise to around 1600 million in 2030 (DaimlerChrysler, 2005). In 1960 there were 42 independent automobile assemblers in the 'Triad' regions of North America, Western Europe and Japan. By 2005, that number had shrunk to just twelve firms, through an intensive process of merger and acquisition. The top five auto assemblers now account for 58 per cent of total automobile output in the Triad regions and the top ten account for 83 per cent of total vehicle output (DaimlerChrysler, 2005). Even the leading automobile firms face threats to their survival arising from the intensity of oligopolistic competition.

In order to survive in this ferocious competition, the leading assemblers must spend large amounts on R&D, in order to make vehicles lighter in weight, and to improve fuel efficiency, safety, durability and reliability. Each of the main automobile assemblers spends between US$ 2–8 billion annually on R&D (DTI, 2005). They also each spend several billion dollars each year on building their brands.

The leading auto assemblers each spend several tens of billions of dollars annually on procurement of materials and components. GM, for example, has an annual procurement spend of around US$ 80 billion. As the leading automobile assemblers have grown in terms of the scope and size of their markets since the 1970s, so also has the intensity of pressure they have imposed upon their supply chains. The pressure upon suppliers is felt most visibly in terms of price. The price pressure on North American assemblers has been so intense in recent years, that several of them have become large loss-makers and entered bankruptcy under Chapter 11.

However, the relationship is far from arms-length. There is a deep interaction between the direction of the core strategic suppliers' R&D and the needs of the assemblers. The leading auto assemblers have put intense pressure on leading components suppliers to invest large amounts in R&D to meet the assemblers' needs. The fourteen giant components suppliers in the *Fortune 500* have an average annual R&D spend of over US$ 1 billion, and the industry leaders, Bosch, Delphi and Denso each spends over US$ 2 billion on R&D (DTI, 2005). The assemblers have selected a group of powerful subsystem integrator firms, that are able to partner them in their global expansion: 'We're looking for the top suppliers to help us grow in the market place. As we grow, they will grow with us' (GM website). The leading auto assemblers work together to plan the supplier firm's investment in new production locations close to the assemblers. Leading components suppliers such as Bosch, Delphi, Valeo, and Michelin, each have more than 100 production plants across the world, close at hand to the assembly plants.

The strategic suppliers themselves are deepening their relationship with their own suppliers beyond a simple price relationship. For example, Delphi, is developing a group of its own 70–80 key 'strategic suppliers': 'These are the suppliers we'd like to grow with, they understand our cost models, where we are going, and being increasingly willing to put more of their research and development and engineering money behind projects for us' (*FT*, 30 June 2003).

The auto components industry has been through a dramatic transition during the past two decades, under intense pressure from the cascade effect. The number of components makers expanded from an estimated 20,000 in 1950 to over 40,000 in 1970. However, by 1990 the number had fallen to under 30,000. During the epoch of revolutionary growth and consolidation of the vehicle assemblers, the number of components makers shrank to fewer than 5000 in 2000, and is predicted to fall still further, to fewer than 3000 by 2015 (DaimlerChrysler, 2005).

A handful of components makers have emerged, mainly through merger and acquisition, to dominate the upper reaches of the auto components supply chain. The combined revenues of the fourteen giant auto components firms in the *Fortune* 500 amounts to a total of around US$ 291 billion (*Fortune*, 31 July 2006), which amounts to around 55–60 per cent of the total estimated spending by the auto assemblers on procurement.[94] In each segment of the vehicle, a handful of subsystems integrators, each with their own supply chains, dominates the global market. For example, three firms (Michelin, Bridgestone and Goodyear) account for 55 per cent of total world production of auto tyres (*FT*, 6 June 2006); three firms (Asahi, Saint-Gobain and NSG) account for 75 per cent of the world output of auto glass (Pilkington, website); three firms (GKN, NTN, and Delphi) account for 75 per cent of the global market for constant velocity joints (GKN and NTN, websites); two firms (Bosch and Delphi) account for around three-quarters of the world's production of diesel fuel injection pumps (*Ward's Auto World*, January 2000); two firms (Johnson Controls and Lear) account for over one half of all the automobile seat systems supplied to auto assemblers in Europe and North America (Lear and Johnson Controls websites, 2006); and two firms (Bosch and Continental) account for around 50 per cent of the global total of ABS/ESC[95] brake systems (Continental and Forbes, websites, 2005).

In addition, the pressure from the cascade effect has been a major stimulus for the high-speed consolidation in the steel industry, and, to a lesser extent, in the aluminium industry. Following their merger, in 2006 Arcelor-Mittal accounted for an estimated 26 per cent of the total global production of automotive steel, and the top five firms (Arcelor-Mittal, Nippon Steel, JFE, US Steel, and ThyssenKrupp) accounted for 54 per cent of global auto steel production (Mittal, 2006). In the aluminium industry, the top five firms (United Company Rusal, Alcoa, Alcan, Chalco and Hydro) now account for 44 per cent of total global production, and the top ten firms for 57 per cent (*FT*, 31 August 2006).

Telecommunications. Privatisation and liberalisation of the telecommunications services industry in the 1990s unleashed a wave of international expansion and consolidation. A small group of super-large telecoms services companies emerged from this process. By 2005, the top ten telecoms firms had revenues of between US$ 35 billion and US$ 95 billion. They were all headquartered in high-income economies. They had mainly built extensive international operations. Where permitted, they had participated heavily in the acquisition of formerly state-owned telecoms assets in developing and former communist countries.[96] The giant telecoms firms benefited from advantages of scale, through their ability to build global brands, offer global services, and lower costs through large procurement budgets. The leading telecoms firms such as NTT, Verizon, Deutsche Telekom and Vodafone have annual procurement budgets of US$ 15–25 billion. Their intimate knowledge of the final customer helped to place them in a position to integrate their supply chains in order to meet their needs.

Alongside the transformation of the telecoms services industry, the telecoms equipment industry experienced high-speed institutional change in the 1990s. Under intense pressure to meet the technical demands of the telecoms service providers, with their enormous procurement budgets, the telecoms equipment industry witnessed intense consolidation as the industry leaders sought increased scale, in order especially to increase their R&D capability both through direct spending and the acquisition of smaller companies with specialist technical knowledge. By 2002, the top ten telecoms equipment makers, all with their headquarters in the high-income countries, accounted for 57 per cent of the total global telecoms equipment market (Xing, 2004). In the mobile handsets market, which only emerged as a mass market in the late 1990s, the sector is already highly concentrated. In 2006, the top five firms in the sector, all with headquarters in the high-income countries, accounted for 81 per cent of the global market, and the top two alone (Nokia and Motorola) accounted for 56 per cent of the global market (*FT*, 29 September 2006).

Institutional change in the industry entered a new phase in 2005–06, stimulated by technical change. New technologies have created the possibility of 'convergent' services that offer a combination of 'triple play', including video, voice and data, which can be provided by broadband and include VoiP ('voice-over-the-internet protocol' telephony). The new technologies have created the possibility of a new form of telecommunications firm providing all these services in a combined 'bundled' package to customers. The telecoms industry is being restructured at high speed, with fixed line, mobile, cable, satellite, internet and media companies all participating in the 'convergent' institutional restructuring of the industry. This places intense pressure on the telecoms equipment makers to meet the needs for 'converged technologies' of the giant telecoms services companies in the new epoch of telecommunications: 'Equipment suppliers are being forced to offer end-to-end solutions to a consolidating base of carrier customers that are in the middle of major network transformations ... As carrier consolidation continues to drive increased vendor instability, existing players will need to seek merger and partnership opportunities to compete within the new market structure' (*FT*, 7 April 2006).

In 2005–06 a new round of industry consolidation was unleashed among the telecoms equipment makers in order to meet the intense pressure to supply new converged technologies. In rapid succession, Cisco acquired Scientific Atlanta, Ericsson acquired Marconi, Alcatel merged with Lucent, and Nokia and

Siemens merged their telecoms equipment divisions. Following the hectic round of mergers and acquisitions, the top three firms in the sector (Ericsson/Marconi, Nokia/Siemens, and Alcatel/Lucent) accounted for 75 per cent of total global sales of wireless telecoms equipment (*Communications Weekly*, 26 June 2006), and were poised to dominate the epoch of convergent technologies. The top five telecoms equipment makers each spend US$ 2–5 billion on R&D, amounting to between 10–17 per cent of their revenue (DTI, 2005).

Pressure from the 'cascade effect' in the telecoms industry does not end with the leading telecoms equipment suppliers. Semiconductors are a critically important part of the technical progress in the equipment industry, just as they are in the computer and consumer electronics industries. The level of industrial concentration in the industry is high. The leading semiconductor firms typically supply products for the whole range of industries using their products, enabling them to benefit from 'economies of scope' in applying new technologies across several closely-related sectors. The top ten firms, all with headquarters in the high-income countries, account for 49 per cent of the total global market for semiconductors (*DigiTimes.com*, March 2006). However, within individual sub-sectors, the level of industrial concentration is even higher. Meeting the needs of the world's leading telecoms equipment makers necessitates large scale and a high level of spending on R&D. In the supply of integrated circuits to the wireless telecommunications industry, the top five firms accounted for 44 per cent of total global sales revenue in the sector in 2005, and the top ten firms, all with headquarters in the high-income countries, for 65 per cent (*IC Insights*, 16 November 2005).

The impact of the 'cascade effect' penetrates even deeper down the industry supply chain. The manufacture of silicon wafers has witnessed high-speed consolidation as the firms in the sector struggle with the large capital costs and high level of R&D spending required to meet the exacting demands of the semiconductor makers. Following the latest round of industrial concentration in the sector, the top two firms in the sector, one American and one Japanese, account for 63 per cent of total global revenue in the sector (*FT*, 21 September 2006). The sector supplying the equipment to manufacture semiconductors is even more highly concentrated. The leading firm in the sector, Dutch-based ASML, accounts for 57 of global sales in the sector (*FT*, 19 January 2006).

Beverages. Since the 1980s, the global beverage industry has witnessed high-speed consolidation. In the carbonated soft drinks sector, just two firms now account for around three-quarters of total global sales. In the broader category of non-alcoholic drinks, just five firms account for over one half of the global market. The beer industry lags some way behind, but the trend towards consolidation is clear, with the emergence of super-large global firms, such as Anheuser-Busch, SABMiller, and Inbev.[97] The closely-related food industry has undergone its own process of consolidation, resulting in the emergence of a group of super-large international firms, such as Nestlé, Unilever and Sara Lee. The beverage and food industry are both experiencing intensifying pressure from the emergence of giant retailers, such as Wal-Mart, Metro, Carrefour, and Tesco.[98]

The massive procurement expenditure on material inputs and services by the world leading beverage producers has increased the pressure for consolidation from the higher reaches of the supply chain. In many areas, the 'cascade effect' pressures on the supply chain from the beverage industry are applied simultaneously by the food industry. This cascade effect has stimulated a wave of consolidation in the beverage industry's supply chain. Moreover, as the higher reaches of the supply chain have struggled to meet the global needs of the world's leading beverage companies, the process of consolidation within their ranks has produced further cascade pressure on the supply chain of these firms, as they struggle to lower costs, and achieve the technical progress necessary to meet the fierce demands of the world's leading systems integrators who stand at the centre of their respective supply chains.

The global consumer packaging industry is a huge industry, worth about US$ 300 billion annually. The top ten global packaging firms account for between 40 and 80 per cent of global markets, depending on the sector. The world's leading beverage firms interact closely with the leaders of the packaging industry to work together for ways to meet their needs better through innovations in product and process technologies. Key pressures on the packaging industry have included cost and weight reduction, improved customer safety, increased product life and enhanced appearance. Technical progress has also been achieved through contributions from the primary material suppliers in the aluminium, steel, PET resin industries, as well as in the suppliers of machinery. The world's leading beverage firms have interacted with this process at every step, acting as 'systems integrators' for the overall process of technical progress, and nurturing institutional change so that leading suppliers have sufficient scale to meet the beverage companies' strict requirements.

Over 200 billion beverage cans are consumed annually. Since the late 1980s, the world's metal can industry has rapidly consolidated. Three firms now stand out as the global industry leaders,[99] with a combined global market share of 57 per cent (*FT*, 2 November 2005). The metal can industry is a major consumer of both aluminium and steel, and places intense pressure on the steel and aluminium industries to achieve technical progress, improve product quality and lower costs. The other major users of primary metals have also consolidated at high speed during the Global Business Revolution, including the automobile, aerospace, construction and household durable goods industries. They also place intense pressure on the steel and aluminium industries, which have experienced intense consolidation. The top five firms produce 44 per cent of total world production of aluminium (*FT*, 31 August 2006), and an even higher share of the aluminium sheet for beverage cans. In the steel industry, leading steel firms focus on high value-added, high technology products for global customers, including steel for beverage cans. Although the top ten firms account for 'only' around 27 per cent of total global output by weight, following the merger of Arcelor and Mittal Steel, they account for around three-fifths of total global sales revenue from the steel industry (Nolan and Rui, 2004b).

Glass bottles are still the main form of primary packaging in the beer industry, and, despite its relative decline, the glass bottle remains an important form of packaging for soft drinks, especially in developing countries. Following successive rounds of merger and acquisition in the 1990s, the glass bottle industry has become highly consolidated. The two super-giants of the industry (Owens-Illinois and Saint-Gobain) now account for around 68 per cent of total glass bottle production in Europe and North America (Owens-Illinois and Saint-Gobain, websites). Between them they produce more than 60 billion glass bottles annually.

PET (plastic) bottles were developed in the late 1960s, and quickly became the most important form of primary packaging in the soft drinks industry, though it still has a less important place in the beer industry. In recent years the industry has become increasingly concentrated. By 2003, excluding the production by beverage companies for self-consumption, the top four firms accounted for almost two-thirds of the total production of PET bottles in North America and Europe respectively. Much of the technical progress in the PET bottle industry has been achieved by the specialist machine builders, which make two different types of machinery, namely 'pre-forms' and the equipment that 'blows' the pre-forms into their final bottle form. Each of these sectors is dominated by specialist high technology firms. One firm alone (Husky) accounts for around three-quarters of the total global market for high volume PET injection machines (Husky, website), while another specialist firm (Sidel)[100] has a near monopoly on the purchase of advanced blowing equipment by the world's leading beverage companies.

In the supply of beverage filling line equipment, the high value-added, high technology segments of the market supplying the world's leading beverage companies are dominated by just two firms (KHS and Krones), the product of remorseless M&A, which together account for almost nine-tenths of global sales of high-speed beverage bottling lines (KHS and Krones, websites). The world's leading beverage companies have bought machines almost exclusively from these two companies because of their high levels of reliability, low operating costs, high speed, more consistent filling height, and low rates of damage to bottles and product. Each of them spends heavily on research and development.

The advertising and communication sector, which is crucial for branding global businesses, has witnessed intense M&A activity, alongside the global expansion of their main customers. The world's top ten spenders each spend an average of US$ 2–3 billion per company annually. They account for a large share of the revenues of the leading advertising and marketing firms. In addition, the advertising and communication companies face increasingly powerful global media companies, such as Disney, News International, Time Warner, and Viacom, with which they place their products. The advertising and communication industry has become polarised into a small number of immensely powerful firms and a large number of small firms. By 2001, the top four firms in the sector[101] accounted for almost three-fifths of total global advertising revenue.

The world's leading beverage companies are among the largest purchasers of trucks.[102] Their truck fleets are enormous, amounting to hundreds of thousands of trucks for the industry leaders. The world's leading truck manufacturers experience intense pressure from their global customers to lower costs and improve technologies. This intensifies the pressure to increase scale in order to achieve greater volumes of procurement and push down costs across their own value chains, including suppliers of truck components (engines, brake systems, tyres, exhaust systems, seats, informatics, and ventilation systems) and materials (steel, aluminium and plastics). Greater scale also enables them to achieve faster technical progress through economies of scope (coordinated technical progress that can be used in different divisions of the company), in order to provide the customer with more reliability, lower fuel costs, greater safety and more effective ability to meet pollution control requirements. Since the 1980s, industrial concentration in the truck industry has greatly increased. By the late 1990s, the world's top five truck makers accounted for one half of total global sales in terms of the number of units sold (DaimlerChrysler, 2005) but an even higher share of the total market value, as the leading truck companies tended to produce far higher technology vehicles. In 2003 industry leader DaimlerChrysler's truck division alone had revenues of US$ 36 billion and operating profits of US$ 1.1 billion, and spent US$ 1.3 billion on research and development.

Conclusion

It is widely believed that in recent years, the landscape of global industrial competition has become 'flat',[103] with the prospect of an ever-increasing role for firms from developing countries within the global economy. In fact, the nature of the competitive landscape facing firms from developing countries is much more challenging than most analysts appreciate. Mainstream, neo-classical, economists consider that opening up developing economies to the 'freedom' to compete against global competition provides broad opportunities for indigenous firms to catch up with firms headquartered in the high-income countries. Their view is based on the belief that the basic tendency of capitalist competitive 'freedom' is competition with strict limits to growth of firm size: they believe that by forcing weak firms to compete with strong ones, the weak can learn from the strong, imitate them and overtake them. In fact, the epoch of the Global Business Revolution since the 1980s has witnessed an unprecedented degree of industrial consolidation and concentration of business power at a global level. The 'commanding heights' of the global business system are almost entirely occupied by firms from high-income countries. This presents a deep challenge for firms and policy-makers in developing countries.

The most easily visible part of the structure of industrial concentration is the well-known firms with powerful, globally recognised technologies and/or brands. These constitute the 'systems integrators' or 'organising brains' at the apex of extended value chains. As they have consolidated their leading positions, they have exerted intense pressure across the whole supply chain in order to minimise costs and stimulate technical progress. However, the challenge is even deeper than it at first appears.

This section has closely examined the value chains in four different sectors. It has shown that these sectors have striking similarities in the way in which the core systems integrators have stimulated a comprehensive transformation of industrial structure across the whole supply chain. At every level there has taken place an intense process of industrial concentration, mainly through merger and acquisition, as firms struggle to meet the strict requirements that are the condition of their participation in the systems integrators' supply chains. This 'cascade effect' has profound implications for the nature of competition. It means that the challenge facing firms from developing countries is far deeper than at first sight appeared to be the case. Not only do they face immense difficulties in catching up with the leading systems integrators, the visible part of the 'iceberg', but they also face immense difficulties in catching up with the powerful firms that now dominate almost every segment of the supply chain, the invisible part of the 'iceberg' that lies hidden from view beneath the water.

At the dawn of the twenty-first century, the reality of the intense industrial concentration among both systems integrators and their entire supply chain, brought about through pressure from the cascade effect, presents a comprehensive challenge for both firms and policy-makers in developing countries. The nature of capitalist 'freedom', with its inherent tendency towards industrial concentration and inequality in business power means that firms from developing countries are in a massively unequal position to take advantage of that freedom.

1.3.4 Class Structure in the Epoch of Globalisation

Global Inequality

Capitalist globalisation is massively unjust. The freedom of the global capitalist market economy has been accompanied by staggering inequality, with a vast, yawning gap between the global elite and the vast mass of humanity.

Identity. Those employees who work in the upper reaches of the value chain of globalising firms inhabit an increasingly homogenised global environment, with a common culture and high global incomes that broadly reflect their scarce skills. The international firm is, indeed, increasingly multinational in terms of the origin of its employees, even at high levels. It is increasingly common even for CEOs of giant global firms to be drawn from nationalities other than those in which the company is headquartered. The global elite is a tiny fraction of the world's population that is made conscious of its special position through many symbols. It shares a common language (English). Its members move their place of residence frequently from country to country. They share common values. They read the same newspapers. They stay in the same global hotels. They communicate across their respective companies continuously, connected by ever-advancing new information technologies, the latest of which is the ubiquitous 'handheld Blackberry' device. The buy the same globally branded luxury goods – Prada, Gucci, Mont Blanc, Mercedes, Lexus and Ferrari. They are experts in global high quality wines. Their children attend the same international private schools and finish their education at the same global elite universities. They share a common culture of charity, care for poor people and concern for the global environment. Their companies' leaders attend the Davos Economic Forum. Their homes are increasingly physically isolated from those of ordinary people.[104] They have less and less attachment to a particular country, both at the level of the company and as a social group. The members of the global elite typically own residences in several countries.

Income. The differences between the life led by the members of this elite group and the mass of poor people are astronomical. Whereas close to three billion people live on less than US$ 2 per day, a few tens of millions of people[105] in the global elite live on upwards of US$ 200 per day.

The long-term trends in global inequality are not disputed. If global inequality is measured in terms of the average per capita income of countries (using the PPP exchange rate, unweighted by population) then the Gini coefficient more than doubled from 0.20 in 1820 to around 0.52 in the 1980s (Milanovic, 2007: 29). If the measurement of inequality weights average per capita income by each country's population, then the trend is the same: the Gini coefficient of global inequality rose from 0.12 in 1850 to 0.52 in the 1980s (Milanovic, 2007: 30). There is considerable debate about trends in global inequality during the epoch of modern capitalist globalisation. The trend in unweighted international inequality was for a steady increase: the Gini coefficient is estimated to have risen from around 0.46 in the late 1970s to around 0.55 by the year 2000 (Milanivoc, 2007: 32). The trend in weighted inequality is ambiguous. If China is included, then the Gini coefficient declines slightly from around 0.55 in the late 1970s to around 0.50 in 2000. However, if China is excluded, the Gini coefficient rises slightly from around 0.52 in the late 1970s to around 0.55 in 2000. In other words, the trend reduction in this measure of global inequality is entirely due to the rise in China's average income. Neither of these two concepts of inequality takes account of the distribution of income within countries. During the epoch of modern capitalist globalisation, within-nation inequalities during this period have 'increased almost everywhere' (Milanovic, 2007: 33).

Attempts have been made to analyse the extent of, and trends in, global inequality that take account of inequality within countries, making use of household surveys. These reveal a far greater extent of global inequality than measures that use the average per capita income of each country. In 1998, using the purchasing power parity (PPP) exchange rate, the Gini coefficient of global income distribution is estimated to be 0.64, far above the figure for measures that use each country's average per capita income. Using the same measure, the income share of the top five per cent is 33 per cent and that of the top ten per cent is 50 per cent, while the bottom five per cent receive just 0.2 per cent of global income, and the bottom ten per cent receive just 0.7 per cent (Milanovic, 2007: 39) The ratio of the top five per cent to the bottom five per cent is 165:1, and the ratio of the top ten per cent to the bottom ten per cent is 70:1 Using this measure there is no trend change in global inequality during the epoch of modern capitalist globalisation. The Gini coefficient is estimated to rise from 0.62 in 1988 to 0.65 in 1993, before falling slightly to 0.64 in 1998. This level of inequality is 'perhaps unparalleled in world history': 'If such extreme inequality existed in smaller communities or in a nation-state, governing authorities would find it too destabilising to leave it alone, or revolutions or riots might break out' (Milanovic, 2007: 32).

However, there are question marks around the appropriateness of using 'purchasing power parity' dollars (essentially using US prices) to measure global inequality. This method of estimating income across different countries systematically over-estimates the output of poor countries. Using purchasing power data, China's level of energy efficiency (GDP produced per unit of primary energy) is on a par with countries such as Sweden, which no one seriously believes to be the case. In addition, it is especially questionable to use PPP data for analysing the upper levels of the income distribution. The main reason for using PPP dollars is that the amount of goods and services that a dollar can buy varies across countries. However, the higher in the income level one is located, the less this is the case. Most of the key items in the budget of rich people are purchased at international price, such as the prices of high quality global education, high quality housing, international travel and tourism, luxury cars and clothing. Expenditure on items such as food and domestic servants, the prices of which are relatively low in developing countries, form a relatively small part of the budget of rich people in developing countries.

Using the official exchange rate to convert national income data to a common standard reveals an even greater extent of global inequality than that which is shown using the PPP data. Using the official exchange rate it is estimated that the global Gini coefficient in 1998 was no less than 0.80, which is 'probably the highest ever recorded' (Milanovic, 2007: 39). By this measure, the top five per cent take 45 per cent of total global income, and the top ten per cent take 68 per cent. The ratio of the top five per cent to the bottom five per cent is 300:1, and the ratio of the top ten per cent to the bottom ten per cent is 150:1 (Milanovic, 2007: 39). There appears to have been a small trend increase in global income inequality by this measure during the epoch of modern capitalist globalisation, from 0.77 in 1988 to 0.80 in 1998.

The World Bank (2006: 73) has divided the global population into three different income categories (using PPP dollars). They estimate that in 2000, the 'global poor', with incomes below the average of Brazil, accounted for 82 per cent of total global population, but accounted for only 29 per cent of global income. The global 'middle class', with a per capita income between that of Brazil and Italy, accounted for only 8 per cent of the global population, and accounted for 14 per cent of global income. The global 'rich', with an income level above that of Italy, amounted to 11 per cent of the global population, but accounted for 58 per cent of global income.[106]

That there should be such extreme inequality after more than two decades of modern capitalist globalisation is a cause for deep reflection on the nature of capitalist freedoms and their ability to produce a just outcome.

Wealth. The world is now more than two decades into the modern epoch of globalisation. The inequality in the distribution of global wealth that has accompanied this process is staggering. In the year 2000, total global household wealth amounted to US$ 125 trillion, roughly three times the size of global GDP (Davies, *et al.*, 2006). The estimates in the study by Davies *et al.* use the official rate of exchange rather than purchasing power parity, since a large share of global wealth is owned by people who can readily travel and invest their wealth internationally. In the year 2000, the top decile owned 85 per cent of total global wealth, while the richest two per cent held more than one half of total global wealth. The richest one per cent alone accounted for 40 per cent of all household assets. The entire bottom half of the world adult population owned barely one per cent of global wealth. The Gini coefficient for the global distribution of wealth is 0.89: 'The same value of Gini would be obtained if US$ 100 were shared among 100 people in such a way that one person receives US$ 90 and the remaining 99 get ten cents each' (Davies, *et al.*, 2006).

The distribution of global wealth is heavily concentrated in the hands of those who live in high-income countries. Although it has only six per cent of the total global population, North America accounts for 34 per cent of global wealth (Davies, *et al.*, 2006). The high-income countries of North America, Europe and the Asia-Pacific account for 88 per cent of the global total. China and India together account for two-fifths of the world's population, but they account for only four per cent of global wealth. Membership of the pinnacle of the world's wealth distribution is even more highly skewed by region. Among the top one per cent of the global wealth distribution, 39 per cent live in North America, 27 per cent in Japan, and 23 per cent in Western Europe (Davies, *et al.*, 2006).

Politics. If the world were governed by a single representative political body elected by the whole global electorate consisting of the 4.5 billion people in the world over the age of eighteen, it is hard to imagine that large-scale redistribution of income and wealth would not command wide support.

Inequality within High-Income Countries

The free movement of capital combined with the impact of modern technology means that it has become possible to establish truly global systems of production. Globally competitive markets ultimately work towards the 'law of one price' in the markets for both goods and services. Global capital is able to move to where labour is cheapest and where markets are growing fastest. Slow-growing markets and high labour costs in high-income countries have encouraged capitalist firms to re-locate production increasingly to fast-growing developing countries in order to sustain profits. This deeply threatens the nature of labour market organisation that has developed over a long period in the high-income countries. Liberalisation since the 1980s has not only opened up a vast world of low-priced, low-skilled labour, but has also opened up a sea of highly skilled labour across the 'transition' and 'developing' countries. In high-income countries even workers with high levels of skills are being forced to work longer hours, accept reduced rates of overtime pay, and other changes in their conditions of work under the threat that their jobs will be 'exported' if they don't agree. Across both the United States and much of Continental Europe this has helped to produce a political crisis, as ordinary people increasingly believe that the multinational corporation is increasingly divorced from their interests.

Initially, the segments of the labour market that were most affected were relatively limited and confined mainly to the manufacturing sector. In the United States between 1970 and 2000, the number of manufacturing jobs fell by around six million (*NYT*, 24 May 2005). However, the impact has spread to almost all segments of the workforce. Labour market competition for employees in high-income countries is mediated through cheap imports of both final and intermediate goods (such as components for final assembly of complex products in high-income countries) as well as through the replacement of production for world markets with production systems in fast-growing low and middle-income countries. Pressure to compete on labour markets that have become effectively global in scope in many sectors has forced large changes in conditions of work, as well as placing downward pressure on real wages across large segments of the workforce. This means that the globalisation of capitalism provides an intensifying threat to the livelihood of a large section of the workforce in high-income countries. Far from producing a homogenisation of class interests, the progressive unification of global labour markets is producing intensified conflict of interest between workers in rich and poor countries, as the latter undermine conditions of work for a large segment of the former.[107]

For lower levels of workers, especially those outside the global value chain of leading global companies, the globalisation of capitalism creates intensifying conflicts across countries. For the global elite the situation is the reverse. Their personal interests and the interests of the firms for which they work, are steadily reducing their attachment to a particular national identity. Instead of companies with names that reflect national identities, names of international firms are increasingly acronyms or newly invented names without any national significance,[108] which give no clue as to the original nationality of the company or its headquarters. Their fastest growing markets and production locations are typically in low and middle-income countries. These countries form the most dynamic part of their revenue and employment growth. Increasingly, their internal knowledge generation through research and development is taking place there.

In order to compete in the ferocious global competition most large American firms are bringing to an end their 'defined pension' schemes, and replacing them with 'defined contribution' schemes, which greatly increase ordinary workers' insecurity about their old age. In Continental Europe, the future of the 'cradle to the grave' social security system hangs in the balance. European-based firms argue for reductions in their contributions to employees' pensions and reductions in corporation tax, in order to compete more effectively on the 'global level playing field'. The possibility of following the Scandinavian path of high levels of public welfare based on high personal tax and low corporate taxes is now being widely mooted as a possible solution to the crisis. It is far from certain that Continental Europe will follow this path.

The profound impact of the integration of global labour markets upon the conditions of employment in high-income countries has been compounded by the impact of explosive technical change achieved by the ferocious oligopolistic competition of the Global Business Revolution. The revolution in information technology has greatly changed the nature of demand for labour in the lower-skilled occupations, with widespread substitution of labour with information systems. A vast swathe of occupations that were formerly undertaken by skilled clerical and manual workers is now undertaken by computer systems, due to the technical achievements of the giant capitalist firms in the information technology sector, resulting in an explosion of growth in the information processing capabilities and a simultaneous explosive fall in their real price. Those who have the skills to make effective use of the new information technologies have achieved large increases in their relative incomes. Across a wide range of high-income countries, the epoch of capitalist globalisation has seen a decline in the relative wages of low-skilled workers compared to skilled workers. Between the late 1970s and the late 1990s, the gap increased by 29 per cent in the United States, 27 per cent in the United Kingdom, 15 per cent in New Zealand, 14 per cent in Italy, and 9 per cent in Canada (World Bank, 2007: 106).

The gap in income between the global elite and the local population has widened sharply during the last two decades. The most marked change in inequality was in the United Kingdom and the United States (World Bank, 2007: 80), which have been the most determined among the high-income countries in their pursuit of neo-liberal policies. The United States' Congressional Budget Office reports that the after-tax income of the top one per cent of American households jumped 139 per cent to more than US$ 700 000 from 1979 to 2001 (adjusted for inflation), while that of the middle fifth rose by 17 per cent and that of the poorest fifth rose only 9 per cent (*NYT*, 15 May 2005). The income of the top 0.1 per cent of the US population includes around 145

000 tax-payers, each with an income of over US$ 1.6 million, with an average income of US$ 3 million in 2004. Their share of America's income rose from around 3.5 per cent in 1980 to over 10 per cent in the year 2000 (*NYT*, 5 June 2005).[109] The widening gaps in income in the United States are reducing the degree of inter-generational mobility.

Inequality within Developing Countries

During the early phase of industrialisation, for a significant period of time the distribution of income typically becomes more unequal (the 'Kuznets curve'). During this phase, the majority of the developing country's workers are under-employed in the farm sector on close to subsistence levels of income. As the modern sector expands, the growing army of rural-urban migrants is pulled into permanent wage employment, but mostly on low incomes in unskilled occupations. This is the so-called 'Lewis' phase of 'economic development with unlimited supplies of labour'. On the one hand, rural-urban migration to permanent wage employment contributes to the decline in absolute poverty in many developing countries in recent decades. On the other hand, although a growing fraction of the urban workforce gradually moves into higher income occupations, a fundamental constraint is set to the growth of real wages for urban unskilled labour by the availability of unlimited supplies of under-employed rural labour.

A large fraction of rural-urban migrants work as unskilled 'lumpen' labour in the urban 'informal' sector, unprotected by trade unions, health and unemployment insurance, effective minimum wage legislation or government supervision of conditions of work. Several hundred million people work in this sector in low and middle-income countries, often in arduous, physically dangerous and psychologically insecure conditions. For example, in India in the early 1990s, out of a total of 93 million people employed in the non-farm sector, 68 million (73 per cent) were employed in the 'informal' sector, vastly outnumbering those working in the formal sector (Breman, 1996: 4).

In China during the period of modern globalisation, the nature of non-farm employment has changed drastically. The total numbers employed outside agriculture expanded at an incredible rate, from 118 million in 1978 to 413 million in 2002, an amazing record of job creation (SSB, ZTN, 2004: 128). However, the numbers employed in the formal sector plummeted from 149 million in 1995 to 106 million in 2002 (SSB, ZTN, 2003: 130). In the state sector alone, under the impact of widespread restructuring after the mid-1990s, in the same period the number of employees fell from 110 million to 69 million (SSB, ZTN, 2003: 134). At the end of the 1970s, over four-fifths of China's non-farm employees worked in secure conditions in the state or collective sector, with regular wages, and health care, housing and pensions provided by the employer. By 2002, only a quarter of them worked under such conditions. The number of employees in the informal sector rose from just 23 million in 1978 to 307 million in 2002. Among these were around 131 million rural-urban migrants, who almost all worked in the informal sector (UNDP, 2005: 75). By 2002, there were 54 million informal sector employees in manufacturing, 42 million in trade and catering, 31 million in construction and 15 million in transport (SSB, ZTN, 2003: 128–9). Employees in the informal sector typically have temporary contracts, no health or old age insurance, and wages are typically around US$ 1–2 per day. Real wages for most informal sector workers have not risen for many years. Official data on the Pearl River Delta show that for manual workers in the fastest-growing region in China wages have stagnated for two decades (Liu Kaiming, 2006).

The huge numbers of people who work in the informal sector across the developing world are employed in millions of small-scale establishments. Conditions in the 'informal' mining, manufacturing, construction, agricultural wage labour, transport and service sectors, and the associated family living conditions, are frequently little different from those described in Frederick Engels' study the *Condition of the English Working Class*, published in the 1840s, during the early phase of British industrialisation (Breman, 1996). Real wages in this sector remain constant, set by the wall of underemployed labour in the agricultural sector. This is the world of the eighteenth century, but with access to the global television of the twenty-first century.

Unlike most previous experiences of late industrialisation, today the world's leading firms have established production systems across the developing world within the fast-growing low and middle-income countries. During the Global Business Revolution, low and middle-income countries have opened themselves to the free flow of foreign direct investment at a point in history at which levels of global industrial concentration and barriers to entry have never been higher. Within the fastest-growing parts of low and middle-income countries, leading multinational firms, almost all headquartered in the high-income countries, have established production systems that dominate large swathes of the host economy.

Global oligopoly has been transplanted from the high-income to the fast-growing low and middle-income countries, in almost all sectors that produce high value-added products with high technology and/or powerful brands.[110] These may be intermediate products supplied to other businesses, final products for relatively affluent local consumers or exports to customers in high-income countries. In a wide range of sectors, including banking, insurance, marketing, telecommunications service, international logistics, commercial aircraft, passenger cars, commercial vehicles, patented pharmaceuticals, medical equipment, carbonated soft drinks, premium beers, modern power stations, telecommunications equipment, semiconductors, automobile components, high value-added steel, aluminium, high technology mining, modern farm equipment, lifts, modern construction and mining equipment, agro-chemicals, modern packaging and packaging equipment, leading global firms have established oligopolies in many fast-growing developing countries. This is quite different to the experience of most previous late-comer countries.

As a result of this development, international firms employ an increasing fraction of their workforce within the low and middle-income countries. However, relative to the total workforce of these countries, the numbers involved are small. For example, in China, employees working for foreign-funded firms' enterprises (excluding those from Taiwan and Hong Kong, which mainly employ workers in the informal sector) totalled 37 million in 2002, amounting to only 9 per cent of total non-farm employment (SSB, ZTN, 2003: 138).

Development economists used to believe that multinational firms would adjust their 'factor proportions' (capital to labour ratios) to the conditions of developing countries, employing relatively large amounts of labour for each unit of capital. In fact, the epoch of globalisation has produced globally standard products using global standard technologies in the high value-added market for final and intermediate products. Global procurement, global branding, globally integrated product design and globally integrated production technologies require homogeneity in capital-labour ratios across countries at every level of income.

Global firms employ international workers at international income levels. Local employees of multinational firms in developing countries, whatever their skill level, tend to work at income levels considerably above those of comparably skilled local workers. Moreover, a disproportionate fraction of these are people with relatively high skill levels. Conditions of work also approximate those in high-income countries, even for manual work. Multinational firms must adopt global employment standards or their reputation will be damaged. Also, it is impossible to manage a multinational firm using a wide variety of different employment practices across different subsidiaries of the company in different locations. Insofar as local firms are able to compete with the global firms, they also must adopt global standards in order to competitively attract high quality local labour.

The presence of larger pockets of multinational firms within fast-growing low and middle-income countries has brought the 'twenty-first century' to these countries in terms of employment and remuneration, with pay and conditions of work determined by global standards. However, those employed in these conditions constitute only a small fraction of the non-farm population.

Surrounding them is a vast and far larger 'sea' of urban informal sector employment, for whom pay and conditions of work are set by the standards of the rural under-employed masses, not by international markets. During the epoch of the Global Business Revolution, the low-wage informal sector, with employment at a constant real wage, has increased its share of non-farm employment, while skilled workers who are within or connected to the supply chain of global firms have achieved increases in real incomes.

During this period, the levels of income inequality have risen within fast-growing low and middle-income countries. Many of them have seen the Gini coefficient of inequality in income distribution rise during this period from 0.2–0.3 to 0.4–0.5. In East Asia, inequality has 'increased significantly over the last several decades' (World Bank, 2007: 80). For example, in China, the reported Gini Coefficient of urban income distribution rose from 0.16 in 1978, to 0.34 in 2002, while the overall Gini Coefficient rose from 0.30 to 0.45 in the same period (UNDP, 2005: 56–8). In Latin America, inequality increased 'almost uniformly' in the 1980s, though the deterioration was 'less pronounced' in the 1990s (World Bank, 2007: 80).

The epoch of globalisation of capitalism has seen the emergence of two worlds within the fast-growing low and middle-income countries. One is the world of the twenty-first century, with modern apartment blocks and villas for the globalised elite, with modern sanitation and water supply; living and working in physically segregated environments; protected by private and public police forces; buying globally branded consumer goods produced to global standards; investing their wealth in global assets; sending their children to 'global' private schools and universities; receiving healthcare from global standard private hospitals using global medical equipment and pharmaceuticals; staying in global 'five star' hotels; and holidaying in foreign countries.

The other and far larger world, is that of the mass of under-employed farmers and the permanent members of the urban informal sector. The latter work in arduous, often dangerous conditions, with a high degree of insecurity; they live in low quality, overcrowded housing, and often inhabit *favellas*, slums, and shanty towns, without running water and modern sanitation; the official police force often fears to tread there, and 'law and order' is often in the hands of the local 'mafia'; the only available schools are those run by the hard-pressed local government staffed with overworked, underpaid teachers; only a small fraction of the children in these schools is able to escape to study in the public sector's hard-pressed universities; 'wealth management' typically means borrowing from the informal banking sector at high interest rates to meet pressing living expenses; illness has to be dealt with by using over-worked, under-staffed public health facilities or entering crippling indebtedness by resorting to private sector medicine.

Conclusion

The period of the global capitalist business revolution has seen a dramatic increase in inequality within the fast-growing low and middle-income countries. In these countries, the 'freedom' of people to migrate out of their underemployed rural environment has stimulated the growth of a vast sea of urban informal sector workers, earning low and stagnant incomes, living in low quality physical environments, with great personal insecurity, with low quality healthcare and educational services. Their conditions of work and life are fundamentally constrained by the existence of a huge pool of rural underemployed workers ready to migrate to the cities. This situation is unlikely to change for several decades, until the industrialisation process has run its course and the rural reserve army of labour has dried up, allowing urban real wages for unskilled labour to be bid up by the market. Alongside them, 'freedom' of global capital to move to low and middle-income countries has stimulated the growth of an enclave of global modernity of working and living. In this enclave, people live 'global' lives, isolated from the realities of daily life for their fellow citizens. This immense inequality has been produced by the freedoms of the global capitalist structure.

The current phase of global capitalist development closely resembles that of Britain in the early nineteenth century, in the sense that the world is still in the phase in which there is a huge global rural reserve army of underemployed people. This sets the parameters within which the global capitalist accumulation process must operate. The class interests of the rulers of the capitalist system dictate that they should support undemocratic systems of government which restrict the 'voice' of poor people in global institutions. However, the contradictions involved in this stage of the capitalist accumulation process are deep, with a yawning gulf between the emerging global elite, which has less and less commitment to any particular country, and the mass of poor people, whose lives are still bound within their nation state. In addition, a large part of the workforce in the high-income countries feels that its interests are threatened in fundamental ways by the economic progress of developing countries. Today's high-income countries all experienced severe class struggle during the comparable periods in their development, but ultimately the capitalist system survived. Global capitalism has arrived today at the equivalent of '1848'. Whether the surging contradictions within countries and across countries are sustainable remains to be seen.

The extent of global inequality is so great, and the difference of class interests is so wide, that in the interests of global capital accumulation the mass of disadvantaged people across the low and middle-income countries cannot be allowed a full 'voice' in global politics. The great paradox for the global capitalist system is that its most dynamic part is the Chinese economy, which does not have Western multi-party democracy. The growth prospects of the world economy, the hub of so many interests of global capitalists, hinge around the capability of the 63 million-member Chinese Communist Party to sustain their rule effectively, and provide a secure home for international and domestic capital. A truly global state, built around one vote per person on a global scale is not remotely in the realm of possibility. If it were, it would have highly problematic consequences for global capitalist development.

People are still tightly bound into the framework of the nation state. Migration across international boundaries from low and middle-income countries is tiny compared with internal migration within those countries. Despite the growth of both sub-national and supra-national institutions, the nation state remains the primary basis of identity. People remain bound to particular countries through the accident of their birth. Fast-growing late industrialising countries have tended to witness an intensified identity with the nation, even in countries that lack the obvious signs of being a 'nation', such as a common language or belief system. Modernisation requires universal literacy, a 'national language', a public health service, and public infrastructure. These in turn require the state to tax the people and build an administrative machine. The expanded role for the state is central to enhancing the sense of national identity.

1.3.5 Finance

Inherent Instability of Financial Markets

Keynes (1936: Chapter 12) provides the foundation of the modern critiques of the potentially de-stabilising effects of uncontrolled financial markets. He strongly attacked the idea that stock markets and currency markets are efficient, and based on rational expectations. He emphasised the influence of speculation in determining prices in financial markets: 'Speculators may do no harm as bubbles on a steady stream of enterprise. But the position is serious when enterprise becomes the bubble on a whirlpool of speculation. When the capital development of a country becomes a by-product of the activities of a casino, the job is likely to be ill-done' (Keynes, 1936: 159). He believed that speculation is 'a scarcely avoidable outcome of our having successfully organised "liquid" investment markets' (Keynes, 1936: 159). Indeed, he believed that as the organisation of investment markets improves, 'the risk of the predominance of speculation increases' (Keynes, 1936: 158).

More recently, Robert Shiller has pointed out the shortcoming in 'many of the major finance textbooks today', which 'promote a view of markets working rationally and efficiently', and 'do not provide arguments as to why feedback loops supporting speculative bubbles cannot occur' (Shiller, 2001: 67). He comments: 'In fact, they do not even mention bubbles or Ponzi schemes': 'These books convey a sense of orderly progression in financial markets, of markets that work with mathematical precision' (Shiller, 2001: 67). Shiller (2001) has shown that bubbles in financial markets are 'so natural that one must conclude that if there is to be debate about ... speculative bubbles, the burden of proof is on the sceptics to provide evidence as to why [they] cannot occur' (Shiller, 2001: 67). The initiating factor is often the optimism generated by a feeling that the economy has entered a 'new era'. Once the speculation process gets under way, powerful positive feedback loops drive markets ever higher. Credit is extended on the basis of increased collateral asset prices, which supports still further increase in asset prices, and still further credit expansion (White, 2006: 9).

The counterpart of the powerful tendency of financial markets to produce self-reinforcing 'bubble' effects is the tendency to produce self-reinforcing market collapse: bubbles tend to burst, rather than slowly deflating (Shiller, 2001). This tendency has been heightened by modern sophisticated measures of internal risk management, which operate through daily, price-sensitive risk limits. These generally used techniques require a bank to reduce exposure to risk when the probability of losses increases as a result of falling or more volatile asset prices (Persaud, 2000). If only a handful of banks uses these techniques, everyone may be better-off. However, if all the banks use the same techniques to reduce risk, and they have similar positions, then the banks will respond simultaneously and in the same way to an initial fall in asset prices, which drives them up against their risk limit. As banks try together to sell the same assets, 'prices plummet and volatility increases, causing more banks to hit their risk limits': 'As long as market participants herd, which they have been doing for as long as markets have existed, the spread of sophisticated risk systems based on the daily evolution of market prices will spread instability, not quell it' (Persaud, 2000).

Kindleberger (1996) has observed that financial markets are subject to frequent crises, which he ascribes to periodic and alternating bouts of irrational exuberance and pessimism of investors largely unrelated to fundamentals. Kindleberger's historical analysis is implicitly endorsed by Alan Greenspan, the Chairman of the US Federal Reserve himself, who commented as follows on the 1987 US stock market crash and the Asian financial meltdown of the 1990s:

> At one point the economic system appears stable, the next it behaves as though a dam has reached a breaking point, and water (read, confidence) evacuates its reservoir. The United States experienced such a sudden change with the decline in stock prices of more than 20 per cent on

October 19, 1987. There is no credible scenario that can readily explain so abrupt a change in the fundamentals of long-term valuation on that one day.... But why do these events seem to erupt without some readily evident precursors? Certainly, the more extended the risk-taking, or more generally, the lower the discount factors applied to future outcomes, the more vulnerable are markets to a shock that abruptly triggers a revision in expectations and sets off a vicious cycle of contraction.... Episodes of vicious cycles cannot easily be forecast, as our recent experience with Asia has demonstrated (Greenspan, quoted in Singh, 2002).

This mirrors the Keynesian view of investor behaviour and the significance of mass psychology in price formation in financial markets. Keynes's insights on this subject have been formalised in current theoretical literature, which is able to provide a 'rational' explanation for the herd-like behaviour, contagion and other irrational manifestations of economic agents in financial markets.

Financial Risk Today

The relationship between finance and the real world of production of goods and services is fundamental to economic activity. In the epoch of the Global Business Revolution, this relationship has assumed a global character. The global financial system stands on the edge of a precipice. The world faces the possibility of a catastrophic financial crisis stemming from the operation of the capitalist free market in the realm of finance. The impending crisis has several inter-related elements.

Rate of interest. The rate of interest in the high-income economies has fallen to unprecedentedly low levels in the past decade. In part this has been due to government policy to serve as an anchor for consumer price inflation by limiting inflationary expectations. The low rate of interest has also been stimulated by the massive increase in foreign exchange reserves in East Asia and the oil-exporting countries. Between 1995 and 2005, world foreign exchange reserves tripled to more than US$ 4000 billion, with an accelerating rate of increase after the year 2000.

The devastating impact of the Asian Financial Crisis on economies in the region prompted intense efforts by East Asian economies in the subsequent period to follow 'mercantilist' policies, increasing export surpluses in order to expand their foreign exchange reserves, in the hope that this would insulate them from the impact of such a crisis in the future. It was hoped that the large accumulations of foreign exchange reserves would enable these economies to 'self-insure' against financial crisis rather than rely on international institutions such as the IMF (*FT*, 9 March 2006). In addition, the rise in oil and gas prices after the turn of the millennium stimulated increased export surpluses and foreign exchange reserve growth in the oil-producing economies.

These reserves have massively increased the supply of financial investments to global markets, especially in the United States. The availability of such vast and rising foreign exchange reserves seeking a return on global financial markets, especially in the United States, means that the US Government finds it relatively easy to borrow from international markets, and has helped to keep the rate of interest low. These developments in turn have helped to stimulate a long-term bubble in asset prices. The inflow of funds has also helped to prop up the US dollar.

Falling price of goods and services. The period of the Global Business Revolution has seen falling prices of final goods and services. The cause of the decline is partly due to the entrance of a vast number of new workers at low wages from the former communist planned economies and from the formerly inward-looking developing countries. The enormous increase in low-cost, low-price exports has underpinned the decline in the price of a wide range of goods and services. The decline has also been due to intense oligopolistic competition among giant firms, who compete by forcing down prices along their respective supply chains and by investing huge amounts in technical progress.

Asset price bubble. Alongside the decline in the prices of final goods and services has taken place an unprecedented asset bubble. The bubble has been stimulated by the feeling that the world has entered a new era of global markets and uninterrupted capitalist expansion across the world. The asset bubble has been self-reinforcing, with speculation driving up asset prices in a classic self-reinforcing cycle around the world. The asset bubble moved from the stock market in general to the IT sector. In the past few years, the asset bubble has increased dramatically in the property market, the market for oil, gold, silver, aluminium, platinum, nickel, and other metals, the bond market (forcing down bond yield), the market for agricultural products such as refined sugar and orange juice futures, and even to exotic areas such as the art market.

For example, the price of copper surged from less than US$ 1000 per tonnes (three-month forward) in 2001–02 to US$ 1800 in mid-2005, before achieving a 'near-vertical take-off', reaching US$ 8500 per tonne in May 2006 (*FT*, 24 May 2006). Between 2001 and 2005, global copper usage rose by less than one-fifth,[111] alongside a more than eightfold rise in the price of copper. It is widely believed by experts in the field that 'momentum investors' have played a central role in the rise in the copper price, as indeed, they have in the increase in other commodity prices.

Property prices have surged across the world. Between 1995 and 2005, average house prices tripled in Australia, almost tripled in the United Kingdom, more than doubled in Spain, and almost doubled in the United States (*FT*, 17 April 2006). The underlying fundamentals of supply and demand for properties have not changed greatly in this period, and differ greatly from country to country, and region to region. What is common is the huge rise in property prices. The most plausible explanation for the explosive growth is that the liberalisation of credit markets in leading economies has allowed lenders to meet the demand for mortgages more easily. The period has seen a wide range of innovations in the range of mortgages on offer, including 'interest only', 'deferred payment of interest', and 'multi-generational mortgages'. House values have become the largest source of personal wealth,[112] and mortgages have become the largest source of household debt.[113]

National monetary authorities target consumer price inflation, not asset price inflation. They are afraid to puncture the asset price bubble through increasing the interest rate, for fear of the socio-economic consequences. However, the longer the asset price bubble continues, the more serious will be the final result when the bubble bursts. Some commentators believe the monetary authorities ought to concern themselves with asset price inflation as well as consumer price inflation. Preoccupation with consumer price inflation is likely to stimulate conditions that lead to asset price bubbles and the eventual collapse of asset prices, with large damaging effects on the economy and society (Eichengreen and Mitchener, 2003).

Sources of liquidity. The expansion of liquidity has been driven in part by the historically low rate of interest. However, it has also been driven by the self-reinforcing process of endogenous money creation:

> Monetary expansion is systemic and endogenous rather than random and exogenous ... The fact is that money, defined as a means of payment in actual use, has been continuously expanded, and existing money has been used ever more efficiently in periods of boom to finance expansion, including speculation. This has occurred despite efforts of banking authorities to control and limit the money supply (Kindleberger, 1996: 45).

Kindleberger warns that 'the problem of "money" is that it is an elusive construct, difficult to pin down and to fix in some desired quantity for the economy' (Kindleberger, 1996: 48). Both the velocity of circulation and the invention of new forms of money make it extremely difficult to control the quantity of money. The Radcliffe Commission in Britain in 1959 claimed that in a developed economy there is an 'indefinitely wide range of financial institutions' and 'many hold highly liquid assets which are close substitutes for money, as good to hold and only inferior when the actual moment of payment arrives' (quoted in Kindleberger, 1996: 48). The period of the Global Business Revolution has seen a proliferation of new financial institutions and new forms of debt.

(a) **New financial institutions.** In the epoch of the Global Business Revolution, the range of financial institutions has expanded beyond imagination. Traditional commercial banks now compete routinely with investment banks, credit card companies, insurance companies, and the financial branches of supermarkets, automobile companies, aircraft manufacturers, oil companies, and diversified conglomerates such as GE.

Hedge funds hardly existed before the 1990s. The amount of money invested in so-called 'hedge-funds'[114] had risen to around US$ 1500 billion by the middle of 2005, almost doubling in the previous two years, and rising from around US$ 170 billion ten years ago (*FT*, 23 May 2005). Hedge funds account for only around 2 per cent of total financial assets. Due to their high leverage, their use of derivatives and their active trading policy, they account for around two-fifths of daily trading in equity markets in the United Kingdom and the United States, and on some days as much as 70 per cent (*FT*, 29 September 2004). Investors in hedge funds are 'impatient for results'. They expect hedge fund managers to be 'more aggressive and to take larger bets in their search for much higher returns' (*FT*, 29 September 2004). The sector has been widely criticised for its aggressive use of leverage, pursuit of short-term momentum trading and heavy involvement in 'increasingly esoteric and illiquid markets in pursuit of high returns' (*FT*, 14 May 2005).

(b) **Endogenous money supply: new sources of debt.** Moreover, the sources of debt have expanded into forms that were unimaginable before the Global Business Revolution. Investors now have 'a dizzying array' of corporate bond and debt instruments to choose from' (*FT*, 17 June 2005). Two decades ago, derivatives didn't exist.[115] A huge variety of 'derivative' products has emerged in recent years, based on predictions of price changes in currencies,[116] interest rates, bonds, equities and equity indices, and commodities. The market for credit derivatives and the associated new types of debt[117] has exploded. Today, derivatives are a hugely important part of the global financial system. By 2004, the global total of outstanding notional amounts of all types of derivatives reached US$ 500 trillion (HSBC, 2005).[118] The rate of growth of liquidity through the use of these instruments has been fantastic. In December 2000, the 'over-the-counter' (OTC) market in derivatives (i.e. excluding those traded on exchanges) stood at around US$ 90 000 billion (i.e. US$ 90 *trillion*).

By January 2006, the OTC derivatives market had increased to US$ 360 000 billion (i.e. US$ 360 *trillion*) (*FT*, 15 January 2007). The issuance of 'collateralised debt obligations (CDOs) is also rising at high speed. Total issuance of CDOs rose from around US$ 30 billion in the first quarter of 2004 to almost US$ 800 billion in the last quarter of 2006 (*FT*, 15 January 2007).

These developments are of immense importance for global financial markets, which in turn have immense potential implications for the real world. The volume of new 'money' that is being created through speculation in newly developed financial instruments now dwarfs the 'real' economy in which tradable goods and services are produced. At the end of 2006, central bank 'power money' amounted to around 10 per of global GDP, but amounted to just one per cent of total global liquidity. So-called 'broad money' amounted to around 122 per cent of global GDP, but still accounted for only around 11 per cent of total global liquidity. Securitised debt amounted to around 142 per cent of global GDP, but still accounted for just 13 per cent of total global liquidity. Derivatives amounted to no less than 802 per cent total global GDP, and fully 75 per cent of total global liquidity (*FT*, 15 January 2007). In other words, 'cyber money' now amounts to more than eight times the total global output of goods and services.

The glut of global savings in search of high yield has stimulated investors into ever more risky asset classes in order to generate high returns. Important segments of risk are located in areas of the economy that are not regulated by financial authorities.[119] The new financial instruments are extremely complex, with risks that are often not fully understood by the investors. Derivatives often invest in each other's products, increasing the leverage and risk for end-investors, so that a collapse in one part of the system could rapidly spread to other parts (*FT*, 16 February 2005). Nor have they been tested in the face of acute economic stress. Financial instruments such as collateralised debt obligations (CDOs) are dispersed throughout the economic system which has spread risk widely. However, the fact that such a wide array of financial institutions, pension funds, banks, hedge funds, and insurance companies, have all 'piled into the sector', means that 'if a nasty accident did ever occur with CDOs it could ricochet through the financial system in unexpected ways' (*FT*, 19 April 2005).

Increased indebtedness in high-income economies. In the high-income economies, the asset price bubble, especially that in property, has formed the foundation for an explosive growth of credit, both to fund speculation and to fund current consumption. Whereas East Asian economies have saved an extremely high share of income, in the high-income countries, based on a self-inflating asset bubble, levels of personal indebtedness have reached extraordinary heights. By 2004, the US population's savings rate stood at minus one per cent, compared with 35 per cent in China (Roach, 2005). The level of household debt in the United States has risen remorselessly, from 60 per cent of household income in the mid-1980s to over 120 per cent in 2004 (*FT*, 16 February 2005). In the United States, the share of consumption has risen from around 65 per cent in the early 1980s to 71 per cent in 2004 (Roach, 2005). The United States accounts for only around 5 per cent of global population, but it accounts for no less than 35–40 per cent of global consumption.

Consequences of asset bubbles. The consequences of the unprecedented asset bubble are extremely serious. They have led to a large redistribution of wealth in the high-income economies towards those with higher incomes and those who already own larger asset holdings. They reward speculation over investment in production of goods and services. They encourage a culture of borrowing and indebtedness.

Most seriously, when the bubbles burst, it will lead to massive global consequences. It will cause a widespread financial sector crisis, penetrating deep into the sectors that have absorbed risk, which are now much more widely distributed throughout the economic system of the high-income economies than before the Global Business Revolution. It will cause a collapse of people's consumption, as the wealth effect takes hold and people in high-income economies seek to rebuild their savings. It will cause widespread anger in high-income economies as people are forced to curtail their spending in the face of a collapse of their wealth. The impact on consumption growth will affect the growth of demand for exports from developing countries, which will affect their socio-economic stability.

Financial risk and developing countries. In the epoch of the Global Business Revolution, greatly increased 'freedom' for the giant global financial firms to allocate capital across international markets has contributed to a rise in global financial instability. The instability has been especially serious for developing countries, where financial crises can cause deep downturns in economic activity and threaten social stability. These have, in their turn, frequently led to the overthrow of national governments.

The number of financial crises has sharply increased since widespread liberalisation of financial markets began in the 1980s. The period since then has seen a succession of huge financial crises among developing countries. These include the Mexican 'Tequila Crisis' of 1994–95; the Asian Financial Crisis of 1997–98; the Russian Crisis of 1998; and the Argentinian Crisis of 2001–02. In addition, there have been numerous smaller financial crises.

There are strong grounds for believing that capital flows to developing countries might be especially volatile. Both internal (e.g. weak domestic financial systems; frequent economic shocks) and external factors, particularly the animal spirits of foreign investors, make these flows volatile. Empirical evidence suggests a close link between financial liberalisation and financial crises in developing countries. The volatility and the pro-cyclicality of private capital flows to developing countries is a well-attested feature of international capital movements during the last two decades. Such in-flows come in surges, often bearing no relationship to the economic fundamentals of the country and leave the country when they are most needed, i.e. in a downturn. Also, the early phases of industrialisation are bound to have a tendency towards social and political instability. This further amplifies the potential for financial instability inherent in naturally occurring speculative bubbles. Moreover, the Bank for International Settlements has concluded that financial instability in developing countries tends to be increased where international financial firms dominate the financial systems of developing countries, as it 'exposes local banking more directly to changes in global conditions' (reported in *Financial Times*, 5 December 2005).

The Asian Financial Crisis has led to a substantial modification of the views of senior officials in the IMF, which formerly was firmly in favour of capital account liberalisation. An IMF study has concluded that there is little hard evidence that developing countries with open capital accounts grow faster than those with closed accounts (reported in *Financial Times*, 21 August 2006). They emphasise that countries 'need to develop well-functioning institutions and reasonably mature capital markets before they can benefit from capital account liberalisation'. They emphasise that they also need to have 'decent corporate governance', appropriate economic and exchange rate policies and 'openness to trade' if they are to avoid financial crises alongside capital account liberalisation.

Absence of global financial system regulation. The global financial system is now deeply integrated across national boundaries, far more deeply even than the integration of production systems. However, the transition from primarily national to global markets has not been accompanied by a strengthening of international regulatory governance. In the view of many financial experts, there is 'no-one in charge at the global level' (*FT*, 15 March 2002). The IMF, the institution that is supposed to guide the global financial system, has been described as a 'rudderless ship in a sea of liquidity' (Barry Eichengreen, speaking at an IMF meeting in September 2005) (quoted in *Financial Times*, 26 September 2005). At the same meeting Fred Bergsten, Director of the Institute for International Economics, said that the IMF's Strategic Review had 'provided too few answers to the questions [it] raised'.

Moreover, the complexity of the new financial instruments has made it extremely difficult for regulatory authorities to understand fully the nature of systemic global financial risk. The problem for regulators has been exacerbated by the fact that the global financial system has now developed instruments of such great complexity and at such a high speed, that no one understands how to regulate the whole system, even assuming that the political mechanisms existed to do so. The spread of financial innovation is so dramatic that 'regulators, lawyers and rating agency officials struggle to keep up' (*FT*, 19 April 2005). Moreover, the massive extent of repacking and sale of debt means that debt is far more deeply distributed throughout the economy than was the case before the Global Business Revolution. This provides a source of stability and enhances the ability of the financial system to ride out relatively small-scale crises, but means that the whole global financial system is far more susceptible to a giant financial crisis should it erupt.

The ease with which lenders can repackage loans and move them off their balance sheets means that they are able to lend even more, as regulatory rules permit banks to reduce their reserves of cash against their loans if these are securitised. The ease of securitising loans has a powerful 'moral hazard' effect for banks, since it means that they feel that they are insured against default. These processes further encourage lending and the inflation of asset bubbles in a self-reinforcing cycle. National regulators now have little idea of the origin of the funds that support the derivatives market. This greatly reduces the effectiveness of national monetary policy.

There is a palpable sense of deep unease among policy makers. In early January 2007, at a variety of different meetings, the following fears were expressed about the absence of control over the global financial system consequent upon the new forms of liquidity creation, due to their complexity, absence of regulatory oversight and their international nature. Malcolm King, managing director of the Bank for International Settlements said: 'Financial innovation has produced vehicles for leverage which are very hard to measure ... liquidity is increasing very rapidly and this is affecting asset prices ... Central banks are scrambling to address the problem ... but international cooperation and data gathering efforts need to be deepened' (quoted in *Financial Times*, 29 January 2007). Jean-Claude Trichet, President of the European Central Bank warned: '[T]here is now such creativity of new and very sophisticated financial instruments ... that we don't know fully where the risks are located. We are trying to understand what is going on, but it is a big, big challenge' (quoted in *Financial Times*, 29 January 2007). Sir John Gieve, the deputy governor of the Bank of England warned that the growing complexity of the derivatives market is a risk to financial stability, 'because the ultimate bearer of risks is no longer clear' (quoted in *Financial Times*, 3 January 2007).

Paul Tucker, executive director of the Bank of England warned that the explosive growth of new financial instruments has profound implications for 'how we gauge money and credit conditions and assess the resilience of the financial system as a whole (quoted in *Financial Times*, 15 January 2007). Stanley Fisher, governor of the Central Bank of Israel said: 'It remains unclear who takes responsibility for the financial system in a time of crisis' (quoted in *Financial Times*, 29 January 2007). Jochen Sanio, Germany's top regulator said: 'Does anyone know who holds the risk [in modern financial deals] ... Market participants are operating in *terra incognito*' (quoted in *Financial Times*, 17 January 2007). Andrew Crockett, former head of the Bank of International Settlement (now President of JPMorgan) said: 'These new instruments ought to make markets more complete. But there is a lack of transparency ... we don't know how much leverage there is in hedge funds, for example' (quoted in *Financial Times*, 29 January 2007).

Also in January 2007, Kenneth Rogoff, former chief economist at the IMF (now professor at Harvard University) issued an alarming warning about the absence of global governance over the financial system (*FT*, 8 February 2007). Released from the burden of official language that was part of his obligation at the IMF, he launched a devastating attack on the absence of a global plan to ensure the safe operation of the financial system. He asked the rhetorical question: 'Whatever happened to all the grandiose plans for improving the global financial architecture?' He answered: 'Over the past couple of years, all introspection seems to have vanished. Instead, the policy community has developed a smug belief that enhanced macroeconomic stability at the national level combined with financial innovation at the international level have obviated the need to tinker with the system ... There is no problem that markets cannot solve'. His observation is scathing: 'Really? How well would markets handle the fallout from a sharp slowdown in India or China? How would they react to a dirty nuclear bomb in a US city that triggered a retreat from US assets, and a sudden reluctance on the part of global investors to keep financing America's 800-plus billion dollar account deficit? Or a rapid escalation of conflict in the Middle-East that encompassed Iran and Saudi Arabia? Or an avian flu pandemic?' He argues that, despite improvement in central cooperation in recent years, 'contrary to market perceptions, global central banks have only very limited instruments for dealing with a genuinely sharp rise in global volatility, particularly one that is geo-politically induced' (*FT*, 8 February 2007).

Lessons of history. The lessons of history suggest extreme caution in considering the potential for a global financial crisis to erupt. The world's largest financial crisis occurred in the early 1930s, following a period of price stability, and, even, price deflation at the end of the decade. The period preceding the crisis was characterised by rapid technological innovation, rising productivity, rapid increases in the prices of equity and real estate, and strong fixed investment. Behind these developments were technical innovations in the financial sector, not least the much greater availability of consumer credit (White, 2006: 7).

Conclusion

In the epoch of the Global Business Revolution, greatly increased 'freedom' for the giant global financial firms to allocate capital across international markets has contributed to a significant rise in global financial instability. The consequences of the exercise of this freedom have been especially serious for developing countries. In these countries, financial crises can cause deep downturns in economic activity and threaten social stability. These have, in their turn, frequently led to the overthrow of national governments. Most experts believe that the global financial system has now developed such complex instruments, that no one understands how to regulate the whole system, even assuming that the political mechanisms existed to do so. The world may stand at the brink of a comprehensive financial crisis. This would have incalculable consequences, not only for the financial system, but also for international, and, even, military relations.

Financial speculation and the matching creation of money to meet the needs of speculation are a natural part of the 'freedom' of capitalism. As Kindleberger has shown in his long-term study of financial crises, the natural working of 'free markets', allied to the motives of fear and greed, have repeatedly produced financial cycles. The lure of 'greed' is deep. Even the genius, Newton, having once been burned in the early phase of the South Sea Bubble, went back into the market again, lured on by greed, which overcame his rational calculation. The crisis facing the world today originates in the 'freedom' of the financial system to pursue profits blindly through speculation, 'money to make more money'. This is exactly the 'unnatural' behaviour that so dismayed Aristotle. The risk for the global community has been greatly increased by the application of sophisticated new technologies to create 'money'. These technologies are the product of many of the most creative minds in the world today. The free exercise of their intelligence in the pursuit of profit places the world on the edge of a financial abyss.

Effective regulation of the global financial system is desperately needed, but the short-term self-interest and power of giant financial firms is combined with the ineffectiveness of international political institutions to prevent such mechanisms being put into place. As the Asian Financial Crisis demonstrated vividly, the 'fire' of a financial crisis moves at high speed, fanned by self-created winds,[120] and swiftly shifts into the economic, social and political sphere.

The next financial crisis is likely to be global in scope, and, if it happens, the consequences will of unimaginable dimensions. A phrase that was much-repeated during the Asian Financial Crisis was 'when the tide goes out, the rocks appear (*shui luo, shi chu*). When this tide 'goes out', as seems increasingly probable, the rocks that appear are likely to make those of the Great Depression appear small indeed.

1.3.6 Conclusion

Capitalist freedom is a two-edged sword. The same force that has propelled forward human ingenuity for over two millennia has reached a new peak in its stimulus of human creativity. However, it threatens fundamentally the very existence of the human species.

The global ecology is profoundly threatened by the consequences of the uncontrolled locked-in pattern of consumption, distribution and energy consumption that is at the heart of capitalist globalisation. Responsibility for the lion's share of past global warming lies with the high-income countries. Developing countries are rapidly increasing their contribution to global warming, and there is the prospect of a sharpening confrontation between rich and poor counties over their respective responsibility for resolving this issue. The world faces an intensifying struggle for energy security among the main importers of oil and gas, which will remain the core of the primary energy supply for the world's transport systems for decades to come.

The large corporation has burst the boundaries of the nation in the pursuit of profit on the global market stage, producing profound contradictions with the separate nation states out of which the world's leading firms grew. On the one hand, giant global firms, occupying the leading position in the battle for survival in the global marketplace, deeply threaten the indigenous firms that are headquartered in developing countries. On the other hand, the fact that global firms are fast attenuating their allegiance to their original home country is creating a fissure within the political system of the high-income countries.

The distribution of income and wealth within both rich and poor countries has become much more unequal as a consequence of capitalist globalisation. A large mass of citizens in both sets of countries believe the other set of countries is largely responsible for this situation. A global capitalist class has developed rapidly, with shared interests that are at odds with those of the people and nations within which the global firms had their origins.

The revolution in the financial system has produced deeply integrated markets, with money creation and associated speculation on an unimaginable scale, powerfully supported by the creativity of financial technicians, facilitated by the revolution in information technology. There is no global entity with the power and authority to regulate the global financial system. The system is 'flying blind', with a high possibility of a global financial crisis. Such a crisis would interact powerfully with the contradictions in the realms of ecology, income and wealth inequality, and the changed nature of the large firm and its relationship to the nation state. Such a crisis would have massive social, economic and political consequences.

Behind all of these issues lies the fact that politics is mainly conducted at a national level, while the capitalist system has become global in scale. The mechanisms for the world's citizens to control the global capitalist system are extremely weak. The interests of individual nations are extremely strong. Military force remains a central part of the reality of international relations. The United States possesses a vast and immensely effective nuclear arsenal. Russia still possesses a huge arsenal. In early 2007, Russia announced a large increase in military spending,[121] in order to 'fund a new generation of intercontinental ballistic missiles, nuclear submarines and aircraft carriers' (Sergei Ivanov, Russia's defence minister, quoted in *Financial Times*, 10 February 2007). France, the United Kingdom, China, India, Pakistan and Israel, all have nuclear weapons. The world could be destroyed in the twinkling of an eye.

If human beings are to resolve these contradictions and avoid the looming disaster, it is urgently necessary to establish global mechanisms to contain the tiger of unconstrained global capitalism. However, to do so requires cooperation between real nations, with real national interests that often diverge from each other. It also requires cooperation between groups of nations at different levels of economic development. The richer group of countries have many interests in common that often diverge from those of the developing countries.

The United States sits at the centre of this question. The reality is that it does lead the global system of political economy. It has the opportunity to grasp the nettle of leadership and build on some of its own traditions to lead the world towards cooperation and harmony, or it can pursue its own self-interest, wrapped in the cloak of ideology, and lead the world towards disaster. Two of the most urgent issues that require resolution both involve the United States, namely the relationship with China and the relationship with the Islamic world. Between them they contain around two-fifths of the world's population. They can use their own rich traditions to contribute to a sustainable future for humanity in the twenty-first century. The possibility of their doing so will be much greater if the United States is able to develop an evolving pattern of 'constructive engagement' with them. Resort to 'destructive engagement' will lead to disaster. The second part of this book examines the challenges of the contradictory character of capitalist globalisation in relation to these centrally important issues.

PART 2.
GROPING FOR A WAY FORWARD: CONFLICT OR COOPERATION?

Those who seek international conciliation may study with advantage the conditions which have made the process of conciliation between social classes in some degree successful. Essential conditions of that process were that the reality of the conflict should be frankly recognized, and not dismissed as an illusion in the minds of wicked agitators; that the easy hypothesis of a natural harmony of interests, which a modicum of goodwill and common sense would be sufficient to maintain, should be consigned to oblivion; that what was morally desirable should not be identified with what was economically advantageous; and that the economic interests should, if necessary, be sacrificed in order to resolve the conflict by the mitigation of inequalities.

(Carr, 2001: 217)

Introduction

Between them, China and the Muslim world contain over 2.5 billion people, over two-fifths of the world's population. China's population is around 1.3 billion. They mostly live in a single country. China's rise is a central fact of political economy in the twenty-first century. At the start of the twenty-first century there were 1.3 billion Muslims in the world, roughly the same number as Chinese people. Unlike the Chinese, the Muslims are spread much more evenly across the world's territory. There are around 900 million in fifty-seven independent Muslim states and 400 million in over 100 communities in the rest of the world (Ahmad, 2003: 190).

Although they are dispersed across many countries, they have common beliefs that give them a united voice on some key issues.

The way in which the United States interacts with these two giant civilisations will be central to the possibility of a sustainable path of global development in the twenty-first century. American foreign policy has been wracked by intense debate about whether to 'engage' in a peaceful or a confrontational fashion with both China and the Islamic world. This issue is still unresolved. The way in which it is resolved will determine the nature of capitalist globalisation in the twenty-first century, and the possibility for a sustainable future for mankind.

2.1 The United States and China

We[Chinese Communists] must unite with the proletariat of all the capitalist countries, with the proletariat of Japan, Britain, the United States, Germany, Italy, and all other capitalist countries, for this is the only way to overthrow imperialism, to liberate our nation and people and to liberate other nations and peoples of the world. This is our internationalism, the internationalism with which we oppose both narrow nationalism and narrow patriotism.

(Mao Zedong, 1939)

Since the late 1970s, under the leadership of the Chinese Communist Party, China's policy of reform and opening up has led to it becoming ever more deeply integrated with the capitalist global economy. This has enabled it to benefit from the 'advantages of the latecomer' and to the release of its latent productive forces based on a long history of capitalist development (Xu Dixin and Wu Chengming, 2000). It has produced remarkable economic growth and transformation of the Chinese people's standard of living. However, the very success of China's engagement with global capitalism has produced deep contradictions, including rising inequality, declining energy security, worsening ecological damage, and serious difficulties in competing with the world's leading firms. These challenges are fully recognised by China's leaders. Resolving them is their central task in the years ahead. This is a 'choice of no choice'. Sustainable development in China requires that it must achieve balanced development and establish a 'harmonious society'.

Capitalist globalisation has had a contradictory impact also on the United States. It has brought great benefits to American firms, American shareholders, and American consumers. However, it has also brought deep challenges. These include a sharp increase in inequality, a decline in energy security and an increased threat to the natural environment, the erosion of national identity among leading US firms, and potential financial instability. China's rise is increasingly the scapegoat for US difficulties that arise from capitalist globalisation.

Despite its increasingly universal character in the epoch of globalisation, capitalism retains deep roots within individual nations, each with its own national interests and internal contradictions that influence its international relations. The tension between the universalising impulse of capitalism and the archaic structure of the nation state remains intense. The contradictory character of capitalist globalisation is crystallised in US-China relations. There is a serious possibility of deep conflict between them, which would be a catastrophe for humanity. Faced with such a terrible possibility, US-China cooperation is the only rational path for the leadership of the two countries to pursue. They can benefit from mutual support in resolving the stresses that capitalist globalisation brings to both countries and to the whole global community.

2.1.1 China

Capitalist development has a long history in China. Prior to the early modern period, China's embryonic capitalism was far more developed than that of Europe. China's capitalist development took place within the context of a powerful state that shaped the pattern of capitalist development in numerous ways to meet common social interests. China's policy-makers today can gain inspiration from this experience ('using the past to serve the present') as they struggle to find their own path through which to relate to capitalism's surging power and contradictory character.

Embryonic Capitalism in China

Agriculture and property rights. The foundation of Chinese civilisation was, and still is, agriculture. D. H. Perkins' (1968) meticulous account of the long-term development of Chinese agriculture between the fourteenth and the mid-twentieth century shows how the responsiveness of Chinese rice-based agriculture was able to both allow huge long-term population growth and absorb productively the huge long-term increase in farm labour force. Total population grew from around 100 million in the twelfth century to over 500 million in the early 1950s (Perkins, 1968). There were several elements in the long-term growth of Chinese farm output, enabling output per person to remain fairly constant over the long run. These included substantial increases in the cultivated area in the earlier period, but these were substantially exhausted by the late seventeenth century. The main path to increased output was an intensification of techniques to raise output per acre. These involved the spread of double-cropping rice, initially introduced in the eleventh century, huge long-term expansion of the irrigated area, the introduction of indigenous dryland crops into new areas, the spread of 'new' dryland crops from the New World, and powerful effects resulting from increased inter-regional trade and specialisation, which continued strongly into the modern period (see especially Li Bozhong, 1998, on the impact of inter-regional trade on farm productivity in Jiangnan between 1620 and 1850).

It is widely thought that the key to the economic development of Western Europe lay in the 'unique' system of private property rights that developed in this part of the world. This view received its most powerful advocacy from Nobel Prize Winner Douglas North: Efficient economic organisation is the key to growth; the development of an efficient economic organisation in Western Europe accounts for the rise of the West. Efficient organisation entails the establishment of institutional arrangements and property rights that create an incentive to channel individual economic effort into activities that bring the private rate of return close to the social rate of return (North and Thomas, 1973: 1).

The development of private property rights is thought to have been caused by the growing pressure of population on the limited supply of farmland. Land replaced labour as the relatively scarce resource. From this developed the concept of private property in physical assets that, it is argued, underpinned the entire edifice of early modern economic development in Western Europe: 'The pressure to change property rights emerges only as a resource becomes increasingly scarce relative to society's wants ... The abundance of land during the high Middle Ages made labour easily the most scarce, and hence the most valuable, factor of production ... [U]nprotected land at the time was almost as abundant as air and of no more economic value. Labour and capital, the scarce factors of production, alone set the boundaries for all output' (North and Thomas, 1973: 30). By the thirteenth century, arable land had reached the limits of expansion with existing technology: 'Throughout the century the rewards to labour declined while land provided ever greater returns to its owners' (North and Thomas, 1973: 51).

'China' does not even appear in the index of North and Thomas (1973). In fact, pressure of population on land occurred in China far earlier than in Europe. As the political power of aristocrats declined and their estates disappeared, this led to the growth of private property in land, including, before long, the right of freed slaves to own their own land. Before the Tang Dynasty (618–907), 'large aristocratic families dominated the countryside, administered huge rural estates, and held their farm labourers in virtual slavery' (Eastman, 1988: 71). During the Tang and Song dynasties, the power of the aristocratic families gradually collapsed: 'With the collapse of the aristocrats' political power and the disappearance of their estates, the peasants working the fields gradually sloughed off their status as slaves, and by about the fourteenth century, most of them had gained the freedom to own and rent land and to move about at will' (Eastman, 1988: 71). By the seventeenth century at the latest China was only 'feudal' in the broad sense that the surplus was extracted mainly from peasants by land rents, not in the narrow sense of a manorial, serf economy.[1] These considerations invalidate the proposition that private property in land was a uniquely European phenomenon which formed the basis of wider concepts of private property, which in turn facilitated capitalist investment and innovation, which in short, was responsible for 'the rise of the West' (North and Thomas, 1974).

Technical progress. Joseph Needham (1954-) has documented the enormous technical advances made in medieval China. From the tenth to the thirteenth century, China set out along the path of the 'Second Industrial Revolution' well before Europe. The list of technical innovations independently developed in China includes such items as the windmill, canal lock gates, mechanical clockwork, power transmission by driving belt, water-powered metallurgical blowing engines, and hemp-spinning machines, gear wheels, numerous naval inventions (for example, the stern-post rudder, watertight compartments), and water-powered trip hammers for forges (Needham, 1965: 222–4). A key feature of industrial advance in the European Middle Ages was the crank: '[T]he powers of the crank were widely used and appreciated throughout the Chinese Middle Ages. For 3-400 hundred years before the time of Marco Polo it was employed in textile machinery for silk-reeling and hemp-spinning, in agriculture for rotary winnowing and water-powered flour-sifting, in metallurgy for the hydraulic blowing-engine, and in such humble uses as the well-windlass' (Needham, 1965: 224). Although the pace of technical progress slowed down after China's medieval 'industrial revolution', a steady stream of significant technical advances was made thereafter through until the nineteenth century (Xu Dixin and Wu Chengming, 2000), without making the leap to a full-fledged modern 'Industrial Revolution'.

Trade. These technological developments were stimulated by powerful long-term growth of both domestic and international trade. For long periods, the Chinese state was able to unite the vast territory of China into a single integrated market. Marco Polo provided a vivid description of the level of commerce on the Chang Jiang (Yangtze) in the thirteenth century:

> This river runs for such a distance and through so many regions and there are so many cities on its banks that truth to tell, in the amount of shipping it carries and the total volume and value of its traffic, it exceeds all the rivers of the Christians put together and their seas into the bargain .... I have seen in this city [Sinju] fully 5000 ships at once, all afloat on this river. Then you may reflect since this city, which is not very big, has so many ships, how many there must be in others. For I assure you that the river flows through more than sixteen provinces, and there are on its banks more than 200 cities, all have more ships than this ... The amount of shipping it carries, and the bulk of the merchandise that merchants transport by it, upstream and down, is so inconceivable that no one in the world who had not seen it with his own eyes could possibly credit. Its width is such that it is more like a sea than a river (Marco Polo, 1974: 170 and 209).

In the eighteenth century, Father Du Halde, the Belgian Jesuit priest wrote: [T]he particular riches of every province, and the ability of transporting merchandise by means of rivers and canals, have rendered the empire always very flourishing .... The trade carried on within China is so great, that all of Europe cannot be compared therewith (quoted in Ho Ping-ti, 1959: 199).

Foreign trade was a crucial part of the Chinese economy along the coastal regions. Although there were periods in which the central state tried to restrict trade with foreigners, such as the early Ming dynasty, for most of the last two thousand years, international trade operated free of government controls, other than the levying of import duties.

In his pioneering account of trade and economic development in South China before 960 AD, Wang Gungwu comments: 'The South China Sea was the main trade route of what may be called the Asian East-West trade in commodities and ideas. It was the second Silk Route. Its waters and island straits were as the sands and mountain passes of Central Asia; its ports were like the caravanserais. It became to the southern Chinese what the land outside the Jade Gate was to the northern Chinese' (Wang Gungwu, 1998: 3).

Guangzhou remained at the centre of the thriving trade with southeast Asia for the next thousand years, except during the relatively brief periods of government restriction on trade with foreigners.

Marco Polo writes of the city of Tinju, which made porcelain bowls that were 'exported all over the world' (Marco Polo, 1974: 239). He records that 'Zaiton' (Xiamen) is 'the port for all the ships that arrive from India laden with costly wares and precious stones of great price and big pearls of fine quality. It is also a port for the merchants of all the surrounding territory, so that the total amount of traffic in gems and other merchandise entering and leaving the port is a marvel to behold' (Marco Polo, 1974: 237).

Shiba's account of the growth of the port city of Ningbo shows the importance of both domestic and international maritime trade in the city's growth (Shiba, 1977: 391–9). After Ningbo moved to its present site in the eighth century, it developed into an outport for the Lower Yangtze region and flourished for the next thousand years as a centre of both the coastal trade and of the long-range trade with other regions of China, with Japan and with Korea. During the Southern Song dynasty, shipping flourished in Ningbo. The concentration of shipping and shipbuilding accelerated the economic specialisation of the city's hinterland, stimulating the production and marketing of materials necessary for the transport industry. After restrictions on international trade were lifted in the mid-Ming dynasty in 1567, silver from Japan, Portugal, and Spain poured into inland China via Ningbo. Numerous other ports up and down the long Chinese coast, such as Guangzhou and Xiamen, had similar paths of development.

Far from Europe dominating the long-term development of the world economy from the late Middle Ages onwards, Europe had little to sell that Chinese people wished to buy until well into the nineteenth century. The persistent pattern of international exchange over many centuries, right up to the early nineteenth century, was the Chinese export of manufactured goods in return for specie, especially silver.

Mercantile capital in traditional China was highly developed. Marco Polo's *Travels* is replete with accounts of teeming mercantile activity, and innumerable cities in which there are 'merchants of wealth and consequence'. Brooks' (1999) study is focused on the extraordinary degree to which the volume of commerce advanced during the Ming dynasty, with a pervasive impact on the culture of the period. In the late eighteenth century, there were reported to be about 5000 seagoing ships in the ports of Shanghai and Zhapu, with a total weight estimated at around 550 000 tons. Large merchants were reported to each own fleets of more than 100 ships employing over 2000 people (Xu Dixin and Wu Chengming, 2000: 364). By the mid-eighteenth century, 'native trade in all but the isolated interior regions of China was dominated by three groups of prominent traders, the Hui-chou merchants of Anhui, Shansi merchants, and Fukienese merchants from the Ch'uan chou-chang-chou region' (Shiba, 1977: 403).

For several hundred years prior to the nineteenth century, Foshan was the centre of the flourishing iron trade in the province, with products 'marketed far and wide: up and down the coast of China and all over Southeast Asia' (Wagner, 1997: 73). Outside merchants came from all over China, 'including the wealthy merchants from the provinces of Shanxi and Shaanxi in the north, who traded throughout China. Remains left by the outsiders must have dotted the Chinese coast' (Faure, 1996: 6). These were increasingly challenged by the merchants from Ningbo, of whom 'several thousand' had settled in Shanghai by the end of the eighteenth century (Shiba, 1977: 436).

Industry. The textile industry was much the most important in traditional China, as it was in early modern Europe. Towards the end of the Ming dynasty (1368–1644), cotton replaced hemp and silk as the principal fabric for daily wear. The spinning and weaving of cloth became the largest handicraft industry (Xu Dixin and Wu Chengming, 2000: 213). By the early nineteenth century, there were around 60–70 million peasant households engaged in the occupation as a subsidiary activity to farming (Xu Dixin and Wu Chengming, 2000: 217). Around one half of the cloth was for self-consumption and one half for sale on the market. Of the marketed cloth, it is estimated that around 15 per cent entered long-distance trade.

By the early Qing (1644–1911), in the late seventeenth and early eighteenth century, there were many examples of large-scale businesses (Xu Dixin and Wu Chengming, 2000: 250–98). Many of these were in the metallurgical industries. In the iron industry many large-scale private enterprises emerged as the market economy expanded. One of the largest was the Guangdong merchant, Ho Xi. In the early eighteenth century, he was recorded as owning 64 iron mines employing 130 000 workers. In the manufacture of iron from iron ore, there were several examples of large iron works that employed two or three thousand workers. Large copper mines also often employed several thousand workers. One report even records a copper mine in which as many as 700 000 were employed. Although this is thought to have been somewhat exaggerated, there are many reliable reports from the early Qing, of copper mines with many thousands of employees. In the coal industry, there are frequent references to large mines with many hundreds or even several thousand employees. However, examples of large-scale businesses were not confined to the metals and mining sector.

In the porcelain industry in the sixteenth century, Jingdezhen was reported to have up to 50 000 people employed in the different branches of the industry. Most of these were employed in private kilns, with around 100–200 employees per kiln (Xu Dixin and Wu Chengming, 2000: 314). In the salt fields of Sichuan there were many large businesses. Reliable evidence from the early nineteenth century records that in the large salt works at Fushun and Jianwei, there were 'several hundred thousand' employees and in the smaller ones, 'several tens of thousands' (Xu Dixin and Wu Chengming, 2000: 338). In Imperial times, Foshan, 'the city of iron and steel' (in Guangdong), was estimated to have a population of close to a million people, 'mostly of the working class' (Wagner, 1998: 73).

Urbanisation. G. William Skinner's pathbreaking research (Skinner, 1977: 286) showed that late Imperial China had a high level of urbanisation for a pre-industrial society. In the nineteenth century there were estimated to have been a total of 35 000 'standard' and 'intermediate' market towns. Above this dense local trading structure were a further 2300 'central market towns', 932 'cities' and 26 huge 'metropolitan trading systems', which in turn formed eight 'great economic systems'. Among these were cities of a size and level of sophistication that far exceeded those of contemporary European cities until late in the latter's economic development.

The Tang dynasty (618–907) capital, Chang An, was the 'largest, richest and grandest city in the world of that time' (Boyd, 1962: 51). The vast eleventh century painting *Ching ming shang he tu* shows in minute detail the city of Kaifeng, the capital of the Northern Song dynasty up until around 1127. It provides a unique visual insight into the immense richness of trade, calmness of atmosphere, cultural profusion, and effectiveness of government administration, as well as the beauty and sophistication of architectural arrangement in a large medieval Chinese city.

Marco Polo's long account of Hangzhou ('Kinsai') around 1280 (Marco Polo, 1974: 213–22), reveals him to have been overwhelmed by the city's size ('the greatest extent of its walls was about fifteen miles, and that of the inner city walls, about eight miles'); booming trade ('as for the merchants, there are so many and so rich and handle such quantities of merchandise that no one could give a true account of the matter'); highly developed civic infrastructure (including '12 000 bridges, mostly of stone' and 'fully 3 000 public baths'); effective government administration ('when [the guards] find a man who is unable to work on account of illness, they have him taken to one of the hospitals, of which there are great numbers throughout the city, built by the ancient kings and lavishly endowed'); with a flourishing manufacturing and service economy ('the city has twelve main guilds, [and] each of these guilds has 12 000 establishments, that is to say, workshops'). Marco Polo considered Hangzhou to be 'without doubt the finest and most splendid city in the world'.

Jiangnan. Jiangnan was much the most developed area of China in the late Ming and early Qing dynasties. This is the Delta Region of the Yangtze River. In 1815 it had a population of around 26 million (Li Bozhong, 1986), out of a total Chinese population of around 330 million (McEvedy and Jones, 1978: 167). This compares with a European population in 1820 of around 190 million, including 31 million in France, 25 million in Germany, and 14 million in Great Britain (Cipolla, ed., 1973: 747). By the end of the seventeenth century Jiangnan was the world's biggest exporter of textiles and fibres and was more highly commercialised and urbanised than any other part of the world (Li Bozhong, 1986). Over many centuries Jiangnan's agriculture became steadily more intensified, with improvements in yields per crop, increases in multiple-cropping and rising real value of output per unit of farmland (Li Bozhong, 1986: 4–16).

By the late sixteenth century textiles had become the largest single part of the Jiangnan industrial economy. Nanjing was the centre of the silk industry. In the 1840s there were nearly 200 000 people engaged in the industry, with more than 35 000 looms (Li Bozhong, 1986: 21). Songjiang prefecture was the most highly developed part of China in terms of the production of cotton cloth for the market, and Suzhou, the country's most important commercial centre, 'teemed with cloth merchants and was also a dyeing centre' (Xu Dixin and Wu Chengming, 2000: 171). During the Qing dynasty about 90 per cent of the marketed cotton cloth produced in Jiangnan was exported to other parts of China or abroad. In the eighteenth century, the fastest growth rates of exports were to Europe: between 1786 and 1798, the export of 'Nankeens' (cloth woven in Nanjing and other places in Jiangnan) to Western Europe and the Americas increased almost fivefold (Li Bozhong, 1986: 27).

The level of urbanisation in Jiangnan in the late eighteenth century may have been as high as 35–45 per cent, if the residents of small towns are included (Li Bozhong, 1986: 51). Around 5000 sea-going ships were based in Jiangnan, with a tonnage that was 2.8 times that of British ships of all kinds in 1700 (Li Bozhong, 1986: 53). The proportion of people who obtained some kind of education was 'very high by pre-modern standards', with a relatively high fraction of ordinary workers educated to a basic level. Jiangnan's farmers and craftsmen, were 'full of commercial awareness', and 'organized their production with an eye to the changing markets'. Its entrepreneurs 'organized their business activities in order to maximize profits' (Li Bozhong, 1986: 58).

Chinese economic development in comparative perspective. Paul Bairoch (1982) has compared national output in different parts of the world historically. He estimates that in 1750, China's share of global manufacturing output stood at 33 per cent, compared with 25 per cent in India/Pakistan and just 18 per cent in the 'West'. Bairoch estimates that in 1800, China's per capita GNP was US$ 228 (at 1960 prices) compared with US$ 150–200 for England and France (Bairoch, 1982). Up until the nineteenth century, the dominant view of China among European intellectuals was of a country that was materially superior to Europe. As late as 1798, Malthus declared China was the richest country in the world (Dawson, 1964: 7). Western travellers praised the quality of its roads and the cleanliness of its cities. In his description of McCartney's mission to China in 1793, Sir George Staunton says that 'in respect to its natural and artificial productions, the policy and uniformity of its government, the language, manners, and opinions of the people, the moral maxims, and civil institutions, and the general economy and tranquillity of the state, it is the grandest collective object that can be presented for human contemplation or research' (quoted in Dawson, 1964: 7).

State and market in Chinese development
(a) The bureaucracy. The key feature of the traditional Chinese state was a combination of a hereditary emperor with a large professional civil service, selected mostly by competitive examination.[2] In addition, there was a much larger number of members of the local 'gentry' (*shenshi*), 'who dealt with many interests of their local communities for which the official government had no time' (Michael, 1964: 60). The dominant ideology of bureaucratic rule was conveyed continuously through the examination system. Confucian ideology, the foundation of the examination system, was the key to the system's long-term stability and cohesion. The over-riding values were those of 'the primacy of order and stability, of cooperative human harmony, of accepting one's place in the social hierarchy, of social integration' (Feuerwerker, 1976: 15). China's long tradition of political philosophy emphasised that the sole test of a good ruler was 'whether he succeeds in promoting the welfare of the common people ... This is the most basic principle in Confucianism and has remained unchanged throughout the ages' (Lau, 1979: 32 and 37). In order to serve the interests of the mass of the people, the bureaucracy must gain the trust of the masses: 'Only after he has gained the trust of the common people does the gentleman work them hard, for otherwise they would feel ill-used' (Confucius, 1976: 154). If the bureaucracy becomes corrupt, losing its moral foundation, the result is

disaster for social order: 'Those in authority have lost the Way and the common people have for long been rootless' (Confucius, 1976: 155).

China's merchants occupied a subordinate ideological and political role. Merchants were placed at the bottom of the bureaucracy's official ranking of social strata, behind the scholars, farmers and artisans. There was no official representation of the merchants' interests in either the local or the central government. Howsever, the fact that the merchants' political standing was degraded, did not mean that trade itself was regarded as undesirable. The successful merchant's wealth 'had always drawn covetous awe if not respect' (Faure, 2001). If merchants wished their families to enter the ruling bureaucratic class, their children needed to go through the laborious and highly competitive examination system. The consequence was thorough absorption of the ideology of the ruling scholar-bureaucrat elite. The merchants were allowed to perform their essential function of stimulating economic interaction through expanding the division of labour, facilitated by trade, but were firmly kept in their place in terms of the political power structure and the ideology that underpinned that structure.

(b) Law. During the long periods in which it functioned relatively effectively, the Chinese state provided a framework of law and order and protection for property rights within which powerful long-term economic development took place and was matched by corresponding technical progress. Chinese merchants were never able to develop the independence from the state that began to develop in increasingly autonomous towns in late medieval Europe (Balazs, 1964). However, the control exercised by the state ensured that in periods when the central government functioned well, the cities provided a secure environment in which to conduct business, not only due to the peaceful environment, but also due to an environment in which their property rights were protected by the state. It is unimaginable that such huge quantities of merchandise could have been stored and traded without security that the corresponding contracts were legally enforceable, or that robbery of the merchants' property was illegal. Rowe's meticulous research on late Imperial Hankow (Rowe, 1984) has shown that before 1850 there were all manner of written commercial agreements, including shipping orders, bills of lading, promissory notes and contracts of sale, all of which were routinely circulated and enforceable in Hankow. Without them the bulk trade of the port would hardly have been conceivable. Local officials in late imperial Hankow played a key role in guaranteeing debt repayment.

(c) The army. The most important function of the imperial state was to provide long periods of relative peace and stability over the vast territory under its rule. Although there were terrible period of state disintegration, for long periods, China was distinguished from the rest of the world by the fact that the central authorities were able to establish peaceful conditions over vast territories. Even in the midst of long dynasties, such as the Ming, China had the world's largest army (Huang, 1981: 160).

Most importantly, the presence of so many troops also provided a source of security for economic activities during the long periods in which they were under effective control from the civilian authorities. They provided merchants with the confidence to undertake trade that far exceeded that in other parts of the world until modern times. The normally peaceful environment over wide areas provided a powerful incentive to those with capital to undertake long-term investments. It also enabled the entire territory of China to form a single unified free trade area. The degree of state interference in trade was small, in normal times confined mainly to taxation of a small number of key items. Estimates for the eighteenth century show that only around 7 per cent of national income went into the central government budget, of which the vast bulk, 74 per cent came from the land tax and just 14 per cent came from the domestic and international customs revenue (Nolan, 1993: 17). Therefore, long before any other comparable region of the world, China was able to enjoy for a long period the powerful 'Smithian' stimulus of specialisation, the division of labour, the rapid spread of best practice techniques, and powerful incentives to accumulate capital.

(d) Money. In the traditional Chinese economy exchange was almost always a monetary transaction (King, 1965: 42). Marco Polo was fascinated by the control exercised by the central authorities over the supply of money. During the Yuan dynasty, the Mongol rulers were the first economy in the world to have paper money. He was amazed that 'all the peoples and populations who are subject to [the Great Khan's] rule are perfectly willing to accept these papers in payment, since wherever they go they pay in the same currency, whether for goods or for pearls or precious stones or gold or silver. With these pieces of paper they can buy anything and pay for anything' (Marco Polo, 1974: 148). For over two thousand years, the Chinese government was aware of the importance of money to a sound economy. One of its ongoing struggles was to ensure that the money supply was not debased and that the quantity of money corresponded to the current economic needs. The central government tried persistently to maintain central control over the amount and nature of currency in circulation. Detailed accounts from the early Qing dynasty show the way in which the central government closely monitored the money supply, frequently changing the specified weight and composition of coins in response to changing economic conditions, and attempting to maintain a constant exchange rate between copper cash and silver coinage (King, 1965: 133–43).

(e) Water control. The most important single function of the state in traditional China was water control, both for drainage and irrigation, as well as for transport. Large water control projects were almost exclusively public, organised either directly by the central government, or by lower levels of the bureaucracy. Water control activities carried a grave moral imperative for government officials, with a similar responsibility to that of national defence: '[B]uilding embankments on the Yellow River is like constructing defenses on the frontier, and to keep watch on the dike is like maintaining vigilance on the frontier' (a high official of the Ming dynasty, quoted in Ch'ao-ting Chi, 1936: 73). The central administration had important functions in inter-district water projects or projects with large expenses. In the Ming and Qing dynasties, the construction of the embankment of the Yellow River was in the charge of a special official ranking high in the bureaucratic hierarchy. The Grand Canal was by far the greatest transport infrastructure achievement of the traditional Chinese state. It played a significant part in providing a transport system linking the productive south with the political north, engaging the attention of the best minds of China for more than ten centuries. It demanded countless millions of lives and a large portion of the wealth of the country for its improvement and maintenance.

Local government officials had an important role in water control. For almost any local water works beyond the capacity of the peasants of a single village, the magistrate intervened with the delegation of the duty of mobilising forced labour, supervising the construction of local works, and regulating the use of water by rival villages. There was a heavy moral burden upon local officials to ensure that the innumerable local water control activities were provided at an adequate level. The ideal magistrate 'is an official close to the people, and flood and drought should be of as much concern to him as pain or sickness of his person' (Ku Shih-lien, an early Qing dynasty scholar and official, quoted in Ch'ao-ting Chi, 1936: 72). The ideal magistrate should make extensive visits to the countryside during the slack season: 'He should survey the topography of the region, ask about conditions of drainage, and investigate sluices and locks ... All these affect the conditions of the public treasury and the welfare of the people and must be carefully considered by the magistrate' (Ku Shih-lien, quoted in Ch'ao-ting Chi, 1936: 72).

(f) Famine relief. Famine relief in the Chinese empire included famine investigation, providing relief funds, supplying relief grain, controlling price, strengthening and rebuilding production (Will 1990).[3] Many of the measures to fight famine demonstrated subtle strategies by the state in providing relief to the poor and the capability of the state in using the market to combat famine problems. Many of the measures adopted anticipate the analysis of famine made by modern writers such as A. K. Sen. The 'detailed and formalised procedures for combating famine' were permitted by 'the sophistication, centralisation, and stability of the (Chinese) bureaucratic system' (Will, 1990: 4).

The local gentry had a prominent part in fighting famine and distributing relief. Collective action at the local level was 'to the advantage of both the bureaucrats and the holders of local power, headed by the great landowners and the gentry, that appropriate measures be taken to prevent the ruin of the economy and social disorder, and this was certainly a powerful factor for cohesion within the global power system' (Will, 1990: 5). Official famine prevention measures had been formulated as early as the Song period. Many of the recommended procedures – surveys of the disaster and its victims, the regular distribution of grain, public soup kitchens, and so forth – had been practised for centuries, albeit on a smaller scale, by the local notables and landlords in cooperation with the bureaucracy (Will, 1990: 74).

(g) Commodity price stabilisation. From early in Chinese history, the Chinese state was deeply interested in ways to stabilise the prices of basic commodities. From very early on, China's bureaucrats were aware of the dangers of speculation for the ordinary people's livelihood. This anticipates the modern interest in 'commodity price stabilisation'. As early as in the Warring States Period, Fan Li's price policy held that fluctuations in the price of grain should be kept within a certain range so that it could benefit both production and distribution. (Hu Jichuang, 1984: 17). Marco Polo described the provision of grain in the Yuan Dynasty (1271–1368). When the harvests were plentiful and the price of crops was cheap, 'the Great Khan accumulates vast quantities of corn and every kind of grain and stores them in huge granaries'. When some crops failed and there was a dearth of grain, he drew on these stocks: 'If the price is running at a bezant for a measure of wheat, ... he supplies four measures for the same sum. And he releases enough for all, ... and this he does throughout all parts of his empire' (Marco Polo, 1974: 157).

Will (1990) provides a meticulous account of the way in which in the Qing Dynasty in the eighteenth century the bureaucracy intervened in the rice market to protect the livelihood of the masses from price fluctuations and speculation. The government established a vast network of 'evernormal granaries' (*changpingcang*) across the country in order to stabilise grain prices. In addition to maintaining emergency reserves, the purpose of the *changpingcang* was 'to cushion the impact of seasonal price fluctuations by buying up grain immediately after the harvest, when prices were low, and reselling it at a low price during the lean period before the new harvest came in'. The 'evernormal granaries' spring sales and autumn purchases were supposed to even out prices by compensating for the weakness of the private sector or by competing with it when it tended to take advantage of and speculate on seasonal and/or regional price differentials (Will, 1990: 182). The sale of public grain became 'one of several strategies available to the State to combat a subsistence crisis' (Will, 1990: 186).

Conclusion. Even economists who have been powerful advocates of the dynamic power of the market in promoting economic development, have sometimes acknowledged the frequency with which market failure necessitates state intervention. The more subtle have distinguished between the different ways and levels of market failure in different countries, at different stages of development, and confronting different challenges in the international economy. Criticism of market failure needs also to be tempered by sharp awareness of the potentialities for state failure. There is nothing intrinsically good or bad about either the state or the market.

The Chinese state strongly encouraged the development of the traditional market economy. The state stepped in where markets failed, not only in respect to immediate growth issues, but also in relation to the wider issues of social stability and cohesion. It nurtured and stimulated commerce, but refused to allow commerce, financial interests and speculation to dominate society. Behind the edifice of authoritarian Imperial rule was a pervasive morality based on the necessity of all strata of society observing their duties in order to sustain social cohesion, to achieve social and political stability and to ensure social sustainability. When these functions were operating effectively, there was 'great harmony' (*da tong*), a prosperous economy and a stable society. When they were operating poorly, there was 'great turmoil' (*da luan*), economic retrogression and social disorder.

China's Rise

Since the 1980s, China's policies of experimental reform and opening-up ('groping for stones to cross the river') have produced a remarkable economic performance. The growing impact of market forces and integration with the global economy produced one of the most remarkable periods of growth the world has ever seen. The contrast with the period of Maoist planning was dramatic.

From 1990 to 2002, China's growth rate of GDP averaged 9.7 per cent per annum, compared with 3.4 per cent among low and middle-income countries and 2.5 per cent for high-income countries (World Bank, WDI, 2004). China rose from being the world's seventh largest producer of manufacturing output in 1990 to the third largest in 2005. Its exports grew at over 13 per cent per annum between 1990 and 2001. It rose from the world's 28th largest exporter in 1980 to the third largest in 2005. Global corporations view China as central to their long-term strategy. By 2002 it had overtaken the United States as the country with the largest FDI inflows (UNCTAD, 2003: Table B.1). Over the course of the past two decades, China's indigenous large enterprises have undertaken large-scale evolutionary institutional change. They have grown rapidly, absorbed modern technology, learned how to compete in the marketplace and a large group of them has floated on international stock markets. The number of Mainland Chinese firms in the *Fortune 500* increased from just three in the late 1990s to fourteen in 2004.

The explosion of market forces in China after the 1970s, alongside the progressive deepening of China's engagement with global capitalism, transformed people's lives. The share of urban dwellers in the total population rose from 17 per cent in 1975 to 38 per cent in 2002 (World Bank, WDI, 2004).[4] The nature of employment changed decisively away from farming: the number employed in the non-farm sector rose from 118 million (30 per cent) to 412 million (56 per cent) in the same period (SSB, ZTN, 2003: 128).[5] The World Bank estimates that the proportion of the rural population in poverty declined from 31 per cent in 1979 to 13 per cent in 1982, 'a speed and scale of poverty decline that is unprecedented in human history' (World Bank, 1986: 30). The proportion of the population with access to sustainable improved sanitation rose from 29 per cent in 1990 to 40 per cent in 2000 (World Bank, WDI, 2004). The infant mortality rate fell from 85 per thousand live births in 1970 to 31 in 2002, and life expectancy at birth rose from 63 years in 1970–75 to 71 in 2000–05. The rate of illiteracy fell from 23 per cent in 1982 to 7 per cent in 2000 (SSB, ZTN, 2003: 99). The number of mobile phone subscribers rose from a negligible level in 1990 to 161 per thousand in 2002 (World Bank, WDI, 2004), and the number of internet users increased from 20 million in 2000 to 110 million in 2005 (*FT*, 13 May 2006).

China's Globalisation Challenge

Alongside the immensely positive impacts, China's deep engagement with capitalist globalisation has been accompanied by surging contradictions. China's leadership is trying hard to identify and implement policies that tackle these problems.

Poverty and inequality. Behind almost every aspect of China's development process in the early twenty-first century lies the harsh reality of the 'Lewis model' of economic development with unlimited supplies of labour (Lewis, 1954). China has a huge population of almost 1.3 billion, almost 70 per cent of whom still live in the countryside.[6] The average per capita income of China's rural dwellers is only around US$ 0.87 (87 cents) per day (UNDP, 2005: 170).[7] China may well become the world's largest economy while it is still locked in the Lewis phase of development.

The great extent of rural underemployment and the low level of average income powerfully stimulate rural-urban migration, and provide severe downward pressure on non-farm wages in unskilled and low-skilled occupations. There are as many as 150 million rural migrants working in the urban areas. They are predominantly unskilled labour, earning US$ 1–2 per day. Around 300 million Chinese workers, a large fraction of whom are illegal 'immigrant' workers, are now employed in the non-farm 'informal' sector, without the protection of trade unions, mainly in small enterprises with little regulation over conditions of work, and without unemployment or health insurance. Furthermore, around 40–50 million workers have lost their jobs due to reform in state-owned enterprises. On the other hand, large amounts of FDI by multinational firms is helping to produce clusters of modern businesses and residential areas, in which the relatively affluent urban middle class is isolated and protected from the surrounding mass of poor people.

The national Gini Coefficient for income distribution rose from 0.28 in the early 1980s to 0.45 in 2001 (UNDP, 2005: 13). Official Chinese data for 2005 reported that the Gini coefficient for income distribution had risen still further to 0.496 (*FT*, 27 December 2006).[8] In 2002, the Gini Coefficient for the distribution of wealth reached 0.55, while that for the distribution of financial assets was 0.74 (UNDP, 2005: 37). In 2002, the top ten per cent of the Chinese population accounted for 32 per cent of national income, 41 per cent of total wealth and 48 per cent of financial assets (UNDP, 2005: 37).

The global business revolution. Since the 1980s, China has implemented industrial policies intended to nurture a group of globally competitive large indigenous firms. However, this period has witnessed a revolution in world business. It has seen a unique intensity of merger and acquisition. An unprecedented degree of global industrial concentration has been established. A veritable 'law' has come into play. Within the high value-added, high technology, and/or strongly branded market segments, a handful of giant firms, the 'systems integrators', occupy upwards of one half of the global market (Nolan, 2001a and 2001b, Nolan *et al.*, 2007a). The process of concentration cascades across the value chain. The leading firms in each sector select the most capable suppliers, in a form of 'industrial planning', adopting 'aligned partners' who can work with them across the world.

A 'cascade effect' has produced intense pressures upon first tier suppliers, forcing them to develop leading global positions, achieved through expanded research and development, and investment in global production networks. The result is a fast-developing process of concentration at a global level in numerous industries that supply the systems integrators.

This intense industrial concentration among both systems integrators and their supply chain, brought about through pressure from the cascade effect, presents a comprehensive challenge for Chinese firms. Not only do they face immense difficulties in catching up with the leading systems integrators, who occupy that part of the 'iceberg' that is visible 'above the water'. They also face immense difficulties in catching up with the powerful firms that now dominate almost every segment of the supply chain, the invisible part of the 'iceberg' that lies hidden from view. Successful late-comer industrialising countries, from the United States in the late nineteenth century to South Korea in the late twentieth century, each produced a group of globally competitive firms. China is the first successful latecomer not to have done so. The fact that the world's sixth largest economy (the second largest in PPP terms) (World Bank, WDI, 2004) has not produced a substantial group of internationally competitive large firms is highly significant in the history of modern capitalist development.

China's firms are mainly far from the forefront of global technology. More than one half of China's exports and around 90 per cent of its exports of electronic and information technology products are produced by foreign-owned factories (Bergsten, *et al.*, 2006: 105).[9] The key components in a wide range of electronic and information technology products manufactured in China are imported from the world's leading firms in the sector. China's imports of semiconductors rose from US$ 3 billion in 1995 to more than US$ 90 billion in 2005, when China's imports accounted for two-fifths of total global semiconductor output (Begsten, *et al.*, 2006: 107).

China's policy-makers recognise that the challenge facing the country's large firms on the 'global level playing' field is far greater than had been imagined prior to China joining the WTO. The policy-makers are intensely investigating ways in which to build powerful Chinese firms that can compete with the global giant firms in a range of strategic industries, including financial services, telecommunication services and equipment, oil and gas, metals and mining, power generation and equipment, and aerospace.[10] The move to investigate ways to build 'national champions' in the face of the intense competitive pressure of globalisation, led the National Development and Reform Commission (NDRC) to call for the establishment of a government body: 'It should rigorously examine major individual foreign acquisitions of state companies and assess the effect of foreign investment, in order to guard against all the kinds of hidden dangers that such investment brings' (NDRC official quoted in *Financial Times*, 4 August 2006). The NDRC said that 'the relevant departments should "strictly guard the pass" when industrial or national security is at stake' (quoted in *Financial Times*, 4 August 2006).

Energy and the environment. China's success in becoming the 'world's workshop'[11] has been achieved at a high price in terms of environmental deterioration. Fast-growing developing countries typically experience a phase of environmental deterioration until average income rises beyond a certain point, at which point the environment begins to improve.[12] China is likely to remain for many years firmly locked into the phase of environmental deterioration unless drastic action is taken by the Chinese state.

China's explosive economic growth has been accompanied by an 'ecological implosion' (Bergsten, *et al.*, 2006: 53). The area affected by serious soil erosion has increased to include around 38 per cent of the entire country (UNDP, 2002b: 70). The area of desert is increasing at the rate of around 2500 square kilometres per year, equivalent to the area of a medium-sized country. China's area of natural forests is falling at an alarming rate. There is 'rampant water pollution', and a serious and worsening shortage of fresh water. China's emission of organic water pollutants is as large as that of the United States, India, Russia and Japan combined (World Bank, 2004: Table 3.6). China contains sixteen of the world's twenty most polluted cities. Nearly 200 Chinese cities fall short of the WHO's standards for airborne particulates (Bergsten, *et al.*, 2006: 54). Four-fifths of the country's air pollution is accounted for by vehicle emissions. China's Vice-Minister of the State Environmental Protection Agency (SEPA) has stated that 'China's economic miracle is a myth', since environmental degradation is costing the country nearly 8 per cent of its annual GDP (quoted in Bergsten, *et al.*, 2006: 54).

The country's explosive industrial growth since the late 1980s, which has been deeply integrated into capitalist globalisation, has been highly 'commodity-intensive' and highly energy-intensive. In 2005, China accounted for around 4 per cent of global GDP, but it consumed 9 per cent of global crude oil, 20 per cent of aluminium, 30–35 per cent of steel, iron ore and coal, and 45 per cent of cement (*FT*, 23 May 2006). Between 1994 and 2004, China's total primary energy consumption increased by 71 per cent and its share of global primary energy consumption increased from 9.8 per cent to 13.6 per cent (BP, 2005).

The rapid growth of passenger vehicles and trucks has significantly contributed to China's accelerating demand for oil. The total number of vehicles is predicted to rise from 24 million in 2005 to 100 million in 2020 (Bergsten, *et al.*, 2006: 54). Between 1994 and 2004, China's oil consumption increased 113 per cent. However, China's oil reserves amount to only around 1.4 per cent of the world total (BP, 2005), and from 1994 to 2004 China's oil production grew by only 19 per cent. By 2004, China was importing 2.5 million barrels of oil per day, and the price of these imports has risen greatly since the mid-1990s. It is forecast that by 2020 China will be importing as much as three-quarters of its total oil consumption (USCESRC, 2003: 8).

National energy security is of central importance for China, and the pressure will intensify as the economy expands. This will increase the incentive to rely on coal as the main form of primary energy supply. China has large coal reserves, estimated to be around 13 per cent of the world total (BP, 2005). The relatively low cost of coal provides a strong incentive to continue to use coal as the main source of primary energy. It accounted for 69 per cent of China's primary energy consumption total in 2004 (BP, 2005). China plans to install nearly 600 new coal-fired power stations by 2012, around one half the world total, and to greatly increase the supply of oil from coal ('coal liquefaction'). By the mid-1990s, China had overtaken the United States as the world's biggest coal producer, accounting for almost 30 per cent of global output. China's high dependence on coal has enormous environmental implications, both for China and the world.

China's per capita consumption of primary energy is only around one-ninth of that in the United States: the United States today consumes around 8 metric tons (oil equivalent) of primary energy per person, compared with around 0.9 metric tons per person in China (World Bank, WDI, 2004: 140–2). By 2001, China was the world's second largest producer of carbon dioxide, standing at 50 per cent of the level of the United States, but its per capita emissions are still a mere 11 per cent of those of the United States (World Bank, WDI, 2004: Table 3.8). In 2007 the International Energy Agency estimated that in that year China would overtake the United States as the world's largest producer of carbon dioxide. This controversial statement caused great anger in China.

China's leaders fully appreciate the need to find a new path of economic development that is less energy-intensive and less polluting than that of the United States today. They need to do so for reasons of national energy security, as well as to protect China's domestic environment and to prevent international conflict over China's impact on the global environment. If China were to climb to the US current level of per capita consumption of primary energy, it would consume more even than the current total world consumption (10 000 million metric tons). If it were to catch up with today's level of per capita income in the United States, and were to use similar technologies, China's emissions of carbon dioxide would be one-fifth greater than those of the entire world today.

China's Eleventh Five Year Plan has called for the ambitious goal of improving the country's energy efficiency by 20 per cent by 2010. In part this will be achieved by technical progress in the world's leading firms that produce complex machines such as power stations, automobiles, and aeroplanes, as well as in the technologies of building construction. In part progress in energy efficiency will take place through greater use of taxation and the price mechanism, as well as through the country's advancing energy efficiency codes. The Chinese government has responded to the intensifying ecological degradation with numerous laws and regulations on resource protection and pollution control, including strict regulations to control emissions from vehicles. From 1 July 2006, all new vehicles will have to meet fuel economy standards that are stricter than those in the United States. New construction codes encourage the use of double-glazed windows to reduce air-conditioning and heating costs. The government is restricting the construction of small power plants, and encouraging the installation of large, modern power plants which use coal-heated steam at high temperatures and generate 20–50 per cent more kilowatts than older Chinese power plants. They are also encouraging the installation of power plants that use 'integrated gasification combined combustion' (IGCC) technologies, which produce more electricity per unit of coal, and allow the possibility of carbon dioxide being separated and pumped underground (carbon sequestration) for storage. Also, all existing coal-fired power plants are required to have sulphur filters on each smokestack by the year 2010.

However, there are still enormous environmental problems facing China. The State Environmental Protection Agency still has a relatively low standing, with just 300 employees, while for local government officials, the priority remains economic growth and employment creation. There is a strong incentive for profit-seeking power generation companies to choose cheaper indigenous power plants that have older technologies. The technology for advanced coal-fired power stations is mainly possessed by the leading international power station producers (GE, Siemens, Alstom and Mitsubishi) and are costly for operators to install. Sulphur filters on power stations are costly to install and costly to operate, putting pressure on operators' profit margins. In 2002, the government vowed to reduce sulphur emissions by 10 per cent. Instead, they rose by 27 per cent (Bradsher and Barboza, 2006). There has been no attempt to challenge the dominance of the automobile as the main form of transport for people and goods. Solutions to urban air pollution, which is increasingly caused by automobile traffic, are sought through technical improvements rather than in alternative transport systems (UNDP, 2002b: 60).

The capability and role of the state. China's outstanding economic performance since the 1980s is inseparable from the firm leadership and political stability provided by the Chinese Communist Party. However, the country's engagement with capitalist globalisation also poses deep challenges for the nature and function of the Chinese state.

China is a vast, poor country with urgent development needs, which can only be met by state action. Despite some increase in the government's fiscal strength in recent years, central government revenue still accounts for only around 7 per cent of GDP (World Bank, WDI, 2004: Table 4.11). The share of central government revenue in GDP is below that of other large developing countries, such as India, Mexico, Pakistan, and Indonesia, as well as Russia. Moreover, the state has given a low priority to welfare expenditure within the government budget. For example, the share of public expenditure allocated to education stands at only 3.2 per cent, compared with an international average of around 3.8 per cent (UNDP, 2005: 51).

There has been a large rise in the share of welfare expenditure from fees paid by private individuals. In 1980 more than 75 per cent of educational funding came from the government, but by 2000 this had fallen to just 54 per cent, which has had 'serious implications for social equity because it excludes many poor children' (UNDP, 2005: 52). Private spending on health care amounts to almost twice as much as public health care expenditure (Bergsten, *et al.*, 2006: 51). China ranks 61st out of 191 countries in overall quality of health, but it ranks 188th in terms of fairness in financial contribution to health expenditure (World Bank, 2002: iv). The country's medical insurance system covers less than half of the urban population and only one-tenth of the rural population (Bergsten, *et al.*, 2006: 52).[13]

The Chinese leadership has devoted great attention in recent years to the importance of establishing a 'harmonious society'. In 2006, the Eleventh Party Congress emphasised the importance of speeding up reforms to improve access to welfare services, especially in poor areas and among disadvantaged groups of the population. The Eleventh Five Year Plan pledged to raise the share of government spending allocated to education from 3 to 4 per cent. The government has promised to improve the provision of medical services for the rural dwellers, but 'so far very little has happened outside the urban areas' (Lindbeck, 2006: 43).

Under the planned economy, their work units guaranteed all Chinese citizens incomes in their old age, though the level of income guaranteed varied hugely depending on the nature and location of the place of work. This system is undergoing comprehensive transformation. China is still in the very early stages of establishing a pension system consistent with the emerging market economy. In 2002, only around 55 per cent of the urban workforce and 11 per cent of the rural workforce were covered by public pensions (Bergsten, *et al.*, 2006: 53). The problems of building an insurance system are hugely complicated by the dramatic changes taking place in China's demography. The one-child policy, introduced in the late 1980s, as well as the effects of urbanisation, produced a huge decline in fertility. Also, there has been a steady rise in longevity. It is projected that the share of the population over the age of 60 will rise from 11 per cent in 2005 to 28 per cent in 2040 (Bergsten, *et al.*, 2006: 47). Unlike the West, which became 'rich' before it became 'old', China is set to become the world's first major economy to become 'old' before it becomes 'rich' (Bergsten, *et al.*, 2006: 47).

The Communist Party leadership is the foundation of China's modernisation. The Party is deeply intertwined with every aspect of socio-economic life. In the late 1980s and early 1990s, Deng Xiaoping warned repeatedly of the dangers of China collapsing into chaos. In his 2001 speech to celebrate the 80th anniversary of the founding of the Chinese Communist Party, Jiang Zemin stated:

> [The Party] must address the two major historic subjects of enhancing the Party's ability of exercising state power and art of leadership, and resisting corruption and warding off risks ... [W]e must be strict in Party discipline. We should have a deeper understanding of the loss of political power by some Communist Parties in the world that had long been ruling parties and learn a lesson from them.

There has been widespread insider dealing and corruption during China's economic system restructuring, notably in the ubiquitous triangular relationship between the local Communist Party, the banks and the 'development' of publicly owned land, as well as in the process of privatising state-owned enterprises. In the view of some Western experts corruption has 'increased dramatically' (Bergsten, *et al.*, 2006: 43). The level at which Party members were sentenced for corruption has risen to include many in high positions.[14] An official report to the National People's Congress in 2005 declared that in 2004, 2960 officials at or above county level had been investigated for corruption. Eleven of these were at the provincial or ministerial level. In 2004 also, the Party's Central Discipline Inspection Commission punished 170 850 Party members for corruption-related crimes, including sixteen provincial-level officials (Bergsten, *et al.*, 2006: 44). In 2005, the CCP launched a rectification campaign to address the problem of 'moral degeneration' among its members (Bergsten, *et al.*, 2006: 44).

Corruption is not unique to China today. India's multi-party democracy has been plagued with corruption. In China itself in the 1930s, the Kuomintang (KMT) regime was enormously corrupt, with deep inter-weaving of politics and business, and concentration of power in the hands of a tiny clique of inter-related families. However, from 1927 to 1936 the economy grew quite rapidly under KMT rule. The regime's downfall was precipitated by the Japanese invasion and the opportunities this provided to the CCP, rather than by the contradictions of capitalist development. Despite intense class struggle and high levels of corruption in the early phase of capitalist development in the nineteenth century, none of today's high-income countries experienced a political revolution. Instead, they all experienced political evolution. Capitalist development led to the gradual unfolding of citizens' opportunities and consciousness, and to the steady advance in their assertion of their rights, rather than to a violent political revolution.

Financial institutions. Engagement with the international financial system is, arguably, the most sensitive and difficult aspect of China's involvement with global capitalism. The Asian Financial Crisis provided a deep insight into the fragility of China's financial institutions. China appeared to escape any effects of the crisis, due to the fact that the *renminbi* was not fully convertible. In fact, the crisis had a deep impact through the medium of Hong Kong and the massive debts accumulated there by Mainland 'trust and investment' and 'red chip' companies, and other Mainland-based entities operating in Hong Kong (Nolan and Wang, 2007b and Nolan, 2008). The most visible of these were GITIC (Guangdong Trust and Investment Company) and GDE (Guangdong Enterprises) which included five floated 'red chip' companies. During the Asian Financial Crisis, GITIC went into bankruptcy while GDE was insolvent and comprehensively restructured. Prior to the crisis, they each had been regarded as model institutions by international lenders. GITIC's bankruptcy and GDE's restructuring allowed the outside world to look closely inside large Chinese companies for the first time. The investigations revealed comprehensive failure in corporate governance, including disastrous lending practices: a large fraction of their loans were made to firms and institutions that were unable or unwilling to repay their debts. A substantial part of their 'investments' were highly speculative, including heavy participation in the property boom in Guangdong Province and Hong Kong.

After the Asian Financial Crisis, the central government began a massive 'clean up' of the country's financial institutions. The clean up revealed shocking evidence about the state of corporate governance in China's main banks. In early 2002, it was revealed that five bank officials at the Bank of China's branch in Kaiping city (Guangdong) had stolen the equivalent of nearly US$ 500 million.[15] The problems penetrated to the apex of the country's banking system. Zhu Xiaohua, who held top positions in China's financial sector, including deputy governor of the People's Bank of China, head of China's foreign exchange reserves and head of China Everbright Bank, was arrested in 1999, and subsequently sentenced to fifteen years imprisonment. Wang Xuebing, formerly head of the China Construction Bank and then of the Bank of China, was arrested in 2002 and subsequently sentenced to twelve years imprisonment.[16]

China's financial firms face escalating international competition under the terms of the WTO Agreement. Since the 1980s the world's leading financial firms have been through a period of unprecedented merger and acquisition. The period saw the emergence of super-large financial services firms, such as Citigroup, JPMorgan Chase, Bank of America and HSBC. They have rapidly acquired dominant positions in Latin America and Eastern Europe. After its acquisition of Banamex, one of Mexico's largest banks, Citigroup proclaimed: 'China is top of our radar screen' (Nolan, 2004a: 57).

Since the late 1990s, the Chinese government has made immense efforts to restructure the country's largest banks, each of which is a state-owned enterprise. Beginning in 1999, specially created asset-management companies (AMCs) relieved the four big banks of an estimated US$ 328 billion in non-performing loans. The government has made intense efforts to improve the level of corporate governance and to upgrade the technical capabilities of the banks, including their capabilities to evaluate risk and their information technology systems. They have sold minority shares of their equity to leading international banks, hoping that this will further help to raise their competitive capabilities.[17] Following reconstruction of their internal operations, the leading state-owned Chinese banks have strong balance sheets. They are floating a minority share of their equity on the Hong Kong stock market. The IPOs of China Construction Bank (October 2005) and Bank of China (June 2006) raised US$ 9.2 billion and US$ 9.73 billion respectively. The flotation of the Industrial and Commercial Bank of China in late 2006 raised over US$ 21 billion, a global record for an IPO.

Despite progress in restructuring their internal operations, large difficulties remain. China's financial institutions suffer from 'endless corruption' (Bergsten, *et al.*, 2006: 25). The party's Central Disciplinary Inspection Commission punished over 1600 employees in the first half of 2005 alone for fraud and other related crimes. Of these, 570 managers and branch heads were imprisoned or fired (Bergsten, *et al.*, 2006: 44). They have 'made only limited progress towards operating on a commercial basis', while having 'high cost structures and limited risk assessment skills' (Bergsten, *et al.*, 2006: 25). Intense debate surrounds the level of non-performing loans in the Chinese financial system. Many analysts have drawn attention to the fact that there is still extensive Party intervention in the loan allocation process. Many outside analysts believe that new non-performing loans may have replaced the old ones on a large scale during the explosive growth of credit in the past few years.[18]

2.1.2 The United States

Capitalist globalisation has stimulated America's economic progress, but also produced deep internal policy challenges for the United States. These challenges are increasingly perceived within the United States as being linked with China's rise, rather than intrinsic to the contradictions of capitalist globalisation.

America's Dominance of Globalisation

The United States sits at the centre of capitalist globalisation. Despite China's rise, the United States still accounts for over 26 per cent of global manufacturing output (excluding production in overseas subsidiaries of firms headquartered in America) compared with around 6 per cent for China and at current rates of growth China will not overtake the US manufacturing output until some time between 2020 and 2025 (World Bank, WDI, 2004, Section 4). The United States is by far the world's most powerful stock market. Its share of the total value of global stock markets rose from 33 per cent in 1990 to 47 per cent in 2003 (World Bank, WDI, 2004: 268). In 2004, firms headquartered in North America accounted for 175 of the *Fortune 500* companies (ranked by sales revenue) (*Fortune*, 26 July 2004). In the same year there were 247 North American firms in the *FT 500* companies (ranked by market capitalisation), accounting for 55 per cent of the total market capitalisation of *FT 500* firms (*FT*, 27 May 2004). The vast bulk of global technical progress takes place in a relatively small number of giant firms. Among these firms, those from North America are dominant. In 2005, out of the world's top 1000 firms ranked by R&D expenditure, 440 were headquartered in North America (DTI, 2005). The so-called 'BRIC' countries (Brazil, Russia, India and China), with a combined population of 2.7 billion (43 per cent of the world's total) between them had a mere nine firms among the world's top 1000 firms ranked by R&D expenditure.[19]

The De-Stabilising Impact of Capitalist Globalisation Upon the United States

Social contradictions. The central drive of American foreign policy in the epoch of globalisation has been opening the global economy to free trade and free movement of capital:

> Promoting free and fair trade has long been a bedrock of American foreign policy ... History has judged the market economy as the single most effective system and the greatest antidote to poverty. To expand economic liberty and prosperity, the United States promotes free and fair trade, open markets, a stable financial system, the integration of the global economy, and secure, clean energy development (Bush, 2006: 25).

Since the 1970s, this is exactly the system that has been established under US leadership, namely capitalist globalisation. There is an old saying: 'Be careful lest your wish is granted'. The United States' wish for a global free market has been substantially granted. However, the contradictions are far deeper than US policy-makers could ever have imagined.

The integration of global markets has had profoundly contradictory results for American people. The liberalisation of capital markets since the 1980s has opened up a vast world of low-priced labour across the 'transition' and 'developing' countries, including skilled and unskilled manual labour as well as scientists, engineers and managers. China is the largest single source of this greatly expanded labour supply to global markets. In the 'BRIC' countries alone, economic liberalisation since the 1980s has added around 1.7 billion people of working age to the international labour market. This is nearly three times the size of the labour force in the high-income economies.[20] China alone has a labour force of around 880 million, compared with 647 million in the high-income countries as a whole (World Bank, WDI, 2004: 38–40). In 2002, the average per capita gross national product in low and middle-income countries was US$ 1170 (4030 in PPP dollars), compared with US$ 26 490 (28 480 in PPP dollars) in the high-income countries (World Bank, WDI, 2004: 14–6). Previously, the labour markets of most low and middle-income countries were, to a significant degree, isolated from international markets by the operation of 'planned economies' or the protectionist, 'inward-looking' strategies of the developing countries in which most poor people lived. The levels of foreign trade and foreign investment before the 1980s were much lower then than they are today.

Global labour markets are being integrated to some degree directly through some increase in international migration, but this remains only a small part of the integrative mechanism, since high-income countries retain tight controls over immigration. Rather, the process of integration has taken place indirectly, through the migration of capital to poor countries and through the export of goods and services from poor to rich countries. This places intense pressure for international equalisation of wages and conditions of work. These pressures add greatly to the impact of technological change, which has replaced a wide swathe of white-collar office jobs that demanded modest skills, while demand for unskilled jobs in the service sector, such as restaurants, retail and domestic help, has surged. It is now increasingly being recognised in the United States that the 'law of one price' operates in fully integrated markets. In this case, the 'market' is the global labour market:

> As China, India and the states of the former Soviet Union have commenced active participation in the global economy in the past ten to twenty years, the global market's workforce has doubled, placing major downward pressure on wages around the world. This is a function of what has been termed the 'law of one price', when capital is relatively unencumbered and the factors of production are mobile, capital will gravitate to regions with the highest rate of return. This has been occurring and continues to occur in China and elsewhere, and it is resulting in the movement of jobs, especially manufacturing jobs but increasingly service jobs as well, from the United States to China and to other countries offering higher returns on capital (USCESRC, 2005: 3).

One recent analysis (Blinder, 2006) has concluded that a wide range of occupations is susceptible to being outsourced from the United States to developing countries. The first round of vulnerable occupations are those in American manufacturing: 'The vast majority of [American] manufacturing workers produced items that could be put in a box, and so virtually all of their jobs were potentially movable offshore' (Blinder, 2006: 120). It emphasises that the information technology revolution means that a much wider range of occupations is capable of being outsourced than most people imagine, including a wide range of service sector activities: 'Eventually, the number of service sector jobs that will be vulnerable to competition from abroad will likely exceed the total number of manufacturing jobs' (Blinder, 2006: 119). It concludes that the only occupations that will be untouched by this revolution in the global labour market will be 'personal services', as opposed to 'impersonal services' that can be 'delivered by wire'.

The study also emphasises that the threat to US occupational security exists at every level of skill and education. This process will have enormous political implications: 'As the transition unfolds, the number of people in the rich countries who will feel threatened by foreign job competition will grow enormously. It is predictable that they will become a potent political force in each of their countries' (Blinder, 2006: 127). Up until now, in the United States, job-market stress has been particularly acute for the uneducated and the unskilled. However, 'the new cadres of displaced workers, especially those who are drawn from the upper educational reaches, will be neither as passive nor as quiet. They will also be numerous' (Blinder, 2006: 127).

American workers are being forced to work longer hours, accept reduced rates of overtime pay, and accept reduced company contributions to health insurance and pensions. There are now 45 million Americans without health coverage, many of whom are full-time workers. During the epoch of capitalist globalisation, US income disparity has greatly increased. The income share of the top decile of the US population was stable at around 32–33 per cent from the 1960s to early 1980s, but thereafter it rose to around 43–44 per cent in 2000–02, which was the same income share that they received in the 1920s and 1930s. The share of the top one per cent of the distribution rose from less than 8 per cent in the late 1960s and 1970s to around 15–17 per cent at the end of the 1990s (Piketty and Saez, 2006). Between 2000 and 2006, the median US household income fell by 3 per cent while the share of corporate profits in GDP rose from 7 per cent to 12.2 per cent (*FT*, 10 June 2006).

Alongside the growing inequality in income, America's social mobility is lower than in every other developed country except for the United Kingdom.[21] America performs poorly in terms of key indicators of social well-being. For example, a survey of thirty-three industrialised nations by Save the Children found that their death rate among babies was the highest among the countries surveyed. Only Latvia had a higher rate (*FT*, 6 May 2006).[22] The report attributes America's poor performance to lack of national health insurance and short maternity leave for mothers.

There is widespread public angst across the whole political spectrum about the growth of inequality within the United States, and its relationship to globalisation. Rob Shapiro, Head of the New Democratic Network's Globalisation Initiative, a centrist advocacy group, said: 'The ripple effect caused by the supply shock of the entry of hundreds of millions of Chinese workers into the global economy has changed the way American workers benefit from trade' (quoted in *Financial Times*, 25 July 2006). Harvard President Larry Summers believes that 'the most serious problem facing the United States today is the widening gap between the children of the rich and the children of the poor' (quoted in *New York Times*, 24 May 2005). Alan Greenspan warned of the dangers of current trends in the distribution of income in the United States: 'For the democratic society, that is not a very desirable thing to allow to happen' (quoted in *New York Times*, 5 June, 2005). The newly appointed chairman of the Federal Reserve, Ben Bernanke, said: 'We want everybody to participate in the American dream. We want everyone to have a chance to get ahead. And to the extent that incomes and wealth are spreading apart, I think that is not a good trend' (quoted in *Financial Times*, 25 July 2006).

As consumers, up until this point American people have benefited enormously from globalisation, with an unprecedented fall in the price of most goods and services. An important part of this fall has been due to the declining price of China's exports. However, as producers, they have faced greatly increased pressures. Ordinary Americans increasingly believe that the interests of nominally US-based multinational corporations and their shareholders are divorced from the interests of American citizens. 'One clear danger is that people will increasingly cast round for scapegoats' (Edward Luce in the *Financial Times*, 3 May 2006). Also, the consequences of the global asset and commodity price bubble, and their potential explosive unwinding, may have damaging effects on the welfare of the mass of US citizens in the near future.

Energy and the environment. The United States is by far the world's largest consumer of primary energy. Between 1990 and 2001 its consumption of primary energy rose by over 18 per cent, and by 2001 its share of the world total had increased to 22.8 per cent (World Bank, WDI, 2004: 142).[23] The United States' oil production fell from 8.4 million barrels per day in 1990 to 7.2 million in 2004, while its oil consumption rose from 17.7 million barrels per day to 20.5 million barrels in the same period (BP, 2005). Net oil imports rose from 45 per cent of total consumption in 1994 to 58 per cent in 2004 (BP, 2005). Oil accounts for over two-fifths of total American primary energy consumption, and it is critically important for the country's transportation system. In President George W. Bush's words, America is 'addicted to oil'. Energy security has become a more important issue than ever in US foreign policy.

The freedom of American citizens to own motor vehicles either for private use or for commercial transport is at the root of the country's 'addiction to oil'. In 2003 the United States had 808 motor vehicles per 1000 people, compared with 570 in Europe (EU), 69 in middle-income countries, just fifteen in China and eight in low-income countries as a whole (World Bank, WDI, 2005: 176). The average level of fuel economy of American motor vehicles increased between 1975 and 1985, in the wake of the first oil embargo, under the combined effect of higher prices and higher government standards for fuel efficiency. However, since then, the fuel economy of American vehicles has actually fallen, due to the proliferation of larger minivans and SUVs, declining from around 30 miles per gallon for new vehicles in 1985 to 29 miles per gallon in 2006 (*FT*, 6 July 2006). In June 2006, American petrol prices remained at only 60 cents per litre, compared with

US$ 1.60–1.70 in the EU (*FT*, 6 July 2006). Transport accounts for around two-thirds of the oil consumed by the United States. It is more accurate to describe America as 'addicted to the automobile' than addicted to oil *per se*.

Over the first six years of his administration, President George W. Bush persistently denounced fuel economy standards as 'a drain on the US economy and a threat to the safety of American drivers' (*FT*, 6 July 2006). The Bush administration increased the resources allocated to alternative fuels and more efficient fuel use technologies, but failed to introduce any measures that might significantly reduce energy consumption in the short-term: 'The Bush administration very much reflects the free market ideology on fuel, which is that the government does not have much to add to the market ... The problems are looming, but the solution the Bush administration proposes is largely in research that will take decades to pay off, if at all' (Bill Prindle, American Council for Energy Efficiency, quoted in *Financial Times*, 6 July 2006). The centrality of oil in US politics is reflected in the fact that President Bush's own family is deeply involved in the energy industry, Vice-President Dick Cheney was CEO of Halliburton, the world's largest oilfield services company, and Secretary of State Condoleezza Rice is a former member of the Board of Chevron, the world's fourth largest oil company.

The United States is deeply locked in to a growth pattern that uses fossil fuels as the main source of primary energy. Between 1990 and 2000, it accounted for 46 per cent of the total global increase in carbon dioxide emissions, and in 2000 it accounted for 24 per cent of total world carbon dioxide emissions (World Bank, WDI, 2004: 146–7). The United States' per capita emissions of carbon dioxide are twenty-two times the average level of those in low-income countries, and nine times those of China (World Bank, WDI, 2004: 146). The United States was unprepared to join the Kyoto Protocol without matching action being taken by the world's poorest countries.[24] This provides an ominous signal for the possibility of the world achieving the collective solutions necessary for global survival under US leadership in the decades ahead. However, in 2006–07 attitudes shifted rapidly among the US public and business leaders. Several individual states announced their own plans to limit carbon dioxide emissions. In late May 2007, President Bush astonished the world, by announcing that he had been persuaded by new scientific evidence on global warming, which had deepened his understanding of climate change (*FT*, 1 June 2007). He pledged to establish 'a new framework on greenhouse gases, when the Kyoto Protocol expires in 2012', and accepted the need for 'a long-term global goal for reducing greenhouse gases'. However, it remained unclear how the United States itself would seek to limit greenhouse gas emissions within its own borders and how its attitudes towards other countries' emissions might change.

Financial contradictions. The vast and growing size of the US fiscal and current account deficits, international borrowing and level of personal debt, stand at the heart of the unfolding global financial fragility. The United States and China present mirror images of each other. China has become a 'supply engine' of the global economy, while the United States has become the world's 'demand engine'. Each is growing in a deeply unbalanced fashion (Roach, 2005).

A large fraction of the demand stimulus for Chinese growth has come from exports, which grew from less than 10 per cent of GDP in the early 1980s to around 36 per cent in 2004. Its export growth has been critically important in sucking low-skilled workers into non-farm employment, which has made a large contribution to poverty reduction. After decades of high levels of welfare security under the planned economy, the transition to the market economy has produced high levels of personal insecurity. In addition, the fact that the distribution of income has become markedly more unequal has helped to stimulate a high rate of savings in China. The share of consumption in China's GDP fell from around 53–54 per cent in the early 1980s to 42 per cent in 2004, while the share of fixed asset investment in GDP climbed from around 30 per cent in the early 1980s, already a high level, to around 45 per cent in 2004 (Roach, 2005).[25]

In the United States, on the other hand, the share of consumption has risen from around 65 per cent in the early 1980s to 71 per cent in 2004 (Roach, 2005). The United States accounts for only around 5 per cent of global population, but it accounts for no less than 35–40 per cent of global consumption. Despite having over 20 per cent of the world's total population, China accounts for less than one per cent of global consumption. The United States is 'addicted to shopping', while China is 'addicted to saving' (Roach, 2005). By 2004, the US population's savings rate stood at minus one per cent, compared with 35 per cent in China (Roach, 2005).

China's high-speed export growth, increasing from 0.7 per cent of world exports in 1978 to 7.7 per cent in 2005, has made an important contribution to the stability of consumer prices in high-income countries, not least in the United States.[26] However, China's rise as a global manufacturing centre has played an important role in the explosive growth of global commodity prices.[27] China's share of global manufacturing output rose from 2.6 per cent in 1990 to 6.4 per cent in 2000, accounting for 19 per cent of the total global increase in manufactured output (World Bank, WDI, 2004). Between 2000 and 2005, China accounted for 33 per cent of the increase in global oil consumption,[28] 54 per cent of the increase in copper consumption, and 73 per cent of the increase in coal consumption, and 90 per cent of the increase in internationally traded iron ore (BP, 2006, and *FT*, 10 April 2006). Speculators have also played an important role in the commodity price boom, following the principle of 'momentum trading'.[29] Also, a critical factor in the global oil price boom has been the impact of US foreign policy failure, including the invasion of Iraq, and its de-stabilising effect on the whole regime; US pressure to achieve regime change in Iran; socio-economic instability in Saudi Arabia, for long the stalwart recipient of US support; the failure of 'regime change' in Afghanistan to stabilise that country; and hostility to the United States from the anti-American governments in Venezuela and Bolivia, leading oil producers in Latin America.

By 2006, the commodity price bubble was beginning to have an important impact on consumer price inflation in the high-income countries. This took place, firstly, through the rising price of oil, gas and coal, which feeds through into the consumer price index via the price of household heating bills and transport. It feeds through indirectly through the impact on transport and commercial energy costs in high-income countries, and through the cost of raw materials such as iron ore, bauxite and oil, which in turn affect the price of metals and plastics. These in turn feed through into the price of a wide range of consumer goods. The commodity price bubble feeds through also via the impact on Chinese producers' costs, which in turn affects the price of China's exports. From 2005 onwards, the price of China's exports began to rise, to a considerable degree due to the impact of higher input costs.

The level of household debt in the Unites States has risen remorselessly, from 60 per cent of household income in the mid-1980s to over 120 per cent in 2004 (*FT*, 16 February 2005). This has been made possible by the low level of US interest rates, which have in their turn been made possible by the willingness of central banks of East Asia and the Islamic oil-exporting countries, to buy US Government debt. China has used a large share of its rapidly rising foreign exchange reserves to purchase US Government debt. The increase in household debt has been stimulated also by the bubble in the US housing market, which has greatly increased household wealth. If house prices ceased to rise, or, even worse, if the house price bubble burst, there would be a large effect on US household balance sheets. Growth of the United States domestic and international imbalances cannot expand indefinitely. In 2004, Alan Greenspan warned:

> Net claims against residents of the United States cannot continue to increase for ever at their recent pace ... Continued financing of today's current account deficits as a percentage of GDP will, at some future point, increase shares of dollar claims in investor portfolios to levels that imply an unacceptable amount of concentration of risk. International investors will eventually adjust their accumulation of dollar assets, or, alternatively, seek higher dollar returns to offset concentration of risk' (quoted in *Financial Times*, 20 November 2004).

The necessary adjustments may occur smoothly. However, it is *'quite likely that the ultimate adjustment will be both swift and brutal'* (Martin Wolf, *Financial Times*, 8 October 2005) (My emphasis: PN).

If the dollar was 'dumped', the consequences would be a sharp rise in US interest rates, a major US recession, and a surge in American protectionist sentiment (Wolf, 2005a). Current asset price bubbles, including that in the housing market, are largely sustained by low interest rates, so that the impact of such a crisis would flow through the entire political economy of the United States and that of the whole world. The Asian Financial Crisis demonstrated that the 'fire' of a financial crisis moves at high speed, and swiftly shifts into the economic, social and political sphere. This time, the setting would be truly global. Deep international integration has brought many benefits. It also means that it is harder for any part of the global political economy to avoid the destructive effects of a global financial crisis.

2.1.3 Resolving the Contradictions: Conflict or Cooperation?

The United States and China will be by far the most important actors in the global political economy in the first decades of this century. The prospect for global sustainable development hinges around the relationship between these two mighty forces. Despite their respective immense strengths, each of them has its own internal contradictions, brought about by the impact of capitalist globalisation on the two economies and societies, one aspect of which is their deepening mutual economic integration. Their growing interaction may end in terrifying conflict. However, the prospect, literally, of the end of the world, may encourage the evolution of a cooperative relationship based on enlightened self-interest, which attempts to resolve through collective action the immanent contradictions of capitalist globalisation, in respect both to their internal development, to their mutual relationship and their joint role in international political-economy.

2.1.4 Conflict?

American Hegemony

The core of the US political establishment recognises unashamedly the fact that America has established global hegemony, albeit that it needs to exercise this hegemony through the 'careful, selective, and very careful deployment of [its] huge resources' (Brzezinski, 1997: 35). 'Eurasia, which contains three-quarters of the world's energy reserves is critically important in the "Grand Chessboard" of American foreign policy' (Brzezinski, 1997: 31).

There is a deep belief that American global hegemony serves the interests of both America and the world:

> A world without US primacy will be a world with more violence and disorder and less democracy and economic growth than a world where the United States continues to have more influence than any other country in shaping global affairs. The sustained international primacy of the United States is central to the welfare and security of Americans and to the future of freedom, democracy, open economies, and international order in the world (Huntington, 1993).

In the early 1990s, following the collapse of communist rule in the USSR and Eastern Europe, and the Tiananmen events of 1989, the US leadership turned its attention towards assessing America's long-term international relations strategy under the radically changed international situation. The first important statement of America's strategic readjustment was contained in the Defense Planning Guidance (DPG) document for 1994–99. The DPG was prepared secretly in the Department of Defense by the Under Secretary of Defense, Paul Wolfowitz, at the instruction of Defense Secretary, Dick Cheney. The DPG was leaked to the press in March 1992. It clearly enunciated the plan for the United States to maintain permanent US global military superiority and world dominance: 'Our first objective is to prevent the re-emergence of a new rival, either on the territory of the former Soviet Union or elsewhere, that poses a threat of the order of that posed formerly by the Soviet Union ... [This task requires] that we endeavour to prevent any hostile power from dominating a region whose resources would, under consolidated control, be sufficient to generate global power' (quoted in Klare, 2004: 68). The leaked document provoked a 'howl of criticism both in Congress and around the world', and the language in the final version was toned down to exclude an explicit call for US dominance. When George W. Bush came to power in February 2001, the principle of overarching US global dominance enunciated in the original DPG became the cornerstone of US foreign policy.

Despite the overthrow of communism in the USSR and Eastern Europe, and the rise of a market economy in China, the United States still feels deeply insecure. Its feelings of vulnerability were increased greatly by 9/11. It seeks to reduce its vulnerability through military and other forms of spending to protect its territory from attack, as well as by trying to nurture a world in which American values dominate. American foreign policy is deeply ideological, explicitly intended to support the construction of a world in which its own values, as well as its economic and political system are the model for all other countries to follow. The equation of [America's] national interests with the liberation of mankind and of its antagonists with hostility to freedom is not something new. From the earliest days of American territorial expansion, it has 'infused the rhetoric of American statecraft to the present day, often to the bemusement and annoyance of other nations' (Foner, 1998: 78).[30]

Following the collapse of communism in Russia and Eastern Europe, the United States felt itself to be leading the world towards a period of unprecedented economic and social progress. In her hugely influential *Foreign Affairs* article in 2000, Condoleezza Rice set out the foreign policy position that guided both Bush administrations thereafter.

Condoleezza Rice observed triumphantly: 'The process of outlining a new foreign policy must begin by recognising that the United States is in a remarkable position. Powerful secular trends are moving the world toward economic openness and – more unevenly – democracy and economic progress. Some hold on to old hatreds as diversions from the modernising task at hand. But the United States and its allies are on the right side of history' (Rice, 2000). Rice proclaimed that the United States was leading the world towards global free markets, and toward the enhanced human rights and personal freedom that would flow from them. American values were asserted emphatically to be universal:

> American values are universal ... The global economy demands economic liberalisation, greater openness and transparency, and, at the very least, access to information technology. International economic policies that leverage the advantages of the American economy and expand free trade are the decisive tools in shaping international politics ... The growth of entrepreneurial classes throughout the world is an asset in the promotion of human rights and individual liberty, and it should be understood and used as such (Rice, 2000).

At the time of the original DPG document, there was an array of possible rivals for the United States to consider as future superpowers. By the end of the decade the possible superpower rivals had been reduced to one, namely China.

In her article in 2000, Condoleezza Rice argued: 'Trade and economic interaction are, in fact, good, not only for America's economic growth but for its political aims as well ... Trade in general can open up the Chinese economy and, ultimately, its politics too. This view requires faith in the power of markets and economic freedom to drive political change, but it is a faith confirmed by experiences around the globe' (Rice, 2000). However, Rice warns that even if there is a case for supporting China's deeper international economic integration, 'China is still a potential threat to stability in the Asia-Pacific region': 'China is a great power with unresolved vital interests, particularly concerning Taiwan. China resents the role of the United States in the Asia-Pacific Region. This means that China is not a status quo power but one that would like to alter Asia's balance of power in its own favour. That alone makes it a strategic competitor, not the "strategic partner" the Clinton administration once called it' (Rice, 2000).

Rice argued that US policy towards China 'requires nuance and balance'. In Rice's view, the United States should 'promote China's internal transition through economic integration', while 'containing Chinese power and security ambitions': 'Cooperation should be pursued, but we should never be afraid to confront Beijing when our interests collide'. The US policy of 'containment' of China was clear: 'The United States must deepen its cooperation with Japan and South Korea and maintain its commitment to a robust military presence in the region. It should play closer attention to India's role in the regional balance ... The United States has a deep interest in the security of Taiwan ... If the United States is resolute, peace can be maintained in the Taiwan Strait until a political settlement on democratic terms is reached' (Rice, 2000). The paper makes no mention of the role of Hong Kong, but after the return of Hong Kong to Mainland rule, it clearly remained a focal point for US attempts to 'contain' China.

America's response to globalisation in general, and the rise of China in particular, has been deeply ambivalent. US politicians for the most part are parochial in their concerns. Few of the representatives in Capitol Hill have spent a lot of time travelling outside the country.[31] Their interests are focused on their constituents. Former House Speaker Tip O'Neill's maxim was that 'all politics is local' (quoted in *Financial Times*, 7 June 2006). It must be assumed that the politicians on Capitol Hill have a good understanding of the views of their voters, since this is vital to staying in power. The preoccupations of US voters also are strongly parochial. Indeed, two-thirds of Americans do not have passports.

The mainstream view on Capitol Hill is fearful of China's rise.[32] The US-China Economic and Security Review Commission (USCESRC) was set up in October 2000 by the US Congress specifically to investigate the implications for the United States of China's growth.[33] The Commission's mandate is to 'monitor and investigate and report to Congress on the national security implications of the bilateral trade and economic relationship between the United States and the People's Republic of China' (USCESRC, 2005: iii). The Commissioners are all appointed by Congress. The Commission has produced a succession of reports, each of which expresses deep apprehensions about the implications of China's economic growth for the United States, including the impact on US employment and conditions of work, and upon the United States' technological and military superiority. At one of its hearings, Vice-Chairman C. Richard D'Amato[34] commented: 'If you can figure out how to integrate a Chinese communist dictatorship with over a billion people who go where they're told to go; who work in the industry they're told to work [in]; who get paid what they're told they're worth; who have no way to answer back, if you can figure out how to integrate that into the world economy, please let me know' (USCESRC, 2004: 9).

America's Need for Enemies

Samuel Huntington has done more than anyone to shape the American establishment's view of international relations, notably through his book *The clash of civilisations* (Huntington, 1996). Huntington's latest book *Who are we?* (2004) identifies the choices that he considers the United States faces today.

Huntington believes that the Unites States faces serious threats to its national identity and unity from various directions. These include the rise in domestic social inequality, the rapid expansion of 'Hispanisation' of American culture, and the 'globalisation' of the American elite. Historically, the existence of an external enemy has played a central role in helping to create American national unity out of a people who came to the country from all over the world. America's sense of national unity was undermined by the collapse of the 'evil empire' of the former USSR: 'The absence of a significant external threat reduced the need for a strong national government and a coherent, unified nation' (Huntington, 2004: 265). Much of American foreign policy debate since then has involved identifying the new 'enemy': 'The ideal enemy for America would be ideologically hostile, racially and culturally different, and militarily strong enough to pose a credible threat to American security' (Huntington, 2004: 266).

For Huntington, there are two possible enemies who might fulfil this role, namely the 'Muslim' world and China: '[China is] still communist in theory if not in economic practice, clearly a dictatorship with no respect for political liberty, democracy, or human rights, with a dynamic economy, an increasingly nationalistic public, a strong sense of cultural superiority, and among its military and some other elite groups, a clear perception of the United States as their enemy.' (Huntington, 2004: 267).

There is a powerful set of interests in the United States that believes serious conflict with China is unavoidable. In the early days of the George W. Bush administration, Joseph Cirincione, of the Carnegie Endowment, warned: 'There are many people in this [Bush junior] administration who think that a war with China is likely, perhaps even inevitable in the next twenty or thirty years.

[They think] China will challenge us [and] we'd better be ready for it' (quoted in *Financial Times*, 20 August 2001). Henry Kissinger warned: the hawks see China 'as a morally flawed inevitable adversary' and believe that the United States should act 'not as a strategic partner, but as it treated the Soviet Union during the cold war, as a rival and a challenge' (quoted in Nolan, 2004a: 38). General Brent Scowcroft, former security advisor to two republican administrations (Gerald Ford and George Bush senior), commented: 'If there is a real division within this [Bush junior] administration, it is probably on China. There is a division between those who see China as inexorably developing into the primary security threat to the United States, and those who feel China is transforming rapidly but ... that it has been overwhelmingly positive' (quoted in *Financial Times*, 20 August 2001). These divisions persisted throughout the first and second Bush administrations.

Energy Contest with China

As we have seen, the United States is becoming progressively more dependent on imported oil, and 'energy security' has risen to the top of the political agenda. China's own search for secure sources of international oil has become an increasingly important aspect of US-China relations. US policy-makers believe that 'China is increasingly active in striving for energy resources in ways that portend direct competition for energy resources with the United States', and that 'this is producing a possibility of conflict between the two nations' (USCESRC, 2005: 171). Richard D'Amato, chairman of the US-China Economic and Security Review Commission argues that 'it is critical to persuade China to abandon its mercantilist spree to lock up attractive energy supplies wherever it can, and instead to participate [in planning] for sharing oil in the case of supply disruptions and begin relying on free markets to promote energy security for everyone' (USCESRC, 2005: 171). The co-founders of the US-China Working Group warn that 'China's massive energy needs have motivated the country to secure ownership of global energy supplies' (Kirk and Larsen, 2006: 28).

China has been heavily criticised by the United States for its fast-growing involvement in Africa. For example, the USCESRC commented: 'China is a source of diplomatic, economic, and/or military support to pariah governments in countries such as Sudan and Zimbabwe, which underscores the amoral nature of China's African strategy' (USCESRC, 2005: 148).

China's oil companies have, indeed, increased their efforts to acquire ownership of international oil reserves. In the 1990s, the leading international oil companies believed that they would greatly increase their role in owning and operating oilfields in developing countries, making use of their superior technologies and financial resources. In fact, flush with funds arising from the increased oil price, the National Oil Companies (NOCs) have by and large ceded only limited control of oil reserves to the leading international oil companies. Chinese oil companies also have been permitted to acquire only limited ownership and operation rights over the resources controlled by the NOCs in Latin America, the Middle East, and the former Soviet Union (USCESRC, 2005: 167–70).[35] By and large, China's oil supplies from these regions have come through open market purchases.

China's efforts to acquire oil assets has met with the greatest success in Africa. There is a deep symmetry of economic interest between China and Africa. Africa has low density of population, huge natural resources, and immense potential to benefit from trade with China based on its comparative advantage. China has intensely increased its efforts to develop supplies of oil from Africa, as well as supplies of other primary produce, including food. Its intense interest in the region as an economic partner is indicated by the fact that in the first half of 2006 alone, three senior Chinese leaders visited the continent.[36] During his trip in June 2006, the Chinese premier, Wen Jiabao, visited no less than seven African countries (Angola, Congo Republic, Egypt, Ghana, South Africa, Tanzania, and Uganda).

China's imports from Africa rose from US$ 5 billion in 2001 to US$ 22 billion in 2005 (*FT*, 20 June 2006). In 2005 Africa had a surplus on its trade with China of around US$ 5 billion. China has grown rapidly to overtake Britain and become Africa's biggest commercial partner after the United States and France, in 'the most sudden change in the continent's international trading patterns since the end of the colonial era' (*FT*, 20 June 2006). If the trade relationship continues to grow at this speed, it could be of enormous importance for African economic development. Africa as a whole now supplies almost one-third of China's oil imports (*FT*, 19 June 2006). Angola was second only in importance to Saudi Arabia as a source of oil supply to China in 2005 (*FT*, 20 June 2006).. Chinese oil companies are fast developing their operations in Africa. China National Petroleum Corporation has the largest international operations in Sudan, as well as being involved in proposals for US$ 4 billion-worth of investment in Nigeria's oil fields. CNOOC recently paid US$ 2.7 billion for a share of a Nigerian oil block stake, and Sinopec has stakes in several Angolan oil areas.

China now has around 900 investment projects in Africa, and there are around 80 000 Chinese workers employed on different projects in Africa. State-owned enterprises have been at the heart of the Chinese expansion in Africa. Their goals are not short-term profit-maximisation. Rather, they operate in order to pursue China's long-term political-economic goals alongside commercial objectives. Chinese state-owned companies operating in Africa typically are supported in their expansion by Chinese state-owned banks. They frequently operate in countries and regions that are shunned by Western companies. For example, Chinese businesses are far ahead of other international investors in Sierra Leone. Unlike Western countries operating in Africa, the Chinese government rules a country that contains a large number of people who have only recently been released from poverty, and many who still live in poverty. China's understanding of African development challenges is often much deeper than that of Western countries, including the United States. China is committing a large amount of development assistance to African countries that are its main partners in natural resource supplies. For example, it has made available a US$ 3 billion line of credit to Angola to reconstruct its war ravaged infrastructure in return for a guarantee of reliable oil supplies.

China has emphasised that its policy in Africa is based on 'mutual respect, equality, mutual benefit, and non-interference in others' internal affairs'. It is recognised by the United States that China 'often champions the interests of developing countries in international fora' (USCESRC, 2005: 147). As a developing country itself, and one that has successfully lifted hundreds of millions of people out of poverty in the last two decades, China is much better able to understand the needs and challenges facing African nations than the United States is able to do. The 'Chinese model' deeply interests poor developing countries and the successor states of the former Soviet Union. In the long term Africa has immense possibilities to expand its exports to China, including food as well as raw materials. If this is associated with intelligently constructed support for building infrastructure, and, even, welfare facilities, then China has the potential to contribute greatly to the advance of African capitalism, and the overall economic and social progress that eluded the continent under Western colonial rule, under inward-looking economic policies post-Independence, and under the policies of free market fundamentalism, 'good governance' and democratisation, led by the IMF and the World Bank in the 1990s. This would be an immense contribution for China to make to Africa. It might also threaten American and European interests in the continent, by exposing the failure of their development strategies in Africa.

In the late 1990s, in quick succession, BP acquired two large US-headquartered oil companies, Amoco and Arco, which greatly increased BP global reserves,[37] including those in North America. Hong Kong's Hutchison Whampoa already owns Canada's Husky oil, which owns a significant share of one of the world's largest deposits of oil sands. However, China's efforts to acquire international oil reserves through its national oil companies led to an extremely hostile response from the United States, reaching a crescendo in 2005. When CNOOC made a bid to acquire Unocal, the American headquartered oil company, it 'sailed into a perfect storm'. It released an outpouring of hostility towards China:

> Congress was furious about the US-China trade deficit and the strength of the *renminbi*, the supposed loss of American jobs overseas, gas prices, China's military build-up, its continued denial of political and religious freedoms and its acquisition of natural resources round the world. The disparate issues converged on CNOOC. One of the most critical issues for the world is that the United States should permit and encourage China's peaceful rise. Killing Chinese takeovers makes one doubt whether the United States understands this (*FT*, 3 August 2005).

William Reinsch, President of the US National Foreign Trade Council observed: 'We are in a time and place where every single one of these deals is going to go through extra scrutiny, because the deals give fodder to the view that China is the enemy' (quoted in *Financial Times*, 3 August 2005). The proposed takeover effectively was blocked by US Congress.[38]

The intensity of feeling in the US Congress is remarkable in view of the massive international reserves owned by the world's leading American and European-based oil companies.[39] These companies typically own 70–80 per cent of their oil reserves in foreign countries, whereas for the leading Chinese oil companies, international oil reserves are still only a tiny share of their total reserves. PetroChina has the largest international reserves of any Chinese oil company, but these are only one-tenth of those of Exxon Mobil, the leading American oil company. The widespread feeling among American politicians that China is involved in unacceptable interference in the internal affairs of oil-producing countries is staggeringly disingenuous, given the remorseless, ongoing and intensifying American involvement in the internal development of oil-producing regions, especially the critically important Gulf Region.

Environmental Battle

In the last few years in the high-income countries there has developed a gathering hysteria over the perceived threat to human civilisation from burning fossil fuels. China is increasingly perceived by Americans as the major threat to the global environment in the coming century. In his apocalyptic book, '*Collapse*', Jared Diamond paints a nightmare vision of the environmental implications for America and the rest of the world consequent upon 'China's rise'.

Diamond warns that China's large population, economy, and area 'guarantee that its environmental problems will not remain a domestic issue but will spill over to the rest of the world, which is increasingly affected through sharing the same planet, oceans, and atmosphere with China': 'China is already the largest contributor of chlorofluorocarbons, other ozone-depleting substances, and (soon) carbon dioxide to the atmosphere; its dust and aerial pollutants are transported eastwards in the atmosphere to neighbouring countries and even to North America; and it is one of the two leading importers of tropical rainforest timber, making it a driving force behind tropical deforestation' (Diamond, 2005: 359). Diamond argues that even more important than all those other impacts will be the 'proportionate increase in total human impact on the world's environment if China, with its large population, succeeds in its goal of achieving First World living standards which also means catching up to the First World's environmental impact' (Diamond, 2005: 350). He believes that if China achieves First World living standards it will 'approximately double the entire world's human resource use and environmental impact'. He doubts whether even the world's current human resource use and impact can be sustained: 'Something has to give way. That is the strongest reason why China's problems automatically become the world's problems' (Diamond, 2005: 373).

He forecasts that if current trends continue, with 'emissions rising in China, steady in the US (sic), declining elsewhere', by the year 2050 China will become the world leader in carbon dioxide emissions, accounting for 40 per cent of the world's total emissions'. He states that China 'already leads the world in the production of sulphur dioxides, with an output double that of the US': 'Propelled eastwards by winds, the pollutant-laden dust, sand, and soil originating from China's deserts, degraded pastures, and fallow farmland gets blown to Korea, Japan, Pacific Islands, and across the Pacific within a week to the US and Canada. Those aerial particles are the result of China's coal-burning, deforestation, overgrazing, erosion, and destructive agricultural methods' (Diamond, 2005: 371).

China will soon overtake Japan as the world's largest importer of tropical timber. Diamond argues that China is, in effect, 'conserving its own forests' by 'exporting deforestation to other countries, several of which (including Malaysia, Papua Guinea, and Australia) have already reached or are on the road to catastrophic deforestation' (Diamond, 2005: 372). Diamond argues that several of China's 'exports' pose a severe environmental threat to the United States: '[T]he three best-known pests that have wiped out numerous North American tree populations - the chestnut blight, the misnamed "Dutch" elm disease, and the Asian long-horned beetle – all originated in China or else somewhere nearby in East Asia' (Diamond, 2005: 371). He believes that the Chinese grass carp, 'now established in rivers and lakes of 45 US states', competes with 'native fish species and causes large changes in aquatic plant, plankton, and invertebrate communities' (Diamond, 2005: 371).

Diamond is concerned at yet another threat to the United States from China's rise: 'Still another species of which China has an abundant population, which has large ecological and economic impacts, and which China is exporting in increasing numbers is *Homo Sapiens*. For instance, China has now moved into third place as a source of legal immigration into Australia and significant numbers of illegal as well as legal immigrants crossing the Pacific reach even the United States' (Diamond, 2005: 371).

Jared Diamond's '*Collapse*' is a bestseller in the United States. It both reflects and helps to nurture popular sentiment, especially in the United States, about the perceived dangers of 'China's rise'. Its popularity spans a wide political canvas, from right-wing anti-immigrant groups to left-wing environmentalists. By linking closely China's rise with people's deep fears about the survival of the planet, the sentiments expressed in Diamond's book are immensely potent politically.

Military Relations

Former US Ambassador to China, J. Stapleton Roy, warned of the awful possibilities if relations between the United States and China, as well as their mutual relationship with Japan, were not handled well: 'If these relations are handled well, there is no danger in East Asia that cannot be effectively addressed. If they are managed badly, chances of destructive collision will be greatly enhanced ... Now, the danger signals are all too evident' (Roy, 2006). He cautions that much depends on whether an increasingly powerful China 'continues to demonstrate restraint in defining its objectives and in using its growing capabilities' (Roy, 2006). However, he also cautions that the response of the United States or other major powers such as Japan, is crucial to the prospects for peace. If they feel threatened by China's rise, 'their reactions could precipitate conflict as easily as the conduct of the emerging country' (Roy, 2006). If the US goal is, indeed, to maintain 'perpetual supremacy', then China's rise 'will become threatening at some point': 'Sooner or later, regardless of Chinese behaviour, the United States would have to adopt a policy of containment toward China' (Roy, 2006).

There is deep concern in the United States that China's rise will transform fundamentally the balance of world economic and military power. In the view of the US Government, China is the one country in the world that has the potential to challenge US supremacy.

In a series of official documents and statements, the US leadership has warned China against military expansion. The Pentagon's latest Quadrennial Defense Review states: 'Of the major powers, China has the greatest potential to compete militarily with the United States and field disruptive military technologies that could over time offset traditional US military advantages absent [sic] counter strategies' (quoted in Roy, 2006).

The US Government has acknowledged that China is far behind the United States militarily. Its latest report on China's Military Power concludes that 'China will take until the end of this decade or later for its military modernisation programme to produce a modern force capable of defeating a moderate-size adversary' (Office of the Secretary of Defense, 2006: 24). However, despite the recognised weakness of China's armed forces, the mainstream of US Government officials have expressed deep concern about China's military capabilities and intentions. China's arms purchases have 'prompted the US Secretary of Defense to publicly question the ultimate purpose of China's military build-up' (USCESRC, 2005: 8). The co-founders of the US-China Working Group note:

> The greatest threat to the growing diplomatic relationship between the United States and China is China's military modernisation and the lack of transparency or clear motive behind the growth. It is against the interests of both China and the United States for the Chinese to develop a military that exceeds the scope of the Asia-Pacific region or directly threatens the United States. China is not a current military threat to the United States. However, for the United States and the rest of the world to feel confident in peaceful China, the PRC has to be clear about its military relationships (Kirk and Larsen, 2006: 27).

In 2002, President Bush warned China:

> In pursuing advanced military capabilities that can threaten its neighbours in the Asia Pacific region, China is following an outdated path that, in the end, will hamper its own pursuit of greatness. It is time to reaffirm the essential role of American military strength. We must build and maintain our defenses beyond challenge ... Our forces will be strong enough to dissuade potential adversaries from pursuing a military build-up in hopes of surpassing, or equalling, the power of the US (quoted in *Financial Times*, 21 September 2002).

Following 9/11, the consensus among the inner core of the Bush administration shifted to the view that 'in the long-term the United States would only find security in a world in which US values were widely held and spread' (*FT*, 6 March 2003). The 'colour revolutions' in Georgia, Ukraine and Kyrgyzstan were strongly supported by the United States, which 'have brought new hope for freedom across the Eurasian landmass' (Bush, 2006: 2). The long-run hope of the US political leaders for China is clear:

> Ultimately, China's leaders must see that they cannot let their population increasingly experience the freedom to buy, sell, and produce, while denying them the rights to assemble, speak, and worship. Only by allowing the Chinese people to enjoy these basic freedoms and universal rights can China honour its own constitution and international commitments and reach its full potential. Our strategy seeks to encourage China to make the right strategic choices for its people, while we hedge against other possibilities (Bush, 2006: 42).

As the world moves towards unified markets and global capitalism, the possibility of military conflict increases rather than diminishes. The world is in the middle of one of the 'great historic changes in relative power', and 'historically such changes have mainly led to conflict' (Wolf, 2005a). Martin Wolf warns: 'Ours is the second era of globalisation since the dawn of the industrial revolution. The first began in the second half of the nineteenth century and ended with a series of political and economic disasters in the first half of the twentieth century. If such calamities are to be avoided, much will depend on relations between the United States and a rising China ... Peaceful and cooperative relations are perfectly possible ... [b]ut they are not inevitable' (Wolf, 2005b).

In 1999, the United States' military budget stood at US$ 253 billion, compared with just US$ 135 billion for NATO Europe (IISS, 1999: 37). In the wake of September 11, the US military budget rose to over US$ 400 billion by 2005, while the military spending by NATO Europe stagnated. In 2006, President George W. Bush requested Congress to increase US military spending to a record level of US$ 439 billion in fiscal year 2007 (*FT*, 7 February 2006).[40] Moreover, this figure did not include requests for US$ 9.3 billion to maintain the US nuclear arsenal, or US$ 50 billion in emergency spending to fund the wars in Afghanistan and Iraq. When all forms of military expenditure are included, it is estimated that the United States is 'on a path to spend US$ 2 billion per day by the end of [the Bush administration's] tenure' (*FT*, 7 February 2006). In the epoch of the global market economy, which has a central impulse towards universalism that breaks down international economic, social and cultural differences, it is remarkable that the United States spends so much on instruments designed to wound and kill human beings from other countries.[41]

Since V-J Day, the United States has been engaged in what Gore Vidal has termed a 'perpetual war for perpetual peace': '[E]ach month we are confronted by a new horrendous enemy at whom we must strike before he destroys us'

(Vidal, 2002: 20). Gore Vidal provides a catalogue (Vidal, 2002: 22–41) of 'several hundred wars against Communism, terrorism, drugs, or sometimes nothing much, between Pearl Harbor and Tuesday 11 September'. Vidal observes: In these wars 'we tended to strike the first blow. But then we're the good guys, right? Right.' (Vidal, 2002: 40). A *New York Times*/CBS poll prior to the US invasion of Iraq after 9/11 noted that only 6 per cent of Americans opposed military action, while a substantial majority favoured war, 'even if many thousands of innocent civilians are killed' (quoted in Vidal, 2002: 20).[42]

'Realists' in American policy-advice circles, such as John Mearsheimer of Chicago University, argue that the United States will 'seek to contain China and ultimately weaken it to the point where it is no longer capable of dominating Asia' (Mearsheimer, 2005). Mearsheimer considers that 'the United States is likely to behave towards China much the same way it behaved towards the Soviet Union in the Cold War'. In fact, the United States is already engaged in efforts to 'contain' China. The strategy can be likened to feeding a baby tiger to make it grow bigger, while making the cage around it ever stronger as the tiger grows.

The United States has an ever-deeper military relationship with Japan. In the US view this alliance is 'the most important pact in the Pacific' (Fallon, 2006). Japan itself has a large stock of military equipment, including 16 submarines, 45 destroyers, 9 frigates, and 360 combat aircraft (mainly American F-2s, F-4s, and F-15s) (IISS, 2004: 177). In addition, the United States has almost 60 000 military personnel stationed in Japan (IISS, 2005: 31). Its stock of military equipment in Japan includes 36 F-16s and 48 F-15 fighters, and an aircraft carrier plus support ships, which form the core of the 7th Fleet, headquartered at Yokosuka. In 2005, Japan expressed its concern at China's growing military power. The two countries have established a 'joint missile defense shield', the primary motivation for which is widely thought to be 'the longer term fear over the potential threat posed by China' (*FT*, 24 June 2006). Japanese and US officers are engaged in joint efforts to improve their forces inter-operability, and smooth the 'interface' between their respective combat and communication systems (Fallon, 2006, and Klare, 2006).

The United States is trying also to nurture 'trilateral military cooperation' between South Korea, Japan and the US (Fallon, 2006). Admiral Fallon, Commander-in Chief of the US Pacific Command (PACOM) has indicated that America's ties with South Korea must adapt to the changing security environment represented by 'China's military modernisation' (quoted in Klare, 2006). South Korea itself has a huge airforce, including almost 500 modern fighter aircraft (all American F-4s, F-5s, and F-16s) (IISS, 2004: 180). In addition, the United States has around 35 000 military personnel in South Korea. Its military equipment includes 84 combat aircraft (60 F-16s and 24 A-10s) (IISS, 2004: 31).

The United States 'continues to encourage [Taiwan's] acquisition of useful technologies and a strong commitment to their own defense': 'Enhancing the ability of Taiwan to defend itself is the focus of [the US's] military engagement with Taiwan' (Fallon, 2006). The United States has strongly supported Taiwan's acquisition of modern military equipment. Taiwan has a large modern airforce, with over 500 combat aircraft, including 236 American F-5s and F-16s (IISS, 2004: 190).

The United States has a stock of 8000 active or operational nuclear warheads, with an average destructive power that is twenty times that of the Hiroshima bomb, which killed around 200 000 people (McNamara, 2005).[43] Of these nuclear weapons, 2000 are on hair-trigger alert, ready to be launched on fifteen minutes warning. The United States has never endorsed the policy of 'no first use':

> We have been and remain prepared to initiate the use of nuclear weapons – by the decision of one person, the president – against either a nuclear or non-nuclear enemy whenever we believe it is in our interest to do so . . . On any given day, as we go about our business, the president is prepared to make a decision within twenty minutes that could launch one of the most devastating weapons in the world. To declare war requires an act of congress, but to launch a nuclear holocaust requires twenty minutes' deliberation by the president and his advisors (McNamara, 2005).[44]

The world has never faced a greater risk of nuclear warfare.

The United State's Annual Report to Congress on 'The Military Power of the People's Republic of China' (USCESRC, 2005) concluded that China will not be ready to fight even a 'moderate-sized adversary' until 2010, and that the People's Liberation Army (PLA) is 'presently unable to compete directly with other modern military powers'. China has a limited nuclear arsenal. China possesses no long-range bombers or modern submarine-based nuclear weapons. China's medium-range bomber force is 'obsolete and vulnerable to attack'. China's entire intercontinental nuclear arsenal consists of eighteen stationary single-warhead ICBMs: These are 'not ready to launch on warning'. Their warheads are 'kept in storage' and 'the missiles themselves are unfuelled' (Lieber and Press, 2006: 49).[45] The lack of any advanced early warning system adds to the vulnerability of China's ICBMs: 'It appears that China would have no warning at all of a US submarine-launched missile attack or a strike using hundreds of stealthy nuclear-armed cruise missiles' (Lieber and Press, 2006: 49).

American military analysts claim that the United States has succeeded in its explicit goal of nuclear primacy. Russia can 'no longer count on a survivable nuclear deterrent'. Despite 'much talk about China's military modernisation', the odds that China will acquire a survivable nuclear deterrent in the next decade are 'slim' (Lieber and Press, 2006: 48–9). The fact that for many years to come the United States may have the capability to destroy the nuclear weapons systems of either Russia or China without risk of nuclear retaliation can be seen as a force for global stability. It may also be viewed as a dangerous encouragement to the United States to threaten or, even, to use nuclear violence in the event of international confrontation.[46]

The US Government regards nuclear weapons as central to its military strategy for 'at least the next several decades' (McNamara, 2005). This provides an intense incentive for other nations to either expand their existing arsenal or develop nuclear weapons if they do not already possess them. McNamara characterises the US nuclear weapons policy as follows: '[It is] immoral, illegal, militarily unnecessary, and dreadfully dangerous. The risk of an accidental or inadvertent nuclear launch is unacceptably high'. The only rational policy, in his view, is to 'move promptly towards the elimination – or near elimination – of all nuclear weapons'.

Fears of 'China's rise' are now deeply embedded in the US intellectual and government elite in relation to China's perceived impact on inequality, conditions of work, energy security, ecology, and financial security, not to speak of the perceived threat to the US global economic, cultural and military dominance. It requires little imagination to visualise the innumerable different ways in which the contradictory impact of capitalist globalisation upon both China and the United States could erupt into a military conflict.

2.1.5 Cooperation?

While there is deep fear of China's rise among Congressional representatives, the leaders of large US firms are deeply enthusiastic about globalisation in general, and China in particular. There is a 'deep and widening rift between business people and the political herd on issues ranging from foreign investment into the United States, to immigration, to America's engagement with multilateral institutions' (*FT*, 7 June 2006). US business leaders have become more and more international in their outlook. Most of them view China's rise as an immense opportunity. Most of them are intensely enthusiastic about China, and try to understand its history and culture.

Apart from the benefit to US firms, there are numerous ways in which US-China cooperation can work to the advantage of the population of both countries. All-out military conflict would be a disaster for the people of both countries. In conventional wars, the front line armed forces are typically recruited disproportionately from the lower income groups.[47] In the event of nuclear, biological/chemical warfare, no one would escape the impact, whatever their level of income or wealth. Also, socio-political disorder in China would harm a large proportion of Americans, not to speak of the mass of Chinese people. However, beyond these disastrous possibilities, there are many practical benefits from US-China cooperation. The surging inequalities in income, wealth and life chances in both countries can only be resolved by each of them identifying a new role for the respective governments, coordinating their efforts, and learning from each other's experience, both today and in the past. The two countries need to cooperate closely to resolve the global energy and ecological challenge, and to establish a stable structure for global finance.

A recent study carried out jointly by the American-based Centre for Strategic and International Studies and the Institute for International Economics draws up a 'balance sheet' of the implications for the United States of 'China's rise',[48] and concludes that the 'areas of mutual interest between the United States and China are more prevalent, and more significant, than their spheres of potential conflict' (Bergsten, *et al*., 2006: 161). US Deputy Secretary of State, Robert Zoellick, has proposed that America tries to work with China to become a 'responsible stakeholder in this international system of systems' (Zoellick, 2006).[49] He argues that there is now a deep inter-connection between domestic developments in the United States and China, and the way in which the two countries interact with each other on regional and global issues. Zoellick believes that this 'duality' is the key to US-China relations. He acknowledges that, 'in contrast to the experience of the Soviet Union', China seeks 'a benign external environment in which to pursue their internal development'. He notes that China's philosophy of 'peaceful rise' and 'peaceful development' emphasise that 'it is not challenging the international system, and it wants to work with the United States and others to calm anxieties'.

Deepening Inter-Connection of US and Chinese Political Economy

In the 1980s, the prime goal of American foreign policy was the overthrow of the 'evil empire' in the Soviet Union. This goal was pursued through acceleration of the arms race and numerous channels of influence upon Soviet policy-makers. US policies played a significant role in the collapse of Soviet communism and the disintegration of the USSR. 'Regime change' resulted in state disintegration, with disastrous consequences for the economy and for the welfare of most Russians. The Soviet economy had only negligible linkages to the US economy. The USSR accounted for a tiny fraction of American exports and there was no investment in Russia by US multinationals. Soviet exports to the United States were trivial in scale. The collapse of the Soviet economy had a negligible impact on the US economy other than the short-term fall in military expenditure.

During the explosive development of capitalist globalisation since the 1980s, the Chinese and US economies have become deeply inter-twined. US consumers benefit from the explosive growth of low-priced Chinese exports.[50] US companies and shareholders benefit from China's absorption of booming American investments and from American companies' access to the low-cost manufacturing supply-chain in China. US primary product producers (including food, oil and mining companies) benefit from exports to China, both directly from the United States and, increasingly, from production bases in other countries.[51] US high technology firms benefit from the export of products such as aeroplanes, medical equipment, telecoms equipment, power equipment, semiconductors, and software. US retailers benefit from low-cost sourcing in China. The US Government benefits from Chinese government purchase of its debt. This in its turn helps to keep US interest rates low, which helps to sustain the US housing bubble. This helps to underpin the growth of US personal consumption through the wealth effect and the ability of US consumers to borrow against the value of their housing wealth.

'System disintegration' in China, such as the United States helped bring about in the USSR, Afghanistan and Iraq, and may help to bring about in Iran (and, in its turn, perhaps more widely in the Islamic world), would have severe economic consequences for the United States. It is in the interests of US business and the mass of US citizens, not to speak of the rest of the world, to support the efforts of China's Communist Party leadership to achieve the country's 'peaceful rise'.

China's deep engagement with global capitalism has resulted in an economy that is far more open to the international economy than were other latecomer countries. By 2003, the ratio of the stock of inward investment to GDP was 35 per cent, compared with 8 per cent in Korea, 5 per cent in India and just 2 per cent in Japan (Wolf, *Financial Times*, 14 September 2005). In 2004, the ratio of China's trade to its GDP reached 70 per cent. China's economy is far more open to trade than any other large economy. The foreign trade ratios of the United States and Japan are both less than 25 per cent (Wolf, 2005b).

The United States is extremely important for the Chinese economy. The United States has become the largest source of foreign direct investment (FDI) inflows into China, amounting to over 10 per cent of total inflows (excluding Hong Kong) by 2002 (SSB, ZTN, 2003: Table 17.15).[52] There are large positive externalities from American FDI in China. Leading global 'systems integrator' firms from the United States stimulate other international firms (both from the United States and elsewhere) within their supply chain to establish production facilities in China. They bring their own managements skills and technologies to China, and exert intense pressure on the whole supply chain within China to advance its business and technical skills (Nolan, 2007a). By 2002, the United States had become much the most important market for China's exports, totalling US$ 70 billion, which amounted to 22 per cent of China's total exports, compared with 18 per cent for the whole of Europe and 15 per cent for Japan (SSB, ZTN 2003: Table 17.7). China's imports from the United States amounted to only 9.2 per cent of China's total imports in 2002. However, these imports consist predominantly of high technology products, which play an important role in upgrading the technological base within China. A serious downturn in the US economy, or the rise of American protectionism, would have large deleterious economic consequences for China.

State and Market

As we have seen, the interpretation of the word 'freedom' has been the object of intense debate in the United States since Independence. At the heart of the struggle for the meaning of 'freedom' in the United States was the battle over the role of the state, and its function in the achievement of 'negative' and 'positive' freedoms.

In the nineteenth century, the United States achieved explosive industrialisation behind protectionist barriers. The 'Gilded Age' at the end of the century witnessed a tremendous concentration of wealth and income.[53] The idea that 'freedom' essentially meant freedom of contract became the bedrock of 'liberal' thinking. The true realm of freedom was regarded as 'the liberty to buy and sell ... where and how we please, without interference from the state' (Foner, 1998: 120). Social Darwinism became the dominant political philosophy, strongly opposing state interference with the 'natural' workings of society. The leading Social Darwinist, Prof William Sumner (Yale) argued that freedom meant the 'abnegation of state power and a frank acceptance of inequality'.[54]

The 1890s saw deep class struggle in the United States, stimulating the emergence of powerful critiques of free market fundamentalism in the years leading up to the First Word War. However, it was only with the onset of The Great Depression that such ideas came into the mainstream of US politics. These ideas remained as the mainstream of US political thought for long into the post-war world, reinforced by the massive task of economic and social reconstruction in war-ravaged Europe.

In the 1950s, a group of conservative thinkers set out to 'reclaim the idea of freedom'. For them, freedom meant de-centralised political power, limited government, and a free market economy.[55] By the 1990s, the dominant view equated 'freedom' with individual choice in the market place and minimal interference from the state. As the US business system became increasingly powerful globally, the idea gained force that the United States should lead the world towards a single universal free market. The collapse of the USSR deeply reinforced Americans' confidence in the free market, and in the country's duty to lead the world towards this as a universal form of socio-economic organisation. By the 1990s, in the United States there was no serious intellectual challenge to the economic philosophy of the free market: 'Market utopianism has succeeded in appropriating the American faith that it is a unique country, the model for a universal civilisation which all societies are fated to emulate' (Gray, 1998: 103–5).

As we have seen, Social Darwinist ideas reached a new apogee under President George W. Bush. However, the roles of state and market are already beginning to be re-thought in the United States in the light of the surging contradictions of capitalist globalisation, and their impact upon the United States. The wisest voices in US political discussion realise that the answer to these contradictions is not to blame 'China's rise', but, rather, to return to an older tradition that attempts to establish a more sophisticated understanding of the appropriate role of state and market. There is an increasing chorus of voices from all parts of the political spectrum that is appalled by the growing inequality of income and life chances.[56] Even *The Economist* magazine, the cheerleader of the global free market economy, has recognised the dangerous explosion of inequality in the United States, publishing a long special report on the topic: 'America's income distribution is likely to continue the trends of the recent past. While those at the top will go on drawing huge salaries, those in the broad middle of the middle class will see their incomes churned' (*The Economist*, 17 June 2006).[57] It warns: 'The political consequences will depend on the pace of change and the economy's general health'.

It is increasingly recognised that the US Government needs to assume greatly increased responsibility for supporting and retraining American blue and white collar workers who become displaced by globalisation (Bergsten, *et al.*, 2006: 77). In common with the other high-income countries, the US Government 'must face up to the massive, complex, and multifaceted challenges that offshoring will bring': 'National data systems, trade policies, educational systems, social welfare programme and politics all must adapt to the new realities' (Blinder, 2006: 114).

It is also increasingly widely recognised among the American business elite that powerful action needs to be taken by the US Government to control the effects of free market capitalism upon the environment. Even a leading US financial institution such as Goldman Sachs has declared: 'Voluntary action alone cannot solve the climate change problem' (quoted in *Financial Times*, 31 May 2006). It is also widely appreciated that the United States sits at the centre of ever-deepening global imbalances, the resolution of which requires sophisticated international government coordination. The US Government has no choice: it must stand at the centre of this process if the imbalances are to unwind without disaster striking.

China also is searching for its own balance of state and market. Under the extremes of Maoist administrative direction, the economy failed to meet the aspirations of Chinese people: 'direction' rather than real planning, which steps in where the market fails, deadened economic life. China is now looking back to its own history for inspiration about the appropriate role of state and market (Nolan, 2004a). Throughout its own long history the Chinese state both stimulated and regulated the market economy. Alongside vibrant market development, the Chinese state guided economic activity through such mechanisms as control over the money supply, commodity price stabilisation, constructing irrigation and transport infrastructure, organising famine relief, regulating urban planning, and spreading knowledge. In periods when the state operated effectively, the economy and society functioned harmoniously.

China and the United States have entered the epoch of capitalist globalisation from fundamentally different starting points. However, they are both groping their way towards a sustainable development path. Despite the huge discrepancy in their levels of development, they are both experiencing profound system de-stabilisation arising from the surging contradictions of raw capitalist globalisation. The United States and China can both learn enormous amounts from their respective political-economic histories. Both countries are trying to 'use the past to serve the present'. China is trying to find a new centre of gravity after the extremes of the Maoist 'instruction economy', and search in its own long history for inspiration. In the United States it is increasingly recognised that the country needs to learn from its own history about the way in which to control the market in the broad social interest. A financial crisis in the United States could lead to war. Alternatively, it could lead to a return to a deeper role for the state comparable with that after the Great Depression, and in the post-war period of global reconstruction, when America's leaders tried to build a 'Great Society'.

Science and Technology

The United States is at the centre of global technical progress. Its firms are by far the most powerful in terms of R&D, with 43 per cent of the world's top 1000 companies by R&D expenditure (DTI, 2005). In 2002, US companies spent around US$ 21.2 billion on R&D undertaken in other countries. Of this total around US$ 2.7 billion was in developing countries, of which around US$ 650 million was undertaken by US companies in China (UNCTAD, 2005: 294). By 2003, foreign companies are estimated to have accounted for around 24 per cent of total R&D spending in China (UNCTAD, 2005: 292).[58] Of this, American companies accounted for around 31 per cent (UNCTAD, 2005: 292–4).

US tertiary education in technical subjects[59] is greatly exceeded by that in China, India and Russia. In 2000-01, there were 2.6 million students enrolled in tertiary education in these subjects in China, 2.4 million in Russia, 1.9 million in India and 1.7 million in the United States (UNCTAD, 2005: 296). In 2006, the US National Academies[60] published the report 'Rising Above the Gathering Storm', which argued for a large increase in both the size and effectiveness of government intervention in US science and technology if the country were to sustain its technological lead. It argued that the American Government needed to greatly increase its involvement in science and technology. The report makes a number of recommendations, for ways in which the United States can attract an even larger share of the world's most able young scientists and engineers to work in the United States, including easing visa requirements, providing priority to doctoral level scientists and engineers in obtaining US citizenship, and providing international students and researchers in the United States with access to information and research equipment in US industrial, academic, and national laboratories comparable with the access provided to US citizens and permanent residents in a similar status (National Academies, 2006).

China was at the centre of global technical progress right up until the Industrial Revolution in the late eighteenth century.[61] Although the pace of technical progress may have slowed down somewhat after China's medieval 'industrial revolution', a steady stream of significant technical advances was made thereafter through until the nineteenth century, without making the leap to a full-fledged modern 'Industrial Revolution'.

Although Chinese firms still face an intense struggle on the 'global level playing field', Chinese people already are making a large and rapidly-growing contribution to global technical progress. Chinese engineers and scientists constitute a large and growing fraction of the research force of leading global firms, working both in the high-income countries, and, increasingly, within research institutes established by global firms in China. American firms are in the vanguard of global technical progress, and, already, Chinese scientists and engineers are making a large contribution to new knowledge within those firms.

There are numerous areas in which science needs urgently to produce solutions in order to allow global sustainable development. Nowhere is the challenge more intense than in China. These challenges include improving human physical and mental well-being, overcoming the exhaustion of non-renewable resources, producing food in sustainable ways, and shifting the structure of consumption towards sustainable paths. China cannot simply replicate the growth pattern of today's high-income countries. Due to its vast size and explosive growth, these challenges are of unique intensity in China. The very survival of China and the world depends on meeting these challenges. By contributing to solutions to these burning problems, Chinese science and technology can make a massive contribution towards global sustainable development. The achievement of global sustainable development is in the long-run interests of US business and the mass of US citizens.

Energy and the Environment

The energy sector is a critical area of interaction between the United States and China. Perceptions of the importance of energy security have dramatically increased in the United States in recent years. In March 2006, the Chairman of the Senate Foreign Relations Committee, Richard Lugar, warned: 'No one who is honestly assessing the decline of American leverage around the world due to energy dependence can fail to see that energy is the albatross of US national security' (quoted in *Financial Times*, 14 March 2006). He compared President Bush's 2006 State of the Union speech, in which the former oil executive warned that the United States was 'addicted to oil', with 'President Nixon using his anti-communist credentials to open up China'. He said that the United States needed to expand international coordination of energy issues, 'especially with India and China', to address the growing global competition for energy resources. He argued that resolving US energy security required 'extraordinary international diplomacy'.

In some ways, China and the United States face common problems and have common incentives to solve their respective energy problems. Both of them have huge coal reserves. There is tremendous potential for them to cooperate in technologies to convert coal to oil (USCESRC, 2005: 171). China's investments in coal liquefaction, using US-South African technology, are already well advanced. Shenhua Coal Group, the giant Chinese state-owned coal company, plans to invest around US$ 24 billion on coal liquefaction technologies over the next few years (*FT*, 27 September 2005). By 2020 Shenhua plans to produce around 30 million tons of coal liquefied oil products and coal chemical products (*FT*, 27 September 2005). China can benefit from American technology in a number of areas that enable it to increase the efficiency of its energy consumption and thereby tend to reduce its reliance on oil. These include energy intensity use reduction through employment of advanced machinery, clean coal technologies, and combustion efficiency improvements (USCESRC, 2005: 172). The United States and China could also work together to develop and implement utilisation of 'next generation fuels' such as hydrogen. The United States and China have a common interest in political and social stability in Islamic countries in order to ensure stability of oil supplies.

Finance

By early 2006, global economic imbalances had reached a record level. The US current account deficit had increased from 0.4 per cent of world GDP in 1997 to around 1.9 per cent in 2006 (*FT*, 24 April 2006). In 1997, 'emerging Asia' had a current account deficit, amounting to 0.1 per cent of global GDP, while Japan and the 'oil exporters' each had a surplus amounting to around 0.2 per cent of global GDP. The experience of the Asian Financial Crisis was searing for emerging Asia. The region resolved to try to insure itself against another financial crisis by generating large export surpluses and accumulating large foreign exchange reserves. By early 2006, the region had achieved a current account surplus amounting to 0.6 per cent of global GDP, compared with 0.4 per cent for Japan, and, largely due to rising oil prices, 0.8 per cent for the oil-exporting countries. By early 2006, the net foreign assets of emerging Asia and the oil exporters had each reached 3 per cent of global GDP and those of Japan had reached 4 per cent, while the US net negative balance in terms of foreign assets had quadrupled from 2 per cent of global GDP in 1997 to 8 per cent in early 2006 (*FT*, 24 April 2006).

China's current account surplus and its role in the overall growing global imbalances was smaller than that of Japan, Germany or the oil exporting countries. However, its role is politically the most sensitive. The debate over the worsening international imbalances is focused disproportionately on the US-China relationship, with an intense confrontation between the two governments over their respective responsibility for global financial fragility stemming from international imbalances: 'Up to now, the debate has been narrowly bilateral, with China insisting the United States must address its low savings rate and the United States insisting that China should revalue the *renminbi*. Partly as a result, neither has been able to diminish what has been described as a global "financial balance of terror"' (*FT*, Editorial, 25 April 2006). Clearly, the problem of international imbalances embraces far more than simply the United States and China, and cannot be solved at a purely bilateral level.

By early 2006, fears intensified that global international economic imbalances might unwind dramatically. There was wide anxiety at the absence of international coordination of the emerging global imbalances. The agency that had been established precisely to deal with international financial coordination, namely the IMF, was widely perceived to have failed in its coordination function precisely when it was most needed. The Governor of the Bank of England, Mervyn King, warned that the IMF 'could slip into obscurity' if it 'failed to reclaim its role as the umpire of the global economy' (quoted in *Financial Times*, 28 April 2006). Against all predictions, in April, 2006, the IMF announced significant changes in its role: 'Even the most sceptical finance ministers, and central bank governors viewed the IMF meeting as a great success' (*FT*, 24 April 2006). There was finally 'a shared understanding [that] huge trade gaps represent the biggest threat to the world economy', and crucially, there was 'a willingness to do something about it' (*FT*, 24 April 2006).

The IMF meeting of April 2006 decided to initiate 'a process that goes beyond analysis and description of problems, and engage in discussions with the specific governments about the linkages and spillovers of the macroeconomic situation, and in relation to the global economy' (Rodrigo Rato, Managing Director of the IMF, quoted in *Financial Times*, 24 April 2006). This meant that the IMF would henceforth report publicly on the effects of, for example, Chinese policies on the US trade deficit, and call together the relevant countries to see whether an agreement on policy changes could be reached. It would decide which countries were relevant for any given issue, and provide a forum to see if agreement could be reached. The Fund decided that where problems arose it would have the right to call 'multilateral consultations', forcing groups of countries to explain how their domestic policies were compatible with Article IV of the IMF and to try to secure agreement on policy changes.[62]

At the same meeting it was decided to initiate major changes to the IMF's methods of operation. Under the current system, voting powers are hugely disproportionate to different countries' role in the global economy. For example, Belgium accounts for 2.16 per cent of the IMF vote, compared with China's 2.98 per cent, even though Belgium's economy is only one-sixth the size of China's in terms of its nominal GDP, and only one-twentieth of its size in terms of GDP in PPP dollars. Of the twenty-four IMF executive directors, nine are European, and the convention is that there is always an American director of the World Bank and a European managing director of the Fund. Of the chairs on the board of the IMF, Europe has eight compared with five from Asia.

The April 2006 meeting approved a plan to give big emerging market economies a greatly increased role in the IMF. China, along with South Korea, Mexico and Turkey, were to be granted an 'ad hoc' quota increase to raise their shareholding. It was agreed that this first step would be linked to 'near-term completion of broad second step reforms'. Under the new system, quotas for the IMF would be calculated on the basis of GDP rather than a complex range of variables as at present. It was agreed that there would be a further increase in emerging market representation, and a shake-up of the current board structure. It was hoped that these changes would increase the IMF's legitimacy and 'bind rising economic powers more tightly into the multilateral financial system' (*FT*, 24 April 2006).

In June 2006 it was announced that the IMF was to set up a 'Group of Five', including China, Saudi Arabia, the Eurozone, Japan and the United States. They would engage in 'multilateral consultations' aimed at 'how to address global imbalances while maintaining robust global growth'. The five economies had been chosen and agreed to participate because their cooperation was crucial for the imbalances to be reduced: 'Their economies are either ones with large current account surpluses or deficits, or they represent a large share of global output' (Rodrigo Rato, quoted in *Financial Times*, 9 June 2006).

Faced with the threat of global financial disaster, at the final hour it appeared to many people that, with the agreement of both rich and poor countries, the IMF was finally assuming the role for which it was originally intended: 'In Washington last weekend, there was unanimous agreement that all IMF members shared collective responsibility for global issues and mutual responsibility to each other, and for the first time also they committed to addressing the fund's governance issues' (Gordon Brown, United Kingdom Chancellor of the Exchequer, quoted in *Financial Times*, 28 April 2006).

Harmonious Society

Capitalist globalisation has contributed to surging inequality of income and life chances in both China and the United States in recent years. In China, there has been a surge of policy debate about the explosive growth of inequality, not only in income, but also in education, health and life chances. The country's leaders have declared their intention to try to establish a 'harmonious society' based on a just distribution of income and life chances. In the United States also there has been a surge of publications about the rapidly growing disparity of income and life chances, with parallels being drawn with the 'Gilded Age' in the late nineteenth century. Today, as then, many Americans, from widely differing political backgrounds, feel that the US Government must play a much larger role in income redistribution if American society is remain stable and just, and if 'freedom' is to mean more than simply the 'freedom' to buy and sell.

From ancient times to the present day, philosophers have sought to find a 'middle way' between competing extremes as the ethical foundation for the good society. If they are to cooperate internationally to solve the challenges created by capitalist globalisation, human beings must find a common ethical ground from across the different world civilisations, 'using the past to serve the present' to form a common ethic for global survival, which answers people's deep spiritual needs from the basis of a simple rational philosophy that all people can understand.

In their search for a good society, China and the United States can look to their respective intellectual traditions and to those key elements that constitute common ethical foundations for social life. The most influential thinkers of all cultures have addressed the fundamental issues of the ethical foundations for human survival. Among the most enduring of these are Confucius (1976), Aristotle (1979) and Adam Smith (1761 and 1776).[63] Each of them is deeply spiritual, attempting to address human being's fundamental fears and needs. Each of them is based on humanistic rationality, which is complementary to, rather than a substitute for, the main religious belief systems.[64] At the core of their common search for an ethic to guide human beings towards a good life has been the concept of benevolence. They agree that the pursuit of wealth, social position and ever-increasing consumption is not the path to human happiness. They share the view that a good society is one in which social harmony is achieved through the whole people sharing a common view of social justice. They each believe that education is critically important for inculcating the ethics that form the foundation of the good society. They share the view that the only rational human goal is happiness, and that this is most completely achieved through the search for tranquillity, not the relentless pursuit of material consumption and pleasure.

2.1.6 Conclusion

The essence of capitalism is its propensity towards universalism. In the pursuit of profit, capitalism has always pushed beyond local boundaries, whether village, town, region or country. However, there has always been a tension between capitalism's universal impulse, and the nation. In the process of constructing modern capitalism, the national state has both propelled capitalism forward and reinforced the sense of national identity and interests, through the mechanisms of mass education, the mass media and government ideology (Hobsbawm, 1990). The rise of modern capitalism in the late nineteenth century erupted into the international conflict that dominated much of the twentieth century. Even in the epoch of capitalist globalisation, there persists a profound tension between the national state and the international impulse of capital. The tension is crystallised today in the relationship between the United States and China. This relationship is central to the prospect for human survival.

Against almost all predictions, the combination of political stability under the leadership of the Chinese Communist Party, and experimental economic system reform and opening up, resulted in the most remarkable epoch of development the world has ever seen. China has been unique among large late-comer countries in its degree of openness to trade, international capital and business, and international culture. China's ever-deepening incorporation into global capitalism has transformed the country's productive forces and social relationships, producing enormous benefits for Chinese people. However, it has also led to wide-ranging challenges that threaten the entire social, economic and political system. These include the growth of inequality, deterioration in the physical environment, the harsh challenge of the 'Global Business Revolution' for large Chinese firms, widespread corruption, and the reform of China's financial sector.

The Chinese government is working hard to devise polices that can meet the intense internal challenges. These include policies to equip the country's leading firms to meet the challenge of the Global Business Revolution, to mitigate the unequal distribution of income, to improve health and educational provision for the mass of the population, to improve energy efficiency, to reduce environmental pollution, and to tackle corruption. No sector is more vital to the government's reform efforts than finance. China is groping for a way to avoid socio-political upheaval in the midst of immense internal challenges and to ensure 'harmonious development', which establishes a balance between China's inland and coastal regions, urban and rural areas, society and economy, and nature and man. This is a 'choice of no choice' for China's sustainable development.

Capitalist globalisation has also brought enormous benefits to the United States. China's increasing involvement in the global capitalist economy has contributed greatly to US prosperity. US firms benefit from their investments in China. US high technology companies benefit by their sales to China and by employing large numbers of Chinese scientists and engineers. US consumers benefit from China's cheap exports. The US Government benefits from China's bond purchases. However, global capitalism has also given rise to intense contradictions within US capitalism in respect to social inequality, energy, the environment, and financial fragility. There is a growing perception that China's rise threatens the dominant position of its firms, as well as its social stability, the identity of American firms, its energy security, its natural environment and its financial stability. These perceptions may influence decisions taken by the leadership or be made use of by them in a time of socio-economic crisis.

Capitalist globalisation has produced intense contradictions within both China and the United States, as well as in their inter-relationship. The possibility that, through a variety of channels, these contradictions might result in the final conflict for humanity is attracting increased attention from commentators across a wide spectrum of political persuasions. The degree of inter-connectedness in world affairs is now so deep that it is no longer possible even for the strongest political economy in the world to establish 'national' security within its own borders.

If the United States seeks long-term security, it faces a 'choice of no choice'. It must cooperate with Communist China to support the construction of a harmonious society internally within China. The areas of necessary cooperation include resolving China's energy needs, its ecological difficulties, its financial system reform, and reform of its health and education system, and supporting China's efforts to establish a just distribution of income. In other words, it must accept and contribute to China's 'peaceful rise', even if that means accepting that the resulting system of political economy will look very different from that of the United States today. China and the United States have no choice but to cooperate to solve the global challenges produced by capitalist globalisation.

2.2 The United States and Islam[65]

The [Muslim] believers, the Jews, the Christians, and the Sabaeans - all those who believe in God and the Last Day and do good – will have their rewards with their Lord ... The East and the West belong to God: wherever you turn, there is his face ... Each community has its own direction to which it turns: race to do good deeds and wherever you are, God will bring you together ... Goodness does not consist in turning your face towards East or West.

(*The Koran, The Cow*, 62, 114, and 148).

*Those heroes that shed their blood and lost their lives,
You are now lying in the soil of a friendly country;
Therefore, rest in peace.
There is no difference between the Johnnies
And the Mehmets to us here;
They lie side by side
Here in this country of ours.
You, the mothers
Who sent their sons from faraway countries,
Wipe away your tears;
Your sons are now lying in our bosom and are in peace,
After having lost their lives on this land, they have
Become our sons as well.*

(Kemal Atatürk, words carved in stone at Gallipoli)[66]

2.2.1 *Islam and the West*

The way in which the Islamic world interacts with capitalist globalisation is determined primarily by its relationship with the world's dominant nation, the United States. In the view of many people, there is a fundamental contradiction between Western capitalism and the Islamic world, which amounts to nothing less than a 'Clash of Civilisations'.

Europe and Islam

Although the United States is central to the relationship between Islam and the West, prior to the Second World War, it was the European powers, especially Britain and, to a lesser degree France, that formed the frontline of Western interactions with the Islamic world. The legacy of this period still affects the way in which Islam interacts with global capitalism, and the European powers remain important actors in the Islamic world.

The deepest hostility in the Islamic world towards Europe has been directed at Britain and France. At the end of the First World War, with the collapse of Ottoman rule in the Middle East, powerful movements emerged among the Arab people for national self-determination, though the nature of such national boundaries was still unclear.

There was considerable sympathy for such views both in the United States and in certain parts of the political establishment in the victorious European states, Britain and France. During the war, the British government had encouraged the hope that in return for their support, the Arab people might be granted political independence: 'For the first time, the claim that those who spoke Arabic constituted a nation and should have a state had been to some extent accepted by a great power' (Hourani, 2002: 316).[67]

By the end of the nineteenth century France and Britain already dominated North Africa, their colonies spanning almost the whole territory. At the end of the First World War, with the defeat of Germany and its Turkish ally, Britain and France together seized control of the Middle Eastern possessions of the Ottoman Empire. They did so under the authority of a 'mandate' granted by the newly established League of Nations, in which they and the United States were the leading forces. Britain was given the mandate for the territory that is now Iraq, the occupied Palestinian territories and Jordan, while France was given that for Lebanon and Syria. In the period 1919–39, the British and French were able to intensify their control over trade and production within the region. The granting of the mandates was greatly resented by the Arab people, who had wished for independence after the downfall of the Ottoman Empire.

British troops occupied Egypt in 1882. The country remained a virtual colony from then until the Anglo-Egyptian Treaty of 1936. Britain defended its rule forcefully against Egyptian nationalist movements. Britain refused to allow an Egyptian government to put its case for independence to the peace conference at the end of the First World War. This sparked a national uprising, which was forcefully suppressed by British troops.[68] In 1956, the Egyptian government nationalised the Suez Canal, which was controlled mainly by Anglo-French shareholders. In a secret tripartite agreement Britain, France and Israel agreed to use the decision as a pretext for overthrowing the socialist government of President Nasser (Hourani, 2002: 167). First the Israeli army invaded and moved towards the Canal. Then Britain and France invaded, demanding that both Israeli and Egyptian forces withdraw. In fact, neither the United States nor the USSR was happy with the Franco-British invasion, and forced them to withdraw. However, the Suez incident added to the anti-British sentiment in the Middle East.

Britain has been deeply involved in the political economy of the Persian Gulf. By the end of the First World War 'British hegemony in the Gulf was unquestioned' (Bullard, 1958: 120). Kuwait remained a British protectorate until 1961 and it was not until 1971 that the British withdrew finally from the states of the lower Gulf, including Bahrain, Qatar, the United Arab Emirates and Oman (Owen and Pamuk, 1998: 217). Further south, in the Gulf of Aden, the port of Aden was a British colony from 1839, and the surrounding territory was a British protectorate from 1896. The area did not gain independence from Britain until 1967.[69]

In the inter-war period, Britain maintained a network of military facilities in the Middle East, including ports, airfields and army bases. In the inter-war period, British forces undertook bloody suppression of revolts in both Iraq and Palestine, including the use of the RAF to drop chemical weapons in Iraq. The British Government's Balfour Declaration was critical to the Jewish colonisation of Palestine. Under British aegis, large-scale Jewish immigration into Palestine was permitted up until the Second World War. Although the United States overtook Britain as the leading diplomatic power in the Middle East, Britain played a significant role in buttressing the authoritarian governments in the Arab oil-producing countries, through the sale of weapons and the provision of military advice and training. Moreover, British policy in the Islamic world was also overshadowed by the catastrophe of the hand-over of power in South Asia in 1947. The appalling violence, with Muslims at the centre, was widely perceived to have been a consequence of bungled policy by the British colonial rulers.

Along with Britain, France's role in the Arab countries in the inter-war period was deeply resented because of its establishment of the *de facto* colonies in the mandated territories of Syria and Lebanon. In Lebanon, France's 'divide and rule' policy exacerbated an already complex situation, through encouraging the different religious and linguistic groups to maintain separate educational systems.

As well as its mandate over the former Ottoman territories in the Middle East, France had for a long period controlled colonies in North Africa, including Tunisia (occupied by the French army in 1881), Morocco, and Algeria. In Morocco, the French defeated an armed movement of national resistance in 1926, and by the late 1920s had conquered almost the whole of the country.[70] The French army and navy had a network of bases spread across the Maghrib, protecting France's extensive economic interests in the region.

Most important among these was the vast territory of Algeria, which is mostly Muslim. Unlike normal colonies, Algeria was fully integrated into France's political structure, in the same way that Corsica still is today, including French as the official language, representation in France's political system and taxes paid to the central government in France. By the early 1950s there were around 1.3 million French immigrants (*colons*) in Algeria, compared with around nine million Arab people. The French colonists dominated the economy, controlling the most fertile land and the most productive agriculture. The national liberation movement, the FLN (Front de Libération Nationale) fought a prolonged and violent war with the French armed forces. By 1962, Algeria achieved independence, but at great human cost. A large part of the Muslim population was displaced in the struggle, and around 300 000 or more (out of a population of around nine million Muslims) were killed (Hourani, 2002: 372).

France played a significant role in relations with the Islamic world in other respects also. France's relationship with Israel helped to cement hostility towards France in the Islamic world. Beginning in 1956, France began to supply Israel with advanced conventional weapons (Karpin, 2006: 68).[71] It was France that provided the technical capabilities in the late 1950s and early 1960s that enabled Israel to build nuclear weapons. In part this was due to strong support for the Zionist movement at high levels of the French government. In part also it was due to the fact that Israeli scientists were able to help the French solve their own technical problems as they moved towards the final stages of building their own nuclear bomb. But a key element was the relationship with the Algerian independence struggle. The Algerian national liberation movement attracted widespread support in the Islamic world, especially in the Arab countries. The French central government believed that Egypt was playing an important role in the struggle against the French. They agreed to help Israel to acquire nuclear technology in return for

Israeli support to provide intelligence information to the French about Egyptian activities in Algeria. Moreover, in the wake of the French humiliation by President Nasser over the Suez debacle, the French government promised to work with Israel to topple President Nasser.

Energy Security, US Foreign Policy and the Middle East

Henry Kissinger, former US Secretary of State, has warned that the global battle for the control of energy resources could become the equivalent of the nineteenth century 'great game', which involved intense conflict between Britain and Russia for control of central Asia: 'The great game is developing again. The amount of energy is finite, up to now in relation to demand, and competition for access to energy can become the life and death for many societies. It would be ironic if the direction of pipelines and locations become the equivalent of the colonial disputes of the nineteenth century' (quoted in *Financial Times*, 2 June 2005). He warned that 'when nuclear weapons spread to thirty or forty countries and each conducts a calculation, with less experience and different value systems, we will have a world of permanent immanent catastrophe'.

American foreign policy is influenced profoundly by the desire to achieve national energy security. Indeed, a large part of international relations in the modern world has been driven by the search for secure supplies of oil. The United States has throughout been at the centre of that drive. The core of this drive has been the Middle East, which contains 62 per cent of the world's oil reserves and 40 per cent of its gas reserves. Ever since oil was discovered in large quantities in the Middle East and Central Asia, American foreign policy has been heavily involved in the region's internal development. The Second World War demonstrated how critical oil was to national power, and the United States was already becoming a more petroleum-based society. It pushed the United States to develop a wider approach to energy security, including preventing the rich oil resources of the Middle East falling into the hands of the Soviet Union.

As the United States' dependency on imported oil has become ever larger, so the importance of secure access to oil has risen ever higher on US foreign policy agenda. Not only does the Middle East have over two-thirds of the world's oil reserves. Its share of global output is predicted to rise from 27 per cent in 2000 to 43 per cent in 2030, and the share of imports in US oil supply is predicted to rise from 54 per cent in 2001 to 68 per cent in 2025 (Klare, 2004: 76). Within the Gulf region, five countries stand out: Saudi Arabia has 22 per cent of the world's oil reserves, followed by Iran with 11.5 per cent, Iraq with 9.6 per cent, Kuwait with 8.5 per cent, and the United Arab Emirates with 8.1 per cent (BP, 2006: 6). The share of the Gulf countries in world oil trade is predicted to rise from 41 per cent to 70 per cent in 2030 (Klare, 2004: 77–8). The US Government's National Energy Policy document of 2001 concluded: 'Middle East oil production will remain central to world oil security ... [and] the Gulf will be a primary focus of US international energy policy' (quoted in Klare, 2004: 78).

The United States has been deeply involved in the political economy of the key Middle Eastern oil-producing states, Saudi Arabia, Iran and Iraq.

Saudi Arabia. The fundamental lines of American policy in the region were established towards the end of the Second World War. The Saudi Arabian monarch, King Ibn Saud, made it clear that if Washington were willing to come forward with foreign aid, they would be willing to offer the US Government special access to Saudi oil. In February 1943, the American President authorised Lend Lease assistance to Saudi Arabia, and the United States began its long and deep involvement in Saudi Arabian politics and oil. A year later, in February 1944, a famous discussion took place between the British Ambassador in Washington (Lord Halifax) and President Roosevelt, in which Roosevelt showed the ambassador a map of the Middle East and said: 'Persian oil is yours. We share the oil of Iraq and Kuwait. As for Saudi Arabian oil, its ours' (quoted in Yergin, 1991: 401). The episode was a 'testament to the importance oil had assumed in world politics' (Yergin, 1991: 401). Ever since, the United States has closely supported Saudi Arabia's autocratic ruling family, politically, and militarily.

At the end of the Second World War, Saudi Arabia became 'the dominant focus of American policymakers' (Yergin, 1991: 427). The United States and Saudi Arabia formed a unique relationship. In October 1950, US President Harry Truman wrote to King Ibn Saud: 'I wish to renew to your majesty the assurances which have been made to you several times in the past, that the United States is interested in the preservation of independence and the territorial integrity of Saudi Arabia. No threat to your Kingdom could occur which would not be a matter of immediate concern to the United States' (quoted in Yergin, 1991: 428). Right through to the present day, the United States has 'provided the basic guarantee of Saudi Arabian territorial integrity and independence': 'It was an unlikely union – Bedouin Arabs and Texas oil men – a traditional Islamic autocracy allied with modern American capitalism. Yet it was one that was destined to endure' (Yergin, 1991: 426 and 428).

Since the end of the Second World War, Saudi Arabia has been closely allied with and dependent upon the United States, which has closely supported the country's autocratic rulers politically, diplomatically and militarily.

Today, many prominent members of the House of Saud are friends of senior American politicians, including both Bush presidents, and are investors in firms managed by prominent Republicans, including former Secretary of State, James Baker and former Secretary of Defense, Frank Carlucci (Klare, 2004: 89).

Iraq. At the end of the First World War, Britain took control of Iraq from Turkey, and ruled it as a colony on the Indian model. At the San Remo Conference of 1920, Britain and France divided the Arab world between them. Britain took control of Iraq and Palestine, while France took control of Lebanon and Syria: 'The British and French held complete sway over the fertile crescent states' (Lapidus, 2002: 539). These areas had been part of the Ottoman Empire, without distinct national identities. The British and French 'created the Arab states, gave them territorial boundaries and central regimes', and 'bequeathed to the future the dilemma of a cultural region partitioned into numerous small states' (Lapidus, 2002: 540). In 1930, Iraq became independent, but Britain still had control over Iraq's foreign and military affairs. In 1963, the Ba'ath party seized power, and set Iraq on its modern course. It declared Iraq to be a part of the Arab nation and a socialist society. It also declared itself to be an Islamic state, but it was far removed from the 'fundamentalist' Islamic government that was to come to power later in Iran, let alone that of the Taliban in Afghanistan. It nationalised the main banks and industries. Saddam Hussein came to power in 1968, and in 1972 Iraq completed the nationalisation of the country's oil resources. Under Saddam, the Ba'ath state created a 'wide base of public acceptance', providing 'extensive subsidies for urban middle-class education and health policies' (Lapidus, 202: 553).

Under Saddam, Iraq attempted to build itself into the leader of the Arab world. First, it attempted to capture the oil resources of Western Iran, which led to the prolonged war between the two countries. Then, it invaded Kuwait, in order to add Kuwait's huge oil resources to its own. The central importance of the region in US foreign policy was made clear through the first Gulf War, in which the United States drove Iraq out of Kuwait, and restored the country's vast oil reserves to its autocratic rulers. The First Gulf War made crystal clear the ultimate dependence of the region's autocratic rulers on the United States' protection. At the end of that war, the giant oil producers, Iraq and Iran, on the Northern and Eastern sides of the Gulf respectively, were both ruled by regimes hostile to the United States, while the oil-producing countries along the Western side of the Gulf, were all broadly sympathetic to, and reliant on, American support, both diplomatically and militarily. The region is characterised by an absence of democratic procedures and extreme inequality in the distribution of income and wealth.[72]

After the defeat of Saddam Hussein and his eviction from Kuwait, the United States stationed large numbers of troops in Kuwait and Saudi Arabia, and maintained no-fly zones over Northern and Southern Iraq. The United States enforced a blockade of Iraq's ports, which drastically restricted its international trade and hugely damaged the economy. The oil industry was crippled under the combined impact of prohibitions in international investment and bans on imported equipment. Iraq's oil production fell to les than one half its capacity (Klare, 2004: 96). It is thought that the direct and indirect effects of the American-enforced blockade contributed to the deaths of hundreds of thousands of Iraqi children due to lack of adequate food and healthcare (Klare, 2004: 95). American policy throughout the 1990s was aimed at stimulating internal dissatisfaction and the overthrow of Saddam Hussein. Instead, the suffering caused by American policies generated much popular support within Iraq and among the wider international Arab community. In March 2001, Secretary of State Colin Powell observed: 'We are being accused, and we are taking on the burden of hurting Iraqi people [and] hurting Iraqi children' (quoted in Klare, 2004: 95). At the same time he acknowledged also that when the Bush administration took office in 2001, America's Iraq policy was in disarray, 'and the sanctions part of that policy was not just in disarray, it was falling apart: We discovered that we were in an airplane that was waiting to crash' (quoted in Klare, 2004: 96–7).

The First Gulf War and the invasion of Iraq were intimately connected with the US search for energy security. Not only has the US position deteriorated sharply in terms of energy security, with a steadily rising share of its oil needs met through imports, but also, the National Oil Companies (NOCs) control around 70 per cent of the world's oil reserves. The top five oil companies are all among the top ten largest global companies (*Fortune*, 24 July 2006). Three of these (ExxonMobil, Chevron and Conoco Phillips) are headquartered in the United States, and the other two giants, BP and Shell, have a large share of their business in the United States. A decade or so ago, the leading international oil companies hoped that they would gain increasing access to the reserves controlled by the NOCs. However, this has not advanced as they had hoped and the international oil giants have been forced increasingly to develop expensive and inaccessible fields out of the control of the NOCs. The oilfields of Iraq (and Iran) are huge and low cost. The prospect of increased access to these oilfields is of perennial interest to the international oil giants.

Prior even to his assumption of power in 2001, several of George W. Bush's top officials believed that the answer to the Iraq question was self-evident: 'Invade Iraq, oust Saddam Hussein, and replace him with a new regime friendly to US interests' (Klare, 2004: 97). Several of his top officials, including Secretary of Defense Donald Rumsfeld and Deputy Secretary of

State Paul Wolfowitz, had indicated their support for such a plan before Bush's election in the form of a highly publicised letter written in January 1998. After Bush's election they continued to push strongly for military action, despite many voices within the US Government urging caution. In the early months of the Bush government, it was China, not the Middle East that was at the forefront of American international relations. The Bush regime came to power viewing China as a 'strategic adversary'. The collision between a Chinese fighter plane (in which the pilot died) and an American reconnaissance plane, which lost power and landed on Hainan Island, pushed US-China relations to the top of the international relations agenda.

However, on 11 September came the attack by Al Qaeda on the twin towers. Following the 9/11 attacks, the United States invaded Afghanistan in order to overthrow the Taliban regime.[73] Having completed the invasion of Afghanistan, in the early weeks of 2002, the Bush government prepared its plans to invade Iraq. In the teeth of widespread international opposition including mass protests across the length and breadth of Europe, the United States invaded Iraq ('Operation Iraqi Freedom') in a military campaign designed to 'shock and awe' the Iraqi population. Despite constant references by the military to a new type of weaponry with precision targeting, it is widely accepted that many tens of thousands of Iraqi civilians died during the American invasion, certainly a vastly greater number than lost their lives in the destruction of the twin towers. In addition, a huge number of people were wounded, lost their homes and were displaced due to the American invasion.

Senior US officials went to great lengths to avoid mentioning oil as a *casus belli*, since this would have undermined the US public's support for the war. Instead, the principal justifications given for the invasion, were that Iraq had played a role in the 9/11 attacks on the twin towers and that Saddam Hussein had developed 'weapons of mass destruction'. Both of these claims were later shown to be false. Instead, a large body of opinion across the world believed that the invasion was intimately connected with the Bush administration's wish to gain access to Iraqi oil. Indeed, in his August 2002 address to the Veterans of Foreign Wars, Vice-President Cheney declared:

> Should all [of Hussein's WMD] ambitions be realised, the implications would be enormous for the Middle East and the United States. Armed with an arsenal of these weapons and seated atop 10 per cent of the world's oil reserves, Saddam Hussein could then be expected to seek domination of the entire Middle East, take control of a great portion of the world's energy supplies, directly threaten America's friends throughout the region, and subject the United States or any other nation to nuclear blackmail (quoted in Klare, 2004: 99).

At its meetings in 2002–03 the US State Department's 'Future of Iraq' Project reportedly called for the opening up of Iraq's state-owned oil sector to outside investment after a period of rehabilitation of the oil fields (Klare, 2004: 99). The Department of Defense developed plans to seize control of Iraq's oilfields immediately after the invasion and prevent their destruction. The multi-billion contract to rehabilitate Iraq's oilfields was awarded to a subsidiary of the American company Halliburton, of which Vice-President Cheney had formerly been the CEO. American oil companies did little to disguise their hopes that they would be at the centre of the Iraqi oil industry under the post-Saddam government. In early 2003, one oil company executive commented: 'For any oil company, being in Iraq is like being a kid in F. A. O. Schwarz' (quoted in Klare, 2004: 104).

For many commentators, the link between oil and the American war to topple Saddam was obvious. Incurring intense hostility for their views, some people even dared to ask the question in relation to 9/11: 'Who gains (*cui bono*)?' Gore Vidal, for example, argued that the negligence of the American intelligence agencies in failing to prevent the 9/11 attacks may have been intentional, with the objective of justifying the US invasion of Afghanistan and Iraq, in order to allow the United States to firmly establish its control over the region's vast oil resources (Vidal, 2002).

The Bush government hoped that the invasion would replace Saddam Hussein with a stable pro-Western government that would boost oil output with large-scale involvement of Western oil companies. Instead, the American invasion massively backfired in terms of the Bush administration's objectives. As most Middle Eastern experts had predicted, the country descended into anarchy and civil war. Instead of being governed by Saddam Hussein's authoritarian regime, Iraq became the scene of violent chaos. Representatives from the dominant Shi'ite population dominated the new Iraqi government, elected in 2005. The overthrow of Saddam Hussein by the United States' violent intervention massively inflamed Arab public opinion on all sides against the United States. It also provided an opportunity for Iran to extend greatly its influence in the region, due to the closeness of its relationship with the Shi'ite majority that now ruled Iraq. The previously dominant Sunni minority entered a bitter civil war with the now dominant Shi'ite majority population.

By late 2006 it was widely acknowledged that the US invasion of Iraq had failed. In December 2006, Brzezinski bluntly summarised the situation: '[The] war has been a disaster' (*FT*, 5 December 2006).

It was widely accepted that the war had resulted in a deterioration in the welfare of the Iraqi population. A report in the UK medical journal *The Lancet*, estimated that there had been 655 000 'excess deaths' in Iraq since the American invasion (*FT*, 12 October 2006). This is equivalent to

2.5 per cent of the total Iraqi population. Of these, the report estimates that 601 000 died because of violence, usually gunfire. It estimates that the mortality rate doubled from 5.5 per thousand people before the invasion to 13.3 per thousand after the invasion.[74] Although the findings in the report were hotly contested, it was indisputable that Iraq had descended into uncontrollable violence, with many tens of killings each day.

The collapse of order in Iraq, and its threat of wider political implications, was a major factor in the rapid increase in the world oil price. This, in its turn, strongly assisted the oil-producing economies by greatly increasing their foreign exchange earnings. It contributed to greatly increased confidence among the governments of oil-exporting countries, including Russia. It provided greatly increased resources for the budgets of anti-American governments, such as Hugo Chavez, the Venezuelan president, with which to support anti-poverty polices, and win political influence. President Chavez was re-elected in December 2006 with a greatly increased share of the vote.

The increased oil price greatly reduced the incentive for NOCs to involve the leading international oil companies in the development of their oilfields. By late 2006, it was widely accepted that Iraq had descended into civil war, and that the United States had 'lost the war' in Iraq, and faced the prospect of a humiliating withdrawal, analogous to that from Vietnam. The disaster in Iraq threatened to produce 'domino' effects in terms of the comprehensive de-stabilisation of the Middle East. The war in Iraq had produced a growing inter-dependence between the formal mortal enemies, Iran and Iraq, bringing together their mainly Shi'ite populations in a way that threatened fundamentally to re-shape the region. Many people in the US Government sought to place the blame for the disaster in Iraq on external forces, especially intervention by Iran.

The bipartisan Iraq Study Group published its report on 6 December 2006. It 'repudiated virtually all of the policies that Mr Bush has pursued towards Iraq since 2002' (*FT*, 7 December 2006). It underlined the 'staggering cost of a war that is failing', both in terms of the almost 3000 US troops killed and the US$ 400 billion spent on the war to date (*FT*, 7 December 2006). The Report disputed the assertion that the violence in Iraq was mainly due to Al Qaeda, arguing instead that it was responsible for 'only small portions of the violence'. The Report argued that instead of viewing the invasion of Iraq as the basis for spreading democracy to the rest of the Middle East, the goal of American foreign policy should be to stop the fires of the conflict reaching beyond Iraq. It argued that the Arab-Israeli conflict is at the centre of the ongoing crisis in the Middle East: 'Instead of occupying Baghdad to open the route to fixing Jerusalem, there must be a renewed and sustained commitment by the United States to a comprehensive Arab-Israeli peace on all fronts. This includes talks between Israel and Syria and Israel and the Palestinians'.

However, the powerful pro-Israeli lobby group, the American-Israel Public Affairs Committee responded by rejecting any assertion that resolving the Israeli-Palestinian conflict was the key to stabilising Iraq (*FT*, 7 December 2006). In response to the Report, Israeli officials were 'confident that Washington would neither ease its policy against Iran's alleged nuclear weapons programme nor exert undue pressure over the Palestinian issue as part of efforts to reverse the crisis in Iraq' (*FT*, 7 December 2006).

It was widely acknowledged also that the war had intensified anti-American feelings throughout the Islamic world. Former US national security advisor, Zbigniew Brzezinski warned of the potentially disastrous impact of US Middle Eastern policies upon American foreign policy interests:

[T]he US role in the world is being gravely undermined by the policies launched more than three years ago. The destructive war in Iraq, the hypocritical indifference to the human dimension of the stalemate in Israeli-Palestinian relations, the lack of diplomatic initiatives in dealing with Iran and the frequent use of Islamophobic rhetoric, are setting in motion forces that threaten to push America out of the Middle East, with dire consequences for itself and its friends in Egypt, Jordan and Saudi Arabia (*FT*, 5 December 2006).

Iran. In 1919 the ancient state of Iran was made a virtual protectorate under the Anglo-Persian Treaty. This was denounced in 1921, and in 1925, the modern Iranian state came into being when Reza Khan, came to power as head of the army, declaring himself the Shah of Iran (Lapidus, 2002: 476). Under his rule, Iran developed towards an authoritarian, secular, and modernising state. It built a powerful army, established a secular education system, and required that every judge hold a degree from Tehran University, which had been founded in 1935. This deeply undermined the authority of the '*ulama*', the scholars or learned men of Islam. The infrastructure of a modern capitalist economy was developed in the 1920s and 1930s. Oil was discovered in Iran in 1908. Production was dominated by the Anglo-Persian Oil Company, in which the British government established a controlling interest in 1914.

In the late 1940s, the United States became deeply involved in Iran's internal political development. It wanted to forestall Soviet acquisition of Iran's oil assets and its advance through Iran towards the warm waters of the Persian Gulf. The United States advised the Iranian government on economic policy, organised Iran's police and army, and supplied it with military aid. British control of Iranian oil production aroused intense national hostility. In 1951, Prime Minister Mosaddeq pushed a bill through Parliament to nationalise Iran's oil assets. In 1953, the CIA helped the army to overthrow Mosaddeq and return power to the Shah. In 1954, the Iranian National Oil Company was formed and jointly operated the oil fields with a consortium of international companies, including the Anglo-Persian Oil Company (renamed British Petroleum) and several American oil companies.

The Shah ruled with virtually absolute powers. Throughout these years, the United States was preoccupied with the possibility that Iran's vast oil resources might fall into the hands of the Soviet Union. Following state-led, inward-looking economic policies, and with the benefit of large oil revenues, Iran made substantial industrial progress. The Shah controlled the army, secret police (SAVAK) and the intelligence agency. He appointed the ministers, selected half of the senate and manipulated parliamentary elections (Lapidus, 2002: 480). A small elite dominated Iran's political life. Iran was closely allied to the United States, and was dependent on US military assistance and financial support. It maintained close relations with Israel. The Shah's authoritarian regime crushed the Communist Party (Tudch) and National Parties, as well as bids for regional autonomy by Kurds, Arabs and Baluchi minorities (Lapidus, 2002: 481).

In the 1970s, the Pahlavi regime became increasingly oppressive. Huge fortunes were earned from oil revenues, but they accrued to a tiny elite and the government spent a large fraction of its income on armaments, mainly supplied by the United States. The fact that the regime was based on American political and military support strongly contributed to intense popular anger against the Shah's regime. In 1979 these discontents spilled over into the Iranian Revolution, which toppled the Shah and brought to power a new Islamic regime, under which the Ayatollah became the official head of government. Ayatollah Khomeini returned from exile to take up this position. The new regime pursued a fiercely puritanical form of Islam. They carried out large-scale purges of national and religious minorities, as well as purges of liberal nationals, Marxists, and the *mujahideen*. Large segments of the Westernised middle class fled into exile, where they remain to this day. Their flight seriously harmed Iran's economic development.

In 1980, Iraq attacked Iran in the hope of capturing the rich oilfields in the West of the country, close to the Iraqi border. The subsequent eight-year war was horrific. Not only was there dreadful human suffering, but also the economy grew by less than one per cent per annum during the 1980s (Pesaran, 2005). Saddam Hussein was confident that the United States would not intervene on the side of revolutionary Iran, and from 1985 the

United States tilted decisively in favour of Saddam Hussein's government in Iraq, supplying it with arms and intelligence information. Throughout the period since the 1979 revolution, the United States has attempted to de-stabilise the Iranian government. Its persistent hope has been that 'regime change' will lead to the emergence of a pro-Western government that will be friendly to the United States and allow large-scale involvement of Western oil companies: 'If the [Bush] administration could have its wish, the clerical junta that now controls Iran would be replaced by a Western-oriented government that rejects terrorism and nuclear weapons and throws open the country's state-owned oil industry to outside – especially American – investment' (Klare, 2004: 105).

The United States has operated trade sanctions against Iran for over two decades since the Iranian Revolution of 1979 (Pesaran, 2005). The first US sanctions against Iran were ordered by the Carter administration in April 1980. In the years 1988–91 the trade restrictions were slightly relaxed. However, after the First Gulf War of 1991 the sanctions intensified. In 1993, the so-called 'dual containment' policy was initiated by the Clinton administration. This policy focused on the 'dual threats' from Iran and Iraq. This was followed by the Iran-Libya investment sanctions (1996–99), which aimed mainly at hampering the development of the Iranian and Libyan oil industries. Non-US firms investing more than US$ 20 million in any one-year period were subject to a series of sanctions from the US Government.[75] Continuation of the sanctions was endorsed by the administration of George W. Bush.

At the end of the 1990s, there was clear evidence that the Iranian regime, under President Khatami, was making moves towards significant change in the country's internal political economy and its international relations, in response to 'overwhelming popular passion for change' (*FT*, 11 August 2006). After the mid-1990s, the Iranian government undertook substantial economic liberalisation, including privatisation of state-owned enterprises, reduction of import controls, reduction of food and energy subsidies, unification of the exchange rate system, and establishment of an oil stabilisation fund, alongside further expansion of the higher education system (Pesaran, 2005). The rate of growth of GDP accelerated to around 6 per cent per annum (Table 3).

Instead of responding positively to Iran's moves towards economic and social liberalisation, President Clinton not only failed to respond, but intensified the regime of sanctions against Iran. President George W. Bush responded even more aggressively to Iran's tentative suggestion of a 'Grand Bargain' in 2003. Instead it deemed Iran to be part of the 'Axis of Evil'. Iran was even designated by the United States (and the UK Prime Minister Tony Blair), to be the leading force in a 'Crescent of Evil' in the Islamic world.

Instead of moving in the direction that the United States wished, Iran's elections in 2005 brought to power, by a large popular mandate, a new President, Ahmadi-Nejad. The new president was more hostile to the United States and to Israel than his predecessor, President Khatami. His populist commitment to the mass of poor Iranians was based on Islamic foundations, and was strongly appealing to large sections of the population. One important consequence of the rise in oil prices, itself powerfully stimulated by the instability produced in the Middle East by American foreign policy, was that it provided resources for Ahmadi-Nejad's populist regime to enhance their government-funded programmes of social welfare.

The disintegration of Iraq and the success of Hizbollah in Lebanon intensified antagonism towards Iran among the policy-making circles around President Bush. From early in its existence, the Shi'ite Hizbollah movement in Lebanon was strongly supported in its battle with Israel by the post-revolutionary government in Iran. In addition, Iran announced that it was pressing ahead with a plan to enrich uranium, which could provide it with the capability at some point to produce nuclear weapons.[76] In the course of 2006, a number of US policy advisors floated the possibility of a major US air attack on Iran, aimed at destroying Iran's nuclear facilities and achieving the goal of 'regime change' that had been sought by the United States ever since the overthrow of the Shah (Hersh, 2006). In order to ensure the success of this endeavour, it was estimated that 'at least four hundred targets would have to be hit' (Hersh, 2006). Moreover, in order to be sure of the destruction of the alleged deeply-buried nuclear sites across Iran, it was argued that the United States would need to use 'tactical nuclear weapons': 'Every other option, in the view of the nuclear weapons experts, would leave a gap ... It's a tough decision. But we made it in Japan' (former senior US intelligence official, quoted in Hersh, 2006).[77]

Israel was a key ally in the debate over Iran's nuclear programme. Its leaders warned that any attempt by Iran to begin enriching uranium would be regarded as a point of no return. In a speech on 20 March 2006, President Bush depicted President Ahmadi-Nejad's hostility to Israel as a 'serious threat': 'It's a threat to world peace. I made it clear. I'll make it clear again, that we will use military might to protect our ally Israel' (quoted in Hersh, 2006). However, one senior diplomat observed that there was much more at stake for the United States than 'simply' the nuclear issue: 'That's just a rallying point, and there is still time to fix it. But the [Bush] administration believes it cannot be fixed unless they control the hearts and minds of Iran. The real issue is who is going to control the Middle East and its oil in the next ten years' (quoted in Hersh, 2006).

The possibility that the United States might attack Iran was being increasingly mooted in the wake of the disastrous campaign in Iraq. Even the *Financial Times*, in an editorial commented:

The president [Bush] seems incapable of acknowledging the scale of the disaster in Iraq. He and his coterie blame the Iraqis and Iran for US failures. They persist in identifying the US national interest and Israeli hegemony as the same thing ... There is a terrifying possibility this administration will raise the stakes and compound the Iraq misadventure into a regional and international catastrophe by attacking Iran – or by acquiescing in an attack by Israel (*FT*, 11 December 2006).

Israel

Israel-Palestine. In addition to its deep involvement in the world's critical oil-producing countries of the Middle East, the United States' relationship to the region has been massively influenced by its remorseless support for Israel.

Palestine (*Syria Palestina*) was a province within the Roman Empire. From AD 66 until AD 135 there was a series of revolts against Roman rule. The final revolt was crushed and a great slaughter of Jewish people was followed by the expulsion of the surviving Jews from Palestine. The Old Testament, and, especially, the books of the Torah (the five books of Moses), was critical to the survival of Jewish culture. At the heart of this was the Biblical account of the Jews' repeated exile and re-occupation of Palestine. For 2000 years, only a tiny number of Jews lived in Palestine. In the late nineteenth century it was part of the Turkish Empire, which had entered its final stages of decay. The question of national identity in the Middle East is vexed. The Ottoman Empire included most of present-day Iraq, Syria, Lebanon, Jordan and Israel. By the late Ottoman period, 'Greater Syria' had developed into an integrated economic unit linked by modern infrastructure, with a consolidated market network (Gelvin, 2005: 95). After the First World War, the division of the region into smaller states under separate British and French rule[78] prevented the further development of Greater Syria into a single geo-political unit.

In 1878 a small group of Hungarian Jews established a pioneering village at Petach Tikvah, and within a few years, around 1000 Jewish farming families had settled in Palestine. A wider Zionist movement was sparked by the publication in 1896 of Theodor Herzl's book *The Jewish State*, written in response to rising European and Russian anti-Semitism. In Herzl's view, if Jews were able to establish their own state in Palestine, they would 'form a rampart of Europe against Asia, an outpost of civilisation as opposed to barbarism' (quoted in Gelvin, 2005: 51). Inspired by Herzl's book, the first Zionist Congress was held in Basle in the summer of 1897. Their programme opened with the sentence: 'Zionism strives to create a home in Palestine for the Jewish people, which is secured by public law' (Samuel, 1969: 29). It called for 'the colonisation of Palestine by Jewish agricultural and industrial workers' (Gelvin, 2005: 52). By 1914, there were around 85 000 Jews in Palestine, almost all first generation immigrants. However, Palestine was not 'a land without a people': despite the large influx of Jews, they made up only around one ninth of the total population of around 750 000 at that time: (Gelvin, 2005: 30).

At the heart of the Zionist vision was the reclamation by Jews of the ancient territory that they had occupied 2000 years previously. However, the rise of Zionist nationalism was a late development in the history of the Jewish people. It emerged in the late nineteenth century alongside the growth of nationalism in Europe, during its modern capitalist development. For centuries, most Jewish people had felt themselves to be part of the culture in which they lived, bound together by a common religion, but with no thought of establishing a separate state based on their ancient religion. To this day, a significant minority of Jewish people feel that their main identity is with the country of their birth rather than with Israel.

For some Jewish socialists, their identity is not with a particular country, but rather with the whole of humanity. The idea of establishing a 'Jewish state', whether in Israel or elsewhere, is anathema for them. They believe that this reinforces the damaging divisions created and reinforced by nationalism, which divides the people of the world. These Jews believe that nationalism in whatever guise encourages conflict between people who are in a common class position and have common interests that are concealed by nationalism. Karl Marx, a Jew,[79] was remorselessly internationalist in his outlook. Among a later generation of Jews, Rosa Luxemburg, who was to become leader of the German Communist Party, was also ferociously internationalist, and, therefore, resolutely opposed to establishing a Jewish state:

> I feel equally close to the wretched victims of the rubber plantations in Putamayo, or to the Negroes in Africa with whose bodies the Europeans play catch-ball.... [T]his 'sublime stillness of the infinite' in which so many screams fade away unheard – it reverberates within me so strongly that I have no separate corner in my heart for the ghetto. I feel at home in the entire world wherever there are clouds and birds and human tears (quoted in Gelvin, 2005: 54).

In the inter-war period, communist Jews such as Eric Hobsbawm,[80] were 'anti-Zionist on principle': 'Ours was a movement for all humanity and not for any particular section of it. It represented the ideal of transcending selfishness, individual and collective. Time and again young Jews who began as Zionists became communists because, obvious as the sufferings of the Jews were, they were only part of the universal oppression' (Hobsbawm, 2002: 137 and 173). In his autobiography, Hobsbawm commented: '[I]f we make the thought experiment of supposing that Herzl's dream came true and all Jews ended up in a small independent territorial state which excluded from full citizenship all who were not the sons of Jewish mothers, it would be a bad day for the rest of humanity – and for the Jews themselves' (Hobsbawm, 2003: 25).

The five books of the Torah (the five 'books of Moses') are at the heart of Jewish culture. The Torah remorselessly chronicles the Lord's promise to the Jewish people to provide them with their own territory. According to the Torah, the Lord said to Abram:

> Get thee out of thy country, and from thy kindred, and from thy father's house, unto a land that I will shew thee; and I will make thee a great nation, and I will bless thee and make thy name great; and thou shalt be a blessing ... and they went forth to go into the land of Canaan ... and the Lord appeared unto Abram, and said, Unto thy seed will I give this land ... For all the land which thou seest, to thee I will give it, and to thy seed forever ... Arise and walk through the land in the length of it and in the breadth of it; for I will give it unto thee (Genesis: 12 and 13).

The Torah chronicles the repeated exile of the Jews from that territory, and its violent re-conquest with the support of the Lord:

> When the Lord thy God shall bring thee into the land whither thou goest to possess it, and hath cast out many nations before thee ... nations greater and mightier than thee ... and when the Lord thy God shall deliver them before thee; thou shalt smite them, and utterly destroy them; and thou shalt make no covenant with them, nor show mercy unto them ... But thus shall ye deal with them; ye shall destroy their altars, and break down their images, and cut down their groves, and burn their graven images with fire. For thou art an holy people unto the Lord thy God: the Lord thy God hath chosen thee to be a special people unto himself, above all people on the face of the earth ... And thou shalt consume all the people which the Lord thy God shall deliver thee; thine eyes shall have no pity upon them ... and the Lord thy God will put out those nations before thee by little and little ... [T]he Lord thy God shall deliver them unto thee, and shall destroy them with a mighty destruction, until they be destroyed (Deuteronomy: 7).

The Israeli people's close identification with the Torah was shown in striking fashion after the Six Day War in 1967, which led to a large expansion of

Israel's boundaries. At the end of the war, Israelis were intoxicated at being able to visit all the places they had read about in the Old Testament:

> Israelis toured all the new territories ... With unquenchable excitement and interest they stood in line to enter the Tomb of Rachel in Bethlehem and the burial place of the Patriarchs of Hebron. They drove through Nablus and Jericho; went on long, uncomfortable trips through the wilderness of the Sinai Peninsula; and picnicked amid the formidable fortifications on the Golan Heights. Everywhere, families took the Bible along as a guidebook, showing enthralled children the places from which they had been barred for so long (Samuel, 1969: 169–70).

Israelis felt that they were 'the natural heirs to the land of their forefathers, living threads in a historic tapestry first woven in this same Land some four thousand years ago'. In these people 'flickered a flame of love for Israel which had first been lit when Abraham, obeying the word of the Lord, led his people into the Promised Land' (Samuel, 1969: 175).

In 1917, Britain began its campaign in Palestine against Turkey. A Jewish Legion assisted in the capture of the Holy Land. In November 1917, the British Government issued the Balfour Declaration: 'Her Majesty's Government view with favour the establishment in Palestine of a national home for the Jewish people, and will use their best endeavours to facilitate the achievement of this object' (quoted in Samuel, 1969: 42). In 1920, Britain was given the Mandate for Palestine by the League of Nations. A British Jew, Sir Herbert Samuel, was appointed to be the first British High Commissioner for Palestine. The Jewish population in Palestine were 'jubilant': 'For the first time in 1850 years, a Jew ruled over the Land of Israel' (Samuel, 1969: 43).[81] In 1922, the United Senate and House of Representatives placed on record that 'the United States favours the establishment in Palestine of a national home for the Jewish people' (Samuel, 1969: 47).

From 1919 to 1925, around 50 000 Jewish migrants arrived in Palestine. The League of Nations described the Jewish settlement of Palestine as 'the greatest colonising enterprise in modern times' and Winston Churchill described it as 'a great event in the world's destiny' (Samuel, 1969: 48). However, there was intense opposition from the people, including both Arabs and Greek Orthodox Christians, who lived in Palestine. Hostility to Jewish colonisation of Palestine helped to forge a sense of Palestinian national identity. Also, from the beginning of the establishment of the state of Israel, there was deep resentment among Palestinians at the role played by the leading international powers, first Britain, and then the United States, in enabling the Jewish colonisation to be carried out effectively. By the mid-1930s, these feelings erupted into full-blown revolts against Jewish settlement. The Jewish settlers also organised their own military self-defence force, the *Haganah*.

The peak of the conflict between the Jewish colonists and the indigenous Palestinians occurred in the Great Revolt of 1936–37.[82] During the violent struggle, the Stern Gang, a Jewish self-defence force,[83] committed 'some of the most appalling atrocities in modern Palestine' including extensive reprisal bombings in Arab markets (Gelvin, 2005: 72). By the autumn of 1937 there were many thousands of Arab guerrillas operating in the countryside. The British imported a special force of 20 000 troops, which worked in tandem with Zionist 'special night squads'. The British and their Zionist counterparts used the usual tactics of counter-insurgency, including the collective punishment of entire villages, targeted assassinations, mass arrests, deportation, dynamiting homes of suspected guerrillas and sympathisers (Gelvin, 2005: 113). It is estimated that upwards of 10 per cent of the male population of Palestine was killed ... wounded, imprisoned or exiled (Gelvin, 2005: 129). Long after its brutal suppression, the Great Revolt continued to provide a symbol of national resistance for Palestine.

As Hitler's oppression of the Jews intensified in the 1930s, the number of Jewish people who migrated to Palestine from Germany and elsewhere in Europe increased. Amos Oz, the Jewish novelist, in his autobiography writes about his uncle Abraham, who migrated to Palestine in 1933: '[H]e was a nationalist, a patriot, a lover of armies and conquests, a passionate, innocent-minded hawk who believed that if only we Jews girded ourselves with courage, boldness, iron resolve, etc., if only we finally rose up and stopped worrying about the Gentiles, we could defeat all our foes and the whole cruel, wicked Gentile world would come and bow down before us' (Oz, 2005: 78). In 1935 alone, nearly 70 000 Jewish immigrants entered Palestine (Samuel, 1969: 51). By 1939 there were almost half a million Jews living in 250 settlements (Lapidus, 2002: 557).

In the inter-war period, despite the Great Depression, the Palestinian economy grew quite rapidly. The population grew from an estimated 752 000 people in 1922, to 1.7 million in 1944. The Jewish population increased at a faster rate than the Muslim population, due almost entirely to immigration. However, the natural growth rate of the Arab population was almost 3 per cent per annum. Consequently, the absolute increase in the two populations between these two dates was remarkably similar, totalling 445 000 for the Jews and 471 000 for the Muslims. By 1944, there were 529 00 Jews (30 per cent of the total) and 1.06 million Muslims (61 per cent of the total) (Owen and Pamuk, 1998: 249).

The Jewish immigrants acquired substantial amounts of land from local landowners. The acquisition of land by Jewish immigrants helped to produce a growing number of landless families among the Arab population. By 1937 they occupied around 10 per cent of Palestine's cultivated land, mainly in the most productive areas along the coast (Owen and Pamuk, 1998: 59). Commercial agriculture grew significantly, with a large increase in the output of higher value crops, especially citrus fruits, which accounted for over a third of the value of agricultural output for the Arab population and two-thirds for the Jews. However, the Jewish immigrants mainly lived in the urban areas. On average, they were better educated and had more capital than the local population. Industrial output increased sevenfold in the period 1922–39 (Owen and Pamuk, 1998: 60). It was mainly produced in small firms in the light industrial sector. On average, the Jewish population had much higher incomes than the indigenous Arab population. However, within the Arab community there were also large differences in income and wealth, with a small group of landowners and merchants enjoying a 'vastly superior' standard of living than the ordinary Arab population (Owen and Pamuk, 1998: 61).

During the inter-war period, nationalist sentiment among the Palestinian community intensified. The most politically vocal part of the community consistently demanded independence for a united Palestine from British rule, and rejected proposals to divide Palestine between Jews and Arabs.[84] Nationalist sentiments among both the Jewish and Palestinian communities was fuelled by use of the vocabulary from the Jewish and Islamic religions respectively (Gelvin, 2005: 109).

The New York World's Fair of 1939–40 provided a vivid insight into the nationalist aspirations of Zionism. The World Fair was based around pavilions constructed by each of the participating nations. The one exception was the 'Jewish Palestine Pavilion', which represented a community, namely the Yishuv colonists in Palestine, rather than a nation. The dioramas in the pavilion portrayed Palestine as an empty wilderness which had been fructified by the arrival of Jewish colonists: 'For centuries this ancient land lay barren and neglected, ravaged by wars fought over its holy sites ... A primitive population lived a semi-nomadic life in this land, which could barely provide them with a meagre sustenance ... Into this land came Jewish settlers, inspired by the hope of the establishing there a new home for the oppressed' (quoted in Gelvin, 2005: 149). The pavilion was designed in the form of a tower and stockade, which had become a key symbol for the settlers. The pavilion was designed to demonstrate the Jewish settlers as an outpost of civilisation in a savage land, and the Zionist settlers as heroic frontiersmen. The American director described the effect the pavilion would have on young visitors.

He imagined they would say to themselves: 'That's just like American history. Those pioneers defending their stockades against the howling Arab terrorists are no different from our ancestors fighting off the howling Indians' (quoted in Gelvin, 2005: 152).

As in many parts of the developing world, the wartime period was one of considerable progress in capitalist, import-substituting development. The sharp reduction in foreign trade due to the conflict acted as a form of protection for the local economy. Capitalism in both the Jewish and Arab communities progressed rapidly during these years, which were thereafter referred to as the 'Prosperity'. From 1939–42 industrial output in Jewish-owned factories increased 200 per cent and in Palestinian-owned factories, output increased by an estimated 77 per cent. During the same period, agricultural output rose by more than 30 per cent. Unemployment was virtually eliminated in Palestine (Gelvin, 2005: 120).

With the onset of the Second World War, Britain shifted its policy in order to placate the Arabs, and gain their support in the struggle against Germany. Jewish immigration was restricted, and there followed intense struggles of Jewish settlers against the British, including many acts of terrorist violence committed against the British forces by the Irgun and Stern Gang (Gelvin, 2005: 123).[85] After the end of the War, the appalling facts of Hitler's death camps for Jewish people came to light. The genocide against Jewish people in the death camps stands out among the many horrific crimes of the twentieth century.[86] It helped greatly to increase international sympathy for the idea of establishing a 'Jewish national home'.

The revelations of the genocide also greatly intensified the determination of the Zionists to establish an independent 'homeland'. In mid-November, the leader of the Jewish people in Palestine, David Ben-Gurion returned from a mission to Germany. He gave a speech on his findings to the Representative Assembly of the Jews in Palestine. A recording of his speech is lodged in the archives of Kol Yisrael, the Israeli state radio station: 'I was in Dachau and Belsen. I saw the gas chambers, where every day they poisoned thousands of Jews, men and women, the aged and the elderly, infants and children, led them naked as if they were going to take showers. The gas chambers are really built as if they are shower rooms, and the Nazis could peep in from the outside to see the Jews writhe and struggle in their death throes'. Ben-Gurion's voice is restrained. From time to time, someone in the audience can be heard sobbing, or emitting a sigh of pain (Gelvin, 2005: 28).

It was also a politically convenient solution for Europe as it meant that they did not have to deal with the re-settlement of millions of displaced Jews. The United States also would not face pressure to support large-scale Jewish immigration. In April 1945, Harry Truman became US President. In August 1945, Truman announced that he would support both the partition of Palestine and the establishment of an independent Jewish state. Truman's advisors argued that the United States had a moral commitment to the victims of the Holocaust and that the Jewish vote was crucial to his political security. In addition the advisors pointed out that with American support, Israel could become a 'Western outpost in a potentially hostile region' (Gelvin, 2005: 125). The fact that there was already a powerful Zionist settler movement in Palestine, aided by an extremely powerful Jewish lobby in the United States,[87] helped to produce the fateful decision to attempt to establish this new state in Palestine.

In 1947, Britain announced that it would relinquish the Mandate to govern Palestine and withdraw its troops by May 1948. It passed over to the newly-founded United Nations the question of how to resolve the Palestinian issue. At this point the UN had just 51 member nations. A large number of countries were not represented because they were still ruled by the colonial powers. By 1965 the UN had grown to include 118 members. The United Nations Special Commission on Palestine (UNSCOP) produced two reports. The minority report recommended the establishment of a single federal state containing both Jews and Arabs. However, the majority report recommended the partition of Palestine into two states, one Jewish and one Arab. This drastically shrank the territory of Palestine.

Some Israeli politicians acknowledged that the land they seized in establishing Israel was, indeed, already occupied, and that its seizure would lead to lasting conflict. Israeli Prime Minister David Ben-Gurion is reported to have said:

> Why should the Arabs make peace? If I were an Arab leader I would never make terms with Israel. That is natural: we have taken their country. Sure, God promised it to us, but what does that matter to them? Our God is not theirs. We came from Israel, it's true, but two thousand years ago, and what is that to them? There has been anti-Semitism, the Nazis, Hitler, Auschwitz, but was that their fault? They see only one thing: we have come here and stolen their country. Why should they accept that? (quoted in Lieven, 2004: 196).

The UN decision to establish an independent state of Israel was forcibly resisted by the Arab League, and a violent war followed. From the outset, Israel received the strong backing of the US Government and support from the American Jewish community. The First Arab-Israeli war ended in defeat for the Arabs and the establishment of the state of Israel in 1948. At the same time the state of

Transjordan absorbed the portions of Palestine west of the Jordan River and Egypt took control of Gaza.[88] Israel remained in a state of war with Egypt until 1979 and with Jordan until 1994. It remains in a state of war with Syria and Iraq.

The war became know as the 'War of Independence' for the Israelis and as the 'disaster' (*nakba*) for the Palestinians. The Israelis fought both the indigenous Palestinians and the surrounding Arab states. The Israelis were assisted by the American Jews, who supplied the foundation of Israeli armaments capacity through their financial aid. Also, the Arab states were divided, with conflicting objectives, and failed to fight as a single army. Jordan aimed to use the war to establish a state of Greater Syria under its leadership, comprising Palestine, Syria and Lebanon as well as Jordan. Egypt, Syria and Saudi Arabia regarded this as a 'Hashemite conspiracy' between Jordan and Iraq to dominate the Arab world.

In the first eighteen months of the existence of the new state of Israel, 341 000 Jews arrived in Israel (Samuel, 1969: 128).

During the war an estimated 750 000 or so Palestinians who had lived within the territory over which Israel claimed sovereignty became refugees, scattered on the West Bank of the Jordan River and exiled into Transjordan, Lebanon, Syria, and other Arab states. Between 65 to 85 per cent of Palestinians living within the boundaries of Israel were forced into permanent exile. Another 25 per cent were uprooted and became internal refugees within Israel. Around 1.3 million Palestinian refugees still live in camps run by the UNRWA (United Nations Relief and Works Agency). It is estimated that the Israeli Government took over approximately 94 per cent of the property abandoned by the Palestinians who had fled, and distributed the property to Jewish Israelis (Gelvin, 2005: 166).

It is estimated that more than 500 Palestinian villages disappeared forever. In a campaign know as 'Operation Hiram', wholesale transfer of population took place in the Galilee region. Zionist forces engaged in 'an unusually high concentration of executions of people against a wall or next to a well in an orderly fashion' (Benny Morris, quoted in Gelvin, 2005: 137). The Israeli 'revisionist' historian Benny Morris has catalogued a total of twenty-four incidents of terror or massacre, the worst of them involving the killing of hundreds of people.

The Palestinians who remained within Israel were subject to martial law until 1966 (Gelvin, 2005: 135). Former Israeli Prime Minister Ehud Barak acknowledged: '[It] was the shattering of a whole society, accompanied by thousands of deaths and the wholesale destruction of hundreds of villages' (quoted in Gelvin, 2005: 127). Israel's constitution affirms the 'right of return' to Israel for Jews from any country. Israel argued that as Arabs, the refugees could find homes in the Arab states. The masses of Palestinians in exile remained in refugee camps and Israel refused to countenance their repatriation. Albert Hourani commented: 'After 1948, the first step to peace was that Israel should recognise its responsibility to the Arabs who lived in its territory but had been displaced by the fighting. Only this could have set in motion a train of events leading towards peace; and only Israel could have taken the step. Israel never did so, and its attitude was accepted by the Western Powers' (quoted in Gelvin, 2005: 134).

A decade of border clashes culminated in the Second Arab-Israeli War in June 1967. In 1964, Israel unilaterally diverted the Jordan River away from Syria. The resulting dispute flared up in May 1967, and Israel massed troops on Syria's border. Egypt was informed by the Soviet Union that Israel was preparing to attack Syria and Nasser sent the Egyptian army into Sinai. He then ordered the closure of the Strait of Tiran, which denied Israel access to the Red Sea. This produced a massively disproportionate response from Israel. In the first few hours of the Six Day War, Israeli air strikes destroyed 90 per cent of the Egyptian air force, about 70 per cent of the Syrian air force and almost all of the Jordanian air force.

The war ended in complete victory for Israel. It took possession of Gaza and the Sinai from Egypt,[89] the West Bank from Jordan (as it had then become), the Golan Heights from Syria. Israel also won control over Jerusalem. In the subsequent years, strong movements developed within Israel calling for the colonisation of the West Bank, and for the annexation of the West Bank and Gaza. Israel expropriated land and water resources. During the 1990s, the number of settlers on the West Bank grew by 50 per cent, four times the rate of growth of population inside Israel proper (*FT*, 4 August 2006). By the late 1990s, there were over 140 Israeli settlements in the West Bank and Gaza (Lapidus, 2002). East Jerusalem was encircled in this period and enclosed by four big blocks of settlements. Housing and zoning restrictions inside the city helped ensure a Jewish majority. In the words of Ariel Sharon: 'In Jerusalem we built and created facts that can no longer be changed' (quoted in *Financial Times*, 4 August 2006).

Following the Israeli victory in 1967, the Palestine Liberation Organisation (PLO) came into being, with the main goal of returning the Palestinian homeland to the Palestinians.[90] Palestinian identity became increasingly strong. This culminated at the end of the 1980s in the so-called '*intifada*' campaigns of protest against the Israeli occupation, and the demand for the formation of a Palestinian state. Palestinian opinion divided. On the one hand there were those who favoured compromise with Israel, and the establishment of a secular state on the West Bank. On the other hand, there were those, mainly the Islamists, who favoured a continuing struggle for the liberation of all of Palestine (Lapidus, 2002: 563). Hamas emerged from the latter group as a distinct organisation.

The defeat of Saddam Hussein in the first Gulf War, and the collapse of the Soviet Union meant that the United States had become the unchallenged hegemonic power in the Middle East. It used the opportunity to broker the Oslo accords in September 1993. The accords provided for the election of a Palestinian Authority on the West Bank, which would take control of local matters, such as education, culture, welfare, tourism and the police, but left Israel in control of military affairs. The PLO (led by Yasser Arafat) favoured the accord, because it provided the chance to form a Palestinian administrative entity within which they were the dominant political force. The PLO was under tremendous pressure from the United States and Israel to suppress violence against Israel as the condition for implementing the Oslo accords.

The Palestinian opposition, led by Hamas, denounced the accords, because it failed to provide assurances about the eventual status of Jerusalem or to guarantee the return of Palestinian refugees, and left Israel in control of military affairs. The Palestinian Authority was a chequerboard of Palestinian '*bantustan*-style' fragmented settlements amidst a sea of Israeli settlements within the territory that the Palestinians considered to be their own. Hamas agreed to participate in the Authority's institutions, but built up its own social and educational services. It called for the formation of an Islamic state in opposition to the PLO's goal of a secular state. In 2006, Hamas was elected the ruling party of the Palestinian Authority. The United States isolated the new regime unless it promised to accept Israel's existence and renounce violence.

America and Israel. Of all the key issues in international affairs, the United States is most isolated in respect to its relationship with Israel. The United States has provided unstinting, uncritical support since its earliest days of existence as an independent state. A large segment of US public opinion has 'come to view the United States and Israel as almost one country. They believe in an 'identity of interests between the Jewish state and the United States' (Lieven, 2004: 189).

For the past quarter of a century, the United States government has contributed around US$ 3 billion annually in direct aid, along with a further US$ 3 billion in indirect aid (including loan write-offs and special grants). In 2004, Israel received more than one-quarter of the entire US foreign aid budget, totalling around six times the amount of US aid for the whole of Africa (Lieven, 2004: 185).

The way in which the Jewish state was established has a strong resonance with the origins of the United States. In both cases the myth of the colonisers was that they were taking possession of an almost empty land and liberating its productive potentialities. John Wayne expressed this sentiment succinctly in his interview in *Playboy* magazine: 'I don't feel that we did wrong in taking this great country away from [the Indians] ... Our so-called stealing of this country from them was just a matter of survival. There were great numbers of people who needed new land, and the Indians were selfishly trying to keep it for themselves' (quoted in Lieven, 2004: 180).[91]

Israel's military is vastly stronger than that of any other country in the region. From the late 1960s onwards, the United States agreed to supply Israel with its most advanced conventional weapons (Karpin, 2006: 294). Its air force has over 400 American-supplied combat aircraft, including 320 F-15s and F-16s (IISS, 2004), which means that it is more powerful than the air force of all the countries in the Gulf region combined. It has almost 4000 modern, mainly America-supplied, battle tanks and over 10 000 armoured personnel carriers (*FT*, 28 July 2006).

However, far more significant is the fact that it is the only country in the region that possesses nuclear weapons. Israel officially denies that it possesses nuclear weapons. However, even leading Israeli commentators such as Martin Van Creveld and Michael Karpin, freely acknowledge that Israel has a large stock of weapons.[92] The International Institute for Strategic Studies estimates that Israel has around 200 nuclear warheads (Table 4).

While the United States deeply abhors any attempt made by other Middle Eastern countries to acquire nuclear weapons, it makes no reference to, or criticism of, the widely accepted fact that Israel possesses a large stock of nuclear weapons. Recent research has shown that Israel's nuclear weapons' capability resulted from its secret agreement with France (Karpin, 2006). However, Edward Teller was crucial in guiding the Israeli government through the prolonged process of acquiring the technology. Teller was a Jew, born in Europe, who emigrated to the United States in the 1930s. He was the leader of the Manhattan Project that developed the nuclear bomb at the end of the Second World War. In this he was supported by a small group of brilliant Jewish émigré scientists, including Leo Szilard, Eugen Wigner and Robert Oppenheimer. Teller and Oppenheimer had a long meeting with the Israeli leader David Ben-Gurion in Tel Aviv in 1952, in which they advised him about the various options that faced Israel in order to acquire the requisite technology. Teller was an ardent Zionist,[93] and visited Israel repeatedly in subsequent years.

In 1956, France agreed secretly to help Israel to acquire the nuclear technology necessary to build nuclear weapons. The French motive stemmed mainly from the liberation struggle in Algeria. France believed that Egypt was a critically important force behind the Algerian liberation movement. Senior French political leaders believed that Israel and France faced a common problem: 'In Israel a million Jews were besieged by Arabs, and, in Algeria, a million Frenchmen were in the same situation' (Karpin, 2006: 62). Israel pledged to support France in any action against Egypt, 'no matter how far France may go' (Karpin, 2006: 70). The task that France assigned to Israel was to provide France with the pretext for a war against Egypt: 'Give us the pretext to go to war and you'll get a nuclear reactor' (Karpin, 2006: 82). It was against this background that Israel invaded Egypt and precipitated the Suez crisis. In addition, Israel's scientists were able to provide key support to the French in the final stages of their own efforts to develop an atomic bomb that would be their own independent nuclear deterrent. France produced its first nuclear weapon in 1960.

The core of French assistance to Israel was the supply of a large 150-megawatt nuclear reactor, which was built at Dimona in the Negev desert, under the pretence that it was a textile plant. From this Israel was to produce the plutonium that would enable it to make its own atomic bombs. In addition, France agreed to supply Israel with enriched uranium and a plant for the extraction of plutonium (Karpin, 2006: 91). Israel undertook to use the plant for civilian purposes only, but 'both sides knew this was a fiction' (Karpin, 2006: 91). Work on the reactor began at the end of 1957, and just ten years later, Israel produced its first nuclear weapons. It is estimated that each year the Dimona reactor complex produces around 40 kilograms of plutonium and that Israel produces ten atomic bombs annually (Karpin, 2006: 109).

Israel needed to pay the French for the nuclear reactor and associated facilities. A secret fund-raising campaign was undertaken in the United States beginning at the end of 1958, and lasted for two years. Some twenty Jewish millionaires (the so-called 'Sonnenberg Institute') between them contributed around US$ 40 million, which enabled Israel to finance the purchase from France (Karpin, 2006: 136).

From soon after the explosion of atomic bombs in Japan, the United States was publicly committed to nuclear non-proliferation. However, in practice, in the late 1950s and early 1960s it turned a blind eye to the fact that Israel was in the process of acquiring the requisite technologies from France. From early in the process, there were persistent US intelligence reports that Israel was acquiring nuclear technology, but the reports produced no action from the US Government. In fact, at the highest levels, the United States was committed to allowing Israel to acquire the nuclear bomb. It soon became clear to the US intelligence services that Israel was engaged in trying to produce nuclear weapons, but 'the upper echelon of the American Government clearly had no intention of making Israel cancel its project or even freeze it' (Karpin, 2006: 160). Many years later, former Deputy Assistant Secretary of Defense, Paul Warnke, wrote: 'Both Kennedy and Johnson waxed eloquent about the dangers of an increase in the nuclear club, but key officials appear to have been either indifferent or ready to accept an Israeli bomb' (quoted in Karpin, 2006: 302).

The long-standing support for Israel runs deep in the highest levels of the American political establishment, and runs across party political boundaries. In part this is due to the power of the Jewish lobby and the importance of Jewish votes. The wish to placate the Jewish lobby and win the support of Jewish voters lay behind President Kennedy's strong support for Israel. In 1958, two years before he became president, Kennedy said: '[T]he removal of Israel would not alter the basic crisis in the area ... the basic rivalries in the Arab world, the quarrels over boundaries, the tensions involved in lifting their economies from stagnation, the cross pressures of nationalism – all of these pressures would still be there, even if there were no Israel' (quoted in Karpin, 2006: 180).

Towards the end of the 1950s, the US Government increasingly perceived Israel as a strategic asset in enabling the United States to achieve its goals in the Middle East. In 1958, John Foster Dulles, Secretary of State, said: 'The critical situation in the Middle East today gives Israel manifest opportunities to contribute, from its resources of spiritual strength and determination of purpose, to a stable international order' (quoted in Karpin, 2006: 184).

In the second half of 1966 Israel had begun to produce nuclear weapons (Karpin, 2006: 268). It has the capability of delivering nuclear weapons by means of both land-based missiles and aircraft. Israel has also acquired three Dolphin-class submarines from Germany, and has armed them with nuclear missiles. One of these submarines regularly cruises the Indian Ocean (Karpin, 2006: 321). On 9 October 1973, Egypt and Syria launched a surprise attack on Israel (the so-called Yom Kippur War). On that evening, it is reported that Israel's Minister of Defence ordered that nuclear bombs be loaded onto fighter planes and nuclear warheads be fitted to Jericho missiles (Karpin, 2006:325). In the event it turned out that Egypt's main goal was not to invade Israel, but, instead, to seize control of the territory within close range of the East bank of the Suez Canal.

In the mid-1970s, Iraq began to acquire the capability of building nuclear weapons. In 1981, Israel launched an attack in which it destroyed Iraq's nuclear reactor. Immediately afterwards, Prime Minister Begin said: 'Israel will not tolerate any nuclear weapons in the region' (quoted in Karpin, 2006: 349). This policy is still in force today. Shortly after the attack, US Secretary of State, Alexander Hague, said: 'The United States recognises the gaps in Western military capabilities in the region, and the fundamental strategic value of Israel, the strongest and most stable friend and ally the United States has in the Mideast ... [W]e share a fundamental understanding that a strong secure, and vibrant Israel serves Western interests in the Middle East' (quoted in Karpin, 2006: 350).

Both the Jewish lobby and much of the Christian fundamentalist right-wing believe that Israel has a 'right' to occupy a large tract of Palestine, since they consider that the Jewish people were the sole ancient inhabitants of the region. This view has been held at the highest level of the US Government. President Johnson was brought up as a Christadelphian Christian. The Christadelphians have a special affinity for Jews. They believe that the Jews are 'the People of the Book'. They are certain that at the End of Days when the Jews are gathered in the Land of Israel, the Second Coming of the Messiah will take place. In his family album, Lyndon Johnson's grandfather had written on a picture of himself: 'Take care of the Jews, God's chosen people. Consider them your friends and help them in any way you can' (quoted in Karpin, 2006: 243). Lyndon Johnson repeatedly told Jewish groups of the depth of his feelings for Jewish people and for Israel. He asserted that there was a special bond between Israel and the United States: 'Our society is illuminated by the spiritual insights of the Hebrew prophets. America and Israel have a common love of human freedom and they have a common faith in a democratic way of life' (quoted in Karpin, 2006: 244).

In a 1996 policy paper, Richard Perle and Douglas Feith, who both became senior figures in the Bush government,[94] advised the Israeli government to abandon the Oslo peace process in favour of permanent occupation of the Occupied Territories: 'Our claim to the land – to which we have clung for hope for 2000 years – is legitimate and noble ... Only the unconditional acceptance by the Arabs of *our rights*, especially in the territorial dimension ... is a solid basis for the future' (quoted in Lieven, 2004: 178). On the Christian right it is commonplace to find the view that 'Israel alone is *entitled* to possess the Holy Land' (Senator James Inhofe, speech in the US Senate, March 2002, quoted in Lieven, 2004: 179) (My emphasis: PN).

In May 2002, Dick Armey, House Majority Leader, called for the deportation of the Palestinians from the Occupied Territories (Lieven, 2004: 180). He argued that Israel's right to occupy the whole of the Holy Land is based on God's command: 'The Bible says that Abram removed his tent and came and dwelt in the plain of Mamre, which is Hebron, and built an altar there before the Lord. Hebron is in the West Bank. It is this place where God appeared to Abram and said: "I am giving you this land" – the West Bank. This is not a political battle at all. It is a contest over the word of God' (quoted in Lieven, 2004: 181). Many of the millenarian Christians in the United States believe that the restoration of Israeli rule over the whole of the kingdom of David is an essential precondition of the Apocalypse (Lieven, 2004: 181).

One reason for America's unconditional support for Israel is the fact that Israel follows the 'American Creed'. It is regarded as the only democracy in the Middle East and deserving of American support for this reason alone. Israel is widely regarded in America as the sole bastion of American values in the midst of 'a sea of savagery' (Lieven, 2004: 179).

Israel came increasingly to be regarded in America as the frontline in the 'global battle against terrorism'. The balance of American political opinion on the Israel-Palestine issue can be gauged from the vote in the US Senate on 6 May 2002, at the height of Israeli-Palestinian violence. The Senate Resolution attacked Palestinian terrorism and declared that the 'Senate stands in solidarity with Israel, a frontline state in the war against terrorism, as it takes the steps necessary to provide security to its people by dismantling the terrorist infrastructure in Palestinian areas' (quoted in Lieven, 2004: 174). The Resolution passed by 92 votes to 2. It contained no hint of any criticism of Israel. The United States 'views the world through its own starkly moral framework' (unnamed European diplomat, quoted in *Financial Times*, 12 August 2006), and this is especially true of its relationship with Israel.

In 2002, President George W. Bush licensed Mr Sharon's capture of Palestinian territory, backing a so-called security barrier well inside the West Bank. In 2004, he endorsed Israel's claim to annex the wall of settlements separating east Jerusalem from its hinterland. The *Financial Times* commented: 'Everything is now in place for Ehud Olmert, the current Prime Minister, to set Israel's borders where Mr Sharon decided they should be on the map he drew in 1982. The idea is to keep the geography without the demography, leaving the Palestinians with about one-tenth of what was Palestine, in the three contiguous Bantustans' (*FT*, 4 August 2006).

Israel-Lebanon. Under French control in the inter-war years, the Mandate constitution of 1926 divided power between the different religious communities in Lebanon. Maronite Christian, Syrian and Shi'ite each had their own political parties, schools and networks of power (Lapidus, 2002: 555). At last, in 1943, Lebanon became an independent state, but the divisions that had been nurtured during French rule persisted. In 1958, Arab nationalists tried to seize power, but were suppressed by American intervention. In the 1960s and 1970s, Lebanon was divided. On the one hand were those who wanted to use the country as a base for the Palestinian struggle against Israel. These were mainly left-wing groups, who favoured a socialist path of development. On the other hand, there were those who wanted to restrict Palestinian activity in Lebanon and avoid confrontation with Israel. These mainly favoured a free enterprise economy. In August 1975 these forces erupted into a civil war.

In June 1982, with 'some degree of American acquiescence' (Hourani, 2002: 431), Israel invaded Lebanon in the hope of driving the PLO out of

South Lebanon, from where it had been mounting attacks on Israel, and from its headquarters in Beirut. Israel hoped that, freed from effective Palestinian resistance, it could pursue its policy of settlement and annexation of occupied Palestine (Hourani, 2002: 431). Defeated by the Israeli attack and under siege, the PLO agreed to withdraw from its stronghold in West Beirut, which was mainly inhabited by Muslims. The agreement was brokered by the United States. Along with the Lebanese government, the United States jointly guaranteed the safety of the thousands of Palestinian refugees in the city. The assassination of the Christian Phalangist leader, head of the Kata'ib political party, precipitated the Israeli occupation of West Beirut. Under the protection of the Israeli occupation, the Kata'ib massacred thousands of Palestinians in the refugee camps of Sabra and Shatila. It is estimated that around 19 000 people were killed during Israel's two-month siege of Beirut (*FT*, 28 July 2006). An agreement was then struck with Israel, under which its forces would withdraw from the country, in return for supporting the Kata'ib's assumption of 'virtual political and strategic control of the country' (Hourani, 2002: 431). The United States '[gave] both military and diplomatic support to the Kata'ib and their Israeli backers' (Hourani, 2002: 431).

Israel's occupation of South Lebanon stimulated the rise of new forces, notably Hizbollah (Party of God): '[Hizbollah's] parents were Israel and a US that declined to restrain its ally until it had nearly razed Muslim West Beirut' (*FT*, 4 August 2006). Hizbollah's roots were among the poor Shi'ite population of South Lebanon. It was backed by Iran and its goal was to establish an Islamic republic in Lebanon. It took the lead in the struggle against Israel. In the 1990s, Hizbollah became a major political party, buoyed by its success in harassing Israeli forces, and by the Israeli withdrawal from Southern Lebanon in 2000. Hizbollah constructed a network of popular social services, including schools and clinics. In the 1990s, Lebanon remained chaotic and internally divided. In 1991 Syria intervened to enforce cooperation between the warring factions. From then up until 2006, under Syrian overlordship, Lebanon enjoyed a period of peaceful capitalist development. During this period, Hizbollah became increasingly integrated into mainstream Lebanese politics: 'In parliament, the party's slogans shifted from condemnation of Israel to the fight against corruption and the pursuit of social justice' (*FT*, 22 July 2006). As of 2006, Hizbollah had won fourteen seats in the Lebanese parliament out of a total of 128 seats, joining the government as a minority partner. It was considered to be the best-organised of the Lebanese parties, but its total number of seats was restricted by the system of sectarian allocation of quotas to the parliament.

This period of sustained and peaceful development was shattered by the Israeli invasion of 2006. Angered by cross-border attacks from Hizbollah,

Israel seized upon the capture of two of its soldiers by Hizbollah to mount a massive assault on Southern Lebanon in order to destroy Hizbollah's fighting capability.

The Israeli attack on Southern Lebanon in July-August 2006 had the full support of the American Government. In the early stages of the crisis, US Secretary of State, Condoleezza Rice, declared that the upsurge of violence legitimated the US vision of 'a different kind of Middle East' and showed that the 'sponsors are in Tehran and in Damascus': 'Things are clarified now. We know where the lines are drawn' (*FT*, 18 July 2006). While most of the world was shocked at the Israeli violence in Southern Lebanon and called for a ceasefire in late July, Condoleezza Rice ruled out 'temporary solutions': 'A durable solution will be one that strengthens the forces of peace and democracy in the region' (quoted in *Financial Times*, 26 July 2006). With full American support, Israel continued its violent offensive in Lebanon for a further three weeks. Condoleezza Rice's reference to the need to construct a 'New Middle East' aroused massive anger across the Middle East.[95] The statement was widely perceived as concealing a plan to 'impose US-Israeli hegemony by eliminating the option of resistance through the destruction of the Palestinian and Lebanese resistance movements' (*FT*, 31 July 2006).

Senior US government officials, past and present, reported that President Bush 'felt more strongly' and was 'more engaged' in his support for Israel's attack on Hizbollah than 'on any other issue' (*FT*, 12 August 2006). Mr Bush's position is similar to that of most other American Christian fundamentalists. The officials said that Mr Bush 'feels passionately that the US should support Israel in what he sees as the frontline in the global battle between democracy and terrorism' (*FT*, 12 August 2006). During the first month of the Israeli invasion of Lebanon, Mr Bush's language toughened from talking about the 'war on terror' to stronger terminology, in which he referred to the war against 'Islamic fascists', and 'Islamofascism', terms long in currency among the neo-conservatives (*FT*, 12 August 2006).

One former senior Bush administration official said: 'People should not underestimate just how strongly [President Bush] feels in support of Israel and in his anger towards Iran and Syria [because of their sponsorship of Hizbollah]' (quoted in *Financial Times*, 12 August 2006). The observers around Bush say that he possesses a 'visceral instinct to support Israel against its enemies, which he sees in terms of democracy versus totalitarianism' (*FT*, 12 August 2006). Across almost the whole Arab world, in its ferocious attack on Hizbollah, Israel was widely perceived as acting as a proxy for the United States in its 'war against international terrorism'. President Bush himself is considered by former government officials in his administration to consider that fighting between Israel and Hizbollah is a 'proxy war between the US and Iran's theocratic regime' (*FT,* 12 August 2006).

The 'neo-cons' roundly stood behind America's support for Israel. The Democrats do not dare to criticise Israel for fear of losing support among the powerful Jewish lobby, especially those in powerful positions in business and the media.[96] In July, the House of Representatives endorsed a resolution supporting Israel's military response to the cross-border raid by Hizbollah. Only eight out of the 418 votes cast opposed the resolution, and not all of these were Democrats (*FT,* 19 August 2006).

The ferocity of the Israeli attack on Southern Lebanon in order to destroy Hizbollah's fighting capacity, strongly recalls the way in which the Americans themselves fought the native Indians. For daring to use asymmetrical warfare against the settlers who came to America and stole their land, the native Indians' warfare was termed 'terrorism'. The early settlers widely destroyed the native Indians' crops and killed women, children and other non-combatants, among whom the native Indian 'terrorists' sheltered. This was the 'First Way of War'.[97]

Sage voices in US foreign policy circles had long expressed their dismay at the American policy towards Israel. In 1996, former Secretary of State, James Baker, warned: 'We have gone from calling the settlements illegal in the Carter administration, to calling them an obstacle to peace in the Reagan and [George H. W.] Bush administrations, and now [under President Clinton] we are saying they are complicated and troubling' (quoted in *Financial Times,* 4 August 2006). In August 2006, Brent Scowcroft, former National Security Advisor to President George H. W. Bush, observed: 'Hizbollah is not the source of the problem: it is a derivative of the cause, which is the tragic conflict over Palestine that began in 1948' (quoted in *Financial Times,* 4 August 2006). In the midst of the Israeli attack on Lebanon Zbigniew Brzezinski, former head of the National Security Council, said: 'it is absolutely baffling to me and almost everyone I know – Republican or Democrat – how Ms Rice and Mr Bush think this strategy will achieve their objectives. The Bush administration is allowing itself to be suckered into believing it can achieve its political goals through military means. They seem to have learned nothing from Iraq' (quoted in *Financial Times,* 1 August 2006).[98] In 2003, Brzezinski had warned: 'American power worldwide is at its historic zenith. American political standing is at its nadir' (quoted in Lieven, 2004: 174). However, the impact of such people on American Middle Eastern policy was negligible.

Israel's attack was almost universally condemned as grotesquely disproportionate. It is estimated that in just three weeks' fighting, nearly a million people had been displaced, and over 1000 people killed, and 3500 wounded (*FT*, 10 August 2006). It is estimated that the Israeli attack killed nine Lebanese civilians – three of them children – for every one combatant (*FT*, 9 August, 2006). The Lebanese economy, which had grown strongly over the previous decade, was devastated.

The Israeli attack had almost universal support in Israel.[99] The mass-circulation newspaper, *Yedioth Aharanoth* headlined a quote from a military commander: 'Every village from which a Katusha rocket is fired must be destroyed' (quoted in *Financial Times*, 28 July 2006). Most Israelis were reported to believe that the attack against Hizbollah was 'morally justified' (*FT*, 7 August, 2006).

American Military Involvement in the Middle East

In recent years the United States has constructed a network of major military bases in the Gulf region under the administration of a much-enlarged Central Command (IISS, 2004: 32 and Klare, 2004: 92). They include bases in Iraq and Kuwait (under 'Operation Iraqi Freedom'), Oman, Bahrain, Qatar and the United Arab Emirates. The US armed forces in the Gulf Region total around 200 000 (IISS, 2004). In addition, Centcom controls US military bases in Afghanistan and Pakistan (under 'Operation Enduring Freedom') (IISS, 2004: 32). Furthermore, European Command has large naval and air force bases in Turkey, which shares a border with Iraq (IISS, 2004: 30). The US Fifth Fleet, with a complete carrier battle group, is stationed in Bahrain. There is a total of six major US air force bases in the Gulf region (including two in Oman alone) and an air force base in Turkey, close at hand.

In addition to the United States' own military capability, America's allies in the region have their own large armed forces, mainly supplied with US weaponry. Saudi Arabia alone has an air force which includes over 80 F-15s, while Bahrain and Kuwait together have a similar number of American-supplied F-15s, F-16s and F-18s (IISS, 2004).

The United States possesses the comprehensive military superiority of the only true global super-power. It smashed the Taliban forces in Afghanistan. It destroyed Saddam Hussein's army with 'shock and awe'. In Palestine, the modern US-armed Israeli army destroyed Southern Lebanon in a short space of time. However, none of these victories was decisive. In each case, the initial victory, won through the most sophisticated of modern armaments, was followed by an indecisive guerrilla war. There are strong parallels with the guerrilla wars in China and Vietnam. In Afghanistan, Iraq and Lebanon, a form of 'asymmetric warfare' is being waged against the United States and/or its proxies. The forces that the United States faces, either directly or indirectly, operate decentralised command structures, are well supplied with conventional weapons, and rely on strong support from the people among whom they live. The guerrilla forces build an extensive defensive infrastructure, with tunnels and large numbers of dispersed arms dumps. Publicity of guerrilla success and of the atrocities committed by the attackers reinforce popular support and nurture a mythology surrounding the guerrillas. Each of the guerrilla movements has mastered the art of propaganda. In the past, it was conveyed by word of mouth, revolutionary art, pamphlets and newspapers. Today, it is conveyed by video. By attacking the civilian infrastructure in which the guerrilla fighters 'swim' like fishes, the United States and its proxies serve only to inflame popular opinion against them, and raise the guerrilla fighters even higher in the esteem of those among whom they live.

By mid-August 2006, the Israeli forces had agreed to a ceasefire and the withdrawal of their troops from Lebanon. This was widely interpreted as a defeat at the hands of the Hizbollah, who refused to be disarmed, and who had inflicted severe damage on the Israeli invading force. The Israelis appeared to have seriously underestimated the strength of the Hizbollah as a fighting force. They also were misled into thinking that their destruction of a large part of the infrastructure in Southern Lebanon would lead the inhabitants to reject Hizbollah: 'Instead of reinforcing Israel's strategic deterrence, the Lebanon war has allowed Hizbollah to claim victory and bolstered its already heroic status in the Arab world. The outcome of the war may allow Hizbollah's backers in Syria and Iran to expand their influence in the region, and further undermine the Middle East's more pro-Western regimes' (*FT*, Editorial, 18 August 2006).

2.2.2 Capitalism, Development and Islam

Islam and Capitalism in the Medieval World

For a large body of the general public in the high-income countries, the attack on the World Trade Centre on 11 September 2001 represented an attack on capitalism by Islamic fundamentalists. For them, the fundamentals of Islam were, indeed, anti-capitalist. The ultimate symbol of capitalism in the modern world was the United States of America, and the World Trade Centre's twin towers constituted the essential icon of American capitalism and its dominant position within the globalised world economy. Such a view was nurtured in the popular mind by powerful writings such as those of Samuel Huntington. The attack appeared to many to vindicate Huntington's thesis, expounded in the mid-1990s, that there was, indeed, a fundamental 'clash of civilisations' between Islam and the West. This view was nurtured by the Zionist lobby in the high-income countries. They used the attack on the World Trade Centre as an opportunity to assert their own civilising role in the midst of the hostile anti-capitalist, anti-democratic, Islamic world that surrounded them. A minority of Jewish people disagreed with this perspective.

The idea that there is a fundamental 'clash of civilisations' between Islam and the West was not invented by Samuel Huntington. An early generation of Cold War scholars also had argued that Islam and capitalism were fundamentally incompatible. Writing in the 1960s, Maxime Rodinson (1974)[100] wrote a comprehensive critique of this perspective. He pointed out that there were many people who are 'hostile to Islam (and who are backed by a horde of publicists who know nothing about the subject)', and 'endeavour to show that this religion, by forbidding those who hold it to engage in any progressive economic initiative, dooms them to stagnation – or else (a recent variant of the same theory) fatally predisposes them to a satanic alliance with communism, itself intrinsically evil': 'The conclusion to be drawn is that these (Muslim) peoples must be vigorously combated, in the interest of progress of civilisation in general' (Rodinson, 1974: 3).

In fact, the Islamic religion is no more fundamentally anti-capitalist than is Christianity. For centuries, the Islamic world had vibrant centres of capitalist business, with widespread production for profit. Of course, as in any pre-modern economy, mainly self-sufficient agriculture dominated the economy. It has been repeatedly pointed out by both Islamic and non-Islamic scholars of the Islamic world that the teachings of the Koran are perfectly compatible with the basic features of capitalism. For over 1000 years there was a thriving commercial economy over much of the Islamic world. Of course, within the Islamic tradition, there have been intense debates about the contradictory character of capitalism. The views adopted span the full range from unrestricted enthusiasm for the free market to extreme revolutionary hostility. Most views lie somewhere in-between. All can be justified using the sacred texts of the Islamic faith.

Careful textual analysis of the Koran by Rodinson (1974: Chapter 2) and Ahmad (2003) show that the Koran is not inherently anti-capitalist (though, of course, it does not specifically use the modern term 'capitalism'). The Koran has nothing against private property. It even provides clear instructions about the practice of inheritance of property. Wage labour is referred to many times in the Koran as a normal and acceptable institution. The Koran 'looks with favour upon commercial activity'. It confines itself to condemning fraudulent practices and requires abstention from trade during certain religious festivals. In the broader Muslim tradition, the search for profit, trade, and production for the market are typically looked upon favourably. Indeed, according to holy tradition, trade is a superior way of earning one's living (Rodinson, 1974: 17). The Prophet is alleged to have said: 'If God let the dwellers in Paradise engage in trade, they would trade in fabric and the spices' (quoted in Rodinson, 1974: 17).

The Islamic scholar, Khurshid Ahmad, summarises key aspects of Muslim economic morality as follows: 'Wealth is not a dirty word; in fact, wealth creation is a desirable goal, subject only to moral values and imperatives ... Individual freedom, the right to property and enterprise, the market mechanism, and distributive justice are inalienable parts of the economic framework of Islam' (Ahmad, 2003: 192). Many Muslim scholars go even further in their defence of private property and the market. According to one twentieth century Islamic scholar: 'The Prophet heaps praise upon those who, far from being parasites, enrich themselves so as to be able to help the deprived' (quoted in Rodinson, 1974: 17). The moral framework of Islam allowed the medieval Islamic world to develop a sophisticated capitalist economy, with thriving trade and urban commercial centres, widespread production for the market, and a powerful capitalist class.

In a relatively brief period after the death of Muhammad in AD 632, Islam spread across a vast territory. By 750 the Islamic Empire stretched from the Indus in the East through into North Africa, Spain and, even, into Southern France.[101] For four or five centuries thereafter Islam was 'the most brilliant civilisation in the Old World' (Braudel, 1993: 73). This period was ended by the re-conquest of the Eastern Mediterranean by Europe in the eleventh century and the intrusion of the Mongols in the thirteenth century.[102] In 1260, Islamic forces crushed the Mongols in Syria, and in 1291 they re-conquered Acre, the last Christian outpost in the Holy Land. However, Mongol attacks continued in the thirteenth, fourteenth and fifteenth centuries, including the destruction of Baghdad in 1401. For much of the period from the seventh to the seventeenth century, a large part of the Old World was united under Islamic rule. Arabic provided linguistic unity for the Arab world, and 'created an essential tool for intellectual exchanges, for business, for government and administration' (Braudel, 1993: 72). 'Classical Arabic was not only a language, it was also a literature, a philosophy, a fervent universal faith and a civilisation, evolving in Baghdad and from there spreading far and wide' (Braudel, 1993: 72).

Mecca was already a vibrant commercial city when Islam was born there, with large-scale trade networks and extensive money-lending at interest: 'Muhammad lived and worked in the urban world of Mecca ... Mecca's prosperity at that time was still recent, born of its caravan links with distant, foreign cities, and confined to large-scale trade and the emerging capitalism of the Meccan merchants' (Braudel, 1993: 50).

The pre-Ottoman Islamic Empire began with the Abbasid revolution of 750, which ushered in the 'classical period of the economic development of the Muslim Empire', especially its commercial development. This continued right down to the fourteenth century (Rodinson, 1974: 30). The Abbasid Caliphate was based in a newly established capital city, Madinat as-Salam, otherwise known as Baghdad, the 'City of Peace' (Lewis, 1993: 87). The ninth century historian al-Ya'qubi records how the Abbasid ruler al-Mansur halted by the village that was to become Baghdad and said:

> This island between the Tigris in the East and the Euphrates in the West is a market place for the world. All the ships that come up the Tigris from Wasit, Basra, Ubulla, Ahwaz, Fars, 'Uman, Yamama, Bahrayn, and beyond will go up and anchor here; wares brought on ships down the Tigris from Mosul, Diyar Rabi'a, Adhurbayan and Armenia, and along the Euphrates from Diyar-Mudar, Raqqa, Syria and the border marshes, Egypt and North Africa will be brought and unloaded here. It will be the highway for the people of the Jabal, Isfahan and the districts of Khurasan. Praise be to those who preserved it for me and caused all those who came before me to neglect it. By God, I shall build it. Then shall I dwell in it as long as I live and my descendants shall dwell in it after me. It will surely be the most flourishing city in the world (quoted in Lewis, 1993: 88).

A great commercial metropolis developed rapidly around the central core of Baghdad, (Lewis, 1993: 88).

The Islamic Empire constituted a huge, virtual free trade area, across which goods and peoples could move relatively freely. The density of commercial relations within the Muslim world constituted 'a sort of world market of unprecedented dimensions' (Rodinson, 1974: 57). This was a world market similar to that of the Roman Empire, but the Muslim 'common market' was much bigger. It was also more 'capitalist' in the sense that private capital played a much greater role in the economy compared with the Roman Empire. The capitalist sector in the Muslim world was more extensive than that in Western Europe until the sixteenth century (Rodinson, 1974: 57).

Until the discovery of America, Islam dominated the Old World. It was the intermediary between the three great cultural zones of the Old World – the Far East, Europe and Black Africa. Islam was at the centre of a huge entrepôt trade between these regions. Arab sailing dhows used the monsoon cycle to pursue active and large-scale trade. By the ninth century they had reached Canton: '[T]he Arabs' maritime epoch was long-lived. Islam owed its ancient glory not only to its horsemen but also to its seamen' (Braudel, 1993: 56).

Caravans might consist of 5–6000 camels, with the capacity of a very large merchant sailing-ship: 'Coral travelled from North Africa to India; slaves were bought in Ethiopia; iron was brought back from India at the same time as pepper and spices. All that implied large-scale movement of money, merchandise and people (Braudel, 1993: 63). Powerful trading towns flourished in Islam, acting as the motors that made possible the circulation of people, money and goods: 'Everything passed through them: merchandise, pack-animals, people and rare acquisitions' (Braudel, 1993: 64).

Although there was a huge trade with the non-Islamic world, a large part of the trade consisted of exchange within the Muslim world, with specialisation and division of labour between different regions (Braudel, 1993: 34). Different towns and districts specialised in silk weaving, cotton, hides and skins, carpets and leather articles. There were even those that specialised in the manufacture of soap, ointments, rose-water and palm-shoots, scent, honey, saffron, or indigo. There were many agricultural crops produced mainly for the market, including dried fruits, various fresh fruits, especially dates, sugar-cane, spices. Horses and camels were bred for the market. The dried fish of the Caspian, the Aral Sea and the Persian Gulf were exported. Various districts specialised in the commercial production of weapons, copper pans and pails, scales, and articles of furniture.

Throughout the Empire, a vast economic system based on the market economy took root. There took place the development of a money economy and a progressive commercialisation of agriculture. The date trade mobilised every year more than 100 000 pack-camels. The cultivation of sugar cane became an industry, and flour milling spread. There were water mills near Baghdad for instance, and windmills by AD 947 at Seistan, while the flow of the Tigris was used to turn the wheels of floating mills:

> This enterprising economy explains the development of numerous industries – iron, wood and textiles (linen, silk, cotton and wool) – as well as the enormous spread of cotton-fields in the East. Carpets from Bokhara, Armenia and Persia were already famous. Basra imported vast quantities of kermes and indigo to dye textiles red and blue. Indian indigo, which came via Kabul, was reputed to be finer than from Upper Egypt (Braudel, 1993: 75).

Huge fortunes were made under a capitalist trading system that extended as far as China and India, the Persian Gulf, Ethiopia, the Red Sea, Africa and Andalusia: '"Capitalist" is not too anachronistic a word. From one end of Islam's world connections to the other, speculators unstintingly gambled on trade' (Braudel, 1993: 71). Enormous cities were built with trade as their central function: 'They included not only Baghdad, which from AD 762 until its brutal destruction by the Mongols in 1258 was a real "city of light", the largest and richest capital in the Old World, but also - not far away on the Tigris – huge Samarra, as well as the great ports of Basra, Cairo, Damascus, Tunis (a reincarnation of Carthage) and Cordoba' (Braudel, 1993: 71). In 1326, the Arab traveller Ibn Batuta said of Mecca: 'Altogether, every kind of merchandise from every country can be found gathered in this town' (Braudel, 1993: 50). For over one hundred years, in the ninth and tenth centuries, Islam dominated the Western Mediterranean: 'This breathed life and prosperity into seaports like Palermo, Alexandria, and Tunis' (Braudel, 1993: 57).

In the late tenth century, the Fatimid Caliphate broke away from the Abbasid Caliphate, which ruled the Empire from its base in Baghdad, and established its own base in Egypt. The new city of Cairo, with its magnificent new Al-Azhar mosque was built as its capital. The Fatimids extended their sway across the whole of North Africa, and into Sicily, Palestine, Syria, and Arabia. For a while they greatly surpassed the power of the Abbasid Caliphs in Baghdad. The peak of the Fatamid period was reached during the reign of the Caliph al-Mustansir (1036–94). The Fatimid period was one of 'great commercial and industrial efflorescence' and prosperity (Lewis, 1993: 123).

The Fatimid government fully understood the importance of trade for the prosperity of their empire. The Fatimids developed plantations and industries in Egypt. They nurtured a powerful export trade, and developed a wide network of commercial relationships, especially with Europe and India. They established close relations with the Italian city-republics. Their ships and merchants sailed as far as Spain. The two main harbours of the Fatimids were Alexandria and Tripoli, both of which were linked to world-wide markets. Their fleets controlled the eastern Mediterranean. In the east, they developed important contacts with India and gradually extended their sovereignty over both shores of the Red Sea. They shifted the Indian trade from the Persian Gulf to the Red Sea, and especially to the great Fatimid port of 'Aydhab on the Sudanese coast (Lewis, 1993: 123). After decades of gradual decline the Fatimid Caliphate was defeated in 1171 by Saladin, who re-united the main parts of the Islamic world (Lewis, 1993: 166).

Ibn Khaldun, fourteenth century sociologist and historian was well aware of the depth of penetration of the commercial economy into Islamic society at this period:

> It should be known that commerce means the attempt to make a profit by increasing capital, through buying goods at a high price, whether these consist of slaves, grain, animals, weapons, or clothing material. The accrued [amount] is called 'profit' (*riba*) ... There are few honest men ... among those with whom one deals when engaging in this

occupation. One is obliged to give credit, and many are those who repudiate their debts. One has to be prepared to face a thousand difficulties in order to get one's money back, for debtors respect only those creditors who bear the reputation of being obstinate and litigious. Those who lack the temperament appropriate to such habits would do better to refrain from engaging in trade. This is an occupation in which one necessarily has to make use of cunning, quibbling, tricks, quarrelsomeness, tactless insistence (quoted in Rodinson, 1974: 30–1).

The term 'Renaissance' has been used to describe the Golden Age of Islam, from the ninth to the twelfth century. In science, the Muslims made significant contributions to mathematics, especially in trigonometry and algebra. In trigonometry, the Muslims invented the sine and the tangent (Braudel, 1993: 80). In AD 820 Mohammed Ibn-Musa published an algebraic treatise which went as far as quadratic equations, and later Muslim mathematicians resolved biquadratic equations. Islamic mathematical geographers developed astronomical instruments and built astronomical observatories, and were able to establish improved methods of measuring latitude and longitude. The Muslims 'deserve high marks for optics, for chemistry (the distillation of alcohol, the manufacture of elixirs and of sulphuric acid) and for pharmacy'. More than half the remedies and healing aids used by the West came from Islam. 'Muslim medical skill was incontestable' (Braudel, 1993: 81).

In philosophy, the Islamic world rediscovered Aristotle: 'The philosophy of Aristotle, transplanted into the Muslim world, inevitably looked like a dangerous explanation of the world and of humanity, confronting as it did revealed religion, Islam, which was also a general explanation of the world, and an extremely rigorous one' (Braudel, 1993: 81) Aristotle was known as the 'first master'. Muslim humanism, based on Aristotle, was widespread and long-lived throughout Islam (Braudel, 1993: 82). The Muslim scholar Averroes (Ibn Rushd) (1126–98) lived in Cordoba, serving as Islamic judge (*kadi*). He edited Aristotle's works and wrote: '[Aristotle] was the son of Nicomachus and the wisest of the Greeks. He founded and completed logic, physics and metaphysics. I say that he founded them, because none of the works written on these subjects before him is worth discussing ... None of those who have followed him until now, that is, over some 1500 years, has been able to add anything to his works, or find in them any significant error' (Braudel, 1993: 82–3).

As admirers of Aristotle, the Arab philosophers were forced into interminable debate between prophetic revelation, that of the Koran, and a human philosophical explanation, that of the Greeks (Braudel, 1993). Greek influence gave Islamic philosophy its internal cohesion. There took place an 'agonising dispute between revelation and explanation', which 'required mutual concessions by both reason and faith': 'Faith, revealed through Muhammad, had imparted to humanity a divine message. Could the thinker, unaided, discover the truth of the world and set his own reason in judgement over the value of dogma?' (Braudel, 1993: 83). Thanks in considerable degree to Averroes' edition of his works, Aristotle's ideas reached Europe, where they sparked off the great philosophical revolution of the thirteenth century (Braudel, 1993: 84).

Merchants' private wealth was from an early stage of considerable importance in the Islamic role in organising the world market. The Islamic conquest of other territories permitted a huge accumulation of wealth in the hands of the mercantile class: '[I]f primitive accumulation of capital never attained the European level – all this was due to factors others than the Muslim religion. It is possible to perceive permanent and fundamental factors operative here, such as the relative density of the population, providing a supply of plentiful and cheap labour-power and so giving little incentive to the making of technical innovations' (Braudel, 1993: 57). In addition to the development of commercial capital in the medieval Islamic Empire, financial capital grew substantially after the establishment of the Islamic Empire. Money-lending, 'was undoubtedly practised very extensively ... despite the Koran's prohibitions of *riba*' (Rodinson, 1974: 35). Credit was widespread under the Ottoman Empire (1300–1600), with concealed interest added to the payment on credit as if it were a loan (Inalcik, 1994: 206). Letters of credit were known from the earliest days of Islam, and became widespread among merchants in the Ottoman Empire (Inalcik, 1994: 208).

The Ottoman Empire was established in 1261–1300, but it was not until 1453 with the conquest of Constantinople by the Ottoman Turks that a new epoch of relatively stable Islamic unity began. By 1683 the Ottoman Empire stretched from Armenia in the East through to Hungary in the Northwest, the Crimea in the Northeast, Mecca in the South, and Algeria in the West. During this period, the commercial forces that had grown up in the Golden Age of Islam revived and achieved further expansion. The Anatolian city of Bursa emerged as a world market in the second half of the fourteenth century. Along with Constantinople and Pera, it became the economic foundation of Ottoman power. Around 1400 Bursa was reputed to be one of the great centres for silk commerce and industry (Inalcik, 1994: 223). In the period 1400–1630, Bursa was the international market for raw silk from Iran and also the emporium of Western fine woollen cloth for the whole of Asia (Inalcik, 1994: 237). Most transactions were on credit and at the end of a certain period accounts were balanced (Inalcik, 1994: 241). The silk trade, like the spice trade, constituted one of the most important economic issues affecting world politics after 1250. The states involved in the silk trade, namely Iran, the Ottoman Empire and the Italian city states, were acutely aware of its importance to their economies and finances (Inalcik, 1994: 228).

Asia Minor became an 'industrialised' region within the Ottoman Empire before the Western and Russian manufactures competed with Turkish and Indian textiles in the late eighteenth century (Inalcik, 1994: 275). An important north-south trade developed across the Black Sea in the fifteenth and sixteenth centuries. Large quantities of silk, cotton, and hemp manufactures were imported from Anatolia to the northern Black Sea ports of Caffa, Akkerman, and Kilia. Through these ports animal and agricultural stuffs were exported to Istanbul. Under the Ottoman Empire, there developed a large market for Anatolian manufactures, with textiles at its centre: 'From Tokat, Corum, Merdizifon, Katamonu, Borlu, and Konya came cotton cloth; from Bursa, silk; from Tosya and Ankara, mohair; and from Trabizon, hemp' (Inalcik, 1994: 275).

Jerusalem became a part of the Ottoman Empire in 1516, along with most of the Arabic-speaking provinces (Cohen, 1989). The population was four-fifths Muslim with small Christian and Jewish minorities. The Ottoman rulers provided an environment in which commercial and industrial activity could flourish, but in which the needs of the different segments of the local population could be met through extensive state regulation of economic life. One of the Ottomans' first tasks was to renovate the ancient city walls.[103] They also rebuilt and improved the city's water supply. The Ottoman authorities undertook to supply the local population with water 'night and day, forever and ever' (Cohen, 1989: 3). These two public works were crucial to the commercial prosperity that Jerusalem experienced in the sixteenth century. In the early years of Ottoman rule in Jerusalem, charitable Muslim endowments proliferated. The most famous was that founded by the Sultan Suleiman's wife, Roxelana, which made 'exemplary arrangements for the establishment and maintenance of a free kitchen for poor people and students in Jerusalem' (Cohen, 1989: 9).

Under Ottoman rule there were two critically important offices of local government. The *kadi* was the Muslim judge, who heard legal cases, recorded and notarised decrees emanating from Istanbul and issued licences and permits. The office of *muhtasib* is 'one of the oldest institutions in the Islamic state' (Cohen, 1989: 11). His duties were to 'promote good and forbid evil', in the spirit of the Koran. The *muhtasib* was responsible for inspecting market activities in the widest sense, including 'patrons, clients, merchandise, and their multi-facetted inter-relations' (Cohen, 1989: 11). Most economic activities were conducted in self-organised guilds. However, the structures within which they operated were tightly regulated by the Ottoman's local representatives, especially the *kadi* and *muhtasib*. They exercised meticulous control over all significant aspects of economic life in Jerusalem including prices, division of labour, market locations, product storage, product quality, weights and measures, and health and safety regulations. Although the central Ottoman authorities set the parameters governing economic and social life in sixteenth century Jerusalem, the Sultan's local representative enjoyed wide discretion in the administration of these principles, adjusting their application to the specific local conditions in Jerusalem.

Under this system, economic activity in sixteenth century Jerusalem flourished. Most notably, Jerusalem became the centre of a thriving soap industry. Soap made in the city not only was sold throughout Palestine and Greater Syria, but also regularly exported to Egypt. The soap industry's growth stimulated the commercial olive industry around Jerusalem, as olive oil was the main raw material for soap. The merchant class gained strength during this period. Merchants were deeply involved not only in trade but also in production. They acquired soap factories and invested heavily in them, as well as buying olive oil and selling the finished soap. In terms of the city's economic and social activity, Jerusalem's merchants 'set the pace and were at the helm, as entrepreneurs and developers, and even as local leaders' (Cohen, 1989: 126). The central role in Jerusalem of the merchants' economic and social life under the Ottoman Empire 'emerges as a continuation of a long historical chain that had not changed either conceptually or pragmatically since the emergence of Islam' (Cohen, 1989: 126).

Modern Islamic Capitalism

In the late nineteenth and twentieth centuries, when there was political stability and some degree of security to pursue production for profit, the economies of the Islamic countries experienced significant economic growth. Even under Western colonialism, which governed most of the Islamic world until the middle of the twentieth century, there was a great deal of capitalist development in Islamic countries. Much of this was stimulated by the 'demonstration effect' of international trade and foreign investment. Partly it was attributable to the infrastructure constructed under the colonial governments. But to a considerable degree it was due to indigenous capitalist business endeavour. By the 1950s, there were around 1.5 million workers in industry in the Middle East, amounting to around 2 per cent of the workforce in Iran and Egypt, and 5 to 6 per cent in Turkey and Egypt (Table 5). In addition, there were many people employed in capitalist businesses in the financial, commercial and infrastructure sectors. By the 1950s, the capitalist sector accounted for 20 per cent of annual investment in Iran and Iraq, 50 per cent in Turkey, and 80 per cent in Syria and the Lebanon (Rodinson, 1974: 118).

Since the middle of the twentieth century, the oil-producing Islamic countries have experienced common problems, which can be summarised as the 'curse of oil'. These problems have been caused by factors such as the large fluctuations in their export earnings; the difficulty of absorbing large quantities of foreign exchange; and the socio-political consequences of the elite's access to large economic rents from the oil revenue. In addition, the world's leading powers, especially the United States, have been deeply involved with them politically and militarily, as their oil production is critical for the advanced capitalist economies. This has helped greatly to reinforce highly unequal systems of political economy, which have been unable to achieve widely-based development. As a result of these factors, the oil-producing countries have tended to have unstable patterns of economic growth since the mid-twentieth century.

It is widely thought that the Muslim economies as a group have performed poorly. In fact, when analysis turns to the wider group of countries in which Islamic beliefs are dominant,[104] the picture of economic development becomes much more complex. In the 1950s and 1960s, in common with most developing countries, a large part of the Islamic world turned towards a form of state-led industrialisation. There was widespread nationalisation of banks, public services, and large-scale industry, and even some attempts to set up agricultural collectives. However, even at the height of state-led industrialisation, the economies throughout the Islamic world maintained a combination of public and private ownership, far removed from the central planning of the communist countries. This was true for Egypt under Nasser,[105] Iraq under Saddam Hussein, Libya under Ghaddafi, Syria under Asad, Tunisia under Habib Bourgiba and Iran after the 1979 revolution. Each of these countries had a substantial private sector economy, and none of them ever approached the degree of hostility to private enterprise that was the case in the USSR or pre-1976 China. Even in Afghanistan under the Taliban, there was an active local exchange economy, albeit with limited international trade and deep hostility to international investment.

After Nasser died in 1970, there was a widespread move away from Arab socialism towards the policy of an 'open door' (*infitah*) towards international trade and foreign investment (Hourani, 2002, 419–23). The collapse of the Soviet Union accelerated this trend. The movement towards 'opening-up' since the 1970s was widespread across the Islamic world, which opened up a wide opportunity for capitalist development, building on the ancient foundations of trade and market-oriented production. In most cases, the move toward liberal economic policies occurred through peaceful means in both democratic and authoritarian Islamic countries.[106]

Trade liberalisation helped to stimulate quite rapid export growth in the non-oil producing Islamic countries (Table 6). Even by 1990, the share of merchandise trade in GDP in the Islamic countries was typically above the average for the low and middle-income countries. By 2004, even in the non-oil economies, the share of exports in GDP had risen to levels that were typically above the average for developing countries. In the case of non-oil dependent countries such as Indonesia, Malaysia, Morocco, Tunisia and Turkey, the foreign trade ratio was far above that for low-income economies, and either close to or above the average for middle-income countries.

The Islamic countries also saw a widespread increase in foreign direct investment (Table 7). By 2004, stocks of FDI relative to GDP had reached high levels in several non-oil dependent Islamic countries, including Egypt (27 per cent),[107] Morocco (36 per cent), Malaysia (39 per cent), Syria (53 per cent), Tunisia (62 per cent), and Bahrain (71 per cent). By 2004 stocks of FDI in the Islamic countries totalled around US$ 220 billion, roughly the same figure as that reported for China (US$ 245 billion in the same year), and greater than that for the whole former Soviet Union and Southeast Europe (US$ 200 billion) (UNCTAD, 2005, Annexe, Table B.2).

In recent years, the financial sector of Islamic countries has undergone dramatic change. Liberalisation of financial markets in Islamic countries has provided large opportunities for global giants of the banking industry to expand their business in the Islamic world. Local financial institutions were restricted by Islamic prohibitions on the provision of interest (*riba*) and financial speculation (*ghara*). The interpretation of these concepts has always been fraught with controversy, and they did not historically prevent the existence of a large financial sector in the Islamic world. However, in recent years, there has taken place a major change in the nature of financial institutions in the Islamic world. This has been stimulated by the revolution in the nature of financial instruments and the flood of financial assets accumulating in the hands of oil-producing countries, consequent upon the increased price of oil.

The region's banks have begun comprehensive transformation. For example, Egypt's banking sector until recently was dominated by the big four state-owned banks, with non-performing loans estimated by Moody's at between 35–50 per cent (*FT*, 13 December 2006). Only 4 per cent of Egyptians use credit cards. There is little development of personal loans or formal sector credit for the small-scale business sector. Until recently, cashing a cheque at the big four banks used to take between three and four hours. Typically, a cheque was handled by at least four people (*FT*, 13 December 2006). In the last few years, large changes have taken place in Egypt's financial institutions. Private sector banks now account for over half of the market. Two of the big four banks (Bank Misr and Banque de Cairo) have been merged. The third largest state bank, Bank of Alexandria, has been privatised and sold to the Italian-based bank, Sanpaolo.[108]

The floodgates have opened for the provision of 'Islamic finance', both by multinational banks as well as indigenous financial institutions. 'Islamic finance' is now formally legitimated through the use of a variety of techniques that enable Islamic banks to avoid the constraints imposed by the prohibitions on interest and speculation. 'Islamic' financial institutions may avoid investments in areas prohibited by Islam, such as alcohol, pork, gambling and weapons manufacture.[109] They can emphasise their 'Islamic' credentials by paying a portion of their profits in *'zakat'* to support social welfare in Islamic countries (Tripp, 2005).[110] There are innumerable ways of paying interest on loans, by redefining *de facto* interest payments as legitimate profit earned through a business partnership. Islamic financial institutions may circumvent the payment of conventional interest by issuing *'sukuks'*, which are bonds that give investors profits from an underlying business that backs a bond (*FT*, 27 November 2006).

The countries in the Gulf region are vying with each other to become global financial centres, by encouraging international financial firms to operate there, and by nurturing local financial institutions in the hope that they will become globally competitive. Most recently, Saudi Arabia is building a massive new international financial centre, the King Abdullah Financial District. Saudi Arabia's largest bank, the National Commercial Bank reported a net profit of US$ 1.3 billion in the first nine months of 2006 (*FT*, 27 November 2006), which can only be achieved by essentially adopting the same practices as international financial firms. Financial institutions in the Islamic world have also built up substantial ownership stakes in conventional international banks.[111]

In order to compete in international financial markets, the financial institutions of the Islamic world have adopted international standards. For example, the US Securities and Exchange Commission (SEC) is closely involved in advising the Gulf region countries to build modern financial markets that conform with international practice in terms of their regulatory structures (*FT*, 27 November 2006). The SEC has provided extensive assistance to the region in addressing issues such as broker-dealer relationships, anti-money-laundering, corporate governance and disclosure. The region's governments have sometimes paid directly for this advice, but often it has been funded by the World Bank or the United States Agency for International Development (USAID). Staff are drawn from within the SEC, and can include specialists from the Financial Services Volunteer Corps (FSVC), 'a sort of Peace Corps for the financial sector' (*FT*, 27 November 2006). The FSVC is itself supported by the Middle East Partnership, a Bush administration initiative to promote 'democratic transformation through economic assistance to the Middle East' (*FT*, 27 November 2006).[112]

The Islamic countries achieved widespread structural change, with large declines in the share of agriculture in national output and employment and large increases in the share of urban population in total population (Tables 8 and 9). Across these countries, levels of energy consumption increased enormously, reflecting the modernisation of the economies (Table 8).

Under some form or another of capitalist modernisation, the non-oil Islamic countries overall grew quite rapidly in recent decades (Table 3). From 1975–2002, the per capita GDP of the five largest Islamic countries (Bangladesh, Indonesia, Pakistan, Turkey and Egypt), with a combined population of around 650 million people, grew at an (unweighted) average rate of 2.7 per cent per annum (Table 3), almost twice the average rate of growth of the middle-income countries and considerably faster than the rate of growth of the low-income countries. Over the course of these 27 years, per capita GDP more than doubled in these five Islamic countries. Indeed, in this period, the growth rate of per capita GDP in the largest of the Islamic countries, Indonesia, was not far behind the Asian 'Newly Industrialising Countries' (NICs). From 1975 to 2002, Indonesia's GDP per capita grew at 4.2 per cent per annum, compared with 4.4 per cent in Hong Kong, 5.0 per cent in Singapore, 5.2 per cent in Thailand and 6.1 per cent in Korea (UNDP, 2004: 184–5).

Across a wide spectrum of Islamic countries, the progress in GDP per capita resulted in substantial advances in key indicators of human development. The proportion of people in absolute poverty fell substantially. For example, in the Middle East and North Africa, the proportion of the population living on less than US$ 2 per day is estimated to have fallen from 29 per cent in 1981 to 20 per cent in 2002 (World Bank, WDR, 2006: 73). Infant mortality fell dramatically and life expectancy advanced enormously in the Islamic countries (Table 9). The performance of Islamic countries in terms of child malnutrition is much better than that in low-income countries and is generally above that even in middle-income countries (Table 10). Enrolment rates in education advanced dramatically. By 2004, in most Islamic countries, most females in the relevant age group were enrolled in secondary education. Whereas in 1965, in Egypt, Iran and Turkey, less than one quarter of the relevant age group were enrolled in secondary education, by 2004, the proportion had risen to 80–90 per cent. This constitutes a huge change in the social structure of the Islamic world. By 2004, enrolment rates in tertiary education in key Islamic countries were far above those in low-income countries, and substantially above those even in middle-income countries (Table 11). In sum, broadly-based capitalist development across large swathes of the Islamic world brought large progress in human development.

As modern capitalism has advanced in the non-oil-producing Islamic countries, alongside high rates of population growth in most of them, levels of inequality in the distribution of income have been quite high. As modern sector enlargement takes place in the context of a relatively large rural sector with widespread underemployment of labour, the 'Lewis Phase' of development makes it likely that, *ceteris paribus*, capitalist growth will be accompanied by high levels of inequality until the rural reserve army of labour dries up. Levels of inequality in the distribution of income in the non-oil-producing Islamic countries are generally considerably higher than those in the high-income European countries, but lower than those typical in Latin America and most of Sub-Saharan Africa.[113] There is some qualitative evidence that the nature of inequality may have changed in recent years as the Islamic economies have become more open. For example, Egypt's Minister of Finance, Youssef Boutros Ghali, has acknowledged that 'sustained and equitable growth is [Egypt's] biggest challenge' (quoted in *Financial Times*, 17 December 2006). As in other parts of the developing world, the rich are increasingly living in their own heavily protected residential areas. On the one hand, on the outskirts of Cairo, 'property developers are building gated communities, with swimming pools, golf courses and nearby shopping malls'. On the other hand, 'packed into teeming slums, there are signs that the poor are getting poorer' (*FT*, 13 December 2006).

The small group of countries in the Persian Gulf accounts for almost two-thirds of the world's oil reserves. The vast oil wealth is controlled by a small number of families that also control the political economy of each of these countries. Because of the limited channels through which rents are generated in oil-dependent economies, it is relatively easy for a dominant group to seize control of the rents, and use them to further bolster their rule. The immense inequalities in the distribution of wealth and income in the Gulf countries have inspired intense anger from different socio-political groups within the region. Naturally, this has typically taken an Islamic form. The ruling families were overthrown in the case of the Ba'athist revolution in Iraq and the Islamic Revolution in Iran. However, in the other Gulf states, family control of the vast oil reserves remains in place. The family-run states have been deeply dependent for their survival on support from the United States (and to a lesser extent, from Britain and other European countries) to maintain their authoritarian rule, which has helped to generate intense anger at the United States.

At the core is Saudi Arabia, with around one-quarter of the entire world's oil reserves. The ruling Al Sa'ud family 'makes no attempt to conceal its ownership of the country's principal natural resources behind the mask of state institutions' (Hourani, 2002: 461–2). Since Saudi Arabia's foundation in the 1920s, the Al Sa'ud family has 'effectively been its owners as well as its rulers': 'Oil is not just the kingdom's primary national resource; it is first and foremost private, family property' (Hourani, 2002: 463). The bulk of the oil revenue is paid directly to the king before it is registered as national income. The royal family decides on its needs, and officials are instructed to act in accordance with these. In the late 1990s, the 6000-odd members of the Saudi royal family were estimated to receive an average of around US$ 1 million each in addition to their regular 'working salaries' and commissions on business deals. Similar arrangements apply in most of the other oil-producing countries where rule is vested in a single family (Hourani, 2002: 463). The fact that Saudi Arabia is also the home of Islam contributes greatly to the deeply-felt anger among Muslims both inside and outside the country. It is widely perceived among a wide range of Islamic people that the country that is the home of Islam is ruled by people who live in a way that contradicts the basic principles of Islam.

Although wealth is concentrated in the hands of a small group of families in each of the Gulf countries, the nature of inequality is complicated. In the first place, the enormous per capita income consequent upon oil production has provided the rulers with the means to deliver a high level of social welfare to their citizens. Typically, the rulers of these countries have provided free health care, education and subsidised housing, for all their citizens. This has helped greatly to ensure political stability. However, they have also been heavily dependent on immigrants, especially from surrounding Arab countries as well as from South Asia.[114] A large fraction of these have been employed in relatively low-income occupations, and it is typically difficult for them to obtain citizenship. Their employment in the Gulf provides an extremely important source of personal income as well as foreign exchange for the countries of origin, but the Gulf countries consequently have sharply polarised societies.

Islamic Responses to Capitalism

The growth of modern capitalism in the Islamic world in the late nineteenth and in the first half of the twentieth century brought an outpouring of writing and political movements that tried to come to terms with the new phenomenon. The responses were diverse,[115] but almost all discussion took place within the context of the Islamic religion. Much of the discussion harked back to earlier Islamic thinkers who had wrestled with the role of the market, private property and the state over centuries. There was a ferment of literature, music and film in response to the realities of modern capitalist development.[116] The debate among Islamic intellectuals and political thinkers fused together sentiments of national liberation from colonial rule and the intrusion of international capital, with analysis of indigenous capitalism, and the associated phenomena of urbanisation, class structure and the impact of the modern market economy on people's consciousness.

The writings of scholars and political thinkers operated at one level. Newspapers, films and popular music operated at a different level, far more deeply penetrating the lives of ordinary people in the Islamic world. Increasingly also, the radio penetrated people's daily lives. By the mid-century, radio sets were imported on a large scale. By 1959 there were 850 000 in Egypt and half a million in Morocco. Each set might be listened to by dozens of people in cafés or village squares. Millions of people who had barely heard of the leading scholars and political thinkers listened avidly to their voices beamed across the whole Arabic world: When Egypt's most famous singer, Umm Kulthum sang, 'the whole Arab world listened' (Hourani, 2003: 393). Umm Kulthum did not sing revolutionary sings by Kurt Weill and Brecht. She sang songs that used traditional Arabic poetry of love, beauty and loss.

Anti-Western violence. In the 1990s there was a spate of terrorist attacks by Islamic groups against symbols of the Western world, especially those of the United States, including an abortive attack on the World Trade Centre in New York, a large explosion at the US embassy in Sudan, an attack on a US warship in the Middle East, and an attack on the US Embassy in Beirut. However, the awareness of Islamic terrorism massively increased as a consequence of the astonishing spectacle broadcast live on global television of the destruction of the twin towers of the World Trade Centre. The brilliantly planned and executed attack was a superlative propaganda coup for the perpetrators.

Since mid-2001, a succession of operations has occurred across the world, carried out by Islamic fundamentalist movements, including the bombing of commuters in Mumbai and Madrid, and London. The most important such attacks are listed in the following table (Table 12). These have sparked a media frenzy and widespread panic in high-income countries. A veritable industry of apocalyptic fears and predictions about global terrorism and 'global *jihad*' has erupted. A large body of people in the high-income countries believe that the future of civilisation is under threat from anti-Western Islamic fundamentalists.

The images of extreme violence make for shocking and riveting television. However, in total the fatalities are miniscule. For example, in the terrorist attack in London in 2005, fewer than 60 people were killed. Anyone killed in terrorist violence is shocking.[117] In a single night during the Blitz (10 May 1941), when the city was brightly illuminated by a 'Bomber's Moon', 1436 people were killed. Over the course of the war, a total of nearly 30 000 people were killed due to German bombing in London (Calder, 1969: 226). The bombings in Mumbai killed around 200 people. Since the 1940s, Hindu-Muslim violence in India has resulted in around one million deaths.

The numbers killed by Islamic fundamentalists in the past five years is trivial by comparison with the numbers killed in automobile accidents in the high-income countries. Of course, daily news coverage of the remorseless carnage from traffic accidents in these countries is less newsworthy than Islamic terrorist attacks. The numbers killed by Islamic terrorists is even more trivial in comparison with the fatalities that have arisen from armed conflicts since the end of the Second World War. In the whole period, over 20 million people have died in armed conflicts (Table 13). In the period since 1990 alone, over 4.5 million people have died in armed conflicts, including around 1.5 million people in Afghanistan (1979–92) and a similar number in the civil war in Angola (1975–2002) (IISS, 2005).

It is possible that the numbers killed due to Islamic terrorism may increase, perhaps through the use of a 'dirty nuclear bomb'. However, up until this point, the threat it poses is dwarfed, not only by the losses during the two World Wars of the twentieth century, but also by the huge loss of life in armed conflicts since 1945, and even by the enormous avoidable loss of life in road accidents. The attacks by Islamic 'terrorists' on international tourist resorts, which have been a main target of Islamic terrorists, have not affected the level of international tourism.[118]

To people in Islamic countries, the few thousand people killed in high-income countries due to attacks by Islamic terrorists since the 1990s pale before the immense number of deaths in violent conflicts in their own societies within living memory (Table 14). These deaths were often the result of military action by outside forces, such as the French in Algeria, the Soviet Union in Afghanistan, the Dutch in Indonesia, the Israelis in Egypt, Lebanon and Palestine, and the Americans in Iraq. These forces appear at least as much as terrorists to the local people, as the Islamic terrorists appear to citizens of the United States or Europe when they attack their citizens. What appear to the external occupying forces as terrorists appear to a large part of the indigenous Islamic people as national liberation freedom fighters. Even among the large sections of the indigenous people who disagree with violence as the solution to conflict, the local fighters against the external forces may still appear as freedom fighters rather than 'terrorists'.

In the minds of many people in the West, 'Islamic fundamentalism' is equated with the intensely anti-Western regime of the Taliban in Afghanistan.

In fact, the Taliban regime in Afghanistan (1992–2002) was unique in the history of Islam, 'with no parallels elsewhere in the Muslim world' (Rashid, 2000: 88). It arose in specific circumstances in which Afghanistan was a battleground for the Soviet Union and the United States. One reason for the eventual success of this particular extreme form of Islam was the strong support it received from the CIA and the Pakistan Interservices Intelligence organisation (ISI).[119] It was, of course, in this environment, that Al Qaeda was able to grow. The Taliban regime was deeply antagonistic to the West and, especially, to the United States. However, it was anathema for the vast majority of Muslims across the world: 'The Taliban [were] poorly tutored in Islamic and Afghan history, knowledge of the Sharia and the Koran ... [T]he rich diversity of Islam and the essential message of the Koran – to build a civilised society that is just and equitable in which the rulers are responsible for their citizens [was] forgotten' (Rashid, 2000: 212).

Anti-capitalist revolution. The Islamic world has a long history of capitalist development. The inequality and injustice that is inseparable from capitalism in its raw form, regularly produced social movements against the established order. In the medieval world, rapid economic development produced severe stresses and strains in the social fabric (Lewis, 1993: 107). Parallel to the flourishing economic and commercial development, there was growing class inequality and class conflict: 'The rich became richer, and arrogant; the poor became poorer still ... Islamic prosperity ... helped to foster a revolutionary climate and an uninterrupted series of urban and agrarian disturbances, often linked with nationalist movements' (Braudel, 1993: 75–6). The composition and origin of these movements was diverse, but the form in which they expressed their motives and purposes was almost always in terms of the Islamic religion: 'Almost every movement, whatever its motivation, sought in religion not a mask, but the necessary and organic expression in public and social terms of the ambitions and discontents that drove it' (Lewis, 1993: 108).

One of the most influential thinkers in the radical 'communist' tradition of Islam is Abu Dharr al-Ghifari, who was one of the Companions of the Prophet. He shocked people by saying that the Koran's teaching required everyone to spend on the service of God or on charity, the whole of their wealth beyond the minimum needed for subsistence. Around ten years after the Prophet's death he declared that the threatening verses in the Koran about rich men unwilling to give alms were applicable to members of the Muslim community no less than to the Jewish and Christians clerics attacked in the preceding verse:

> Believers, many are the clerics and monks who defraud men of their possessions and debar them from the path of God. To those that hoard

gold and silver and do not spend it on God's cause, proclaim a woeful punishment. The day will surely come when their treasures shall be heated in the fire of Hell, and their foreheads, sides, and backs branded with them. They will be told: 'These are the riches which you hoarded. Taste then what you were hoarding' (The Koran, 9: 34–5).

Abu-Dharr is said to have been banished to a remote locality as a danger to society (Rodinson, 1974: 25). In the twentieth century, Abu-Dharr enjoyed enormous popularity in the Muslim world. He was viewed by the socialist and communist Left as a distant precursor of modern communism, or, at least to show that socialism is not alien to the Muslim tradition (Rodinson, 1974: 25).

In Iran and Southern Iraq in the eighth and ninth centuries there were a succession of major uprisings. These included the rebellion of the Iranian heretic al-Muqanna (the 'Veiled One') which lasted from AD 776 to 789. He allegedly preached and practised 'communism of both property and women' (Lewis, 1993: 111). The most serious Iranian rebellion was that of Babak, which lasted from AD 816 until 837. Babak led large-scale attacks on the landowners and plundered their possessions (Lewis, 1993: 111). Between AD 869 and 883 there was a huge slave revolt in southern Iraq and south-western Iran. It began among the slaves who worked for large merchants and entrepreneurs on the salt flats east of Basra. The slaves worked in gangs of 500 to 5000, extracting the salt and preparing the ground for agriculture. In one gang there were as many as 15 000 slave workers. Even though many of the slaves were African and not Muslims, the revolt used Islamic language to express its rebellion against intolerable conditions.

At the beginning of the tenth century, 'the social crisis in the [Abbasid] Empire was reaching breaking point' (Lewis, 1993: 116). The slaves and peasant revolts had been defeated, which nourished resentments in the countryside, while 'the growing concentration of capital and labour had created a large, discontented town proletariat' (Lewis, 1993: 116–7). The Isma'ili was the most important of a number of sects that flourished in this period, attracting widespread popular support among ordinary people. They were highly egalitarian. Their orthodox opponents frequently alleged that they practised 'communism of property and women' (Lewis, 1993: 118).[120] One contemporary account of their activities records: 'The duty of *Ulfa* (union) ... consisted of [the inhabitants] assembling all their goods in one place and enjoying them in common without anyone retaining any personal property, which might give them an advantage over the others ... They did not need to own property because all the land belonged to them and to no one else' (quoted in Lewis, 1993: 118). The mainstream of the Isma'ili movement formed the foundation for the Fatimid Caliphate in Egypt. At the beginning, the Isma'ilis 'attacked acquired wealth very sharply', but once they came to power, first in Tunisia and then in Egypt, they 'did nothing to encroach upon the right to riches' (Rodinson, 1974: 26).

The revolts of the medieval Islamic world came in many forms. They had in common hostility to the rich, and the use of language and ideals from the Koran. Some of them took the form of ascetic and religious criticism, but many of them were truly revolutionary in purpose. However, all of the revolts in the medieval Islamic world eventually were crushed or disintegrated of their own accord. They had only a limited influence, or else 'abandoned on their road to power the essentials of their programme regarding this aspect of life' (Rodinson, 1974: 26). They 'left no permanent mark on the course of Islamic history and wrought no radical change in the structure of Islamic society' (Lewis, 1993: 115). None of these uprisings was able to seize the seat of power at the heart of the Islamic Empire. The only major long-term internal challenge to the Abbasid Caliphate in the medieval Islamic world was the Egyptian-based Fatimid Caliphate, but this also was founded on thoroughly capitalist principles of the market economy. Moreover, it is unclear to what degree different rebellions were protests against oppression as opposed to attempts to establish a millennial, egalitarian society.

As modern capitalism evolved in Islamic societies so there arose a strand within Islam that argued for a revolutionary interpretation of Islam, harking back to medieval Islamic thinkers such as Abu-Dharr and revolutionary leaders such as Babak. The Iranian scholar Ali Shari'Ati stands at the forefront of such thinkers. In Shari'Ati's view, when the Koran talks of property as belonging to God, it means that capital belongs to the whole people (Tripp, 2005: 161). In his view, there is a binary opposition running through the whole of human history, represented metaphorically by Cain and Abel: '[T]he system of Cain [stands for] economic monopoly and private ownership ... slavery, serfdom, feudalism, bourgeoisie, industrial capitalism and imperialism (the culmination of capitalism)'. By contrast, the system of Abel stands for 'economic socialism (collective ownership), pastoral and hunting modes of production and the industrial mode of production (in the classless and post-capitalist society' (quoted in Tripp, 2006: 160).

Shari'Ati believed that the establishment of a non-capitalist egalitarian society depended on leadership by an enlightened vanguard. Members of the vanguard would be people who 'through their understanding of Islam and direct apprehension of the true nature of society (and thus its ills), would be unaffected by seductions and intimidations represented, respectively, by capitalism and tyrannical power' (Tripp, 2006: 163). Shari'Ati believed that the *mujahid* should not only be armed with the Koran, but must also engage in violent struggle to overthrow the 'false gods of capitalism and state power'

(Tripp, 2006: 163). In a speech to his students in April 1972 he urged them: 'Die! So that others may live' (quoted in Tripp, 2006: 164). He believed that the spectacle of violent struggle between small groups of *mujahideen* and the state would awaken public consciousness. He recognised that the *mujahideen* would probably be defeated, but believed that the martyrs would expose the hollowness of the rulers and lead to their eventual downfall. He was contemptuous of debating 'scientifically' with his opponents in the face of 'people's hunger and the pillage of the capitalists' (quoted in Tripp, 2006: 165).

Only a small segment of the Islamic movement has adopted such a revolutionary anti-capitalist position. Armed struggle within Islam in recent decades has mainly consisted of actions against Israel; against the American presence, and the lesser presence of America's allies, in the Middle East, including actions in the region itself or in other parts of the world; civil war between different Islamic factions, neither of which is anti-capitalist; separatist struggles by armed Islamic groups; or armed struggle against Islamic regimes with a view to replacing them with a regime that is more just, but still recognizably capitalist.

An Islamic 'third way'. From the late nineteenth century onwards, there was a ferment of discussion among Islamic scholars about the significance of capitalist modernisation, and the ways in which it might be made compatible with Islamic values.[121] There began a prolonged and ongoing engagement with the ways in which it might be possible to build a morally acceptable society under capitalism. Tripp (2006) explains as follows the goal for which the scholars searched: 'Avoiding extremes of wealth and poverty, to sustain a harmonious relationship between the members of society, become important parts of the restored moral framework for a distinctively Islamic society, seeking to give meaning, effectiveness and ethical purpose to property in the restoration of a moral economy which has been disrupted by capitalism and by the attitudes it encourages towards property and wealth creation' (Tripp, 2006: 84). The debates that swirled around this central issue harked back to discussions within Islam over the course of more than 1000 years. These debates, which have formed the focus of intellectual thought within the Islamic world over the last century, have much in common with the debates in the West, which have wrestled with ways in which to tame capitalist forces in the interests of the wider society, albeit that the language is distinctively Islamic and the frame of reference for analysing the moral economy is the Koran.

In the two centuries prior to Muhammad, there had arisen a group of thinkers in Iran who had advocated a form of communism, involving the collectivisation of private property (Rodinson, 1974: 22). There had been 'much talk in Arabia about the communistic experiment carried out in the powerful neighbouring empire'. Muhammad also preached against riches and the rich, especially at the start of his preaching in Mecca. He condemned wealth for turning people away from God. The earlier passages in the Koran express hostility to the pursuit of wealth for turning people away from God and from a harmonious relationship with the rest of society. In places, the Koran exhorts the rich to give away all their possessions to the poor if they wish to be rewarded in the after-life, in the same way that Jesus urged in celebrated passages of the New Testament:[122] 'The righteous man is he who ... though he loves it dearly, gives away his wealth to kinsfolk, to orphans, to the destitute, to the traveller in need and to beggars, and for the redemption of captives ... ' (The Koran, 2:177).

However, unlike the views of many thinkers at the time, later passages in the Koran do not attack private property as such. Muhammad's solution to the evils of inequality of possessions was to urge the rich to give alms to the poor, and to tax them. These were 'reformist' solutions, even for those times. The main body of medieval thinkers and political activists who used Islam to criticise the existing state of society in the Muslim world operated within the reformist framework. They tried to ensure that the state operated according to the ideals of the Koran. For them, this meant treating all believers as equal before the Divine Law. It meant practising within the Muslim community 'an advanced form of mutual aid, at the expense of the better-off and to the benefit of the poorer people': 'This is the ideal that the reforming and revolutionary movements so numerous in Muslim history strove for, again and again' (Rodinson, 1974:26–7). However, these movements almost all accepted it as inevitable that there should exist 'distinctions between free men and slaves, landowners and tenants, rich and poor' (Rodinson, 1974: 27).

Throughout its history, Islam has emphasised that justice is the 'very soul of the Islamic economic system' (Ahmad, 2003: 193). In the eleventh century, Al-Mawardi argued that comprehensive and multi-dimensional justice promotes solidarity, law and order, national economic development, expansion of wealth, population growth, and national security: 'There is nothing that destroys the world and the consciousness of the people faster than injustice' (quoted in Ahmad, 2003: 193). Ibn Khaldun wrote that economic development is only sustainable if there is justice: 'Oppression brings development to an end', and 'decline in property is the inevitable result of injustice and transgression' (quoted in Ahmad, 2003: 193).

However, in the mainstream of Islamic thinking, a just society has been pursued within realistic constraints about the nature and importance of the market economy. Three centuries before Adam Smith, Ibn Khaldun (died in AD 1406) emphasised the rationality of the division of labour and the market mechanism: 'It is well known and well-established that human beings are not themselves capable of satisfying all their economic needs. They must cooperate for this purpose. The needs that can be satisfied by a group of them through mutual cooperation are many times greater than what individuals are capable of satisfying themselves' (quoted in Ahmad, 2003: 195). Ibn Khaldun emphasised the positive function that could be played by extension of the market: '[Tools require savings which is the] surplus left after satisfying the needs of the people. Increase in the size of the market boosts the demand for goods and services which promotes industrialisation, raises income and furthers science and education, and accelerates development' (quoted in Ahmad, 2003: 196).

The great Islamic university al-Azhar was founded in AD 970. In 1948 in an important judgement, it strongly affirmed the reformist view of The Koran. Radical Egyptian Islamists argued that Islam was inherently communist, making use especially of the writings of Abu-Dharr to support their view. The doctors at al-Azhar issued a *fatwah*, proclaiming: 'No communism in Islam' (quoted in Rodinson, 1974: 26).

Across much of the Arab world, in the 1950s and 1960s, 'Arab socialism' was put into practice, at the core of which was extensive nationalisation of the means of production and state planning. Egypt under Nasser was the leading force in this movement. This was typically justified with reference to the Islamic tradition with the state allegedly taking the lead in ensuring that the whole society's interests were met. Nationalisation was justified on the basis that property was God's not the individual's, and the best way to ensure that it operated in the interests of the whole community was to take it into common ownership. After attracting much support from the region's Islamic intellectuals, there took place a widespread backlash among the region's Islamic intellectuals against the authoritarian regimes, and their materialist culture, which came to be viewed as little better than raw capitalism. However, even at the height of Arab socialism, there was still a large role for the private sector. The political economy remained far removed from that of the USSR, despite the fact that the Arab socialist countries were firmly in the Soviet camp in international relations. The model of political economy followed by the Arab socialist countries was not fundamentally different from that in numerous developing countries in the post-colonial period. In 1960, Nasser's own Minister of the Economy, Ibrahim Qaissouni, said: 'Our socialism ... does not aim at allowing the state full ownership of the means of production; but protects private property and stipulates the freedom of private initiative and its equality of opportunity with the private sector' (quoted in Tripp, 2006: 87).

Even during Nasser's lifetime, intense intellectual debate took place among the reformist mainstream about capitalism in the Islamic world. After Nasser's death, the discussion centred even more firmly around the mechanisms that could guide an essentially private enterprise capitalist economy towards Islamic ideals. Policy liberalisation after the death of Nasser in 1971 took the Arab socialist countries much more firmly towards mainstream capitalism. It became commonplace among Islamic intellectuals to refer to an Islamic 'Third Way' between raw capitalism and state-controlled, materialistic communism.[123] There was intense discussion among Islamic intellectuals about how best to restore harmony to a society 'disrupted by class antagonisms and driven by the acquisitiveness, competition and commodification unleashed by capitalism' (Tripp, 2006: 95).

The Egyptian scholar Sayyid Qutb (1906–66) is arguably the most influential internal critic of Islamic governments in the twentieth century. Initially, he was supportive of President Nasser's 'Egyptian socialism'. Nasser was a Muslim, and he made extensive use of Islamic symbols. He was regarded with enormous respect in the Islamic world. However, Qutb came to believe that Nasser had betrayed the fundamental principles of Islam, that he had nurtured a cult of personality, and that he had constructed an authoritarian dictatorship under the flag of 'socialism'. Sayyid Qutb's trenchant criticism led to his being jailed for ten years (1954–64). He was eventually tried and executed by Nasser in 1966.[124]

Qutb had considerable support among the Muslim Brotherhood, which had helped to bring Nasser to power.[125] The Muslim Brotherhood were prepared to use violence and to suffer martyrdom in their pursuit of a just society. In 1981 a group of the Brothers assassinated Nasser's successor, President Sadat. Sadat's successor, President Mubarak has remained longer in power than almost any other political leader, during which time the Muslim Brotherhood have remained an important political force, albeit with large restrictions on their freedom of operation.

Qutb was a sophisticated, highly educated scholar, who had obtained a Masters degree in the United States, taught in higher education in his native Egypt, and served as a senior official in the Ministry of Education.[126] There is a widely-held view in the West that Islamic scholars and Islamic schools (*madrassas*) are 'fundamentalist', anti-Western and anti-capitalist. Given the fact that Qutb is immensely influential in the Islamic world among scholars and students, it may be useful to look at his views in some detail.

Qutb's most influential book is *Social Justice in Islam* (Qutb, 2000), originally published in 1949. Qutb believed that the Koran constituted the sole basis of morality, and that 'justice is the greatest foundation of Islam' (Qutb, 2000: 131).[127] He explains that the Koran's ethical perspective has a profoundly rational core, which enables human beings to construct a good society that meets their essential human needs. Far from being based on a 'fundamentalist' view of ethics, Qutb attempts to find a middle way between the extremes of collectivist communism and free market capitalism. He shows that the Islamic approach to social justice has the potential to make a powerful contribution to an ethic of sustainable development.

Islam's foundation is human beings' nature as social beings, who only prosper as a species through mutual support: 'The Islamic belief is that humanity is an essential unity ... [B]ecause individuals are as atoms, dependent upon and related to the world, therefore they must have the same dependence upon and relation to one another' (Qutb, 2000: 41). The human race is at a critical juncture in its long evolution due to the contradictory character of capitalism: '[T]he world today is in that state of insecurity and instability where it must look for new foundations and search for some spiritual means of restoring to man his faith in the principles of humanity' (Qutb, 2000: 278). Islam can contribute fundamentally to solving the challenges posed by capitalist materialism: 'We are indeed at a crossroads ... [Islam] can offer mankind this theory [of social justice] whose aims are a complete mutual help among all men and a true mutual responsibility in society' (Qutb, 2000: 318).

One of the essential principles to be derived from the Koran is citizens' mutual responsibility: 'Life is like a ship at sea whose crew are all concerned for her safety; none of them may make a hole in his own part of the ship in the name of his individual freedom' (Qutb, 2000: 86). There is 'an embracing identity of purpose between the individual and society' (Qutb, 2000: 92). Islam attempts to find a balance between individual and social interests: 'Justice demands that the social system shall conform to the desire of the individual and satisfy his inclinations – at least so far as will not injure society – as a return for his contribution to it in the way of ability and labour ... [J]ustice is not always concerned to serve the interests of the individual. Justice is for the individual, but is for society also, if we are willing to tread the middle way' (Qutb, 2000: 131).

While law has a key role in ensuring that people behave correctly towards the rest of society, the more important regulator of social behaviour is the individual conscience, which is developed through education: 'Character is the most essential foundation for the building of a firmly based society, for the joining together of earth to Heaven, the temporal to the eternal in the human consciousness with all its finitude and its frailty' (Qutb, 2000: 95). The twin forces of law and the human conscience 'appeal to the depths of feelings in the human consciousness' (Qutb, 2000: 94).

Private property is an integral part of the Muslim economy (Qutb, 2000: 84). The important role of private property is reflected in the elaborate instructions in the Koran on the rules of inheritance and the strict attitude of Islam towards theft of personal property. Islam finds it acceptable for individuals with surplus capital to 'put it to some profitable use in manufacture or trade or agriculture ... [or] in vesting it in share-issuing companies, where the share values may rise or fall' (Qutb, 2000: 310).

However, the owner of property is 'not allowed absolute freedom to dispose of his money as he may wish': 'Property is a trust in the hands of its possessor, who is obliged to use it for the general good of society' (Qutb, 2000: 149). Under Islam, 'everything belongs to the community, and, therefore, all permission for personal ownership must come from the law, virtually or actually' (Qutb, 2000: 138): 'Allah is the only true owner of anything' (Qutb, 2000: 132).

Wealth should be taxed for the benefit of society. Islam prescribes the levying of *zakat* on the usufruct from property. *Zakat* is a 'compulsory duty on property', which is 'as much a right of those who receive it as it is a duty of those who pay it' (Qutb, 2000: 164). It is the 'most essential part of the economic theory of Islam' (Qutb, 2000: 162). *Zakat* means 'purification': 'It is a purification of the soul and the heart from the natural instinct of avarice and from the disposition to love one's self' (Qutb, 2000: 162). Islam 'gives the ruler wide powers to assign levies on capital – that is to say, forced levies from capital at a reasonable rate – subject always to the permanent limitations of its own welfare' (Qutb, 2000: 167). *Zakat* and other state levies are to be used for social welfare: 'Islam disapproves of people being in poverty or need, because it wishes to preserve them from the material cares of life and give them leisure for better things, for things which are more suitable for human nature and to that special nobility with which Allah has endowed the sons of man' (Qutb, 2000: 163). Islam should ensure that medical care and education are 'provided free to every individual in the country: the rich must not be able, by money, to get more than the poor in schools or hospitals' (Qutb, 2000: 308).

Islam 'does not teach any communistic doctrine of property, for the right of personal ownership is firmly established in Islam' (Qutb, 2000: 134). On the one hand, the individual must realise that he is 'no more than the steward of this property', and must, therefore, 'accept the restrictions that the system lays upon his liberty, and the bounds that limit his rights of disposal' (Qutb, 2000: 134). On the other hand, 'society must realise its fundamental rights to such property and must thus become bolder in laying down the laws which concern it': 'Only thus can we arrive at principles that will ensure complete social justice in the profitable use of property' (Qutb, 2000: 134).

Zakat and other levies on property should be provided as a right to the poor and destitute. It should provide them with 'some little enjoyment over and above a bare livelihood' (Qutb, 2000: 163). In addition these collective resources should be used for the provision of education and health services

(Qutb, 2000: 166). Islam does not advocate a life of asceticism: 'Life should be made pleasant and agreeable and cheerful, without wantonness or waste', and 'Islam does not command austerity or asceticism or absence from the good things of life' (Qutb, 2000: 154). However, it wishes the whole community to enjoy these things: 'Hardship and poverty constitute the greatest possible denial of the beneficence of Allah, and He disapproves of such a denial' (Qutb, 2000: 155). When Islam allocates poor people *zakat* money, 'it is giving him comfort and the enjoyment of more than the bare necessities': 'Thus his life may become pleasant and agreeable, and thus the soul may find a freedom from purely material cares to think great thoughts, formulate lofty ideals, ponder the problems of the universe and human nature, and take up the search for perfection and beauty' (Qutb, 2000: 155).

Islam is deeply hostile to the accumulation of capital through usury: 'Mutual help is one of the fundamental principles of the Islamic society, but usury destroys mutual help and it vitiates it at its very root' (Qutb, 2000: 150). It views usury as the means of 'amassing a vast amount of capital wealth that does not depend on labour and effort ... Although Allah has allowed bargaining, he has forbidden usury' (Qutb, 2000: 149–50). Usury is viewed as a key mechanism for producing socio-economic inequality, and exploitation of those in a vulnerable position. Instead, money should be 'loaned to those in need freely and without interest; this is the way to increase affection, cultivate generosity, and create a sense of mutual responsibility between rich and poor, between powerful and weak' (Qutb, 2000: 150).

Islam recognises the need to motivate people through material incentives to work hard, which will be for the benefit of the whole society. Selfishness is deeply ingrained in human beings: 'Islam is aware of the instinct to love oneself and to love money' (Qutb, 2000: 109). Human beings are naturally endowed with different capabilities, and the employment of these talents is to the benefit of the whole society. Those with special talents should be rewarded accordingly: 'On no account must we close off the outlet for such endowments or discourage them by making them equal in reward with lesser abilities; we must avoid shackling such gifts and stifling them, and thereby depriving the community and the human race alike' (Qutb, 2000: 48).

Finding the 'mean' is critical to establishing a good society. Islam aims to 'create a balance of wealth, to oppose destitution, to establish the responsibilities that exist between rich and poor, and thus to shape a society that has a sense of mutual relationship and mutual help and that is therefore a healthy society' (Qutb, 2000: 109). There should be 'a lower level of duty that is prescribed by law', which is demanded by the welfare of society, but above that, there is a 'higher level of conscience, which is so [sic] desirable and towards which individuals and nations have striven in every age and century' (Qutb, 2000: 110). An Islamic society should find a 'just middle course' between luxury and privation (Qutb, 2000: 160): 'The Islamic principle is that it is undesirable to have wealth concentrated in the hands of a few members of the community' (Qutb, 2000: 136).

Islam is internationalist in outlook, embracing diverse peoples from West Africa through the Middle East and Central Asia to Southeast Asia (Qutb, 2000: 267). Islam is 'not isolated from the human caravan' (Qutb, 2000: 286). Islam seeks to provide answers to human beings' deepest spiritual needs. Islam can make a fundamental contribution to global challenges presented by the contradictory character of capitalist materialism:

> [I]t is apparent ... that the philosophy of Western materialist civilisation is a danger to the continued existence of man. It breeds in human nature a ceaseless anxiety, a perpetual rivalry, a continuous strife, a degeneration of all human qualities. And this is in spite of all the triumphs of science that could have tended to human happiness and peace and content had it not been that the bases of the Western philosophy of life were purely materialistic and hence unable to guide men along the path to perfection (Qutb, 2000: 286).

The society that Qutb saw around him in the Islamic world in the 1940s was 'not Islamic in any sense of the word': '[T]he basis of our economic life is usury; our laws permit rather than punish oppression; the *zakat* is not obligatory and is not spent in the requisite ways. We permit the extravagance and luxury that Islam prohibits; we allow starvation and destitution ...' (Qutb, 2000: 262). However, Qutb's solution to these ills was not a violent revolution that would establish an Islamic fundamentalist, ascetic, communist society. Rather, his goal was to construct a socially just Islamic society. This society would be based on social solidarity; balancing the mutual interests of different social groups; protecting private property; acknowledging the importance of material incentives; while strongly encouraging charitable giving, alongside powerful state action to tax the rich in order to redistribute to the poor and fund universal free education and healthcare.

Today, there is a hysteria in the West about the alleged threat from Islamic fundamentalism. There is a widespread view that there is, indeed, a 'clash of civilisations' between Islam and the Judaeo-Christian 'West'.[128] However, as we have seen, the views even of Sayyid Qutb, arguably the most influential Islamic thinker of the twentieth century, were far from Islamic 'fundamentalism'. Qutb was concerned with building a harmonious society that sought a balanced middle way between the extremes of the free market and communist Islamic utopianism. The mainstream of Islamic thinking today, both among scholars and ordinary people, occupies the 'reformist' ground, just as it did in the medieval world. The core values of the reformist mainstream constitute a form of 'Third Way', which accepts the institutions of private property and the market, but which tightly constrains the conditions under which these institutions function, with an ethic that is derived from the Koran. Thinkers and political activists in the reformist approach agree that the *shari'ah* is the basis for providing the moral framework within which private property and entrepreneurial activity work towards the collective interest.

The Islamic mainstream reformists have no objection to globalisation. They point out that the Islamic concept of *Tawhid* (the Oneness of God) implies the oneness of all human beings. They note that the Muslim concept *ummah* is a universal community. For them globalisation in itself is not worrying, 'indeed it could be a great blessing for mankind': 'What must be ensured, however, is that the process is equitable, and does not become a camouflage for hegemony and the exploitation of the weak by the powerful' (Ahmad, 2003: 197).

2.2.3 Conclusion

The widespread anger in the Islamic world against the 'West' has little to do with 'Islamic fundamentalism'. The anger is a consequence of a set of inter-related historical factors that have little to do with religion, let alone class struggle. However, the fact that the Islamic people have an identity that transcends national boundaries has contributed to an anger and resentment that is international, and unites much of the world's Islamic population. Naturally, the form in which this anger is expressed employs language and imagery from the Koran and the surrounding belief system. This does not mean that the conflict has religious origins.

Islamic Unity

The 1.3 billion people who speak different dialects of Chinese and read a common written language, mainly live within a single state, the People's Republic of China. The 1.3 billion Islamic people live in several tens of countries, albeit that in numerous of these countries, the Islamic people constitute a majority of the population. Even the smallest of these countries, such as Kuwait, Bahrain and the United Arab Emirates, have each attempted to build a sense of national identity in the modern epoch. As is normally the case, this identity is often based on a mythical history of national unity. Islamic people are divided by the fact that they speak a diversity of languages.

There are profound differences of culture, language, ethnic and national identity between the Islamic people of African countries such as Nigeria, Sudan or Sierra Leone, those of the Arab Middle East, those of Central Asia in Iran, Afghanistan and Uzbekistan, and those of South and Southeast Asia, in Pakistan, India, Malaysia and Indonesia. There are also violent conflicts within the Islamic community. The Islamic Kurds have fought a ferocious, long-lasting battle for independence with their fellow Muslims in Turkey, Iraq and Iran. Islamic Iran and Islamic Iraq fought one of the longest-lasting and most horrific wars of modern times. Much of the Islamic world is riven by the schism between the Sunni and Shi'ite Muslims. The attempts to build Islamic institutions that cross national boundaries have, for the most part, not advanced far. For example, the Arab League, which was founded in 1945 as an 'Arab United Nations', has never progressed much beyond a talking-shop.

However, despite the facts of deep divisions within the Islamic world, the Islamic people are united by a religion, which remains fundamentally important as a guide to the conduct of their lives for a large fraction of these 1.3 billion. It continues to permeate their daily lives in a way that Christianity has ceased to do for a large fraction of those who are nominally 'Christian'. There is a profound sense of Islamic identity that transcends the boundaries of nationality, culture, language, and religious interpretation.

There is a long legacy in modern times of anti-Western feeling within the broad Islamic world. There are many causes of this hostility, including the late and violent end to colonialism, the inter-twining of oil and international relations, and the role of Israel. The language in which this has been expressed among the Islamic people has been mainly couched in terms of the Islamic religion. This also is unsurprising, as this is the ethical framework for Islamic people and is the realm of the language with the most powerful emotional appeal with their culture.

Islam and Oil

Oil lies in every sense at the heart of the Islamic world. By far the largest oil reserves in the world are located within the national boundaries of the country that was the birthplace of the Prophet Muhammad and which is where the Islamic religion arose. It is where the key sites of the Islamic religion are located, including Mecca, which all Islamic people wish to visit at least once in their life. A large fraction of the remaining reserves of oil are located in the surrounding territories in the Arab world that formed the early core of Islam. Together, the Islamic countries of the Middle East dominate the world's oil reserves. Once it became apparent that the Middle East contained a large fraction of the world's oil reserves, the region became a central focus for the foreign policy of the world's dominant economies.

The world's giant publicly-quoted oil companies are all headquartered in the high-income countries. Several of these have been, and some still are, wholly or partially owned by the respective national governments, reflecting the key role that oil plays in international relations. National energy security has formed a central focus for the governments of the high-income countries. Oil is at the centre of this, because of rising demand for oil in the high-income economies, which is closely related to the fact that they are deeply dependent on combustion engines, and because of declining output from their own oil reserves. The governments of the high-income countries have interacted closely with the leading international oil companies in shaping policies towards the oil-producing countries of the Middle East.

The governments of the leading high-income countries have without exception remorselessly intervened in the political evolution of the oil-producing countries of the Middle East in order to ensure their national energy needs. In the early phase, the lead was taken by Britain, but as British economic, political and military power waned, the United States increasingly took the lead in attempting to shape the region's political economy in order to meet its own interests.

These remorseless geo-political and military interventions, right through to the present-day invasion of Iraq, in the pursuit of oil supplies from the region that is the core of the Islamic religion, has resulted in common sentiments of hostility among Islamic people towards Western governments. It is unsurprising that such sentiments exist. Although the Islamic world is not a single nation, the language and sentiment has much in common with that of national liberation movements against colonial governments across the world in much of the twentieth century.

The United States and Islam

The Middle East has been the focal point of American international relations, alongside its Cold War struggle with the USSR, and the unresolved relationship with China. The United States has persistently and deeply intervened in the region. America's remorseless pursuit of oil and 'energy security', combined with deeply ideological goals and with support for the Jewish state, have together helped to undermine capitalist development in the Middle East. It has nurtured the most important source of instability in the world today, namely the attack upon the United States by Islamic groups across the whole Islamic world. The United States has consistently adopted an ideological position in its foreign policy, supporting democracy and free markets. However, the interpretation of these ideological goals has been systematically undertaken in a fashion that serves the American national interest. Over a long period, American foreign policy has antagonised large segments of the Islamic population.

The United States has deeply intervened in the internal development of oil-producing Islamic countries. It helped to bring about the downfall of the democratically elected Mossadeq government in Iran in 1953 and the installation of the Shah in its place. It has consistently supported authoritarian, pro-American governments in the oil-producing Islamic countries, including the Saudi royal family, the leaders of the small Gulf states, and the Shah of Iran. It is widely perceived in the Islamic world to be bolstering corrupt and highly unequal systems of political economy.

Since the overthrow of the Shah it has tried ceaselessly to bring about the overthrow of the Iranian regime. It supported Iraq in its war with Iran. It has exercised a long-term and intensifying economic blockade of Iran. In the latter phase of Saddam Hussein's rule, for many years it administered an economic blockade of Iraq, with serious consequences for the welfare of Iraqi people. Having long supported undemocratic regimes in the interest of *realpolitik*, it belatedly attempted to implement a policy of establishing a so-called 'New Middle East', based on democratic institutions throughout the region. This was widely perceived in the Islamic world as a fig-leaf to disguise the attempt to put into place regimes sympathetic to American interests in the region, notably access to oil for US oil companies. Despite widespread dislike of the Saddam Hussein regime, the US war invasion of Iraq was deeply resented by a large body of Islamic opinion throughout the Islamic world. The invasion has brought chaos to Iraq, and threatens to engulf the surrounding regimes. This also has brought even deeper resentment among Islamic people worldwide. The fact that the United States stations a massive military force in the Middle East is widely resented in the Islamic world as an intrusion upon the region's sovereignty.

In 1947, the United States led the drive in the UN General Assembly to vote in favour of the partition of Palestine and the establishment of an independent state of Israel. Much of the subsequent conflict in the Middle East flowed from this fateful decision. The United States was widely seen in the Islamic world to have acted in the interests of the Zionists, in the teeth of opposition from almost the entire Islamic world. The United States turned a blind eye to Israel's acquisition of the atomic bomb in the late 1950s and early 1960s, and to the destruction of Iraq's nuclear capabilities by an Israeli military attack. American Jewish scientists, most notably Edward Teller, were central to Israel's acquisition of nuclear weapons technology. American Jews were crucial to the supply of funds for Israel to build armaments in the late 1940s, that enabled it to survive in the 1948 War. They were fundamental also to funding Israel's acquisition of nuclear weapons technology. The United States has been by far the major supplier of advanced non-nuclear weapons to Israel, including the Israeli air force, which holds a commanding lead over the combined air forces of the Arab nations that surround Israel. The United States has supplied massive amounts of foreign aid to Israel.

American foreign policy has hindered the development of modern capitalism in the Middle East, despite capitalism's powerful ancient roots in the region. The seeds of modern capitalist development in the twentieth century were choked off, in no small degree due to the selfish and ignorant intervention of the United States and its proxy in the Middle East, Israel.

The fact that the United States has so deeply supported the autocratic Islamic regimes of the Gulf region, most notably, Saudi Arabia, as well as remorselessly supporting Israel, has contributed powerfully to 'blow-back' against the United States (Johnson, 2000). Saudi Arabia has been deeply hostile to Israel ever since it was established. It has provided extensive support for Islamic education across the Islamic world, and is alleged to have provided extensive support for Islamic organisations that perpetrate violence against both Israel and the United States. However, the Saudi rulers are themselves the object of deep hostility from Islamic people inside and outside the country, due to the rulers' long and deep relationship with the United States, whose support has been critical to the corrupt regime remaining in power and to the maintenance of a highly unequal society.

The attack on the twin towers was not perpetrated in the pursuit of class struggle. The attack on the World Trade Centre on 11 September 2001 was perpetrated by nineteen Arab hijackers, of whom fifteen were from Saudi Arabia. The Al Qaeda network is funded and presided over by the Saudi dissident, Osama Bin Laden. Al Qaeda was founded with the explicit purpose of attacking the United States (Al Qaeda, 1998). Al Qaeda's hatred of the United States was due to American occupation of the Middle East, particularly Saudi Arabia, and its support for Israel. Al Qaeda's founding statement in 1998 pronounced:

> The Arabian peninsula has never ... been stormed by any forces like the crusader armies spreading in it like locusts, eating its riches and wiping out its plantations ... [F]or over seven years the United States has been occupying the lands of Islam in the holiest places, the Arabian Peninsula, plundering its riches, dictating to its rulers, humiliating its people, terrorising its neighbours, and turning its bases in the Peninsula into a spearhead through which to fight the neighbouring Muslim peoples ... The

best proof of this is the Americans' continuing aggression against the Iraqi people using the Peninsula as a staging post ... [D]espite the great devastation inflicted on the Iraqi people by the crusader-Zionist alliance, and despite the huge number of those killed ... the Americans are once again trying to repeat the horrific massacres ... [I]f the American aims behind these wars are religious and economic, the aim is also to serve the Jews' petty state and divert attention from its occupation of Jerusalem and the murder of Muslims there ... The ruling to kill the Americans and their allies – civilians and military – is an individual duty for every Muslim who can do it in any country in which it is possible to do it, in order to liberate the Al-Aqsa Mosque and the Holy Mosque [Mecca] from their grip, and in order for their armies to move out of all the lands of Islam, defeated and unable to threaten any Muslim (Al Qaeda, 1998).

Israel and Islam

The colonisation of Palestine by Jewish immigrants and the subsequent establishment of a separate Jewish state of Israel has been, and still is, a festering sore in the heart of relations between the Islamic world and the West. Instead of migrating to the region to become part of a larger state to which they might have made an invaluable contribution, the Jewish immigrants set out to build a state in which people of the Jewish religion would constitute the overwhelming majority. The colonisation of Palestine was conducted in an extremely aggressive fashion through the purchase of farmland, and the establishment of a powerful military machine to defend the colonists in the face of opposition from the native population. The Jewish colonists angered Islamic people by their propagation of the myth of an 'empty land', by their claim to bring enlightenment to a benighted native population and by the myth that God had always intended his 'Chosen People' to re-occupy the 'Promised Land'.

The fact that it was able to construct an immensely powerful military machine capable of defeating its Arab neighbours in a succession of military conflicts intensified hostility towards Israel. Islamic people deeply resented the way in which Israel remorselessly pushed its boundaries beyond those initially established, including the territories seized after the 1948 War and those seized after the Six Day War. Israel's refusal to countenance the return of East Jerusalem, that it strongly resisted the return of the Occupied Territories on the West Bank, Gaza, and the Golan Heights, and that it settled large numbers of Jewish people in the Occupied Territories, all deeply angered a large body of Islamic people.

The fact that Israel received such powerful support from Western powers, including Britain and France, but especially the United States, deeply angered a large fraction of Islamic people.

Islam and Capitalist Development

Islam is not fundamentally opposed to capitalism. The Islamic religion is perfectly compatible with private property, profit-seeking, commerce, hired labour, and an unequal class structure. For hundreds of years, the medieval Islamic world achieved levels of commercial and industrial development that were far in advance of those in Europe, and even after Europe entered the phase of accelerated capitalist development in the late Middle Ages, Islamic capitalism remained highly dynamic. For a long period, the Islamic world constituted a huge unified free trade area, with all the benefits for specialisation, the division of labour and the diffusion of knowledge that flowed from this. In the medieval and early modern period, large cities such as Damascus, Baghdad and Cairo were the core of flourishing commercial development, surrounded by intensive commercial agriculture, sophisticated irrigation systems, highly developed trade networks, and a rich culture of philosophy, science, art, architecture and literature. Relatively minor Islamic cities such as Jerusalem, also were often highly dynamic centres of capitalist development.

Most of the Islamic world was ruled by the colonial powers until the middle of the twentieth century. Strong rule by the colonial powers ensured a degree of political stability, and there was some progress in the provision of public infrastructure. International capital penetrated most countries. In addition, a national capitalist class that invested in modern businesses emerged. Despite widespread anger at the long period of rule by foreign powers, the late nineteenth and early twentieth century saw a significant advance of modern industrial capitalism across the Islamic countries.

In the wake of colonialism, for several years the main body of the non-oil-producing Islamic countries pursued some form of socialist planning, within the overall context of a mixed economy. This period saw considerable economic progress, but with constraints imposed by inward-looking, import-substituting patterns of development. From the late 1960s onwards, most of the non-oil exporting countries began to implement some form of '*infitah*', or 'opening up' to international trade and capital flows, alongside privatisation of nationalised industries. A broad swathe of non-oil-producing Islamic countries achieved quite rapid growth of output from the 1970s onwards under different forms of modern capitalism. Between 1975 and 2002, the growth of per capita output per annum was: Turkey (1.8 per cent), Bangladesh (1.9 per cent), Tunisia (2.1 per cent), Pakistan (2.6 per cent), Egypt (2.8 per cent), Indonesia (4.2 per cent), and Malaysia (4.0 per cent). Although this fell short of the growth rate of per capita output in the Asia Pacific region (5.9 per cent) in the same period, it substantially exceeded the average for middle-income countries (1.4 per cent). The non-oil-producing Islamic countries achieved wide-ranging improvements in health and education indicators under capitalist modernisation.

Islamic Responses to Capitalist Injustice

Since the earliest days, capitalist development in the Islamic world has been characterised by the same inequalities in wealth, income and power as capitalism in other parts of the world. As in those places, both in the medieval and the modern world, revolutionary social and political movements have arisen that seek to overthrow capitalism. As in other parts of the world, they have sought to establish communist societies based on collective ownership and egalitarian income distribution. Like Christianity, Islam can be used as the basis for a fundamental and often violent opposition to the injustice, inequality, individualism and commercialisation that is inherent in capitalism. In the Islamic world, these millenarian movements have used the language of Islam to express their protest at the injustice of capitalist development. However, from the medieval world through to the early twenty-first century, these movements have rarely, if ever, been able to topple the existing socio-political structures. The attempt violently to overthrow a society based on private property and to establish a form of communism has almost always remained at the margins of the Islamic world, both physically and intellectually. The notion that there is a fundamental 'clash of civilisations' between an anti-capitalist Islam and the capitalist West is refuted by over 1300 years of Islamic history.

Both in the Islamic Middle Ages and in the world of modern Islamic capitalist development, there has been an intense debate about how best to ensure that Islamic society can peacefully produce social harmony. The critical discussion of capitalist injustice has centred on the ways in which private property and material incentives can be constrained to serve the social interest while allowing society to benefit from the acknowledged dynamic character of market competition and private property. The main body of Islamic critical thought has been preoccupied with achieving harmonious development between different social interests. Critical Islamic thought has emphasised finding a 'mean' between the extremes of individual rights and social duties, and between the pursuit of profit and using the usufruct from capital to serve the social interest. It has recognised the benefit to society of competitive markets while wishing to surround commercial behaviour with laws and individual conscience in such a way as to serve the social interest.

Edward Said on Conflict

[T]o most people in the Islamic and Arab worlds, the official United States is synonymous with arrogant power, known mainly for its sanctimoniously munificent support not only of Israel but of numerous repressive Arab regimes ... Israel is now cynically exploiting the American catastrophe by intensifying its military occupation and oppression of the Palestinians ... Political rhetoric in the United States [flings about] words like **terrorism** *and* **freedom***, whereas, of course, such large abstractions have mostly hidden sordid material interests, the efficacy of the oil, defense, and Zionist lobbies now consolidating their hold on the entire Middle East, and an age-old religious hostility to (and ignorance of) 'Islam' that takes new forms every day ...*

The New York and Washington suicide bombers seem to have been middle-class, educated men, not poor refugees. Instead of getting a wise leadership that stresses education, mass mobilisation, and patient organisation in the service of a cause, the poor and desperate are often conned into the magical thinking and quick bloody solutions that such appalling models provide, wrapped in religious claptrap ...

'Islam' and 'the West' are simply inadequate as banners to follow blindly ... [F]or future generations to condemn themselves to prolonged war and suffering ... without looking at interdependent histories of injustice and oppression, and without trying for common emancipation and mutual enlightenment seems far more wilful than necessary. Demonisation of the Other is not a sufficient basis for any kind of decent politics ... It takes patience and education, but it is more worth the investment than still greater levels of large-scale violence and suffering ... Those of us with a possibility for reaching people who are willing to listen – and there are many such people in the United States, Europe, and the Middle East, at least – must try to do so as rationally and patiently as possible.

Edward Said, 'Collective Passion',
in *The Observer* (London, 16 September 2001).

The military solution hasn't worked at all and never will work. Why is that so hard for the Israelis to see? We must help them to understand this, not by suicide bombs but by rational argument, mass civil disobedience, and organised protest ...

Edward Said, 'Dignity and Solidarity', in *El-Ahram*, (26 June–2 July, 2003)
[Edward Said died in September 2003]

(The above articles are reproduced in Said, 2004).

CONCLUSION: SEARCHING FOR THE MIDDLE WAY

Once your crew has rowed you past the Sirens a choice of route is yours. I cannot advise you which to take, or lead you through it all – you must decide for yourself ... On one side there loom two enormous crags. One thrusts into the vaulting sky its jagged peak and halfway up that cliffside stands the fog-bound cavern gaping towards Erebus, realm of death and darkness ... Scylla lurks inside it – the yelping horror, yelping no louder than any suckling pup but she's a grisly monster, I assure you. She has twelve legs, all writhing, dangling down and six long swaying necks, a hideous head on each, each head barbed with a triple row of fangs ... The other crag is lower. Beneath it awesome Charybdis gulps the dark water down ... Don't be there when the whirlpool swallows down – not even an earthquake god could save you from disaster.
(Homer, *The Odyssey*, Book 12)

Zhao ci Baidi cai yun jian,
Qian li Jiangling yi ri huan,
Liang an yuan sheng ti bu zhu,
Qingzhou yi guo wan chong shan.

Early in the morning, leaving Baidi town, splendid amidst the clouds,
In one day returning 1000 *li* back to Jiangling,
On either river bank, monkeys screech unceasingly,
The quick craft has already passed by the serried ranks of 10 000 mountains.
(Li Bai, AD 710–62)

If everyone really desired a 'world-state' or 'collective security' (and meant the same thing by those terms) it would be easily attained ... [N]o progress is likely to be made along this path, and no political utopia will achieve even the most limited success unless it grows out of political reality.[1]
(Carr, 2001: 9)

America's most difficult task, but historically the most critical, will be to embody to the world at large an idea whose time has come.
(Brzezinski, 2007: 210)

Introduction

The contradictions of capitalism in the early twentieth century are, for the first time truly global in nature.

Capitalist globalisation has provided immense benefits, liberating human beings from the tyranny of nature, achieving large declines in the real costs of goods and services, and lifting a large fraction of the world's population out of poverty. However, it has a Faustian duality to its nature, producing profound threats to sustainable development in relation to inequality, ecology and financial stability, and, ultimately, posing the threat of violent international conflict.

The solution to the challenges produced by the nature of capitalist globalisation are immanent within capitalism itself. Capitalist globalisation has produced unprecedented technical progress, which can be harnessed to meet the needs of all human beings. Capitalism has become truly global and global institutions are emerging slowly to meet the global challenges. It is increasingly widely understood that market forces need to be heavily guided and powerfully restrained globally in the common social interest in order to contain socio-economic inequality, ensure an ecologically sustainable future, prevent a global financial crisis and prevent violent international conflict. More and more people, from a wide variety of backgrounds, realise that strict global rules and deep international cooperation are needed to constrain global capitalism in order to build a sustainable future. More and more people talk from different perspectives about humanity being at a crossroads.

In the process of fettering capitalism to serve collective social interests globally, capitalism would be altered radically. Raw, unconstrained capitalism does not exist anywhere. Even the United States today would appear to nineteenth century economists and social thinkers as a highly regulated economy and society. However, the focus of efforts to solve the challenges posed by the internal contradictions of the capitalist system has mainly been confined to individual countries. The range of solutions attempted in different countries has been wide, including communist administrative planning, Arab and Nordic socialism, the United States under the New Deal and post-war state capitalism in Europe. Socialism, in whatever guise, has mainly been confined within the borders of given countries. Indeed, socialist countries have often fought bitterly with each other, sometimes even invading each other's country.[2] It is no longer feasible to pursue either 'socialism in one country' or 'capitalism in one country'.

The new phase in the unleashing of capitalism in the epoch of modern global capitalism poses deeper challenges and requires more profound answers than in the past. These answers are essential to human beings' survival as a species. They require cooperation and collective action on a scale that has not so far been realised, but which exists in potential in the nature of human beings and has been revealed in their past cooperation on a smaller scale to solve common problems. This is the Darwinian challenge facing the human species in the twenty-first century.

The Contradictions of Capitalist Globalisation

The contradictory character of capitalist globalisation manifests itself in a number of ways. The full incorporation of 2.5 billion workers from low and middle-income countries into the global workforce has been a central force in drastic changes in the labour markets of both rich and poor countries in the period of capitalist globalisation. In low and middle-income countries incorporation into global capitalism has not only stimulated rising average incomes, but also contributed to greatly increased inequality. It will be several decades before 'unlimited' supplies of underemployed labour in developing countries are exhausted, and these countries have finally passed through the 'Lewis' phase of development. In high-income countries, capitalist globalisation has helped to lower the price of most goods and services. Simultaneously, it has contributed to the stagnation of median wages and the deterioration of conditions of employment, alongside a dramatic increase in incomes for the global elite.[3] This process needs careful international coordination between rich and poor countries in order to avoid international conflict consequent upon the de-stabilising effect of capitalist globalisation upon the social structure of both rich and poor countries.

The Global Business Revolution has unleashed to the full the potential within capitalism for industrial concentration. Leading global firms benefit from superior technologies and systems integration capabilities, as well as from global marketing and global procurement. Through organic growth and through explosive merger and acquisition, global leaders in each sector occupy dominant oligopolistic positions in global markets. Moreover, through the 'cascade' effect, they have stimulated high-speed industrial concentration far down into the supply chain, in the invisible segment hidden beneath the water of the 'iceberg' of industrial structure. The lion's share of the world's globally dominant firms is headquartered in the high-income countries. This presents an immense challenge for firms from developing countries, in both international markets and their own domestic markets, as leading global firms build oligopolistic position within developing countries at both the level of systems integrators and far down into the supply chain. The explosive growth of global firms' international operations is fast attenuating the relationship with their home nation within which they have their headquarters and where their initial expansion was based. This explosive process requires careful international coordination in order to avoid conflict. Business leaders, answerable to their separate shareholders and focused firmly on business success in their segment of the world market, cannot be expected collectively to lead this coordination process.[4]

The ecological consequences of raw unconstrained capitalist globalisation have become dramatically self-evident in recent years. The destruction of flora and fauna is accelerating alongside rising global economic activity. The list of 'endangered' species grows ever larger. This applies to the world's land masses, but even more seriously to the global commons of the world's seas and all that they contain. However, the most dramatic tragedy of the global commons is that of the earth's atmosphere, with uncontrollable natural forces swirling across the skies, without regard to international boundaries. Human ingenuity has produced the triumph of the internal combustion engine and its continuous technical improvement, and the ever-expanding supply of fossil fuels, including almost limitless supplies of oil from coal, from tar sands and from shale, in order to meet the ever-expanding global stock of automobiles and aeroplanes. The private costs of transport have fallen dramatically thanks to the power of technical progress driven by competition between global capitalist firms. Alternative fuels, such as wind, wave and solar power are a long way from commercial viability, as are commercially viable techniques to sequester carbon dioxide in underground deposits. For several decades, there is the possibility of intense international conflict surrounding global warming from carbon dioxide emissions produced by burning fossil fuels, and, even, a deep threat to the very existence of the human race. Global warming, 'the ultimate externality', has done more than any other issue to impress upon people across boundaries, cultures and income levels, that global cooperation is essential: it is a 'choice of no choice' for human survival. However, the huge differences between countries in levels of economic development and per capita emissions of carbon dioxide make international cooperation especially difficult to achieve. This difficulty is increased due to the fact that the distribution of the impact of global warming (both negative and positive) is likely to be highly uneven across different parts of the world.

For the foreseeable future, oil will be the critical source of primary energy for the internal combustion engine, which will remain the key source of motive power for several decades to come. The Middle East dominates global oil reserves and will increasingly dominate global oil production and trade. There is a high potential for international conflict over access to this finite resource, both directly, but also through the indirect impact of intervention in the region by the United States. Unravelling the damaging consequences of past US foreign policy in the region will take a long time.

The international financial system has made enormous progress during the epoch of capitalist globalisation. Flows of financial firms from high-income countries have brought their high standards of corporate governance and sophisticated techniques for risk management to developing countries. Dramatic advances have taken place in financial risk management through improved risk modelling, the securitisation of bank loans and the proliferation of instruments to hedge risk, especially the huge array of derivatives, covering every conceivable area of financial activity.

However, there are deep system risks embedded in the global financial system. There is an ever-widening 'scissors' between the falling real price of most goods and services on the one hand, and the unprecedented speculative bubble affecting every conceivable asset, from property to works of art on the other. There is an imbalance between the huge trade surplus and foreign exchange reserves of China and the oil-producing countries, on the one hand, and the yawning US trade deficit, on the other. There is an ever-growing level of personal debt in high-income countries, deeply intertwined with the speculative bubble in asset prices, especially property. There are the uncertain prospects for behaviour in the vast speculative derivatives market in the event of an initial crisis in world financial markets. There is an absence of a central regulatory body to ensure order in the global financial system.

The global financial system has weathered a succession of financial crises in recent years, including the Mexican Tequila crisis, the Asian Financial Crisis, the crisis at Long-term Capital Management, and the Argentinian Financial Crisis. However, none of these was truly global. Financial markets have now become so deeply integrated that there is a real possibility that a global financial crisis could erupt with profound consequences for the whole global political economy. The global financial system is 'flying blind', with no one at the controls. It is of the utmost urgency that global coordination mechanisms are established before a financial crisis of cataclysmic dimensions erupts. The interaction of this with other destabilising aspects of capitalist globalisation is extraordinarily dangerous for international relations and the prospects for human beings' very survival.

It is an extraordinary paradox of the epoch of capitalist globalisation that nuclear weapons still exist in large quantities, with vast stocks held by the world's dominant power, the United States, as well as those held by Russia, the United Kingdom and France. Nuclear weapons technologies have progressed enormously, so that their explosive power is many multiples of those that destroyed Hiroshima and Nagasaki.[5]

A growing number of countries have acquired nuclear weapons since the early 1960s, including Israel, China, Pakistan, India and North Korea. The United States turned a blind eye to Israel's acquisition of nuclear weapons. The United States and the United Kingdom justified their invasion of Iraq with the claim, later proved to be false, that it was capable of producing 'weapons of mass destruction' within a month or so. Japan is considered by most nuclear experts to be capable of producing nuclear weapons within a few weeks. The Gulf states announced in late 2006 that they would coordinate a programme for the acquisition of civilian nuclear technologies in the region. Iran is pressing ahead with plans to build nuclear reactors and process uranium. The United States has agreed to increase its support for India's civilian nuclear programme, while agreeing to exclude India's military nuclear programme from international inspection. The threat of global warming is likely to lead to a proliferation of civilian nuclear technologies, which, other things being equal, greatly increases the likelihood of the proliferation of nuclear weapons. In the eyes of an increasingly wide spectrum of commentators, including Robert McNamara, the former US Secretary of Defense under Kennedy and Johnson, there has never been a more dangerous moment in human history.

Globalisation and the Clash of Civilisations

A central issue in humanity's attempt to grope a way forward in this extraordinarily dangerous time is the relationship between the world's dominant power, the United States, and the two most powerful unified cultures, China and Islam, which between them embrace two-fifths of the world's population. The capability of human beings cooperating in order to ensure a sustainable future will stand or fall on these relationships. If their engagement is confrontational rather than constructive, the prospects for humanity are bleak. Many people within each of these cultures believe that there is an unavoidable 'clash of civilisations', between the West, on the one hand, and China and Islam on the other. They believe that it is utopian to imagine that a confrontation can be avoided. They believe that the central task of national policy is to prepare for the inevitable clash in order to ensure victory. Many of them believe that it is better to ensure mutual destruction rather than endure defeat. It is impossible to measure the probability of such a confrontation. Even if the chances are, indeed, high, all possible efforts must be made to avoid such a confrontation from taking place, as this would be a disaster for the human race.

There is no fundamental clash between Western capitalism and the civilisations of China and Islam. Despite their differences in culture, political structure and belief systems, it is the common elements in the long-term evolution of socio-economic systems of China, Islam and the West that are the outstanding feature when viewed from the perspective of the early twenty-first century and the swelling tide of globalisation. In both the East and the West, in both the medieval and the modern world, private property, extension of the market, and pursuit of profit, have been the central forces stimulating human ingenuity to achieve technical progress. The Western world has a great deal to learn from both China and Islam about ways in which to ensure that market forces are harnessed for the collective social good.

Capitalism has demonstrated its unique dynamic force in these different contexts for than 1000 years. It has equally consistently demonstrated its contradictory character. In each of these contexts, social forces have arisen which have attempted to rectify the inequality, the damaging psychological and interpersonal impact, the economic instability and, even, the environmental impact of raw capitalism. These have sometimes taken the form of revolutionary attempts to overthrow the existing social order entirely and establish egalitarian communist societies based on common ownership of property. However, up until the twentieth century, revolutionary communist movements rarely were able to seize state power, whether in China, Europe or the Islamic world. Almost always, the revolutionary movements used religious or quasi-religious language as their ethical foundation. The anti-capitalist epoch of common ownership in the Soviet Union (from the late 1920s until the mid-1980s) and in China (from the mid-1950s until the mid-1970s) appear increasingly as relatively brief interludes and geographically limited in the long span of the history of capitalism.

In both China and the Islamic world, the main focus of responses to the contradictory character of capitalism has been to try to find a 'mean' or 'middle way', which recognises capitalism's unique dynamic power, while constraining the way in which capitalism operates in order to meet the needs of diverse social groups. These constraints have operated through ethics, conscience and self-motivated social behaviour, conveyed through education, religion and common traditional value systems. They have operated also through the law and through state action to provide public goods and regulate the economy. Both in China and in the Islamic world, in both medieval and modern times, intellectuals and political leaders have wrestled with the conundrum of attempting to 'civilise' capitalism and establish a harmonious, stable society. In China this took the ideological form of Confucianism and the attempt since the 1980s to construct a form of Chinese socialism that 'learns from the past in order to serve the present'. In the Islamic world, in both medieval and modern times, the dominant discourse for taming and civilising the market, has been the Islamic faith, based on the Koran. Both China and the Islamic world have a rich potential contribution to make in resolving the contradictions inherent in the nature of capitalist globalisation.

International peace in the early twenty-first century necessitates the United States dealing with China and the Islamic world in a non-ideological fashion. It necessitates America accepting that the nature of capitalism in these parts of the world may be very different from that in the United States. It necessitates America accepting that Chinese Confucian traditions and the Chinese

Communist Party, along with the Koranic tradition of the Islamic world will, in their different ways, contribute to a world in which capitalist markets are more tightly constrained in the interests of the whole global society than has been the case in the United States for most of the past century. It necessitates the United States understanding and recognising the historical role played by capitalism in both China and the Islamic world, and the contribution that this has made not only to these societies, but also to the common heritage of human beings.

It is likely to take a long time to fully develop trust between the United States on the one hand, and the Islamic world and China on the other. The United States' remorseless intervention in the Islamic world, driven by ideology, the pursuit of energy security, and support for Israel, has resulted in a legacy of deep animosity to the United States across all social strata that will take a long time to erase. Although constructive engagement has come to be the *leitmotif* of US relations with China since 9/11, there are still powerful forces across the US political spectrum that favour confrontation and containment of China. It will take a long time for China fully to trust US intentions.

Possibilities for Cooperation and Mutual Understanding

Energy security and ecologically sustainable development are crucial areas of potential conflict. They are also areas in which there are immense and obvious potential gains from cooperation between the United States on the one hand, and China and the Islamic countries on the other. The United States and China have the deepest mutual interest in developing and applying technologies to ensure that both countries increase their degree of self-sufficiency in the supply of oil and renewable sources of energy. They also have the deepest mutual interest in trying to find ways to produce political stability in the Middle East so that the supply of oil from the region is stabilised.

America's policies in the Middle East have been disastrous. It has followed its own narrow self-interest in energy security; allowed foreign policy to be driven by global oil companies; followed a narrowly ideological goal in trying to spread 'democracy' and build a 'New Middle East'; blindly supported Israel, including allowing it to develop a nuclear weapons capability; supplied massive quantities of arms to the region; and supported authoritarian, undemocratic oil rulers over many decades. However, American policies in the region have been subjected to scathing international and domestic criticism, and defeat in Iraq has provoked deep reflection on US policy failures in the region.

The United States, China and the Islamic world would all be deeply affected by a global financial meltdown. Policy-makers in each of these societies deeply fear such an outcome, though no one can predict exactly how the ripple effects from such a crisis would affect their economies and societies. The lessons from the 1930s suggest that they would be enormous. Halting efforts have been made to try to resolve mutual financial imbalances, but with little in the way of concrete results. The efforts to establish a global system of financial control has made little headway, despite the optimistic statements from the IMF in 2006. The world waits with bated breath for a global financial disaster, while financial institutions continue to profit from the vast expansion of global financial markets and the myriad associated instruments of speculation guided by ever-more sophisticated techniques to minimise short-term risk. The very fact of the extraordinary depth of the financial system's inter-dependence between the United States, China and the Islamic countries makes it possible to have some hope that they will struggle to find a way to avert disaster through mutual action, even if the global institutions are not yet able to fulfil their necessary function.

The dramatically unequal nature of the 'global playing field' has become obvious as globalisation has advanced since the 1980s. On the one hand, China and the Islamic world face the political challenge of seeing their national markets overwhelmed by global giant firms. On the other hand, the United States must accept the reality that in the past, along with the other high-income countries, it intervened massively to support indigenous firms. Whatever agreements were entered into on joining the WTO, it is highly likely that China and the Islamic countries will use industrial policy to nurture a group of their own globally successful firms. The United States cannot expect simply to 'pull up the ladder' through which their firms became globally powerful. The core of the Chinese industrial system consists of 150 giant enterprises that are majority owned by the state and partially floated on international stock markets. The core of the Islamic oil-producing economies consists of giant nationally-owned oil companies, which dominate the world's oil reserves. Between them already these two sets of state-owned firms have a large impact on the global business system. The United States also must accept that its most successful multinational firms are increasingly losing their American identity. These are complex, inter-related processes requiring sophisticated understanding of the real nature of the challenge of the Global Business Revolution and of its mutual implications for the different cultures.

The United States on the one hand, and China and the Islamic world on the other hand, need to understand fully the destabilising impact of capitalist globalisation upon their respective class structures. Capitalist globalisation is causing intensified socio-economic differentiation in each of these cultures. In each case, these forces can be mobilised for nationalistic purposes and intensify international hostility, by blaming the other culture for the uncomfortable changes. Deep study of each others' fast-transforming class structure is essential for mutual understanding. The task is not only that of creating a 'harmonious society' in a poor country locked in the 'Lewis' phase of development, but also in the world's most powerful economy undergoing radical transformation of its class structure in the face of the rise of China and significant parts of the Islamic world. The political leaders and intellectuals of the United States, China and the Islamic world need to study deeply the changing nature of the global business elite, and the challenge this poses for each of them by the increasing divorce of the elite from any country. These are common challenges faced by the ordinary people and by politicians in all societies. It is not just the United States that is asking Samuel Huntington's question: 'Who are we?'

Nationalism and Globalisation

America's constructive engagement with both China and the Islamic world would contribute positively to the economic rise of parts of the world that contain over two-fifths of the world's population, and each of which has its own identity and belief systems. This would bring large benefits to many American firms and many advantages for American people. However, China's rise already poses large economic, cultural and military adjustment challenges for the United States. China is still a developing country with a long way to go in terms of its potential growth of per capita output. Despite widespread capitalist development in Islamic countries in recent decades, they have under-performed their potential, due in no small part to the way in which the United States has engaged damagingly with the Islamic world. Positive, constructive engagement by the United States would be likely to stimulate accelerated growth in these countries, which would pose further adjustment challenges for the United States.

For most human beings, 'global' is not their framework of reference or source of identity. Only a tiny fraction of the world's population, systematically roam around the world as a regular part of their life. A much larger number, but still a tiny minority of the world's population, participates in global tourism. A still larger number, but still a small minority of the global population, migrates in search of long-term employment. For most people, apart from the family and religion, the 'nation' is the primary source of identity and the main forum within which they have a political voice. The forces of capitalist globalisation are increasingly international. The markets, employees, production facilities, and supply chains of leading international firms are, indeed, global. The outlook of their leaders is increasingly global and divorced from considerations of the national interest of any given country. More than one CEO of a major international firm has threatened to move the company headquarters away from its current location if the political-economic conditions of the country concerned do not change in ways that the company finds congenial. While the identity of leading firms is increasingly global, the national interest of citizens and national governments remains an immensely potent force.

The United States retains a profound sense of its national interest, with intense debate at all levels of society about the challenges posed to the country's dominant position by the economic rise of a new generation of 'latecomer' countries. Capitalist modernisation has almost always been associated with the creation and reinforcement of a sense of national identity. People within the same national border often with different dialects and, often, different languages, and distinct histories, are welded together into a single entity through a central state, employing unified national tax and legal systems, constructing unified national transport, telecommunication and broadcasting systems, and, critically, building unified national education systems using a common national language.[6] An increasingly urbanised population loses touch with their original local identity, but in a setting of a deep socio-economic inequality, in the early phase of industrialisation. Constructing a unified national identity was a crucially important way in which to create a socially harmonious society amidst the conflicts and strains of capitalist modernisation. Nowhere was this more so than in the United States. In the 'Gilded Age' in the late nineteenth century, not only was America a melting-pot of different national cultures, but also a massively unequal society. The large scale of immigration today, especially from Central America, means that the United States continues to face serious challenges to its cultural unity. The fact that it is a highly unequal society increases the incentive to mobilise strong nationalist sentiments as a unifying force.

Nationalism was an immensely powerful force also in the rise of Britain in the late eighteenth and early nineteenth centuries, as well as in Continental Europe and the Far East at a later date. Trade and financial capital were international, but people, governments, the mass media, education systems, and firms were deeply rooted within given industrialised nations. The dominance of each industrialised nation's sense of its own national interest was inseparable from feelings of national superiority and intense national rivalry. The intense nationalism of advanced industrial capitalism contributed directly to the violent intrusion of rich countries into the less industrialised regions, whose population was viewed as 'backward' and in need of the civilising benefits of being ruled by the colonial powers.[7] The tide of nationalist-inspired colonialism was not finally rolled back until the 1960s, when the French were driven out of Algeria. Seen through the lens of nationalism in the industrialised capitalist countries, indigenous nationalist movements, whether Chinese, Indian, Egyptian, Iraqi, Algerian, Vietnamese, or Palestinian, were alike viewed as 'terrorist organisations' by the industrialised colonial powers. The view that 'native' indigenous people in poor countries are not fundamentally part of the same human race was deeply rooted in nationalist-driven colonialism. This feeling helped to justify incredible acts of barbarism by the strong against the weak.

The intense nationalism of the advanced industrial nations contributed also to their violent struggle with each other. Militarism and nationalism went hand-in-hand in the industrialised capitalist countries. Teeming millions of dead soldiers littered the battlefields of the twentieth century. Teeming millions of civilians were buried or burned in the century's war-torn cities. In the late nineteenth century it would have been unimaginable that, in the epoch of advanced civilised capitalism, human beings fighting to fulfil their patriotic duty to their respective nation, could inflict such devastating violence on each other, using the most sophisticated products of industrial civilisation, culminating in the atom bomb. For Homer, author of both *The Odyssey* and *The Iliad*, it would have been unsurprising, as he recognised that human beings' dualistic personality contains a deep drive both towards love and cooperation as well as towards destruction, annihilation and death. Having witnessed the horrors of the First World War, Sigmund Freud moved reluctantly towards the view that human beings contained two contending forces: 'Our views have from the very first been dualistic, and today they are even more definitely dualistic than before – now that we describe the opposition as being, not between ego-instincts and sexual instincts, but between life instincts and death instincts' (Freud, 2001a: 53).

Capitalist Contradictions and Revolution

Many critics of the injustices and irrationality of advanced nineteenth century capitalism hoped that the solution to the contradictions of the capitalist system would lie in the form of violent revolutionary seizure of power. Others emphasised both the dangers and illogical nature of such a political path. Marx himself was preoccupied with the political dangers of a revolutionary *coup d'etat* led by a 'vanguard' force of workers and intellectuals. He was deeply disconcerted by the negative examples of the French Revolution of 1789, which descended into authoritarian violence, and the further examples of the failed French Revolutions of 1848 and 1870. Marx's belief was that when the conditions of advanced capitalism had fully matured, when most people lived in cities and education had spread to the whole population, the mass of people would seize control of the state through peaceful means and assert collective control over the irrationalities and injustices of capitalism. Capitalism created simultaneously both the contradictions and the means to solve them. Moreover, for Marx, the inherent nature of capitalism was international, and therefore the solution to its contradictory nature had to be found internationally also.

In fact, the course of capitalist industrialisation has normally witnessed the failure of vanguard revolutionary movements, including 1848 in Europe, the

United States in the late nineteenth century, and China in 1927, through to the revolutionary movements in Latin America[8] and South Asia in recent decades. Despite the injustice and inequality that are central to the 'Lewis' phase of capitalist economic development, capitalism has typically survived attempts at its revolutionary overthrow. The great exceptions were societies in this phase of development in which violent military struggle and invasion created a power vacuum, which could be occupied by well-organised vanguard parties. In the long-run, the attempt to organise administratively-planned economies which rejected capitalism entirely, ('capitalism is like a dog in the water to be beaten and drowned')[9] and were led by a vanguard communist party, failed. Despite many achievements, there were deeply negative consequences resulting from the attempt by vanguard revolutionary parties to lead non-capitalist economies in isolation from the rest of the world (and, in the case of Russia and China between 1960 and 1976, in isolation from each other). The former communist administratively-planned economies are all groping their different ways to find a new path through which to come terms with capitalism internally and internationally.

The contradictions of capitalist globalisation can only be resolved by a form of revolution. However, this is not a violent revolution. It is, rather, the process of patiently constructing global institutions that enable global markets to serve the needs of the whole of humanity. This is an evolutionary process that flows from the achievements and contradictions inherent within capitalism, which have reached their high point today. It is unnecessary to give a name to this evolving structure. Its essence is global cooperation to solve commonly acknowledged contradictions while preserving the benefits of the market system.

Conclusion

The period of capitalist globalisation has liberated human productive capabilities in ways that were formerly unimaginable, which benefit most people. However, the destructive aspects of capitalism have intensified, in relation to inequality and injustice within both rich and poor countries, ecological damage, the battle for scarce resources, and potential global financial instability. In the epoch of capitalist globalisation, these problems can only be solved at a global level. However, despite some progress in the construction of global institutions of social control, these institutions remain weak. They are overshadowed by the immense power of profit-seeking global firms, which have little incentive, either individually or collectively, to resolve these contradictions.

The internationalisation of business activity stands in striking contrast to the predominantly national basis of politics. Even regional political groupings of countries, whether in the Far East, the Islamic world, Africa, Latin America or, even, Europe,[10] have run up against large barriers to political integration.

Nationalism remains a powerful political force. Having been created in the process of capitalist modernisation, the *genie* of nationalism has proved hard to put back into the bottle. The intensification of nationalism in the rising latecomer countries of the early twenty-first century sits uneasily alongside the widespread fear of the damaging effects of capitalist globalisation upon the lives of the populations of the high-income countries.

Since ancient times the exercise of individual freedoms has been inseparable from the expansion of the market, driven by the search for profit. This force, namely capitalism, has stimulated human creativity in ways that have produced immense benefits. As capitalism has broadened its scope in the epoch of globalisation, so these benefits have become even greater. Human beings have been liberated to an even greater degree than hitherto from the tyranny of nature, from control by others over their lives, from poverty, and from war. The advances achieved by the globalisation of capitalism have appeared all the more striking, when set against the failure of non-capitalist systems of economic organisation.

However, capitalist freedom is a two-edged sword. In the epoch of capitalist globalisation, its contradictions have intensified. They comprehensively threaten the natural environment. They have intensified global inequality. They have stimulated a high degree of instability in global finance. The world's dominant economic, political and cultural power refuses to dismantle its vast stock of nuclear arms, sufficient to obliterate the entire global civilisation. This country benefits in numerous ways from global capitalism. It also feels under intense threat, both internally and externally from those same forces.

The present stage of development of global capitalism has produced in even more intense form the contradictions latent within the system. As human beings have taken to new heights their ability to free themselves from fundamental constraints through the market mechanism, so they also have reached new depths in terms of the uncontrollability of the structures they have created. Global capitalism has created uniquely intense threats to the very existence of the human species at the same time that it has liberated humanity more than ever before from fundamental constraints. The Astronomer Royal, Lord Rees, believes that 'the odds are no better than fifty-fifty that our present civilisation on Earth will survive to the end of the present century' (Rees, 2003: 8).

Modern capitalist globalisation began in the 1970s. The removal of constraints on the operation of the market mechanism has proceeded remorselessly across the whole world. The first 'wild' phase of modern capitalist globalisation is drawing to a close, as the intensifying multiple contradictions become ever more apparent. The resolution of these multiple contradictions necessitates globally coordinated regulation of the capitalist system. As the 'wild animal' of global capitalism becomes ever larger and more powerful, it becomes ever more important that human beings, who have given birth to and nurtured this animal, establish a moral framework to regulate its activity, and thereby prevent the wild animal from devouring its creator, humanity.

The capitalist system is the product of the collective exercise of human intelligence. The way in which people choose collectively to exercise that intelligence is governed by their ethics. Ethics are the 'pole star' to guide humanity on its journey through history. The possibilities for a sustainable future for human beings is, in turn, deeply related to human being's psychological needs. There have, since ancient times, been sharply polarised views of the fundamental human needs and the ethical systems corresponding to those needs.

Capitalist globalisation creates unprecedented challenges that can only be resolved at a global level through international cooperation. However, nationalism among both old industrialised and newly industrialising countries stands in the way of achieving the requisite cooperation. Human beings face a race against time.

The contradictory character of human psychology has been recognised since the great thinkers of antiquity. One may interpret Homer's great legends, *The Odyssey* and *The Iliad*, as concerned respectively with the 'life instinct' and the 'death instinct'. The former was a joyous celebration of human creativity and the pleasure of the human voyage of discovery. The latter was a remorseless pageant of horror and mutual destruction by men motivated by 'heroism'. Sigmund Freud, the founder of modern psychology, also came to the conclusion that the fundamental driver of human psychology was the struggle between the constructive, loving, 'life instinct' ('Eros'), and the destructive, selfish, death instinct ('Thanatos'). The 'life' instinct came from man's sense of his place within an infinite realm of being. The 'death' instinct came from man's deepest fears, especially the fear of death itself. The death instinct inclined people to distrust and compete with their fellow beings, while the life instinct inclined people to trust and cooperate. In the wake of the horrors of the First World War, Sigmund Freud posed the question of the survival of the human species in stark terms:

> The fateful question for the human species seems to me to be whether, and to what extent, their cultural development will succeed in mastering the disturbance of their communal life by the human instinct of aggression and self-destruction ... Men have gained control of the forces of nature to such an extent that with their help they would have no difficulty in exterminating one another to the last man. They know this, and hence comes a large part of their current unrest, their unhappiness and their mood of anxiety. And now it is to be expected that the other of the two

'Heavenly Powers', eternal Eros, will make an effort to assert himself in the struggle with his equally immortal adversary. But who can foresee with what success and with what result?[11] (Freud, 2001b: 145).

If humanity cannot find a 'mean', its prospects for survival are bleak. The destruction of human civilisation may arise either from the internal self-destructiveness of extreme free market individualism, or from the nihilistic response of those excluded and angered by the globalisation of the free market.

The challenges that are faced by human beings are the product of people's own purposive activities, expressed mainly through the economic system. It is within their collective power to resolve these contradictions. The very depth of the challenges they now face may shock them into the action necessary to ensure the survival of the species. Alongside human beings competitive and destructive instincts are their instincts for species survival through cooperation. However great the challenge may be, human beings have the capability of solving the contradictions that are of their own making. It may only be the approaching 'final hour' which finally forces human beings to grope their way towards globally cooperative solutions. The falling of the 'dusk', as humanity looks into the abyss, may be the final impulse to produce the cooperative solution that is immanent within the unfolding of global capitalism: 'The owl of Minerva spreads its wings only with the falling of the dusk' (Hegel, 1952: 13).

TABLES

Table 1. **Dominance of the Global Business Revolution by Firms Based in High-Income Countries**

	Population (2000)		GNP (2000) (a)		GNP (2000) (b)		*Fortune 500* companies (2003) (c)		*FT* 500 companies (2003) (d)		Top 700 companies by R&D spend (2002–03)	
	Million	%	$b	%	$b	%	No	%	No	%	No	%
HIEs	903	15	24 828	80	24 781	55	472	94	480	96	697	100
L/MIEs	5 152	85	6 336	20	20 056	45	28 (e)	6	20 (f)	4	3	negl.

Notes: HIEs = high-income economies.
L/MIEs = low/middle-income economies.
(a) at official rate of exchange.
(b) at PPP dollars.
(c) ranked by sales revenue.
(d) ranked by market capitalisation.
(e) China = 14, India = 4, Brazil = 3, Russia = 3, Mexico = 1, Malaysia = 1, Venezuela = 1, Thailand = 1.
(f) Russia = 7, China* = 4, India = 3, Mexico = 3, Brazil = 2, India = 1.
*All floated in Hong Kong.
Sources: *FT*, 27 May 2004; World Bank, 1998 and 2002; *Fortune*, 26 July 2004; DTI, 2003.

Table 2. **The World's Top 700 Firms by Research and Development Expenditure, 2003**

	Total (US$ billion)	Average (mean) R&D expenditure per firm (US$ million)	Share of total (%)
Top 17 (a)	66	6000	25
Top 33 (b)	147	4500	40
Top 300	291	970	80
Next 400	75	188	20
Top 700	366	522	100

Notes: (a) firms with over US$ 4 billion in expenditure on R&D.
(b) firms with over US$ 3 billion expenditure on R&D.
Source: *FT*, 25 October 2004.

Table 3. **GDP Growth in Islamic Countries**

	\multicolumn{4}{c}{GDP growth, real average growth per annum (%)}	Growth of GDP per capita (% per annum)	Total population (million)
	1965–80	1980–90	1990–2000	2000–2004	1975–2002	2004
Algeria	–	3.1	1.9	4.8	−0.2	32
Bangladesh	1.7	4.3	4.8	5.2	1.9	139
Egypt	7.3	5.0	4.7	3.4	2.8	73
Indonesia	7.0	5.5	4.2	4.6	4.2	218
Iran	6.1	2.5	3.5	6.0	−0.4	67
Iraq	10.5 (a)	–	–	−11.4	–	(26) (c)
Jordan	–	–	5.0	5.5	0.3	5
Kuwait	1.6	0.7	4.7	4.7	−1.2	2
Lebanon	–	–	5.8	4.4	3.6	4
Libya	4.2	–	–	5.5	–	6
Malaysia	7.4	5.2	7.0	4.4	4.0	25
Morocco	5.7	4.0	2.3	4.7	1.3	30
Oman	13.0	12.8	4.5	3.0	2.2	3
Pakistan	5.2	6.3	3.8	4.1	2.6	152
Saudi Arabia	10.6	−1.8	2.1	3.4	−2.5	24
Syria	9.1	2.1	5.0	3.5	0.9	19
Tunisia	6.5	3.6	4.7	4.3	2.1	10
Turkey	6.2	5.1	3.8	4.2	1.8	72
United Arab Emirates	–	−4.5	4.8	7.9	−2.8	*4*
West Bank/ Gaza	–	–	3.4	−13.3	−4.9 (b)	4
Yemen	8.4 (a)	–	6.0	3.6	2.5 (b)	20
LMIEs	5.9	3.2	3.9	4.8	–	–
LIEs	–	–	–	–	2.2	–
MIEs	–	–	–	–	1.4	–
East Asia/ Pacific	–	–	–	–	5.9	–

Notes: (a) 1970–79; (b) 1990–2002; (c) estimate

Countries in *italics* are oil-exporters. For these countries, fuel exports amount to over 68 per cent of total exports in each case in 2004.

Countries not in italics all have a small or negligible role for fuels in their total exports in 2004.

Sources: World Bank, WDR, 1992: Table 2; World Bank, WDI, 2006: Table 4.1; UNDP, HDR, 2004.

Table 4. **Operational Nuclear Warheads Aligned to an In-Service Delivery System, Excluding Artillery Shells and Mini-Nukes**

	Strategic	Sub-strategic				Grand total
		Delivery system				
		SSM	SLCM	Aircraft	Sub-total	
US	5968	–	320	800	1120	7088
Russian Federation	4978	–	240	1540	2980	7958
France	338	–	–	10	10	348
PRC	252	120	–	30	150	402
UK	185	–	–	–	–	185
Israel	–	90 (+)	'some'	100	200	200
India	–	–	–	40 (+)	40 (+)	40 (+)
Pakistan	–	'some'	–	40 (+)	40 (+)	40 (+)
North Korea	–	–	–	2 (?)	2 (?)	2 (?)

Notes: SSM: surface-to-air missiles.
SLCM: sea-launched cruise missiles.
Source: IISS, 2004: 251.

Table 5. **Industrial Workforce in Selected Arab Countries**

Country	Population (m.)	Workforce (m.) (a)	Industrial workers	
			Thousands	Share of total workforce (%)
Egypt (1958)	24.6	13.5	280	2.1
Iran (1958)	19.7	10.8	209	1.9
Iraq (1952–04)	4.9	2.7	163	6.0
Lebanon (1958)	1.6	0.9	21	2.3
Turkey (1957)	23.0	12.7	280	2.1

Note: (a) Derived, on the assumption that 55 per cent of the population are of working age. This is the average for all low and middle-income countries in 1960. (World Bank, WDR, 1979: Table 19).
Source: Rodinson, 1974: 120.

Table 6. **Exports from Islamic Countries 1965–2004**

Country	Average annual growth rate of exports (% p.a.)				Merchandise trade as a share of GDP (%)	
	1965–80	1980–90	1990–2000	2000–04	1990	2004
Algeria	*1.5*	*5.3*	*3.3*	*4.1*	*36.6*	*59.7*
Bangladesh	n. a.	7.6	13.1	6.7	17.6	35.7
Egypt	−0.1	2.1	3.4	6.7	36.8	26.0
Indonesia	9.6	2.8	5.9	3.8	41.5	49.4
Iran	–	*21.1*	*−1.3*	*4.4*	*32.9*	*48.4*
Iraq	–	–	–	–	*55.4*	*155.9*
Jordan	11.2	10.3	2.4	9.1	91.1	104.9
Kuwait	*18.5*	*−11.1*	*−1.6*	*0.2*	*59.8*	*73.1*
Malaysia	4.6	10.3	12.0	4.5	133.4	195.9
Morocco	3.7	6.1	5.4	4.4	43.4	54.7
Pakistan	−1.8	9.0	1.7	13.1	32.6	32.6
Saudi Arabia	*8.8*	*−9.7*	–	*2.2*	*58.6*	*68.2*
Syria	*11.4*	*8.7*	*12.0*	*−0.5*	*53.7*	*46.7*
Tunisia	10.8	4.8	5.2	1.4	73.5	79.6
Turkey	5.5	9.1	11.7	12.1	23.4	53.1
United Arab Emirates	*13.3*	–	*5.5*	*12.2*	*103.1*	*125.1*
LIEs	5.1	5.4	8.2	9.6	24.1	37.8
MIEs	3.9	3.8	7.2	10.1	34.4	61.5
LMIEs	–	–	7.3	10.1	32.5	58.1

Notes: (a) value.

Countries in *italics* are oil-exporters. For these countries, fuel exports amount to over 68 per cent of total exports in each case in 2004.

Countries not in italics all have a small or negligible role for fuels in their total exports in 2004.

Sources: World Bank, WDI, 2006: Tables 4.9 and 6.1; World Bank, WDR, 1992: Table 14.

Table 7. **Stock of Foreign Direct Investment in Selected Islamic Countries (US$ Billion) (a)**

Country	1980(i)	1990(ii)	2004(ii)	FDI stocks as % of GDP (ii) 1990	2004
Algeria	1.3	1.3	7.4	2.5	9.1
Bahrain	negl.	0.8	7.6	13.0	70.5
Bangladesh	negl.	0.3	3.4	1.1	6.1
Egypt	2.2	11.0	20.9	25.6	27.1
Indonesia	10.3	38.9	11.4	7.7	4.4
Iran	1.2	2.0	4.1	2.2	2.4
Malaysia	6.1	14.1	46.3	23.4	39.3
Morocco	0.3	1.0	18.0	13.9	36.1
Pakistan	0.7	1.9	7.6	4.7	9.2
Qatar	0.2	0.2	4.1	1.0	10.8
Saudi Arabia	2.2	21.5	20.5	13.8	8.2
Syria	negl.	0.4	12.5	3.0	52.6
Tunisia	0.6	2.7	17.6	62.0	61.7
Turkey	0.1	1.3	35.2	7.4	11.7
United Arab Emirates	0.7	1.1	4.4	2.2	4.6

Note: (a) only countries with a total stock of over US$ 4 billion of FDI in 2004 are included in this table.
Sources: (i) UNCTAD, 1994, Annex, Table 3, and (ii) UNCTAD, 2005, Annex, Tables B.2 and B.3.

Table 8. **Structural Change in Selected Islamic Countries, 1960–2004**

	Share of labour force in agriculture (%) 1960	2000–04 (a)	Share of agriculture in GDP (%) 1960	2004	Energy consumption per capita (kilograms of oil-equivalent) 1965	2003
Egypt	58	28	30	15	313	735
Iran	54	–	29	11	537	2 055
Iraq	53	–	17	9	399	1 029 (c)
Syria	54	24	29 (b)	23	212	986
Turkey	78	24	41	13	258	1 117

Note: (a) males only; (b) 1965; (c) 1990.
Sources: World Bank, WDR, 1990: Table 37; World Bank, WDI, 2006: Table 3.7.

Table 9. **Social Indicators for Selected Islamic Countries, 1965–2004**

Country	Life expectancy (years) 1960	2004	Infant mortality (no/1000 live births) 1960	2004	Urbanisation (% total population) 1960	2004
Egypt	46	70	172	26	38	42
Iran	46	71	152	32	34	67
Iraq	47	62 (a)	119	40 (a)	43	70 (a)
Syria	50	74	114	15	37	50
Turkey	51	70	165	21	30	67

Note: (a) 1990.
Sources: World Bank, WDR, 1981: Tables 20–1; World Bank, WDR, 1990: Table 28; World Bank, WDI, 2006: Tables 2.19 and 3.10.

Table 10. **Prevalence of Child Malnutrition in Selected Islamic Countries, 1995–2004**

	Proportion of under-five children with malnutrition (%) Underweight	Stunting
Egypt	8.6	15.6
Iran	10.9	15.4
Iraq	15.9	22.1
Syria	6.9	18.8
Turkey	3.9	16.0
LIEs	43.4	43.1
MIEs	11.1	26.9

Source: World Bank, WDI, 2006: Table 2.17.

Table 11. **Educational Achievement in Selected Islamic Countries, 1965–2004 (Gross Enrolment Rates, % of Relevant Age Group)**

	Primary 1965	2004	Secondary 1965	2004	Tertiary 1965	2004
Egypt	75	100	26	87	7	29
Iran	63	103	18	82	2	22
Iraq	74	98	28	45	4	15
Syria	78	123	28	63	8	n.a.
Turkey	101	95	16	85	4	28
LIEs	73	100	20	46	2	9
MIEs	92	105	26	61	6	17

Sources: World Bank, WDR, 1990: Table 29; World Bank, WDI, 2006: Table 2.11.

Table 12. **Fatalities During the Main Attacks by Islamic Fundamentalist Groups, 2001–06 (a)**

Date	Location	Number of Fatalities
Sept 2001	New York: World Trade Centre	2996
May 2003	Casablanca, Morocco	41
Nov 2003	Turkey: HSBC, UK Consulate, and Synagogues	57
May/Nov 2003	Saudi Arabia: housing compounds	43
March 2004	Spain, Madrid: commuter trains	191
Oct 2002, Aug 2003 and Oct 2005	Indonesia: Bali bombings; Jakarta Marriot Hotel bombings	240
July 2005	London: commuters (underground and buses)	56
July 2005	Egypt: Sharm el-Sheikh tourist resort	88
Nov 2005	Jordan: Amman hotel bombings	60
Nov 2005	India, Mumbai: commuter trains	207

Note: (a) these exclude deaths from Islamic terrorist attacks in Afghanistan, Iraq, the Occupied territories, and Lebanon. It is impossible to disentangle these from other sources of violent deaths, including attacks on military forces by local armed militia, civilians killed by the Israeli army, and deaths due to conflict between Islamic groups.

Table 13. **Fatalities in Selected Conflicts, 1945–2004**

Region	Fatalities
Caribbean and Latin America	688 000
Europe	127 000
Middle East and North Africa	935 000
Sub-Saharan Africa	6 219 000
Central and South Asia	2 534 000
East Asia	9 787 000
Total	20 290 000

Source: IISS, 2005.

Table 14. **Fatalities Through Armed Conflict in Selected Islamic Societies, 1945–2006**

Country/region	Nature of conflict	Date	Fatalities
Turkey	Terrorism and military coup	1977–80	5 000
Algeria	National liberation struggle against France	1954–62	100 000
	Rebels/government	1962–3	2 000
	Civil war after cancellation of election victory of Islamic Salvation Front	Early 90s	100 000
Egypt	Suez crisis: invasion by France/Britain/Israel	1956	4 000
	Six Day War and border conflict with Israel	1967–70	75 000
Iran	Islamic Revolution and its aftermath	1978–89	1 000
	Iran-Iraq War	1980–88	500 000
Iraq	Shammar insurgency against government	1959	2 000
	Kurdish rebellion	1961–70	105 000
	US invasion, anti-US actions and civil war	2003–06	601 000
Lebanon	Civil War	1958	2 000
	Civil War	1975–90	100 000
Nigeria	Islamic rebellion	1980–81	5 000
	Islamic rebellion	1984	1 000
India	Muslim/Hindu violence	1946–48	800 000
	Kashmir: conflict between Islamic forces and Indian government	1971	10 000
Pakistan	Baluchi rebellion against central government	1973–77	9 000
Indonesia	Anti-colonial independence struggle	1945–6	5 000
	Inter-communal violence, mainly directed against Chinese	1965–66	500 000
	Rebellion in East Timor	1975–00	203 000
	Kalimantan rebellion	1997–3	6 000
Syria	Muslim Brotherhood rebellion	1982	20 000
Kuwait	Iraq invasion	1990–91	20 000
Yemen	Civil War in South Yemen	1994	7 000
Afghanistan	Soviet invasion	1979–92	1 500 000
	Civil War	1992–02	130 000
Tajikistan	Civil War	1992–02	26 000

Note: Fatalities resulting from Arab-Israeli conflicts are not included in the data given by IISS, 2005.

Sources: IISS, 2005, except for data for Iraq, 2003–6 (*FT*, 12 October 2006); Algeria in early 1990s and Syria in 1982 (Hourani, 2002: 463).

Table 15. **Growth in GDP Per Head, 1820–1998 (Average Annual Compound Growth Rates, Per Cent)**

Region	1820–70	1870–1913	1913–50	1950–73	1973–98
Western Europe	0.95	1.32	0.76	4.08	1.78
Western offshoots (a)	1.42	1.81	1.55	2.44	1.94
Japan	0.19	1.48	0.89	8.05	2.34
Eastern Europe/ former USSR	0.64	1.15	1.50	3.49	−1.1
Latin America	0.10	1.81	1.42	2.52	0.99
Asia (excluding Japan)	−0.11	0.38	−0.02	2.92	3.54
Africa	0.12	0.64	1.02	2.07	0.01
World	0.53	1.30	0.91	2.93	1.33

Note: (a) United States, Canada, Australia, New Zealand.
Source: Wolf, 2004: 107.

Table 16. **Oil Majors' Regional Distribution of Oil Reserves at 31 December 2005**

Company	Region	Oil reserves (mb)	Total oil reserves (mb)	International oil reserves as a % of total reserves
Exxon Mobil	USA	2 113	7 813	73
	International	5 700		
BP	UK	659	10 407	94
	International	9 749		
Shell	Europe	871	4 793	73
	International	3 522		
Total	Europe	978	5 582	82
	International	4 604		
Chevron	USA	1 831	5 626	67
Texaco	International	3 795		
Conoco	USA	1 675	3 336	50
Phillips	International	1 661		
Marathon	USA	189	704	73
	International	515		
PetroChina	China	10 935	11 536	5
	International	601		
Sinopec	China	3 294	3 294	n. a.
	International	–		
CNOOC	China	1 358	1 457	7
	International	99		

Sources: Companies' *Annual Reports*.

NOTES

Prologue: Conflict or Cooperation?

1 *Tokos* ('offspring').
2 For a recent example, see Wolf's (2004) polemic in favour of capitalist globalisation: 'In this book, the liberalism is essentially that of John Stuart Mill' (Wolf, 2004: 321).
3 Mill passionately believed in the political rights of minorities. He believed that diversity was desirable in its own right, but was also essential to socio-economic progress. His motive for writing his classic text *On Liberty*, was mainly to defend the rights of minorities against the 'tyranny of the majority' (Mill, 1988: 62). Mill believed that 'the present civilisation tends so strongly to make the power of persons acting in masses the only substantial power in society, that there never was more necessity for surrounding individual independence of thought, speech and conduct, with the most powerful defences, in order to maintain that originality of mind and individuality of character, which are the only source of any real progress, and of most of the qualities which make the human race much superior to any herd of animals' (Mill, 1998: 328).
4 In fact, as Foner points out, Hayek's views were far more complex than the interpretation they were given by the New Right. *The Road to Serfdom* endorsed measures that later conservatives would 'denounce as tantamount to socialism' – a minimum wage, laws limiting maximum hours of work, antitrust enforcement, and a social safety net guaranteeing all citizens basic needs of food, shelter, and clothing (Foner, 1998: 236).
5 Different families' human capital can be viewed as predominantly a genetic inheritance or a product of the family environment, depending on one's stance in the 'nature versus nurture' debate.
6 Smith considers education to be one of the critically important areas of 'market failure', which necessitates state intervention. He says that the state of society means that 'the greater part of individuals do not naturally form in them, without any attention of government, almost all the abilities and virtues that the state requires'. Therefore, the government must act in order to 'prevent almost the entire corruption and degeneracy of the great body of the people' (Smith, 1776, Vol. 2: 302).
7 Twentieth century writers such as Eric Fromm (1991, Chapter 8, *'Roads to Sanity'*) also have placed their hope in the cooperative movement as the feasible transition path to a benevolent society. The giant Spanish cooperative Mondragon was established in the 1950s. It remains the world's largest and most successful cooperative, with around 70 000 members and an annual turnover of more than 10 billion euros. Israel's kibbutzim were also an inspiration to those seeking for a path to create a new social ethic through common property. However, the blunt reality is that in the non-communist

world, the cooperative movement failed to grow in the way that Mill hoped. It remains a marginal part of the socio-economic structure with an uncertain future.

8 Mill was acutely aware of the complexity of the topic of government intervention, and the absence of simple rules: '[T]he admitted functions of government embrace a much wider field than can easily be included within the ring-fence of any restrictive definition', and 'it is hardly possible to find any ground of justification common to them all, except the comprehensive one of general expediency; nor to limit the interference of government by any universal rule, save the vague and simple one, that it should never be admitted but when the case of expediency is strong' (Mill, 1998: 165).

9 For example, Mill was emphatic on the desirability of public provision of elementary education in the interests of the 'positive freedoms' of poor people: 'I hold it to be the duty of government to supply ... pecuniary support to elementary schools, such as to render them accessible to all the children of the poor, either freely, or for a payment too inconsiderable to be sensibly felt' (Mill, 1998: 341).

10 For example, Mill believed that 'in many parts of the world, the people can do nothing for themselves which requires large means and combined action: all such things are left undone unless done by the state' (Mill, 1998: 367). In the same fashion as Smith, Mill devotes careful attention to ways in which public provision may be combined with private resources, and in which public ownership may be combined with private operation (Mill, 1998: 349). While Mill was deeply opposed to international protection he fully recognised the justice of the 'infant industry' argument: 'The only case in which, on mere principles of political economy, protecting duties can be defensible, is when they are imposed temporarily (especially in a young and rising nation) in hopes of naturalising a foreign industry, in itself perfectly suitable to the circumstances of the country. The superiority of one country over another in a branch of production, often arises only from having begun it sooner. There may be no inherent advantage on one part, or disadvantage on the other, but only a present superiority of acquired skill and experience. A country which has this skill and experience yet to acquire, may in other respects be better adapted to the production than those which were earlier in the field' (Mill, 1998: 302).

11 Darwin was an ardent advocate of eugenics.

12 This quotation is from a speech delivered by Kessler at the Russian Congress of Naturalists in January 1880.

13 Boserup's path-breaking research (Boserup, 1981) has chronicled the way in which growing population densities force people to work harder and to achieve technical progress in order to support even higher population densities.

14 Childe (1942) describes the central role of women in the Neolithic Revolution as follows: '[W]omenkind had not only to discover suitable plants and appropriate methods for their cultivation, but [had] also to devise special implements for tilling the soil, reaping and storing the crop, and converting it into foods ... [Women] may also be credited [with] the chemistry of pot-making, the physics of spinning, the mechanics of the loom, and the botany of flax and cotton' (Childe, 1942: 58–9).

15 It is an extreme irony that one hundred years later, the AEA should have become the vehicle for conveying the most stultifying form of orthodoxy, which eliminated from the subject of 'economics' anything other than formal mathematical modelling, largely based on free market models, leaving the subject far removed from the open-minded analysis of the real world from which AEA originally derived its inspiration.

16 In the end, Wilson argued that 'the history of liberty is a history of the limitation of government power, not the increase of it'.

Part 1. Capitalism's Contradictory Character

1. Balzac wrote the two novels Cousine Bette and Cousin Pons as a symmetrical pair to illustrate the duality of human nature: 'The two sketches [Cousin Pons and Cousine Bette], which I dedicate to you represent the two eternal aspects of a single reality. *Homo duplex*, said our great Buffon; why not add *res duplex*? Everything always has two faces, even virtue. For this reason, Molière always presents both sides of every human problem ... My two stories are therefore placed together as a pair, like twins of different sex. It is a literary fancy in which one may indulge once, especially in a work which seeks to represent all the forms in which thought may be clothed' (Balzac, 1965: 10).
2. Of course, capitalist development is inherently uneven. Many authors object to the term 'globalisation' (e.g. Hirst and Thompson, 1999), because large parts of the world have been little affected by capitalism's recent expansion. In my view, the recent renewed surge of capitalism, penetrating large areas of the world that were formerly only weakly integrated into the global economy, fully justifies the use of the term 'globalisation'.
3. By far the most profound and interesting account of this is to be found in Boserup (1981).
4. See especially, Braudel, 1981, 1982 and 1984; Dobb, 1963; Cipolla, 1972 and 1973; and Hilton, 1976.
5. On the development of capitalism outside Europe see especially, Braudel, 1984; and Frank, 1998.
6. On the development of Chinese capitalism see especially, Li Bozhong, 1986, 1998, and 2000; Shiba, 1977; and Xu Dixin and Wu Chengming, 2000.
7. On the development of capitalism in South Asia see especially, Chaudhuri, 1985 and 1990; Habib, 1969; and Raychaudhuri and Habib, 1982.
8. On the development of capitalism in the Middle East see especially, Islamoglu-Inan, 1987; and Rodinson, 1974.
9. See especially, the monumental research of Needham, 1954-; and Frank, 1998.
10. In the case of China, these included gunpowder, steel-making, the canal lock gate, the compass, the wheelbarrow, the windmill, mechanical clockwork, water-powered metallurgical blowing machines, water-powered trip hammers for forges, hemp spinning machines, gear wheels, power transmission by driving belt, the sternpost rudder, watertight compartments, and the crank.
11. The share of merchandise exports in global GDP in 1950 stood at just 5.5 per cent substantially below the level of 1913 (Wolf, 2004: 110). The growth of world merchandise trade fell from 3.4 per cent per annum in 1870–1913 to just 0.90 per cent per annum in 1913–50 (Wolf, 2004: 108).
12. The agricultural sector, on the contrary, saw high levels of protection maintained through to the present day.
13. Manufactured exports grew by 8.4 per cent per annum in Western Europe in the period 1950–73 (Wolf, 2004: 108), to a substantial degree due to the impact of reduction of tariff barriers within Europe. By 1973, the share of merchandise exports in global GDP had risen to 10.5 per cent, almost double the level of 1950 (Wolf, 2004: 110).
14. Foreign assets as a share of world GDP fell from 17.5 per cent in 1914 to 8.4 per cent in 1930, and in 1960 stood at just 6.4 per cent (Wolf, 2004: 113).
15. In China during the Cultural Revolution, capitalism was likened to 'a dog in the water', which must be 'beaten with sticks until it is drowned'. Of course, all of the communist economies contained more or less thriving black and 'grey' markets. Also, despite the

elimination of the profit motive from a large part of the economy, these economies developed their own form of anarchy. The communist economies were 'planned' only in name. In fact, they produced their own form of anarchy, being unable to achieve their stated goals of output and living standard growth, due to the very nature of the administrative planning system. The fact that the economy was based on administrative instructions stimulated a vicious circle of 'heavy industry'-biased growth unable to achieve economical use of capital or labour, and consistently failing to achieve hoped-for technical progress.

16 In fact, the issue of 'unequal exchange' is notoriously complex and the subject of endless debate in the academic literature.

17 The list of globally powerful former state-owned enterprises which became world leaders by the end of the 1970s includes: in aerospace, Rolls-Royce, BAE, Snecma, Thales, and Aerospatiale (which became a key part of Airbus); in automobiles, Renault and VW; in oil, BP, ENI, and Total (which combined the main oil companies, both state and private of France and Belgium, including Total, PetroFina and Elf Aquitaine, the former French state-owned 'national champion'), Repsol and Statoil; in telecommunications, France Telecom, Deutsche Telekom, Telefonica, and BT; in steel, Arcelor (which combined the principal steel assets of France, Spain and Belgium); in pharmaceuticals, Aventis (which combined the pharmaceutical business of Rhône Poulenc and Hoechst, and later merged with Sanofi); in glass and building materials, Saint-Gobain; in financial services, Crédit Lyonnais (which later merged with Crédit Agricole); in logistics, Deutsche Post (which includes DHL).

18 It had been only the fourteenth largest as recently as 1990.

19 In fact, political turbulence over much of the region greatly damaged the economy. The former USSR had massively under-utilised human and technological resources. These would have provided the basis for high-speed economic advance if the USSR had managed to maintain a stable political environment and suitable economic reform policies (Nolan, 1995). Instead political collapse combined with unsuitable economic policies, including 'wild privatisation', to destroy the economy. Large parts of the region suffered massive output declines and deep falls in the living standards of a large part of the population, including a huge increase in death rates in the former USSR. The privatisation of state assets across much of the region was hugely corrupt (Goldman, 2003), producing a massive increase in wealth and income inequality, and wide popular discontent. Wide popular dissatisfaction with the reforms of the 1990s laid the basis for President Putin's attempt to reconstruct a strong central Russian state. By 2005, it appeared that the former USSR had gone full circle from one form of authoritarianism to another, with massive economic and welfare costs along the journey.

20 The OECD's Centre for Economic Development, for example, produced landmark studies of India, Brazil and Mexico, which argued that there were high costs attached to the inward looking strategies. The results of this research was summarised in the highly influential book by Little, Scitovsky and Scott, 1970. This was followed by a large number of studies by academics and leading international institutions, notably the IMF and World Bank, which argued for liberalisation of developing countries' economic policies, including privatisation, trade liberalisation and integration with world capital markets.

21 In fact, the relationship of economic performance to economic policies has been extremely complex. Far from accelerating, the growth of GDP per head was substantially faster in the period 1950–73 than in the period of liberalisation, from 1973 to 1998. Across the whole world, the rate of growth of GDP per head fell sharply, from

4.08 per annum in 1973–98, to 1.78 per cent per annum in 1973–98 (Table 15). In Western Europe, the average growth rate (per cent per annum) fell from 4.08 to 1.78; in 'Western offshoots', it fell from 2.44 to 1.94; in Eastern Europe, it fell from 3.49 to minus 1.11; in Latin America, it fell from 2.52 to 0.99; in Africa, it fell from 2.07 to 0.01; and in Japan, it fell from 8.05 to 2.34. Only in 'non-Japan Asia' did the growth rate rise, from 2.92 to 3.54. This was largely attributable to the acceleration of China's growth. However, although China was moving towards a market economy, it still was far from the liberal economists' ideal. For most of the period, large sectors were (and still are) under state ownership; there was substantial protection until after the country joined the WTO in 2001, and throughout this period there were tight controls on international capital movements.

22 Of course, there still were exceptions. High-income countries still intervened heavily to support the farm sector. Some sectors, such as European banks, still maintained controls over cross-border mergers and acquisitions. Some countries, such as France, still operated a form of industrial policy to nurture indigenous 'national champions'.

23 In the pre-modern world, China's system of rice cultivation in paddy fields in the centre and south of the country was peculiarly conducive to high population densities and, therefore, to the non-zero-sum benefits from the division of labour and exchange.

24 Europe's population is estimated to have fallen from a peak of 79 million in 1400 to around 60 million in 1400, and then to have begun a steady climb, reaching around 120 million in 1700, and 180 million in 1800 (McEvedy and Jones, 1978: 18).

25 In Lilley's view, there have been two great technological revolutions in human history. The first began around 8000 BC, and the second began in the early Middle Ages, and 'has been going on continuously from [then] up until our time' (Lilley, 1973: 190).

26 It is estimated that around the time that Gutenberg was perfecting his printing system, the entire annual salary of a professor at Pavia University would have purchased just two volumes of law books and ten of medicine (White, 1972: 162). The parchment necessary for a large Bible is estimated to have needed the hides of between 200–300 sheep.

27 This brief discussion has not, for example, discussed warships, armaments, metallurgy, mining, pumping, textile machinery, or building, all of which made great progress during the Middle Ages.

28 Although he does not write within the confines of formal economics, his analysis has been influential on this branch of modern economics.

29 He does, however, caution, that, 'on the other hand, we could blow up the world': '[W]hile I'm basically optimistic, an extremely bleak outcome is also possible' (Wright, 2000: 9).

30 In 1997, stock market capitalisation in low and middle-income countries stood at US$ 1726 billion compared with US$ 18 451 billion in the high-income countries (World Bank, 1999: 221). In 1990, domestic credit to the private sector amounted to 39 per cent of GDP in low and middle-income countries compared with 108 per cent in the high-income countries (World Bank, WDI, 2004: 256).

31 Defined as 'net inflows of investment to acquire a lasting management interest (10 per cent or more of voting stock) in an enterprise operating in an economy other than that of the investor. It is the sum of the equity capital flows, reinvestment of earnings, other long-term capital flows, and short-term capital flows as shown in the balance of payments' (World Bank, 2000: 286). World Bank data on FDI do not include capital raised by multinational firms in host countries, which has become an important source of their expansion.

32 The countries are Argentina, Brazil, Chile, China, Hong Kong, Indonesia, Korea, Singapore, Thailand, and Venezuela.
33 These include (in descending order of revenue within Brazil in 2001) Volkswagen (2), GM (3), Fiat (5), Unilever (7), Bunge Foods (9), Phillip Morris (10), Nestlé (11), Ford (12), Cargill (13), DaimlerChrysler (16), Siemens (20), Ericsson (21), BASF (22), and Motorola (24).
34 Such sectors include automobiles, automobile subsystems, patented pharmaceuticals, IT hardware, lifts, high value-added steels, many types of complex engineering products (such as modern printing presses and mining equipment), soft drinks and premium beers.
35 In low and middle-income countries, FDI as a share of GDP rose from 0.8 per cent in 1990 to 2.5 per cent in 2002 (World Bank, WDI, 2004: 256).
36 South Korea provides a striking example of such changes in recent years.
37 There remain barriers to cross-border acquisitions in certain East Asian countries. However, even these barriers are slowly falling, including the rapid growth of international acquisition of South Korean financial institutions. Some significant barriers remain to international mergers and acquisitions within the EU, especially those affecting Italian, German and French financial institutions. While EU-based financial services firms push strongly for the rest of the world, especially developing countries, to allow them free access to their markets for merger and acquisition, certain EU countries are reluctant to allow international financial firms to merge with and acquire local financial firms.
38 Formed from Salomon Brothers Investment Bank, Travellers Group, Citicorp, and Schroders' investment banking business.
39 Formed, inter alia, from Deutsche Bank, Morgan Grenfell and Bankers Trust.
40 Formed, inter alia, from HSBC Holdings, Republic New York, and Banque Hervet.
41 Formed, inter alia, from JPMorgan, Chase Manhattan, Robert Fleming and Bank One.
42 Formed, inter alia, from Bank of America and Fleet Boston.
43 These were Banamex, acquired by Citigroup; Bancomer, acquired by BBVA; Bank Serfin, acquired by Bank Santander; and Bital, acquired by HSBC.
44 Sandy Weill (then) chairman and CEO of Citigroup portrayed the acquisition as 'part of the thrust to strengthen US-Mexican ties that have been championed by the (then) new leaders of both countries, George W. Bush and Vincente Fox' (quoted in *FT*, 18 May 2001).
45 Banks have diversified risk as never before, via derivatives such as structured credit which can be used to transfer risk to insurance companies, pension funds, hedge funds and others outside the banking system.
46 This is the second epoch of modern 'globalisation'. The first epoch was brought to a halt by the wars of the twentieth century, the rise of communism and the inward-looking economic policies of non-communist developing countries.
47 Pratten (1971) analysed industrial structure in a number of UK industries. Prais (1981) analysed industrial structure in several industries in the United Kingdom, Germany and the United States. Chandler (1990) analysed industrial structure in the United States, Great Britain and Germany. Chandler (1997) extends the analysis to include small European nations, Italy, Spain, France, Japan, South Korea, Argentina, the USSR and Czechoslovakia. Scherer (1996) analysed the structure of a number of industries in the United States.
48 Global mergers and acquisitions rose from an annual level of around US$ 260 billion in the early 1990s to a peak of US$ 3173 billion in 2000, falling to US$ 1060 billion in 2002.

Thereafter, mergers and acquisitions rose to US$ 2507 billion in 2005 (Moore, 2006), and it seemed likely that the total for 2006 would exceed the previous peak of 2000.

49 See, for example, Wolf, 2004: 'Global M&A activity rose more than five-fold between 1995 and 2000. Yet the surge in cross-border M&A does not seem to have increased concentration' (Wolf, 2004: 224).

50 Meeks, 1977, is the classic study of this topic. The view that 'most mergers fail' is repeated remorselessly among mainstream academics of all ideological persuasions.

51 Like many other writers who hold similar views, Seabright's analysis of the firm (Chapter 10 of *The Company of Strangers*) provides no empirical evidence whatsoever.

52 Friedman's book is a best-seller. It was hugely popular among participants at the Davos Economic Forum in 2006, and won the *Financial Times*/Goldman Sachs 'Business Book of the Year' award.

53 Many products that were once thought to be 'non-traded' such as personal services are increasingly being traded internationally due to progress in information technology.

54 For example, BP is not only one of the world's leading petro-chemical producers, but it alone accounts for around two-fifths of the world's total PTA production. GSK not only is one of the world's top pharmaceutical companies, but within the therapies for anti-asthma and anti-herpes drugs, it accounts for around one-third and almost one-half respectively of total global sales. Samsung, Hynix, Micron, Infineon and Toshiba are all leading semiconductor producers, but in the market for NANDflash memory chips, Samsung, Toshiba and Hynix together account for around nine-tenths of the world total, and in the market for DRAMS, Samsung, Micron, Infineon and Hynix together account for around three-quarters of the world total. Within the telecommunications equipment market, Nokia accounts for over one-third of the total world - market for mobile phones, while Cisco accounts for over two-thirds of the total global market for routers. Not only is Microsoft one of the world's leading software companies, but in the market for PC operating systems it accounts for over 80 per cent of the total global market, while IBM, Microsoft and Oracle between them account for around nine-tenths of the total global market for database software.

55 These are: United States, Japan, Germany, France, United Kingdom, Switzerland, South Korea, Netherlands, Sweden, and Finland.

56 Economists' reduction of 'technical progress' to the so-called 'residual' in the 'production function', which remains after account has been taken of the contribution to economic growth of increased inputs of 'capital' and 'labour', is embarrassingly superficial.

57 Indeed, the common response of most economists, both 'radical' and mainstream, is denial, and endless manipulation of data to attempt to 'prove' that industrial concentration is not in fact taking place, and to suggest that technical progress, insofar as it is acknowledged to be taking place, is the product mainly of small and medium-sized firms. However, the reality of the technical transformation of this epoch and the consequences of oligopolistic competition for real price declines, are obvious to most people through their daily lives.

58 The proportion of the rural population of low-income countries with access to improved water sources (defined as 'the availability of at least 20 litres per person per day from a source within one kilometre of the dwelling) rose from 59 per cent in 1990 to 70 per cent in 200 (WB, WDI, 2004: 134).

59 In low-income countries, the proportion of the urban population with access to improved sanitation facilities (defined as 'at least adequate excreta disposal facilities, private or shared but not public, that can effectively prevent human, animal and insect contact with

excreta') rose from 58 per cent in 1990 to 71 per cent in 2000, while in the rural areas it rose from 20 per cent to 31 per cent in the same period (WB, WDI, 2004: 154).
60 In high-income countries, infant mortality fell from 22 per thousand live births in 1970 to 5 per thousand in 2002, while life expectancy at birth rose from 71 years to 78 years.
61 Even in low-income countries, by 2002 there were 139 radios per thousand people and 91 TV sets (UNDP, 2004: 298).
62 For example, in Brazil, the share of male employment in agriculture fell from 34 per cent in 1980 to 24 per cent in 2000–02; in Malaysia it fell from 34 per cent in 1980 to 21 per cent in 2000–02; and in Egypt it fell from 45 per cent in 1980 to 27 per cent in 2000–02 (WB, WDR, 2004: 46–7).
63 By 2002, developing countries contained 69 per cent of the total global urban population (UNDP, 2004: 155).
64 These studies all use 'purchasing power parity' (PPP) data. Using PPP data of national product, the GDP of developing countries in 2002 increases from US$ 6.2 trillion to US$ 19.8 trillion (UNDP, 2004: 187). Of course, the two different measures show hardly any difference for rich countries. If the PPP figures are used, the energy efficiency of countries such as China (measured in energy use per dollar of GDP) rises to a level equal to that of the countries with the very highest incomes, such as the Nordic countries, which is highly implausible. Clearly, neither PPP nor the current exchange rate are adequate measures of GDP for purposes of international comparison.
65 Kant considered that there is an underlying evolutionary force at work, strikingly similar to that of Adam Smith's 'invisible hand': 'Individual men and even entire nations little imagine that, while they are pursuing their own ends, each in his own way and often in opposition to others, they are unwittingly guided in their advance along a course intended by nature. They are unconsciously promoting an end which, even if they knew what it was, could scarcely arouse their interest' (Kant, 1991: 41). He thought that it would require 'a long, perhaps incalculable series of generations, each passing on its enlightenment to the next, before the germs implanted by nature in our species can be developed to that degree which corresponds to nature's original intention' (Kant, 1991: 43).
66 The most extreme example was the United States of America, which waged a violent war of national unification, heavily protected the national economy and ensured that immigrants all learned the national language, English. However, Germany, Italy and, to a somewhat lesser degree, France, all saw a similar process. At that time the most powerful expression of the philosophy of state-led industrialisation was that offered by List in his *National System of Political Economy* (1885).
67 In the 1980s, the GATT introduced Trade Related Intellectual Property Rights (TRIPS) and Trade-related Investment Measures (TRIMS).
68 The term 'global level playing field has frequently been applied to this development. Zampetti and Sauve (1996) coined the term 'internationally contestable market' to describe this situation, by which they mean 'the conditions prevailing in the market that allow for unimpaired market access for foreign goods, services, ideas, investments and business people, so that they are able to benefit from opportunities to compete in that market on terms equal or comparable to those enjoyed by local competitors. Hence, market access conditions and, more generally, the competitive process should not be unduly impaired or distorted by the totality of potential barriers, including traditional border barriers, investment conditions,

NOTES

315

structural impediments, regulatory regimes as well as private anti-competitive practices'.

69 Of course, the existence of a common ideological enemy in the shape of the communist countries, and the consequent creation of international entities for military cooperation, notably NATO, also helped to mitigate the possibility of military conflict among the capitalist countries.

70 Indeed, for many people, the internationalisation of the capitalist class constitutes a deep threat to national identity. For a striking illustration of this fear, see Huntington, 2004.

71 Information taken from their respective *Annual Reports*.

72 For variants on this view see Ohmae, 1990, and Fukuyama, 1992.

73 In 2003, the share of nationally protected areas stood at 21 per cent in the United Kingdom, 26 per cent in the United States, 30 per cent in Switzerland, 32 per cent in Germany and 33 per cent in Austria (WB, WDI, 2004: 128–30).

74 It goes without saying that there are numberless species that will be lost without ever having been recorded.

75 Already, measured in PPP dollars, the low and middle-income countries account for 45 per cent of global Gross National Income, and their growth rate is over double that of the high-income countries (WB, WDI, 2006: Table 1.1). However, their per capita income is only 15 per cent of that of the high-income countries (in PPP dollars).

76 Throughout the period of human life on earth, levels of carbon dioxide in the atmosphere fluctuated between around 190 ppm (during 'Cold Periods') and around 260 ppm (during 'Warm Periods'). Human civilisation in its present form is usually thought to have begun with the onset of a Warm Period around 60 000 years ago (King, 2005).

77 Burning oil releases about 50 per cent more carbon dioxide than burning natural gas, and burning coal releases about twice as much (World Bank, WDI, 2004: 147).

78 The main negative impact is likely to take place in developing countries. In high-income countries it is possible that global warming could lead to increased yields.

79 Mainstream economists have argued that the world is likely to witness increasing per capita incomes and technical progress, so that future generations are more able to deal with the environmental challenge. Accordingly, the main body of economists has argued that the time discount rate used for measuring the resources allocated today to solving the problem of global warming should be set at a high level. If the world does, indeed, face a threat of the order of seriousness suggested by the new consensus among the world's leading scientists, then the arguments about the time discount rate are as useful as shifting the chairs on the Titanic while the ship sinks.

80 The agreement specifies that the signatories will ensure that in 2012 their carbon dioxide emissions will be 5.2 per cent below those of 1990.

81 Japan consumes 6.4 per cent of the world total, China consumes 8.5 per cent and the rest of the Region consumes 14.1 per cent (BP, 2006: 11).

82 Japan's oil imports were stagnant.

83 It is forecast that by 2020, China will be importing as much as three-quarters of its total oil consumption.

84 With 4.7 per cent of the world's population, the United States accounts for 24 per cent of the world's carbon dioxide production (WB, WDI, 2006: Table 3.8).

85 GDP (in PPP dollars) per kilogram of oil equivalent in low and middle-income countries rose from 3.1 in 1990 to 4.2 in 2003 (WB, WDI, 2006: Table 3.8).

86 The low and middle-income countries have already overtaken the high-income countries in terms of the production of nitrous oxide. In 2002, they accounted for 71 per cent of the global total (WB, WDI, 2006: Table 3.8).
87 The number of motor vehicles increased from 758 per 1000 people in 1990 to 808 per thousand in 2003. The distance covered by road traffic rose from 2.5 trillion vehicle kilometres in 1990 to 4.2 trillion in 2003 (WB, WDI, 2006: Table 3.12).
88 Of course, many of the marketing campaigns combine 'global' with 'local' styles of consumption, typically through the mechanism of local subsidiaries of global marketing companies.
89 Even in less well-known sectors, the share of systems integrators has typically become very high. For example, the global market share of the top two firms in the financial information sector stood at 86 per cent and at 77 per cent in electronic games; the share of the top three firms stood at 71 per cent in legal publishing and at 62 per cent in artificial joints; the share of the top five firms stood at 77 per cent in recorded music; and the share of the top six firms stood at 60 per cent in water management (Nolan *et al.*, 2007a).
90 In fact, these data under-state the true degree of concentration, because many firms focus on specific sub-branches of their sector. For example, within the pharmaceutical industry, in many therapies, just one or two firms account for almost the entire global market.
91 These included the United Kingdom's de Havilland (Comet), Vickers (VC10), Hawker Siddeley (Trident), and BAC (BAC 111), Germany's VFW (VFW 614), France's Sud Aviation (Caravelle), and the Netherlands' Fokker.
92 Tupolev alone produced almost 2000 Tu-134s and 154s, which placed it roughly on a par with McDonnell Douglas, though far short of Boeing. Antonov and Ilyushin also produced large commercial aircraft.
93 President Putin is reconstructing a unified Russian aerospace industry with majority state ownership, but it remains to be seen how successful this endeavour will be in catching up with the global industry leaders.
94 This is a rough estimate based on the fact that GM spends around US$ 80 billion on procurement, and accounts for around 16 per cent of total global automobile sales.
95 Anti-locking Brake Systems and Electronic Stability Control Systems, respectively.
96 There still are important restrictions on the international expansion of the leading telecommunications firms, notably in China and India, and, to some extent, still within Western Europe.
97 In the United States, the top three firms account for around four-fifths of the market. In Japan and Europe, the top two or three firms account for over 70 per cent of the respective markets.
98 There are now more than thirty giant retail groups with annual revenues of more than US$ 10 billion, including seven super-giants with revenues of over US$ 50 billion (*Fortune*, 26 July 2004).
99 These are Ball, Crown and Rexam.
100 In 2003, Tetra Laval, the Swedish/Swiss packaging giant, acquired Sidel. With the weight of Tetra Laval behind it, Sidel will be in an even better position to maintain its leading position in the global PET pre-form blowing industry.
101 WPP, Omnicom, Interpublic, and Publicis.
102 Either directly, or through their 'third party' logistics suppliers. Most beverages are delivered to customers by truck.

NOTES

103 This view has been given its most powerful recent expression in the prize-winning book by Thomas Friedman, *The world is flat* (2005). However, this view is of considerable antiquity. In the mid-nineteenth century, the British Government refused to allow India to protect its industries with tariffs. It argued that an open economy would encourage local Indian firms to catch-up with British firms through the stimulus of competition.

104 In the United States these include places such as Nantucket Island, Palm Beach, Aspen, the Hamptons and Sun Valley. Nantucket has become a preserve for the super-rich, a 'castle with a moat around it'. The average house price on the island in 2004 reached US$ 1.7 million (*NYT*, 5 June 2005). Membership of the Nantucket Great Harbour Yacht Club and the Nantucket Golf Club costs over US$ 300 000 each.

105 We may very loosely define the globalised elite as those earning more than US$ 50,000 per year.

106 The World Bank speculates that by 2030, the global 'middle class' will have expanded to 16 per cent of the global total, and the global 'rich' will have increased to 21 per cent of the global total. However, these are highly speculative.

107 This is not inconsistent with benefits that accrue to the rich country workers as consumers of cheaper imports. Moreover, there have also been important effects on the nature of employment and conditions of work in all countries due to the radical changes brought about by the application of information technology and the acceleration of the replacement of human beings with artificial intelligence.

108 Such as 'Aventis', 'Novartis', 'Arcelor', 'BP', 'BAE', 'E.ON', WPP', 'Xstrata', 'GSK' and 'HSBC'.

109 Their share fell slightly after 2000, reaching 7.4 per cent in 2004, still more than double the share in the 1970s.

110 This is quite consistent with the existence of a huge number of small and medium-sized local firms that produce goods and services for poor people and for other small and medium-sized firms. Markets in low and middle-income countries are highly segmented.

111 US mortgage debt has reached around US$ 12 000 billion (*FT*, 17 April 2006).

112 From 14.8 million tonnes to 16.4 million tonnes (*FT*, 24 May 2006).

113 For example, in the United Kingdom by 2006 housing wealth had reached 59 per cent of personal wealth (*FT*, 25 July 2006). By 2006, letting of dwellings had become the largest single sector in the UK economy, exceeding sectors such as banking and finance, construction, and even health services (*FT*, 21 August 2006).

114 In fact, the term 'hedge funds' is a misnomer in relation to hedge funds today. There is now little difference between the strategy employed by hedge funds and that employed by a traditional asset manager, except that the hedge fund manager is more aggressive. Contrary to popular myth, hedge funds are 'merely vehicles through which people invest in underlying assets: equities, bonds, currencies, commodities and real estate': 'The time has come to stop talking about hedge funds versus non-hedge funds, and to think about asset management as comprised of active and passive investors, with hedge funds as ultra-active management' (*FT*, Editorial, 18 August 2005).

115 Derivatives products are so called because they derive from the price of another product.

116 Turnover on global foreign exchange markets has soared since the 1980s, driven by investor interest in currencies as an asset class. The foreign exchange market is 'by far the world's biggest financial market' in terms of trading volume. Trading on the world's foreign exchange markets soared to a record level of US$ 1900 billion per day

in April 2004 from around US$ 1100 billion in 1995 (*FT*, 29 September 2004). The growth in the foreign exchange market includes currency bets by hedge funds, often in the form of 'macro funds' making big currency bets (*FT*, 29 September 2004). Turnover in currency and interest rate derivatives has also soared in recent years.

117 These include such structured credit instruments as 'residential mortgage-backed securities' (RMBS), 'commercial mortgage-backed securities' (CMBS), and numerous other 'asset-backed securities' (ABS) including 'collateralised loan obligations' (CLOs), and 'collateralised debt obligations' (CDOs). CDOs consist of re-packaged pools of credit derivatives based on dozens of corporate credits. Although each CDO includes hundreds of corporate names, the same firms appear in almost all CDOs.

118 In 2004, within the total derivatives market, interest rate derivatives accounted for 43.0 per cent of the total, currency derivatives accounted for 24.9 per cent of the total, commodity derivatives for 24.7 per cent, and various other types, for the remaining 7.4 per cent (HSBC, 2005).

119 For example, most 'hedge funds' are based 'offshore' to minimise tax liabilities for the fund and the investors, and are 'unrestrained' (*FT*, 11 March 2005).

120 Hot air rises, causing air to be sucked into the fire-stricken area, further exacerbating the intensity of the fire. In the case of the Asian Financial Crisis, China was only able to escape unscathed due to the bold decision to allow GITIC (Guangdong International Trust and Investment Corporation) to go bankrupt. If the Chinese government had assumed responsibility for its debts, the consequential 'domino' effect upon the other offshore debts amassed by the trust and investment companies and other mainland entities threatened to undermine the stability of the entire Chinese financial system.

121 Its military budget in 2007 was set to increase to US$ 31 billion compared with US$ 8 billion in 2001.

Part 2. Groping for a Way Forward: Conflict or Cooperation?

1 See especially, Dobb, in Hilton, ed., 1976, for an extensive discussion of the broad and the narrow interpretation of the term 'feudal'.

2 At the end of the Qing Dynasty, there was a substantial increase in the number of lower level positions in the Civil Service that were sold in order to meet the state's pressing budgetary needs.

3 Will (1990) provides a meticulous account of famine relief in late Imperial China.

4 If the proportion of unregistered urban dwellers were to be included, the share of urban population would be even higher. The absolute number of officially registered urban dwellers rose from 193 million in 1980 to 482 million in 2002.

5 Of these, the number employed in manufacturing and construction rose from 61 million to 122 million, and the number employed in transport, wholesale and retail, and catering, rose from 19 million to 71 million (SSB, ZTN, 2003: 128).

6 Many of these now work in the non-farm sector, albeit that they reside in villages.

7 Of course, in terms of PPP dollars, the income level is somewhat higher.

8 The data were collected by the Chinese Academy of Social Sciences.

9 For example, Taiwanese companies account for around 80 per cent of the notebook computers produced in China, and for the vast majority of China's exports of these products (Bergsten, *et al.*, 2006: 106).

10 In June 2006, the Chinese Government announced that it wished to create Chinese accountancy firms that could take their place alongside the existing global giants (Ernst & Young, PwC, KPMG and Deloitte), which dominate the accountancy functions for Chinese firms floated on stock markets outside China.
11 China is far from being the 'workshop of the world' in the sense that nineteenth century Britain was. Not only was Britain the dominant centre of world manufacturing. It was also the centre of global technical progress.
12 Lomborg (2001) provides an extended account of this argument.
13 It is estimated that around 74 per cent of the permanent urban population in 2002 was covered by health insurance, compared with only 10 per cent for the temporary workers (Lindbeck, 2006: 34).
14 These include a former deputy governor and former mayor of Shijiazhuang, Hebei's largest city; the mayor of one of China's largest cities, Shenyang; a former vice-minister of public security; a former chief of military intelligence; and a deputy chairman of the National People's Congress.
15 The prospectus for the flotation of Bank of China in 2006 reported that in recent years a total of US$ 737 million had been embezzled from BoC's branches in Kaiping, Heilongjiang Province, and Beijing.
16 The chairman of China Construction Bank, Zhang Enzhao, resigned just six months before the bank's IPO, amid a corruption investigation. In 2003, the head of Bank of China (Hong Kong), Liu Jinbao, was detained and subsequently convicted of embezzlement, along with three other BoC (Hong Kong) senior executives.
17 For example, in 2005, Bank of America spent US$ 3 billion to acquire a 10 per cent ownership stake in China Construction Bank, and Bank of Scotland and Temasek (Singapore) spent US$ 4.6 billion to acquire a joint 14.4 per cent stake in Bank of China.
18 In 2006 Ernst & Young, PwC and McKinsey all produced reports saying that China's original stock of bad loans had not been fully dealt with and that a huge stock of new NPLs has been created in the meantime (*FT*, 4 May 2006). Many analysts have pointed out that the surge in the stock price of the recently-floated Chinese banks is a reflection of 'irrational exuberance' and 'momentum buying', rather than reflecting improved fundamentals of the newly listed banks. One of the directors of the Hong Kong Stock Exchange warned: 'I don't believe in listed [Chinese] banks. They've listed too soon. We'll have a Mainland banking crisis within ten years' (David Webb, quoted in *Financial Times*, 2 June 2006). Upon its listing, Bank of China leaped to the top of Hong Kong's market capitalisation tables. The Mainland now has 344 companies, mostly SOEs, listed in Hong Kong. In almost all cases they remain firmly under the control of the Chinese government. They have raised a total of US$ 150 billion from listing in Hong Kong since 1992. Mainland companies now account for 42 per cent of Hong Kong's total market capitalisation. Dividend yields from the listed Mainland companies have been 'paltry'. Only two of China's ten largest IPOs have paid out more than 2.7 per cent (*FT*, 1 June 2006). The territory's financial and social stability now depend heavily on the performance of the Mainland companies floated on its stock market.
19 A group of five small European countries (Denmark, Finland, The Netherlands, Sweden, and Switzerland) have a total of 92 firms in the world's top 1250 companies ranked by R&D expenditure (DTI, 2006).
20 The workforce in the high-income countries in 2002 was 647 million, compared with 3.3 billion in the low and middle-income countries as a whole, and 1747 million in the four 'BRIC' countries (Brazil, China, India, and Russia) (WB, WDI, 2004: 38–40).

21 Recent research shows that an American child born in the bottom-fifth income group has just a one per cent chance of becoming 'rich' (defined as the top 5 per cent of American income earners), whereas a child born rich has a 22 per cent chance of remaining rich as an adult (*FT*, 3 May 2006).

22 The US death rate per 1000 babies is nearly five per thousand. The US ties with Hungary, Malta, Poland and Slovakia, countries with far lower levels of per capita income.

23 Between 1950 and 2005, the size of the average US house increased from 1000 square feet to nearly 2500 square feet. American homes routinely contain a gamut of energy-intensive appliances, such as outdoor kitchens, professional-sized appliances, and heated towel racks. In 2005, the average American automobile achieved 21.0 miles per gallon of petrol. This was even lower than in 1985 (Kolbert, 2006). One-third of American households have more than three cars. The average distance driven by Americans has risen 80 per cent in the past two decades.

24 Under President Clinton, America negotiated and eventually signed the Kyoto Protocol. However, the protocol was never presented to the US Senate for ratification. This was despite the fact that the US Vice-President was Al Gore, who had published in 1992 a best-selling book on global warming. It is widely thought that whoever wins the 2008 US election will respond to rising energy prices by lowering the tax on petrol.

25 China's pattern of growth is heavily skewed towards manufacturing, which accounts for 46 per cent of GDP, compared with 40 per cent in South Korea, 39 per cent in Brazil, and 27 per cent in Mexico. Moreover, the pattern of industrial growth is skewed strongly towards heavy industry. The share of heavy industry in total industrial output (value-added) increased from 62.5 per cent in 2000 to 67.6 per cent in 2004 (SSB, ZTN, 2005: 488). China's incremental capital-output ratio (ICOR) (the ratio of increases in capital stock to increases in GDP) rose from 3.3 in 1990–95, to 4.6 in 1996–2000, reaching 4.9 in 2000–04, compared with ICORs of 4.1 in India (1995–2004), 3.7 in South Korea (1981–90) and 3.5 in Japan (1961–70).

26 China's impact on global export markets should not be exaggerated. Between 1990 and 2002, it accounted for 10 per cent of the total increase in global manufactured exports (WB, WDI, 2004). This is highly significant, but not as large an impact as might be imagined from reading the popular press.

27 Between January 2003 and April 2006, the price index of orange juice rose by 40 per cent, sugar, by 186 per cent, crude oil and silver by 133 per cent, and copper by 290 per cent (*FT*, 10 April 2006).

28 China's total share of world oil consumption is still far below that of the US (8.5 per cent compared with 25 per cent) (BP, 2006).

29 It is almost impossible to disentangle the relative contribution of (i) demand growth, within which China has been the most dynamic element, (ii) sluggish supply response due to gestation lags in capacity expansion, and (iii) pure speculation, to the explosion in commodity prices in recent years. Also, these elements interact in complex ways. For example, most copper mining companies base investment decisions on a long-term planning price of 80–90 cents a pound. However, between 2002 and 2006, the copper price quadrupled to around US$ 2.7 per pound. Speculators argue that mining companies' conservatism merely helped to stimulate still higher prices: 'You have this stand-off between producers who think these commodity prices are not real, and are, therefore, not investing enough in new supply, and the hedge funds who are putting more money into the commodity market because they see that the producers are not

reacting quickly enough by bringing on new supplies' (hedge fund manager, quoted in *Financial Times*, 10 April 2006).

30 From early in the history of the United States, there has been tension between the conception of the 'manifest destiny' of the white majority population and the rights of other civilisations. From 1791 until 1850, no fewer than eighteen new states entered the Union: 'National boundaries made little difference to expansion; in Florida, Louisiana, Texas, and other areas, American settlers rushed in to claim land under the jurisdiction of Spain, France, Mexico, and Indian tribes, confident that American sovereignty would soon follow in their wake' (Foner, 1998: 50). Sitting Bull, the leader of the Sioux Indians proclaimed: 'The life my people want is a life of freedom' (quoted in Foner, 1998: 51). However, the Native American idea of freedom was 'incompatible with that of western settlers, for whom freedom entailed the right to expand across the continent and establish farms, ranches and mines on land that the Indians considered their own. Indian removal – accomplished by fraud, intimidation and violence – was indispensable to the triumph of manifest destiny and the American mission of spreading freedom' (Foner, 1998: 51). Thomas Jefferson was clear that the vast Louisiana purchase from France in 1830, which doubled the then size of the 'Empire of Liberty', would 'push far into the future the dreaded day when an overpopulated, class-divided America would cease to be the home to freedom' (Foner, 1998: 50). This massive territorial expansion depended on the 'energetic exercise of public authority' (Foner, 1998: 53).

31 For example, the visit by Senator Charles Schumer to China in March 2006 was his first official congressional visit abroad in a career in national politics that began more than 25 years ago (*FT*, 7 June 2006).

32 A poll held in 2005 found that among Congressional staff, only 19 per cent saw China positively, while 36 per cent saw it as a military threat and 54 per cent saw it as an economic threat (*South China Morning Post*, 20 May, 2006).

33 The Commission was established by the US Congress in October 2000 by the Floyd D. Spence National Defense Authorisation Act for 2001 sec. 1238, Public Law 106-398, 114 STAT. 1654A–334 (2000) (codified at 22 U.S.C., sec. 7002 (2001), as amended, and the 'Consolidated Appropriations Resolution of 2003', Public Law 108-7, dated February 20, 2003. Public Law 108-7 changed the Commission's title to US-China Economic and Security Review Commission.

34 He subsequently took over the Chairmanship of the Commission.

35 For example, in Venezuela, the government has permitted Chinese oil companies to operate fifteen mature fields (USCESRC, 2005: 168).

36 President Hu Jintao, Premier Wen Jiabao, and Foreign Minister Li Zhaoxing. The three leaders between them visited fifteen African countries.

37 It also greatly increased its stock of petrol stations and its capabilities in chemical production.

38 The takeover was reviewed by the House Committee on Armed Services. The Chairman of the USCESRC, Richard d'Amato, testified before the Committee. He said: 'China's strategic approach to secure its oil supply at source is mercantilist in nature and conflicts with US energy policy that relies on open markets and promotes sharing arrangements in the event of supply disruptions'. He also pointed out 'other features of the proposed transaction that were troublesome, including CNOOC's use of essentially unlimited Chinese government resources, including below market financing, in what purportedly was a free-market acquisition' (reported in USCESRC, 2005: 171).

39 See (Table 16).
40 The 2006 budget proposals also included cuts totalling US$ 65 billion in government spending on health insurance for the elderly and other welfare entitlement programmes over the next five years.
41 It should also be borne in mind that Japan is 'already a formidable military power in its own right'. Its navy is 'more than a match for China's' and is 'technologically more advanced'. Also, 'Japan has the edge over China in modern fighter aircraft and in airborne warning and control systems' (Roy, 2006).
42 This was in sharp contrast to the views of the American public on the Second World War. At the outbreak of the war in Europe, 60 to 80 per cent of Americans were against US involvement. In November 1940, Franklin D. Roosevelt was elected to a third term with the pledge that America would not enter a foreign war unless it was attacked (Vidal, 2003: 9). It was not, of course, until Pearl Harbour that the United States finally entered the Second World War.
43 The United States has been the only country to use nuclear weapons. It dropped the first atomic bomb on Hiroshima on 6 August 1945 and the second one three days later, on 9 August. After the attacks, British Prime Minister Winston Churchill stated: 'The whole burden of execution, including the setting up of the plants and many technical processes connected therewith in the practical sphere, constitutes one of the greatest triumphs of American – or, indeed, human – genius of which there is record' (quoted in Weale, 1995: 172). When he was informed of the attack on Hiroshima, President Truman declared: 'This is the greatest thing that has ever happened' (quoted in Weale, 1995: 171).
44 For the detailed procedures, see McNamara, 2005.
45 China's ICBMs use liquid fuel, which corrodes the missiles after 24 hours. Fuelling them is estimated to take two hours.
46 Even though China is far weaker then the United States in both nuclear and conventional weapons, in the epoch of modern information technology, there are new forms of warfare that may to some degree outweigh ordinary military superiority, including attacks against IT networks in finance, power distribution, telecommunications, and the mass media.
47 This is the case, for example, in the US campaign in Iraq. George W. Bush and Bill Clinton share the distinction of avoiding active service in the Vietnam War.
48 The study is the first step in the 'China Balance Sheet Project', to be carried out jointly by the two institutions. The Project is funded by a group of leading US-based corporations, including American International Group, Boeing, Caterpillar, Citigroup, Coca-Cola, FedEx, General Electric, Goldman Sachs, Microsoft, Pfizer, Proctor and Gamble, and Tyco (Bergsten et al., 2006: xii–xiii).
49 In 1998 Robert Zoellick was one of the eighteen signatories of a letter to President Clinton, which urged him to 'act decisively' to pre-empt Iraq's possible acquisition of weapons of mass destruction before it was too late. Other signatories included Francis Fukuyama (author of *The End of History and the Last Man*), Donald Rumsfeld, Paul Wolfowitz, and Richard Perle (Brzezinski, 2007: 128). About two-thirds of the signatories became officials in George W. Bush's administration. Paul Wolfowitz subsequently was chosen by President Bush to be President of the World Bank, a position from which he resigned in May 2007. President Bush then nominated Robert Zoellick to succeed him.
50 By 2003, China accounted for 16 per cent of total US imports. Its share of US imports of toys and games stood at 77 per cent, while its share of office equipment etc, stood at 24 per cent and its share of clothing stood at 17 per cent (Glyn, 2006: 91).

NOTES

51 We know of no estimate of the total amount of revenue for US firms derived from their production from their branch plants in China and from their sales to China of food and raw materials from their operations in other countries. If these figures were added together, they would greatly reduce the 'real' Chinese balance of trade surplus with the United States. If the contribution of US firms exporting to the United States from their production bases in China was also included, then the 'real' Chinese export surplus to the United States would be even further reduced.

52 By 2002, the flow of FDI from the United States into China stood at US$ 5.4 billion, compared with US$ 4.1 billion from Europe, and US$ 4.2 billion from Japan (SSB, ZTN 2003: Table 17.15). Inflows from Hong Kong totalled US$ 17.9 billion, but it is impossible to disentangle the proportion of this that is accounted for by re-investment in China by Chinese Mainland firms' operations outside China, especially in Hong Kong, and by firms from other parts of the world operating through Hong Kong (Taiwan is especially important in this process, due to the restrictions on direct investment in the Mainland).

53 By 1890, the richest one per cent of the population received the same total income as the bottom 50 per cent, and owned more wealth than the bottom 99 per cent (Foner, 1998: 117).

54 In his view society faced only two possible alternatives: 'liberty, inequality and the survival of the fittest; not-liberty, equality, survival of the unfittest' (quoted in Foner, 1998: 122).

55 The immediate intellectual origins of the movement can be traced back to the publication in 1944 of Friedrich Hayek's book, *The Road to Serfdom*. The theme of the book was simple: 'planning for freedom' was an oxymoron, since 'planning leads to dictatorship' (Foner, 1998: 235).

56 Former Harvard President Larry Summers believes that 'the most serious problem facing the United States today is the widening gap between the children of the rich and the children of the poor' (*NYT*, 24 May 2005). In 2005 Alan Greenspan warned of the dangers of current trends in the distribution of income in the United States: 'For the democratic society, that is not a very desirable thing to allow to happen' (quoted in *New York Times*, 5 June 2005). In an interview in 2005, Hank Paulson, CEO of Goldman Sachs, said that the images of US poverty in the wake of Hurricane Katrina 'were really shocking': 'We need to hold a discussion about the gap between the poor and the rich in America' (quoted in *Financial Times*, 1 June 2006).

57 In true '*Economist*' fashion, its main concern is for its middle-class readers, not the mass of American workers at the bottom of the heap of the income distribution.

58 The comparable proportions for other selected countries were: South Korea:1.6% (2002); Japan: 3.4% (2001); Mexico: 33% (2001); Brazil: 47.8% (2003); and Singapore: 59.8% (2003) (UNCTAD, 2005: 292–3).

59 Science, engineering, and mathematics.

60 National Academy of Sciences, National Academy of Engineering, and Institute of Medicine.

61 Among the most significant examples of technical progress in pre-modern China were gunpowder, steel-making, the canal lock gate, the compass, the wheelbarrow, the windmill, mechanical clockwork, water-powered metallurgical blowing machines, water-powered trip hammers for forges, hemp spinning machines, gear wheels, power transmission by driving belt, the sternpost rudder, watertight compartments, and the crank (Needham, 1954-).

62 Article IV allows IMF member countries to choose their own economic and exchange rate policies, so long as they 'avoid manipulation of payments adjustment and do not seek to gain unfair advantage over other members'.
63 See Nolan (2004a, 145–55) for an analysis of the common ethical ground in Confucius and Adam Smith.
64 For example, at the height of early Islamic civilisation, from the tenth to the twelfth century, Muslim scholars preserved the intellectual heritage of Aristotle, and combined this with their own commitment to Islam and the Koran (Braudel, 1993: 81–4). Muslim philosophy was 'trapped between Greek thought on the one hand and the revealed truth of the Koran on the other' (Braudel, 1993: 82).
65 It will be obvious to experts in the field that I am not a scholar of Islam or the Islamic world. I apologise to those who are experts in these complex subjects. However, I hope that the arguments presented in this section will contribute to the debate about the nature of capitalist globalisation, the possibilities for resolving its inherent contradictions and the critical role that the inherently internationalist Islamic culture may be able to play in this process, alongside that of Chinese culture.
66 Gallipoli, in Turkey, was the scene of a military campaign in the summer of 1915 in which it is estimated that around 160 000 allied servicemen (from Canada, India, New Zealand, Australia, France and Britain) and over 250 000 Turkish servicemen died. Kemal Attaturk was the first president of modern Turkey, and had been a divisional commander at Gallipoli.
67 T. E. Lawrence ('Lawrence of Arabia') wrote: 'Some of us judged that there was latent power enough and to spare in the Arabic peoples, a prolific Semitic agglomeration, great in religious thought, reasonably industrious, mercantile, politic, yet solvent rather than dominant in character' (Lawrence, quoted in Hourani, 2002: 317).
68 The first volume of Naguib Mahfouz's Cairo trilogy concludes with the violent end to one of the demonstrations, and the death of one of the book's main characters, shot by the British troops (Mahfouz, 1991).
69 They then became the People's Democratic Republic of Yemen. South Yemen had long been independent. In 1990, the two segments of Yemen united into a single country.
70 Morocco was jointly ruled by France and Spain until the end of the 1920s (Hourani, 2002: 317).
71 The first batch of French Mystère fighters arrived in Israel in April 1956.
72 Among the Arab states, in 1999 only four out of seventeen had multi-party electoral systems (UNDP, 2002: 15). All observers are aware that the distribution of income and wealth in the Gulf states, excluding Iraq and Iran, is extremely unequal, but there is painfully little data available. The World Bank's table on the distribution of income and wealth (World Bank, WDI, 2006: Table 2.8) contains no data for Kuwait, Oman, Saudi Arabia, or the United Arab Emirates.
73 In fact, the Taliban is far from defeated, and in 2006, there was still fierce fighting in Afghanistan.
74 The estimate is based on research by two medical teams, who surveyed 1849 households in forty-seven randomly selected sites across Iraq between May and July 2006. The editor of the *Lancet* commented: 'It is worth emphasising the quality of the latest report, as judged by four expert peers who provided detailed comments to the

editors ... [The findings] corroborate the impression that Iraq is descending into bloodthirsty chaos' (quoted in *Financial Times*, 12 October 2006).
75 The previous level at which US sanctions for investment in the Iranian oil and gas industry were to be imposed had been set at US$ 40 million.
76 In 2006, the International Atomic Energy Association believed that Iran was five years away from being able to produce a nuclear bomb.
77 In January 2006, the National Institute for Public Policy, a conservative think-tank, produced a report recommending that 'tactical nuclear weapons' be deemed to be an essential part of the US arsenal, to be used on 'those occasions when the certain and prompt destruction of high priority targets is essential and beyond the promise of conventional weapons (quoted in Hersh, 2006). Several signatories of the report were later to join President Bush's Administration.
78 The League of Nations gave Britain the mandate to present-day Iraq, Palestine and Jordan, while France was given the mandate to Syria and Lebanon.
79 Although Marx's family was Jewish, he was not brought up in the Jewish faith.
80 Like Marx, Hobsbawm was not brought up in the Jewish faith, but feels a strong sense of identity with his Jewish ancestors.
81 Sir Herbert's first official visit when he arrived in Jerusalem was to the main synagogue. Long afterwards he wrote: 'The emotion that I could not help but feel seemed to spread through the vast congregation. Many wept. Once could almost hear the sigh of generations'.
82 In April 1936 two Jews were murdered in Nablus. The murder provoked retaliation, and retaliation provoked confrontation (Gelvin, 2005: 109).
83 The Stern Gang was a spin-off from the Irgun, a fascist-style militia in terms of its uniforms, drills and fervent nationalism.
84 The most significant such suggestion was contained in the Peel Report of 1937. The Report recognised the growing antagonism between the two communities, and advocated dividing Palestine into two separate states, one Jewish and one Arab, with a British mandatory zone retained in Jerusalem, Nazareth and some other areas (Gelvin, 2005: 117). The Arab High Committee rejected this solution, and demanded 'complete independence for Palestine, and an end to Jewish immigration and land sales'. The Peel Report helped to exacerbate feelings among the Arab community in Palestine and helped intensify the Great Revolt. The White Paper of 1939 reversed the conclusions of the Peel Report, but this was rejected by the Jewish and the Arab sides (Gelvin, 2005: 118). Although the Report promised independence for a united Palestine, the conditions it attached, such as continuing Jewish immigration (albeit at a reduced level) and regulation of land sales remaining in the hands of the high commissioner for Palestine, were unacceptable to the Arab population (Gelvin, 2005: 118). The Arab Committee said: 'The last word does not rest with the White or Black Papers; it is the will of the nation itself that decides its future. The Arab people have expressed their will and said their word in a loud and decisive manner. And they are certain that with God's assistance they will reach the desired goal – Palestine shall be independent within an Arab federation and shall forever remain Arab' (quoted in Gelvin, 2005: 118).
85 The most notorious of these was the blowing up of the British headquarters in Palestine at the King David Hotel in July 1946 (Gelvin, 2005: 123). The attack was executed by the future Prime Minister of Israel, Menachem Begin.
86 The denial of the horrific reality of the Holocaust among a variety of different groups, from the ultra-right in Europe to elements within certain Islamic countries is an important

and complicated issue, far beyond the scope of this study. Iran's President, Ahmadi-Nejad, is the latest addition to the list of people who deny that the Holocaust took place.

87 The so-called 'Sonnerborn Institute' is composed of seventeen of the richest Jews in America. In 1945 they pledged to finance the acquisition of weapons that the new state would need. They donated millions of dollars to this cause. By January 1947, some 950 shipments of dismantled machinery left New York for Palestine. These shipments 'became the foundation of the Israeli military industry' (Karpin, 2006: 27).

88 Jordan came into being at the end of the First World War. It has been described as an 'unnatural' state and 'even more than Iraq, a British creation', (Lapidus, 2002: 544). Jordan is a constitutional monarchy, based on military and bureaucratic elites, wealthy merchants and East Bank tribal leaders. In 1958, socialist opposition was crushed with the help of British paratroopers (Lapidus, 2002: 545).

89 Israel returned Sinai to Egypt in 1979.

90 The left wing within the PLO, including the PFLP (Popular Front for the Liberation of Palestine), supported the goal of comprehensive revolution in the Arab countries, followed by a full-scale showdown with Israel (Lapidus, 2002: 560).

91 This is a pithy, if unintended, précis of the argument made by John Locke in the seventeenth century to justify the white settlers conquest of North America.

92 The standard formula for satisfying the Israeli censors is to refer to Israel's stock of nuclear weapons in terms of 'foreign estimates'.

93 He 'never hesitated to dismiss technicians or scientists who expressed doubts about the justice of Israel's case' (Karpin, 2006: 292).

94 Perle became Chairman of the Defense Advisory Board, and Feith became Deputy Under-Secretary of Defense.

95 In 1993, Shimon Perez, had published a book entitled *The New Middle East*, in which he argued that Jews and Arabs should promote economic relations in order to promote peace. This view was widely regarded across the Arab world as a plot to control Arab lands without withdrawing from occupied lands.

96 Hilary Clinton, a potential presidential candidate, scolded Nouri al-Malaki, the Iraqi Prime Minister, during his visit to the United States, for having criticised Israel: 'His refusal to denounce Hizbollah and his condemnation of Israel sends exactly the wrong message about the importance of fighting terrorism and bringing stability to the Middle East. He should recognise that Israel has the right to defend itself against the terrorist aggression' (quoted in *Financial Times*, 1 August 2006).

97 It is estimated that between September 2000 and 2005, around 4200 Palestinians and 1100 Israelis were killed in the Israel-Palestine conflict (*FT*, 8 August 2006).

98 Brzezinski called Israel's response 'dogged, heavy-handed, politically counter-productive ... and morally unjustifiable'. He said: 'The US is in the process of learning that it cannot impose solutions on the Middle East by force alone. Nor can Israel' (quoted in *Financial Times*, 22 July 2006).

99 In a poll conducted on 29 July 2006, seventeen days after the Israeli invasion of Lebanon began, four out of five Israelis wanted the military to use more force to eliminate Hizbollah or remove it from the border (*FT*, 30 July 2006).

100 The French edition of Maxime Rodinson's study *Capitalism and Islam* was published in French in 1966.

101 The Arab conquests included Syria in 634, Egypt in 639, Persia in 642, and Spain in 711.

102 The Mongols conquered Baghdad in 1258.

103 They financed their reconstruction with local taxes.

104 This includes countries in which most people follow the Islamic religion, but the state's laws are derived from secular not religious principles.
105 Egypt was a partial exception to this. For a relatively brief period in the early and mid-1960s, Egypt's large scale industrial and financial institutions mostly were under state ownership and operated a form of centralised administrative planning. By 1964, public sector firms accounted for 90 per cent of the value-added in plants that employed ten workers or more (Owen and Pamuk, 1998: 131). However, even during this period, a large sector of the economy was in private hands, including all small businesses in the cities and most of agriculture. Moreover, in the wake of the disastrous defeat by Israel in the Six-Day War in 1968, Nasser immediately began the reform process that would later grow into the '*infatah*' movement (Owen and Pamuk, 1998: 134–5).
106 In the case of Algeria in the 1990s, this occurred through violent suppression of the indigenous fundamentalist movement. As many as 100 000 people may have lost their lives during a bloody struggle to suppress the Islamic fundamentalist movement, which appeared to have legitimately won power through the ballot box. However, it cannot be assumed that the Algerian Islamic fundamentalists would have pursued comprehensively anti-capitalist policies had they been allowed to claim the power they had won through the ballot box.
107 Egypt's constraints on FDI have been further liberalised in recent years. In addition, the boom in oil prices has stimulated FDI from other Islamic countries. FDI in Egypt accelerated from US$ 2 billion in 2003, to US 6.1 billion in 2005, and is estimated to reach over US$ 6 billion in 2006 (*FT*, 13 December 2006).
108 In October 2006, Sanpaolo paid US$ 1.6 billion for an 80 per cent stake in the bank.
109 There are deep inconsistencies in this approach. For example, 'Islamic' banks are free to invest in the stock market, commodity markets and property 'development', as well as in derivatives of all types, all of which constitute legal forms of gambling. Nor is it inconsistent with large-scale purchase of weapons by Islamic governments, which often are the owners of the same financial institutions.
110 All global banks set aside a portion of their profits for charitable purposes. It is a moot point whether these are larger or smaller than the charitable allocations of Islamic financial institutions to '*zakat*'.
111 For example, the Dubai government investment arm, Istithmar, has spent US$ 2.5 billion to acquire a 2.7 per cent stake in Standard Chartered Bank (*FT*, 27 November 2006).
112 A special problem for the Gulf states is that there is a lack of depth in the markets, due to the fact that the 'participants tend to come from a small, affluent community that may be quite influential', which 'presents enforcement challenges' (*FT*, 27 November 2006).
113 The Gini coefficient of income inequality is 0.31 in Pakistan, 0.32 in Bangladesh, 0.34 in Egypt and Indonesia, 0.35 in Algeria, 0.40 in Morocco and Tunisia, 0.44 in Turkey, and 0.49 in Malaysia. The Gini coefficient of income inequality is 0.25 in Denmark, 0.25 in Sweden, 0.28 in Germany, and 0.33 in France. The Gini coefficient of income inequality is 0.43 in Kenya, 0.44 in Nigeria, 0.45 in China, 0.53 in Argentina, and 0.58 in Brazil (WB, WDR, 2006: 76–9).
114 By 1990 in the small oil-exporting countries in the Gulf, more than 40 per cent of the population consisted of foreigners, more than one half of whom came from other Arab countries (Owen and Pamuk, 1998: 234).

115 Tripp (2006) provides a thorough analysis of the different strands within this immense literature, very little of which is accessible to those who cannot read Arabic or other languages in which Islamic people write.
116 See for example, the collection of translations of modern Arabic literature edited by Jayyusi, 2005. Naguib Mahfouz's *Cairo Trilogy* (first published in Arabic in 1956–7) gives a penetrating insight into the way in which an individual Islamic family dealt with the challenges of capitalist modernisation.
117 I regularly sit on a bench in Tavistock Square which commemorates one of the young people killed in the attack on a London Transport bus, the top of which was blown off in Tavistock Square. In my own home city of Plymouth, in just two nights in March 1941, more than 18 000 houses were destroyed by German bombing (Calder, 1969: 211). The entire city centre simply disappeared under the barrage of bombing. I remember the many thousands of fellow citizens killed in Plymouth alone during the blitz when I return to Plymouth. Similarly, as I travel around Germany, to Hamburg, Munich, Dresden and other cities firebombed by the vengeful British and American bombers, I recall the enormity of the violence and death during the Second World War. Of course, the horrors of the war in Western Europe pale before those in the Soviet Union, where are many as 28 million people perished due to the conflict.
118 For example, Egypt has seen some of the most severe attacks on international tourist sites by Islamic terrorists. Between 2004 and 2006 there were three major bomb attacks on Egyptian tourist sites. These were all in the Sinai Peninsula, and killed a total of around 150 people (*FT*, 13 December 2006). The motive for the attacks is uncertain. Some people believe they may be directed against Israel, since the resorts are heavily patronised by Israelis. However, the impact on tourism has been negligible. It is still one of the most important sectors in the Egyptian economy, bringing in around US$ 6.4 billion in revenue in 2005. The number of tourists grew from 8.6 million in 2005 to 9.1 million in 2006 (*FT*, 13 December 2006). More than one-third of Egypt's tourist hotel beds are now in the beach resorts in the Sinai Peninsula, the area targeted in the terrorist attacks of recent years. The objective is to achieve 14 million tourists by 2011. The goal of Egypt's Ministry of Tourism is to attract a new type of clientele, including tourists from India and China. They also wish to introduce new products, 'to attract high spenders and play up to the country's many strengths as a destination'. The Ministry plans to establish 'big integrated high-end resorts ... offering luxury accommodation, residential property, marinas for private yachts, spas and golf courses' (*FT*, 13 December 2006).
119 In 1997, the *Wall Street Journal* had proclaimed: 'Like them or not, the Taliban are the players most capable of achieving peace in Afghanistan at this moment in history' (quoted in Vidal, 2002: 41).
120 Lewis observes: 'There is no evidence in the Isma'ili sources to support any such charges which are not uncommon in hostile descriptions of unpopular and secretive sects in the Islamic world and elsewhere' (Lewis, 1993: 119).
121 Tripp (2006) provides a comprehensive account of these debates.
122 In the New Testament, Jesus says: 'It is easier for a camel to pass through the eye of a needle than it is for a rich man to enter the Kingdom of Heaven'.
123 For example, in 1962, the Egyptian scholar, Muhammad Ismail wrote: '[In the Islamic system] the individual is not acquisitive at the expense of the community, and the community does not impose upon the individual. It secures the shelter of human justice, the good of both the individual and the community' (quoted in Tripp, 2006: 98).

124 Qutb was executed along with two other members of the Muslim Brotherhood.
125 The Muslim Brotherhood was founded in 1928. The Brotherhood strongly supported ideas such as those of Sayyid Qutb for establishing an Islamic society in Egypt. The movement was extremely critical of the path Egypt took under President Nasser. In 1954, there as an assassination attempt on President Nasser. The incident was surrounded in controversy. Following it, Nasser banned the Brotherhood, and arrested more than 1000 of its members, including Qutb. Seven of its leaders were sentenced to death. In 1957, a further group of twenty-one members were massacred at the Liman Tura military jail. In recent years also, the Government has jailed many of its members. However, for a long period, the Brotherhood has avoided head-on confrontation with Egypt's rulers. Instead it has focused on charitable and social welfare programmes, including running schools, health clinics and, even, sports programmes. Its members are allowed to stand as independent candidates in Egypt's elections, and in 2005, they won eighty-eight seats (*FT*, 13 December 2006).
126 He was said to have been offered the post of Minister of Education in Nasser's government, but refused (Alger, 2000: 5).
127 It goes without saying that for Qutb, the Koran records the word of God as mediated through the Prophet, Muhammad.
128 It ignores, inter alia, the common origin of the three religions in the Middle East.

Conclusion: Searching for the Middle Way

1 Carr originally intended to call his book *Utopia and Reality* (Carr, 2001: xxxvii).
2 The Soviet Union crushed the Hungarian uprising in 1956 and the Prague Spring in 1968. China invaded Vietnam in 1979. China and the USSR engaged in a vitriolic war of words for over a decade and clashed frequently along their common border.
3 Technical progress and changes in labour laws, as well as changes in the extent, nature and function of trade unions, have also played their part in the changing nature of work and income distribution in the high-income economies.
4 The Davos Economic Forum constitutes the most significant collective institution for the elite global firms. Although its agenda has become increasingly preoccupied with issues that worry global business leaders, including climate change, 'Islamic terrorism' and the global distribution of income and wealth, the Forum produces no agreed proposals on concrete ways to tackle the contradictions of advanced capitalism. It is a talking-shop and a club for mutual self-congratulation.
5 Van Creveld estimates that Israel's largest atomic weapons, weighing 200 kilotons, are ten times more powerful than that which annihilated Hiroshima (Van Creveld, 2004: 135).
6 As late as the 1840s, schoolchildren in the Catalan region of France were punished for speaking their own language rather than French.
7 This view was expressed with great force by Karl Marx. While he greatly deplored the arrogance, violence and hypocrisy of British colonialism in China and India, he welcomed the 'progressive' impact of industrial capitalism upon 'Asiatic Despotisms'.
8 In spite of widespread anger at the deep injustices and inequality of Latin American capitalist development, South America's elected left-wing leaders, including President

Lula, Evo Morales, and, even Hugo Chavez, have all tried to grope their way towards some form of middle course between raw capitalism and collectivist communism.
9 Red Guard slogan in the Chinese Cultural Revolution.
10 In 2005, the voters of France and the Netherlands rejected the new European Constitution, thereby setting back the momentum of European political integration.
11 The final sentence was inserted in 1931, when the menace of Hitler was beginning to become apparent.

BIBLIOGRAPHY

Ahmad, K., 2003, 'The Challenge of Global Capitalism: an Islamic perspective', in Dunning, ed.
Algar, H., 2000, 'Introduction' to Qutb, 2000.
Al Qaeda, 1998, *Founding Statement of Al Qaeda*', (23 February 1998), in Halliday, 2002.
Aristotle, 1976, *Ethics*, Harmondsworth: Penguin Classics edition.
Aristotle, 1992, *The Politics*, Harmondsworth: Penguin Books.
Avineri, S., 1968, *The Social and Political Thought of Karl Marx*, Cambridge: Cambridge University Press.
Bairoch, P., 1982, 'International Industrialization Levels from 1750 to 1980', *Journal of European Economic History*, Fall.
Balazs, E., 1964, *Chinese civilisation and bureaucracy*, London: Yale University.
Balzac, Honoré de, 1965, *Cousine Bette*, Harmondsworth: Penguin Books.
Bergsten, F., B. Gill, N. R. Lardy and D. Mitchell, 2006, *China: the balance sheet*, New York: Public Affairs.
Berlin, I., 1969, *Four Essays in Liberty*, Oxford: Oxford University Press.
Bernal, J. D., 1965, *Science in History*, 2 Vols., Harmondsworth: Penguin Books.
Blinder, A. S., 2006, 'Offshoring: the next industrial revolution', *Foreign Affairs*, March/April.
Boserup, E., 1981, *Population and Technical Change*, Oxford: Basil Blackwell.
Boston Consulting Group, 2004, *Growing Through Acquisitions*, Boston: BCG Publishing.
Boyd, A., 1962, *Chinese Architecture and Town Planning, 1500 BC–AD 1911*, London: Alec Tiranti.
BP, 1999, *World Energy Review*, London: BP.
BP, 2005, *World Energy Review*, London, BP.
BP, 2006, *World Energy Review*, London, BP.
Braudel, F., 1981, *The Structures of Everyday Life: civilisation and capitalism, 15th–18th century, Vol. 1,* London: Collins.
Braudel, F., 1982, *The Wheels of Commerce: civilisation and capitalism, 15th–18th century, Vol. 2*, London: Collins.
Braudel, F., 1984, *The Perspective of the World: civilisation and capitalism, 15th–18th century, Vol. 3*, London: Collins.
Braudel, F., 1993, *A History of Civilisations*, Harmondsworth: Penguin Books.
Breman, J., 1996, *Footloose Labour*, Cambridge: Cambridge University Press.
Broers, A., 2005, *The Triumph of Technology*, Cambridge: Cambridge University Press.
Brooks, T., 1999, *The Confusions of Pleasure: commerce and culture in Ming China*, Berkeley: University of California Press.
Browne, Lord, 2005, Presentation at China Executive Learning Programme, Cambridge.
Brzezinski, Z., 1997, *The Grand Chessboard*, New York: Basic Books.

Brzezinski, Z., 2007, *Second Chance*, New York: Basic Books.
Bullard, R., 1958, *The Middle East: a political and economic survey*, Oxford: Oxford University Press.
Bush, G. W., 2002, *National Security Strategy of the United States of America*, Washington DC: The White House.
Bush, G. W., 2006, *National Security Strategy of the United States of America*, Washington DC: The White House.
Calder, A., 1969, *The People's War*, London: Pimlico.
Carr, E. H., 2001, *The Twenty Year Crisis*, with a new introduction by Michael Cox, Basingstoke: Palgrave (originally published 1939).
Castells, M., 2000, *The Rise of the Network Society*, Oxford: Blackwells (2nd edn.).
Chandler, A., 1977, *The Visible Hand*, Cambridge, Mass.: Harvard University Press.
Chandler, A., 1990, *Scale and Scope: the dynamics of industrial capitalism*, Cambridge, Mass.: Harvard University Press.
Chandler, A., F. Amatori and T. Hikino, eds, 1997, *Big Business and the Wealth of Nations*, Cambridge: Cambridge University Press.
Chang, Song, 2005, 'Consolidation and Internationalization in the Global Banking Industry Since 1980s, and the implication for Chinese Banking Reform', University of Cambridge Doctoral Dissertation.
Chaudhuri, K. N., 1985, *Trade and Civilisation in the Indian Ocean: an economic history from the rise of Islam to 1750*, Cambridge: Cambridge University Press.
Chaudhuri, K. N., 1990, *Economy and Civilisation of the Indian Ocean from the Rise of Islam to 1750*, Cambridge: Cambridge University Press.
Chi, Ch'ao-ting, 1936, *Key Economic Areas in Chinese History*, New York: Paragon Reprint.
Childe, V. G., 1942, *What Happened in History*, Harmondsworth: Penguin Books.
Cipolla, C. M., ed., 1972, *The Fontana Economic History of Europe, Vol. 1: the Middle Ages*, Glasgow: Collins.
Cipolla, C. M., ed., 1972, *The Fontana Economic History of Europe, Vol. 2: the Sixteenth and Seventeenth Centuries*, Glasgow: Collins.
Cipolla, C. M., ed., 1973, *The Fontana Economic History of Europe, Vol. 3: the Industrial Revolution*, Glasgow: Collins.
Coase, R. H., 1988, 'The nature of the firm', reprinted in R. H. Coase, 1988, *The Firm, the Market and the Law*, Chicago: University of Chicago Press (originally published 1937).
Cohen, A., 1989, *Economic Life in Ottoman Jerusalem*, Cambridge: Cambridge University Press.
Comrades from the Shanghai Hutong Shipyards, and the Sixth Economic Group of the Shanghai Municipal May Seventh Cadre School, 1974, 'Two kinds of society, two kinds of wages', in Selden, 1979.
Confucius, 1979, *The Analects (Lun Yu)*, translated, with an Introduction by D. C. Lau, Harmondsworth: Penguin Books.
DaimlerChrysler, 2005, 'Challenges, measures and opportunities', DaimlerChrysler.
Darwin, C., 1985, *The Origin of Species*, London: Penguin Books (originally published 1859).
Darwin, C., 2004, *The Descent of Man*, London; Penguin Books (originally published 1871).
Davies, J., S. Sandstrom, A. Shorrocks, and E. N. Wolff, 2006, 'The global distribution of household wealth', *WIDER Angle*, World Institute for Development Economics Research, No. 2.
Dawkins, R., 1976, *The Selfish Gene*, Oxford: Oxford University Press.
Dawson, R., 1964, 'Western conceptions of Chinese civilisation', in Dawson, ed., *The Legacy of China*, Oxford: Oxford University Press.

DTI (Department of Trade and Industry), 2003, *R&D Scoreboard, 2003*, London: DTI.
DTI (Department of Trade and Industry), 2005, *R&D Scoreboard, 2005*, London: DTI.
DTI (Department of Trade and Industry), 2006, *R&D Scoreboard, 2006*, London: DTI.
Diamond, J., 2005, *Collapse*, Harmondsworth: Penguin Books.
Dobb, M., 1963, *Studies in the Development of Capitalism*, London: Routledge.
Dreze, J. and A. K. Sen, 1989, *Hunger and Public Action*, Oxford: Clarendon Press.
Dunning, J., ed., 2003, *Making Globalisation Good*, Oxford: Oxford University Press.
Eastman, L., 1988, *Families, Fields, and Ancestors*, New York: Oxford University Press.
Eichengreen, B., and K. Mitchener, 2003, 'The Great Depression as a credit boom gone wrong', *BIS Working Papers*, No. 137.
Engels, F., 1969, *The Condition of the English Working Class*, London: Granada (originally published in German 1845, and originally published in English 1892).
Fallon, W. J., 2006, 'US Pacific Command Posture: statement before the House Armed Services Committee', Washington, DC.
Faure, D., 1996, 'History and Culture', in Hook, 1996.
Faure, D., 2001, 'Beyond Networking: an institutional view of Chinese business', mimeo.
Feuerwerker, A., ed., 1964, *Modern China*, Englewood Cliffs, N.J.: Prentice-Hall.
Feuerwerker, A., 1976, *State and Society in Eighteenth Century China: the Ch'ing Empire in all its glory*, Ann Arbor, Michigan: Center for Chinese Studies.
Financial Times, (*FT*) various issues.
Foner, E., 1998, *The Story of American Freedom*, New York: W. W. Norton.
Fortune magazine, various issues.
Frank, A. G., 1998, *ReOrient*, Berkeley: University of California Press.
Freud, S., 1920, 'Beyond the pleasure principle', in Freud, 2001, Vol. xvii.
Freud, S., 1930, 'Civilisation and its discontents', in Freud, 2001, Vol. xxi.
Freud, S., 2001, *Complete Works of Sigmund Freud*, London: Vintage.
Friedman, M., 1962, *Capitalism and Freedom*, Chicago: University of Chicago Press.
Friedman, T., 2005, *The World is Flat: a brief history of the twenty-first century*, New York: Farrar, Straus and Giroux.
Fromm, E., 1997, *The Anatomy of Human Destructiveness*, London: Pimlico (originally published 1973).
Fromm, E., 1991, *The Sane Society*, London: Routledge.
Fukuyama, F., 1992, *The End of History or the Last Man*, Harmondsworth: Penguin Books.
Gelvin, J. L., 2005, *The Israel-Palestine Conflict*, Cambridge: Cambridge University Press.
Glyn, A., 2006, *Capitalism Unleashed*, Oxford: Oxford University Press.
Goldman, M., 2003, *The Piratisation of Russia*, London: Routledge.
Gray, J., 1998, *False Dawn*, London: Granta Books.
Habib, I., 1969, 'Potentialities of Capitalist Development in the Economy of Mughal India', *Journal of Economic History*, Vol. 29, No. 1, March, 32–78.
Halliday, F., 2002, *Two Hours that Shook the World*, London: Saqi Books.
Hayek, F. A., 2004, *The Road to Serfdom*, London: Routledge (originally published 1944).
Hegel, G. F, 1952, *The Philosophy of Right*, English edition, Oxford: Oxford University Press (originally published in German1820).
Held, D., and A. Kaya, 2007, eds, *Global Inequality*, Cambridge: Polity Press.
Hersh, S., 2006, 'The Iran plans', *The New Yorker*, 17 April.
Hilton, R., ed., 1976, *The Transition from Feudalism to Capitalism*, London: New Left Books.
Hirst, P., and G. Thompson, 1999, *Globalization in Question*, Cambridge: Polity Press (2nd edn.).

Ho, Ping-ti, 1969, *Studies on the Population of China, 1368–1953*, Cambridge, Mass.: Harvard University Press.
Hobsbawm, E., 1990, *Nations and Nationalism since 1780*, Cambridge: Cambridge University Press.
Homer, 1996, *The Odyssey*, Harmondsworth: Penguin Books (translated by Robert Fagles).
Homer, 1998, *The Iliad*, Harmondsworth: Penguin Books (translated by Robert Fagles).
Hook, B., 1996, ed., *Guangdong, China's Promised Land*, Hong Kong: Oxford University Press.
Hourani, A., 2002, *A History of the Arab Peoples*, London: Faber.
HSBC, 2005, 'Risk identification, management and derivatives'.
Hu, Jichuang, 1984, *Chinese Economic Thought Before the Seventeenth Century*, Beijing: Foreign Language Press.
Huang, R., 1981, *1587, A Year of No Significance (Wanli shiwu nian)*, New Haven and London: Yale University Press.
Huntington, S. P., 1993, 'Why international primacy matters', *International Security*, No. 83, Spring.
Huntington, S. P., 1996, *The Clash of Civilizations and the Remaking of World Order*, New York: Simon and Schuster.
Huntington, S. P., 2004, *Who Are We?*, London: Simon and Schuster.
Hymer, S., 1972, 'The multinational corporation and the law of uneven development' reprinted in Radice, 1975.
Inalcik, H., 1994, *An Economic and Social History of the Ottoman Empire, Vol. 1*, Cambridge: Cambridge University Press.
IISS (International Institute of Strategic Studies), 1999, *The Military Balance, 1998/99*, London: International Institute of Strategic Studies.
IISS (International Institute of Strategic Studies), 2004, *The Military Balance, 2003/4*, London: International Institute of Strategic Studies.
IISS (International Institute of Strategic Studies), 2005, *The Military Balance, 2004/5*, London: International Institute of Strategic Studies.
Ismoglu-Inan, H., ed., 1987, *The Ottoman Empire and the World Economy*, Cambridge: Cambridge University Press.
Jayyusi, S. K., ed., 2005, *Modern Arabic Fiction, An Anthology*, New York: Columbia University Press.
Johnson, C., 2000, *Blowback*, New York: Metropolitan Books.
Kant, E., 1784, 'Idea for a universal history with a cosmopolitan purpose', in Kant, 1991, *Political Writings*, Cambridge: Cambridge University Press.
Karpin, D., 2006, *The Bomb in the Basement*, New York: IB Tauris.
Keynes, J. M., 1936, *The General Theory of Employment, Interest and Money*, London: Macmillan.
Kindleberger, C. P., 1996, *Manias, Panics and Crashes: a history of financial crises*, New York: Wiley (3rd edn.).
King, D., 2005, 'The challenge of global warming', Presentation to China Executive Learning Programme, Cambridge.
King, F. H., 1965, *Money and Monetary Policy in China*, Cambridge, Mass.: Harvard University Press.
Kirk, M., and R.Larsen, 2006, 'Helping Congress to understand China', *Far Eastern Economic Review*, May.
Klare, M., 2004, *Blood and Oil*, London: Hamish Hamilton.
Klare, M., 2006, 'Target China: The Emerging US-China Conflict', *The Nation Institute*.

BIBLIOGRAPHY

Kolbert, E., 2006, 'Can America Go Green?', *New Statesman*, 19 June.
Kropotkin, Prince Petr, 1939, *Mutual Aid*, Harmondsworth; Penguin Books (originally published 1902).
Lapidus, I. M., 2002, *A History of Islamic Societies*, Cambridge: Cambridge University Press.
Lau, D. C., 'Introduction', to Confucius, 1979.
Lewis, A., 1954, 'Economic development with unlimited supplies of labour', *The Manchester School*, May.
Lewis, B., 1993, *The Arabs in History*, Oxford: Oxford University Press.
Li, Bai, (lived AD 710–762).
Li, Bozhong, 1986, *The Development of Agriculture and Industry in Jiangnan, 1644–1850*, Hangzhou: Zhejiang Academy of Social Sciences.
Li, Bozhong, 1998, *Agricultural Development in Jiangnan, 1620–1850*, Basingstoke: Macmillan.
Li, Bozhong, 2000, *The Early Industrialisation of Jiangnan, 1550–1850*, Beijing: Shehui kexue wenjian Publishing House (in Chinese).
Lieber, K. A., and D. G. Press, 2006, 'The rise of US nuclear supremacy', *Foreign Affairs*, March/April.
Lieber, K. A., and D. G. Press, 2006, 'The rise of China's nuclear supremacy', *Foreign Affairs*, March/April.
Lieven, A., 2004, *America Right or Wrong*, London and New York: Harper Perennial.
Lilley, S., 1973, 'Technological Progress and the Industrial Revolution', in Cippola, ed., 1973, Vol. 3.
Lindbeck, A., 2006, *Economic Reforms and Social Change in China*, Stockholm, mimeo.
List, 1856, *National System of Political Economy*, Philadelphia: Lippincott.
Little, I., T. Scitovsky and M. Scott, 1970, *Industry and Trade in some Developing Countries*, London: Oxford University Press.
Liu, Kaiming, 2006, 'Migrant workers and the work of the Institute of Contemporary Observation', Denmark: Copenhagen Business School.
Lomborg, B., 2001. *The Skeptical Environmentalist*, Cambridge: Cambridge University Press.
Lorenz, K., 1966, *On Aggression*, London: Methuen.
Maddison, A., 1994, *Dynamic Forces in Capitalist Development*, Oxford; Oxford University Press.
Mahfouz, N., 1991, *Palace Walk*, London: Black Swan (Vol. 1 of the Cairo Trilogy).
Mahfouz, N., 1991, *Palace of Desire*, London: Black Swan (Vol. 2 of the Cairo Trilogy).
Mahfouz, N., 1992, *Sugar Street*, London: Black Swan (Vol. 3 of the Cairo Trilogy).
Malone, T. W., and R. L. Laubacher, 1998, 'The dawn of the e-Lance economy', *Harvard Business Review*, September–October.
Mao, Zedong, 1939, 'In memory of Norman Bethune', in Mao Zedong, 1965, *Selected Works of Mao Zedong, Vol. 2*, Peking: Foreign Languages Press.
Marshall, A., 1920, *Principles of Economics*, London: Macmillan (originally published 1890) (8th edn.).
Marx, K., 1960, *The German Ideology*, New York, International Publishers.
Marx, K., 1967, *Capital, Vol. 1*, New York: International Publishers (originally published in German 1867, and originally published in English 1886).
Marx, K., and F. Engels, 1968, *The Communist Manifesto*, in Marx and Engels, 1968, *Selected Works*, London: Lawrence and Wishart (originally published 1848).
McEvedy, C., and R. Jones, 1978, *Atlas of World Population History*, Harmondsworth: Penguin Books.
McNamara, R., 2005, 'Apocalypse Soon', *Foreign Policy*, May/June.

Mearsheimer, J. J., 2005, 'Better be Godzilla than Bambi', *Foreign Policy*, January/February.
Meeks, G., 1977, *Disappointing Marriage*, Cambridge: Cambridge University Press.
Michael, F., 1964, 'State and society in nineteenth century China' in Feuerwerker, ed., 1964.
Milanovic, B., 2007, ' Globalisation and Inequality', in Held and Kaya, eds, 2007.
Mill, J. S., 1998, *Principles of Political Economy*, Oxford: Oxford University Press (originally published 1848) (7th edn.).
Mill, J. S., 1988, *On Liberty*, Harmondsworth: Penguin Books (originally published 1859).
Mittal, L., 2006, 'Leading the Steel Industry', ArcelorMittal, September.
Moore, D., 2006, Presentation on Global Mergers and Acquisition, China Executive Leadership Programme, Cambridge.
Moore, J., and A. Desmond, 2004, 'Introduction' to Darwin, 2004.
Mottershead, C., 2005, 'Energy and Climate Change', London, BP.
Murman, E. *et al.*, 2002, Lean Enterprise Value: insights from MIT's Lean Aerospace Initiative, New York: Palgrave.
National Academy of Sciences, 2006, *Rising above the Gathering Storm*, Washington: National Academies Press.
Needham, J., 1954, *Science and Civilisation in China*, Cambridge: Cambridge University Press.
Needham, J., 1965, *Science and Civilisation, Vol. 4, Pt. 2, Mechanical Engineering*, Cambridge: Cambridge University Press.
New York Times (NYT), various issues.
Nolan, P., 1993, *State and Market in the Chinese Economy*, Basingstoke: Macmillan.
Nolan, P., 1995, *China's Rise, Russia's Fall*, Basingstoke: Macmillan.
Nolan, P., 2001a, *China and the Global Business Revolution*, Basingstoke: Palgrave.
Nolan, P., 2001b, *China and the Global Economy*, Basingstoke: Palgrave.
Nolan, P., 2004a, *China at the Crossroads*, Cambridge: Polity Press.
Nolan P., and H. Rui, 2004b ' The Cascade Effect and the Chinese Steel Industry' mimeo.
Nolan, P., J. Zhang and C.Liu, 2007a, *The Global Business Revolution and the Cascade Effect*, Basingstoke: Palgrave.
Nolan, P., and Wang Xiaoqiang, 2007b, 'China in the Asian Financial Crisis', in *Integrating China: towards the coordinated market economy*, London: Anthem Press (forthcoming).
Nolan, P., 2008, *Guangdong in the Asian Financial Crisis*, London: Routledge (forthcoming).
North, D. C., and R. P. Thomas, 1973, *The Rise of the Western World*, Cambridge: Cambridge University Press.
Office of the Secretary of Defense, 2005, *The Military Power of the People's Republic of China: Annual Report to Congress*, Washington DC: Department of Defense.
Office of the Secretary of Defense, 2006, *The Military Power of the People's Republic of China: Annual Report to Congress*, Washington DC: Department of Defense.
Ohmae, K., 1990, *The Borderless World*, London: Collins.
Oliva, P., 2005, 'Energy and the Environment: the case of the automobile industry', Presentation to China Executive Learning Programme, Cambridge.
Owen, R., and S. Pamuk, 1998, *A History of Middle East Economies in the Twentieth Century*, London: I. B. Tauris.
Oz, A., 2005, *A Tale of Love and Darkness*, London: Vintage Books.
Penrose, E., 1995, *The Theory of the Growth of the Firm*, Oxford: Oxford University Press, (2nd edn.).
Perkins, D. H., 1968, *Agricultural Development in China, 1368-1968*, Edinburgh: Edinburgh University Press.

Persaud, A., 2000, 'Sending the Herd off the Cliff: the disturbing interaction between herding and market-sensitive risk management practices', New York: State Street Bank.

Pesaran, H., 2005, 'The Iranian economy in a global context', presentation to Workshop on Economic and Social Policies and Wealth Distribution in Muslim Countries, University of Cambridge.

Piketty, T., and E. Saez, 2006, The evolution of top incomes: a historical and international perspective', National Bureau of Economic Research, Working Paper 11955.

Piore, M., and C. Sabel, 1984, *The Second Industrial Divide: possibilities for progress*, New York: Basic Books.

Plato, 1987, *The Republic*, Harmondsworth: Penguin Books.

Polo, Marco, 1974, *The Travels*, Harmondsworth: Penguin Books (written circa AD 1280).

Porter, M., 1990, *The Competitive Advantage of Nations*, London: Macmillan.

Prais, S. J., 1981, *Productivity and Industrial Structure*, Cambridge: Cambridge University Press.

Pratten, C., 1971, *Economies of Scale in Manufacturing Industry*, Cambridge: Cambridge University Press.

Qutb, S., 2000, *Social Justice in Islam*, New York: Islamic Publications (originally published 1949).

Radice, H., ed., 1975, *International Firms and Modern Imperialism*, Harmondsworth: Penguin Books.

Rashid, A., 2000, *Taliban: Islam, Oil and the New Great Game*, New York: I. B. Tauris.

Raychaudhuri, T., and I. Habib, eds, 1982, *The Cambridge Economic History of India, Vol. 1, 1220–1750*, Cambridge: Cambridge University Press.

Rees, M., 2003, *Our Final Hour*, New York: Basic Books.

Rice, C., 2000, 'Campaign 2000: Promoting the National Interest', *Foreign Affairs*, January/February.

Roach, S., 2005, Presentation to China Executive Learning Programme, 24 October 2005, London, Morgan Stanley.

Rodinson, M., 1974, *Islam and Capitalism*, London: Penguin Books.

Rowe, W. T., 1984, *Hankow: commerce and society in a Chinese city, 1796–1889*, Stanford: Stanford University Press.

Roy, J. S., 2006, 'Troubling Signs in East Asia', *Pacific Forum PacNet Newsletter*.

Sacks, O., 1982, *Awakenings*, London: Picador.

Said, E. W., 2004, *From Oslo to Iraq and the Roadmap*, London: Bloomsbury Publishing Company.

Samuel, R., 1969, *Israel: promised land to modern state*, London: Valentine Mitchell.

Scherer, F. M., 1996, *Industry, Structure, Strategy and Public Policy*, New York: HarperCollins College Publishers.

Seabright, P., 2005, *The Company of Strangers*, Princeton: Princeton University Press.

Sears, M., 2001, 'The Bottom Line on Lean: a CFO's Perspective,' a speech given on the Lean Aerospace Initiative, 10 April.

Selden, M., 1979, *The People's Republic of China*, New York: Monthly Review Press.

Shiba, Y., 1977, 'Ningpo and its Hinterland', in G. W. Skinner, ed., 1977.

Shiller, R., 2001, *Irrational Exuberance*, Princeton: Princeton University Press.

Singh, A., 2002, 'Globalisation and Financial Liberalisation', mimeo.

Skinner, G. W., ed., 1977, *The City in Late Imperial China*, Stanford: Stanford University Press.

Smith, A., 1982, *The Theory of Moral Sentiments*, Indianapolis: Liberty Classics edition (revised edition) (originally published 1761).

Smith, A., 1976, *The Wealth of Nations*, (2 Vols), Chicago: University of Chicago Press (Cannan edition) (originally published 1776).
Stapledon, O., 1930, *Last and First Men*, London: Victor Gollanz.
Stapledon, O., 1937, *Star Maker*, London: Victor Gollanz.
SSB (State Statistical Bureau), various years, *Chinese Statistical Yearbook*, (*Zhongguo tongji nianjian*) (ZTN), Beijing: Statistical Bureau Publishing House.
Stiglitz, J., 2002, *Globalisation and its Discontents*, Harmondsworth: Penguin Books.
Sutcliffe, B., 2002, *A More or Less Unequal World? World Income Distribution in the 20th Century*, Bilbao: University of the Basque Country.
Tripp, C., 2005, *Islam and the Moral Economy: the challenge of capitalism*, Cambridge: Cambridge University Press.
UNCTAD (United Nations Conference on Trade and Development), 2003, *World Investment Report 2003*, Geneva: UN Publications.
UNCTAD (United Nations Conference on Trade and Development), 2005, *World Investment Report 2005*, Geneva: UN Publications.
UNDP (United Nations Development Programme), 2002, *China Human Development Report 2002: making green development a choice*, Washington DC: Oxford University Press.
UNDP (United Nations Development Programme), 2004, *Human Development Report, 2004*, New York: UNDP.
UNDP (United Nations Development Programme), 2005, *China Human Development Report 2005: towards human development with equity*, Beijing: China Development Research Foundation.
USCESRC (US-China Economic and Security Review Commission), 2003, *China's Energy Needs and Strategies*, Washington DC: US Government Printing Office.
USCESRC (US-China Economic and Security Review Commission), 2004, *Hearing on China's Impact on the US Manufacturing Base*, Washington DC: US Government Printing Office.
USCESRC (US-China Economic and Security Review Commission), 2005, *Report to Congress*, Washington DC: US Government Printing Office.
Van Creveld, M., 2004, *Defending Israel*, New York: St Martins Press.
Vidal, G., 2002, *Perpetual War for Perpetual Peace*, New York: Clairview Books.
Vidal, G., 2003, *Dreaming War*, New York: Clairview Books.
Wagner, D., 1997, *The Traditional Chinese Iron Industry and its Modern Fate*, London: Curzon.
Wang, Gungwu, 1998, *The Nanhai Trade*, Singapore: Times Academic Press.
Weale, A., 1995, *Hiroshima*, London: Robinson.
White, L., 1972, 'The expansion of technology, 500–1500', in Cipolla, ed., 1972.
White, W., 2006, 'Is price stability enough?', *BIS Working Papers*, No. 205.
Will, Pierre-Etienne, 1990, *Bureaucracy and Famine in Eighteenth-Century China*, Stanford: Stanford University Press.
Wolf, M., 2004, *Why Globalisation Works*, London and New Haven: Yale University Press.
Wolf, M., 2005a, Presentation to China Executive Learning Programme, Cambridge.
Wolf, M., 2005b, 'China's rise need not bring conflict, *FT* 14 September.
WB (World Bank), 1986, *China: long-term development issues and options*, Washington DC: World Bank.
WB (World Bank), 2000, *Global Economic Prospects*, Washington DC: Oxford University Press.
WB (World Bank), 2007, *Global Economic Prospects and the Developing Countries*, Washington DC: Oxford University Press.

WB (World Bank), 2000, (WDR) *World Development Report, 1999/2000: entering the twenty-first century*, Washington DC: Oxford University Press.
WB (World Bank), 2002, (WDR) *World Development Report, 2002: building institutions for markets*, Washington DC: Oxford University Press.
WB (World Bank), 2004, (WDI) *World Development Indicators*, Washington DC: Oxford University Press.
WB (World Bank), 2006, (WDI) *World Development Indicators*, Washington DC: Oxford University Press.
Wright, R., 2000, *Nonzero*, London: Abacus.
Xing, Weixi, 2005, Globalisation And Catch-Up In The Chinese Telecommunications Industry: the case of Huawei, University of Cambridge Doctoral Dissertation.
Xu Dixin and Wu Chengming, 2000, *Chinese Capitalism, 1522–1840*, Basingstoke: Macmillan.
Yergin, D., 1991, *The Prize*, London: Simon and Schuster.
Yergin, D. and J. Stanislav, 1998, *The Commanding Heights*, New York: Touchstone Books.
Zampetti, A. B., and P. Sauve, 1996, 'Onwards to Singapore: the international contestability of markets and the new trade agenda', *The World Economy*, Vol. 19, No. 3, May.
Zoellick, R., 2006, 'Balancing international and domestic forces [are the] key to China's development', *International Economic Studies (Guoji jingji yanjiu)*, Beijing, 17 April.

INDEX

acid rain 97
aggression, as factor of capitalism 3–4
    as factor of human advancement 9–12, 32, 34
agriculture, modernization of 84
air quality *see* pollution, atmospheric
air transport, advances in 75, 83, 91, 108–111
altruistic benevolence 20–21, 23, 26
Argentinian Financial Crisis 65, 138, 285
Aristotle 4–5, 20–21, 205, 248–249
Asian Financial Crisis, the 60, 65, 133, 138, 139, 142–143, 169, 179, 202, 285
asset price bubble 134–135
    consequences of 138
automobile industry *see* vehicular transport
aviation industry *see* air transport

banks and banking systems 62, 64–65, 136, 170, 253–254
'battle for talent', the 70
benevolence, altruistic *see* altruistic benevolence
beverage production and distribution industry 75–76, 115–118
Brazil, and deforestation 93
    and FDI 61–62
Bretton Woods institutions, the 59
Bush, President George W. 16–18, 198, 214–215, 220, 237, 239

'capitalist irrationality' 92–103
'cascade effect', the *see* industrial structure
China, acid rain and desertification in 97
    agriculture and property rights historically in 147–149
    and capitalism/capitalist practices 146–147, 196, 204, 287
    and FDI 62, 196
    and nuclear energy 80
    and the United States 144, 146, 161, 165–166, 171, 172–173, 175, 177–179, 181–183, 186–207, 285–293
    as coal-using electricity generator 82, 101, 165–166, 201
    as economic superpower 40, 48, 51, 68, 160–161, 163, 177–178, 187
    atmospheric pollution in 95, 102, 165–167
    commodity price stabilisation in 159, 178, 199
    corruption among those in authority in 168–170, 206
    energy in 164–167, 177, 184, 201
    environmental degradation in/and 95–97, 164–167, 188
    financial institutions in 167, 169–171, 206
    global business revolution in 162–164
    Jiangnan 154
    mammal species extinction rate in 93
    poverty and inequality in 161–162, 204
    state apparatus, development of the 155–157, 160, 167–171
    technical progress from medieval times in 149–150, 164–167
    trade and industry of 150–153, 162–167
    urbanisation in 153–154, 198
    water, control of 158, 199
clocks and watches, invention of 52
collateralised debt obligations (CDOs) 137

collective good, the 6, 32
communism, communist principles 25–26, 36–37, 46, 243, 252, 260–261, 263–265, 287
competition/competitiveness, as factor of capitalism 3–4, 7–8, 14, 66–68, 107–108, 119
  as factor of human evolution 12, 27, 92
Confucius and Confucianism 205, 287
core systems integrator *see* firm

Darwin, Charles, *Descent of Man* 11–12, 27–28
  natural selection 27, 29
Darwinism, Social *see* Social Darwinism
deforestation worldwide 93, 95, 188
democratisation worldwide 85

energy, and international relations 101–103, 143, 201–202
  and the world economy 78–81, 100
  global use/consumption of 98, 143
  nuclear power 79–80, 99, 100
  renewable (hydro, wind, solar) 80–81, 99, 100, 284
English, as the global language 91, 120
equity ownership, changes in distribution of 90
ethics, ethical principles 9, 11, 15–16, 24, 40, 59, 287, 295

FDI *see* foreign direct investment
fertility rate(s) 83
financial markets, fundamental instability of 131–133, 138
financial services institutions 63–65, 136
firm, as value chain with core systems integrator 106–107
  evolution of the 56, 58
  internationalisation of the 90
  nature of the 68–70, 106
  ownership of the 90, 105–106
fishing industry, and global capitalism 94, 284
Food and Agriculture Organization (FAO), the 88
food production, overall increase in 84

foreign direct investment 61–62, 253, 301
fossil fuels and reserves 78–79, 81, 99, 100–101, 176, 187, 284
  oil 79, 101, 175–176, 284
  see also global warming
freedom, definitions of 12–15, 18–38, 197
  economic as essential for political 15, 35
  from control by others 84–86
  from poverty 86
  from war 86–89, 91
  'negative' 15, 37, 40, 197
  political 15, 35, 85
  'positive' 18–38, 40, 197
free market as a moral concept 17–18
French colonies in North Africa 210
Freud, Sigmund 9, 31–32, 41, 292, 295
Friedman, Milton 13, 15–16, 66
Fromm, Erich 32–34

General Agreement on Tariff and Trade (GATT), the 88
Global Business Revolution, the (era of the) 58, 59, 61–63, 72, 74–76, 78, 84–86, 92, 97, 104, 106, 116, 119, 125, 127, 129, 130, 133, 134, 136, 138, 142, 162–164, 206, 282–283, 289, 297
global financial risk 65–72, 131–142
global financial system 139–142
globalisation, class structure in 120
  definitions of 44–48
Global 1250 DTI annual survey of worlwide R&D spending 72–73
global warming 81–83, 94, 97–103, 143, 284
  airborne particulates and 82–83, 95, 99
  carbon dioxide and 81–82, 98–99, 101–103
  Kyoto Protocol/Agreement, the 81, 99–100, 102
  sea level rise rate 99
  temperature rise rate 99
  see also fishing industry
Gulf states 211–213, 241–242, 254, 256–257, 286
  and Britain 209
Gulf War(s), the 213–218, 220, 232

INDEX

Hayek, Friedrich von 13–15, 59, 67
health, improvement in popular 83
Hiroshima 1, 34, 193, 285
history of capitalism 44–48
humanity at the crossroads 2–3, 92
human nature, and the market economy 2–3, 39–41
human rights, and capital 59
hydroelectric power generation and supply *see* energy, renewable

IMF, the 59–60, 88–89, 203–204
   as a 'rudderless ship' 139
India, and nuclear energy/programme 80, 286
   atmospheric pollution in 95, 102
   mammal species extinction rate in 93
Indonesia, mammal species extinction rate in 93
Industrial Revolution, American 56
   British 50
   European 45, 50, 52, 56, 59, 77
   Second 57–58
   Third 58
industrial structure, nature and determinants of 66, 70–72, 104–119
   the 'cascade effect' 71, 105, 112, 113, 115, 116, 119, 163
inequality, in distribution of world incomes 85–86, 120–123, 129–131, 143
   within developing countries 126–130
   within high-income countries 123–126
informal sector employment 126–129
   in China 126–127
information technology (IT)
   see technical progress
inheritance of property, as element of Islam 243
   as factor of classical liberalism 16
instability of financial markets, the inherent 131–133
interest on loans 5
interest rates 133–35
International Labour Organization (ILO), the 88
International Monetary Fund, the *see* IMF

Iran 213, 216, 218–222, 240, 286
Iraq 213–218, 273
Islam, the Islamic/Muslim world 40, 51, 207–237, 242–278, 285–293
   and capitalism from medieval times 242–258, 260, 263–271, 277–278, 287
   and Europe (especially Britain and France) 208–211
   and Israel 222–237, 274, 276
   and oil 252–253, 256–257, 272–273, 289
   and science from medieval times 248–249
   and the United States 144, 146, 207–222, 273–276
   anti-Western violence and attacks 258–263
   inequality of incomes distribution 256, 278
   the Abbasid Caliphate and economic development 245–247, 261–262
   the Fatimid Caliphate, based in Egypt 247, 261–262
   the Ottoman Empire 249–251
   unity of/in 271–272
Israel-Palestine 222–237

Jerusalem, under the Ottoman Empire 250–251

Kropotkin, Pyotr 29–31
Kyoto Agreement/Protocol, the *see* global warming

labour, division of 50–51
Lebanon 237–241
liberalism, classical 15–16
life expectancy, rising 83
Lorenz, Konrad 9–11
love, as a human instinct 27, 31

Mao Zedong 36–38, 146
market economy, the 4
   and human nature 2–3
Marshall, Alfred, *Principles of Economics* 66–67, 69

Marx, Karl 37, 39, 49, 68, 76, 77, 87, 223, 292
matriarchal society 33
 and the changeover to patriarchal 34
mean, between self-interest and pure altruism 38–41, 296
mergers and acquisitions 63, 67, 71, 90
Mexican 'Tequila' crisis 65, 138, 285
Mill, John Stuart 7–8, 25–26, 39, 77–78
morals and morality 28
mortality rate(s) 83
Muslims, the Muslim world   *see* Islam, the Islamic world

negative freedom 3–18, 37, 40
9/11 (11 September 2001) 65, 180, 190, 192, 215–216, 242, 275, 288, 304
non-capitalist systems, failure of 2, 48, 66, 181, 198, 287, 293
non-zero-sum outcomes/interactions 51, 55–56
nuclear power   *see* energy
nuclear weapons/arms 2, 18, 40, 144, 194, 233, 285, 294, 299

oil   *see* fossil fuels; Islam, and oil; United States, oil production/importation
oligopolistic competition 57–58, 76, 107, 111, 125

packaging industry   *see* technical progress
Palestine 222–237
Penrose, Edith, *The Theory of the Growth of the Firm* 69
Persian Gulf   *see* Gulf states
Plato 19–20
pollution, atmospheric 81–83, 95, 97, 99, 284
 marine 94, 96–97, 284
Polo, Marco 149–151, 153, 157, 159
poverty reduction, overall 86
price/pricing mechanism, the 14
 and non-price competition 57
private capital flows 59–61
Progressivism, the Progressive movement 35–36
property prices, recent surge in 135

property rights, and Islamic principles 243, 267–268
 history of 148–149

Qutb, Sayyid, Egyptian scholar/writer 266–270

R&D expenditure worldwide 72–76
renewable energy sources   *see* energy
Russian Financial Crisis, the 65, 138

Sacks, Oliver, neurologist 31–32
Saudi Arabia, and its oil-wealthy ruling family 257, 275
self-interest, and human society 6, 16, 25, 38, 55
 serving the collective good 6
Six-Day War, the 231, 276, 304
Smith, Adam 5–7, 21–24, 39, 50–51, 54, 76–77, 86, 205
Social Darwinism 11–13, 16, 27, 197–198
solar power   *see* energy, renewable
stock markets 62–63

talent, the battle/war for   *see* 'battle for talent'
technical progress and industry 72–76, 83–84, 97–98, 173, 282
 agricultural technology 84
 information technology (IT) 74–75, 125, 173
 packaging technology 75–76, 98, 116–117
 telecommunications 83–84, 113–115
 see also energy
technical progress and nature 76–78, 81–83, 284
 carbon sequestration technology 82, 284
telecommunications, advances in
 see technical progress
tourism, as a mass phenomenon 91

UN Conference on Trade and Development (UNCTAD), the 88
United States, and Afghanistan 215
 and carbon dioxide emissions 102, 176, 188

and China 144, 146–147, 161,
 165–166, 171–173, 175, 177–179,
 181–183, 186–207
and economic philosophy 34–36, 172,
 196, 199–200
and Iran 218–222, 240
and Iraq 213–218
and Israel/Lebanon 237–241
and Israel/Palestine 222–237, 274
and Japan 188, 192
and Saudi Arabia 212–213
and the Islamic world 144, 146–237,
 273–276
as coal-using electricity generator 82
as consumer of primary energy 175,
 184, 201
as primary capitalist power 2, 13,
 16–18, 40, 144, 171–175, 177–178,
 180, 183, 241, 286
inequality, growth of 174, 195, 198,
 204, 291
military budget 190–191
military involvement in the Middle
 East 213–218, 222–242
oil production/importation in 101,
 175–176, 211, 215–216
potential conflict with China 40,
 183–184, 187, 189–191, 193–194
refusal to sign the Kyoto Protocol 102,
 176
the Great Depression 36, 197
urbanisation of populations 84–85,
 153–154
utopianism 20, 198, 286

vehicular transport, advances in 75, 76,
 82, 83, 98, 111–113, 118
ownership rates worldwide 98, 111

Washington Consensus, the 59, 60
wealth, inequality in global distribution of
 121–130
negative consequences of 22–24
wind power generation and supply
 see energy, renewable
World Bank, the 60, 88–89, 254
World Health Organization (WHO),
 the 88
World Trade Organization (WTO),
 the 88, 289

Zedong, Mao *see* Mao Zedong